Items should be returned on or before the last date shown below. Items not already requested by other borrowers may be renewed in person, in writing or by telephone. To renew, please quote the number on the barcode label. To renew on line a PIN is required. This can be requested at your local library.
Renew online @ **www.dublincitypubliclibraries.ie**
Fines charged for overdue items will include postage incurred in recovery. Damage to or loss of items will be charged to the borrower.

Leabharlanna Poiblí Chathair Bhaile Átha Cliath
Dublin City Public Libraries

Dublin City
Baile Átha Cliath

Date Due	Date Due	Date Due
	1 0 JUL 2019	

To my sister, Linda.

MARIA EDGEWORTH'S LETTERS

FROM

IRELAND

———————

SELECTED & EDITED BY
VALERIE PAKENHAM

THE LILLIPUT PRESS
———————
MMXVIII

First published 2018 by
THE LILLIPUT PRESS LTD
62–63 Sitric Road, Arbour Hill, Dublin 7, Ireland
www.lilliputpress.ie

Text © Valerie Pakenkam, 2018

ISBN 978 1 84351 719 1 (hbk)
ISBN 978 1 84351 734 4 (pbk)

A CIP record is available from the British Library.

3 5 7 9 10 8 6 4 2

Set in Adobe Caslon Pro
Design by Niall McCormack
Printed in Spain by Graphy Cems

CONTENTS

7   Introduction

17   Acknowledgments

21   I   March 1776 – May 1798

55   II   June 1798 – August 1802

75   III   August 1803 – October 1807

113   IV   January 1808 – March 1813

165   V   July 1813 – May 1817

215   VI   June 1817 – October 1825

269   VII   December 1825 – April 1830

311   VIII   July 1831 – August 1834

339   IX   January 1835 – December 1838

375   X   January 1839 – December 1844

399   XI   January 1845 – May 1849

421   Postscript

426   The Descendants of Richard Lovell Edgeworth

427   Maria Edgeworth's Family Circle

433   Main Events of Maria Edgeworth's Life

438   Manuscript Sources and Bibliography

441   Index

Colour plates between pages 192 and 193

INTRODUCTION

I FIRST CAME across Maria Edgeworth more than fifty years ago. The Pakenham family into which I had just married were the Edgeworths' neighbours and also relations. Maria's grandfather had been brought up by Thomas Pakenham, the first Lord Longford, after his parents died and her father Richard Lovell Edgeworth had been a close friend of the next two generations. In his *Memoirs* he claimed to have been cured as a wild young man of a passion for field sports and card playing by being given the key to the library at Pakenham Hall and encouraged to serious reading. The second volume (partly written by Maria) described the family's frequent journeys from Edgeworthstown to Castlepollard, seventeen miles away, across a 'vast Serbonian bog' with a perilous crossing of raft or 'float' across the River Inny en route.

I did not know much about Maria herself but several friends had already pressed on me copies of *Castle Rackrent* (perhaps as a warning!). And in a bedroom I discovered a charming illustrated set of her novels, reissued in 1832, and read my way through the ones set in Ireland, *Ormond, Ennui* and *The Absentee*. Then in the library I found a modest clothbound three-volume *Memoir of Maria Edgeworth* by her stepmother, Mrs Frances Edgeworth. Privately printed in 1867, it was made up largely of Maria's letters to her family. To my delight, they included detailed descriptions of our house in the early 1800s, when the 2nd Earl of Longford was busy transforming it inside and out to a Gothic Revival castle, complete with a hot air central-heating system designed by Maria's father. Maria seemed to have had rather a *tendresse* for 'dear hospitable Lord Longford', and did not like his English wife when he finally married aged forty in 1816.

In the 1970s my interest in Maria Edgeworth received another boost. We were given two magnificent volumes, *Maria Edgeworth's Letters from England, 1813–1842* and *Maria Edgeworth in France and Switzerland*, edited by Christina Colvin, a direct descendant of Maria's youngest half-brother, Michael Pakenham Edgeworth; and a brilliant new literary biography of Maria Edgeworth by Marilyn Butler, married to Christina Colvin's brother, David. Both had drawn on the private Edgeworth family papers, which Christina Colvin had only recently catalogued in full. Then, twenty-five years later again, my daughter Eliza embarked on a composite biography of the Pakenhams of Maria's generation. It involved her reading through many of Maria's original letters, now accessible in the National Library of Ireland, and in the New Bodleian library in Oxford. Reading Eliza's notes reminded me just what a delightful letter writer Maria was, full of stories and wild humour and affection – and also of how many of her letters remained still unpublished and unknown. Partly this was because of Maria's own strong disapproval of the publication of private letters. How could she write 'naturally with any ease or pleasure' with 'one eye squinting at the public and celebrity and the other pretending to look only to my dear friend or correspondent'. Even Augustus Hare, who published *The Life and Letters of Maria Edgeworth* in 1894, had not been granted access to Maria's original letters but simply shortened and re-printed those from the *Memoir* of 1867, which, as Christina Colvin pointed out in the preface to her own books, had already been heavily cut and sanitized from the originals by Maria's younger sisters so as not to offend the living or their descendants

Nearly 170 years after Maria's death, there seemed to me an overwhelming case for a book of Maria's unbowdlerized letters from Ireland if only to redress the balance of Christina Colvin's two large volumes of Maria's letters from abroad. Christina Colvin had dismissed Maria's letters from home as largely of 'domestic interest' only. But Maria had always proclaimed herself as above all a 'domestic being', happiest living at home among her beloved family. Ireland was the country she knew and loved and where she lived for nearly all her adult life, and Edgeworthstown, away from the social whirl of London, Paris or Dublin, was the place where, she wrote, she could best find time to write and think.

How to go about it? From the beginning it was clear that, as in the original *Memoir*, many of her letters could be printed in part only. Some of them run to thirty pages of close writing, punctuated largely by dashes. (Like her contemporaries, Maria preferred the dash to the comma or full stop.) During his lifetime her father was constantly reproving her for writing long letters instead of directing her energies to useful work for publication. And even when not engaged on composing stories for children or novels (or 'Moral Tales' as she preferred to call them), Maria was expected to act as his secretary and bookkeeper for estate business. However he grudgingly acknowledged Maria's letters were 'excellent' and came to rely on her to relay the family news. After his death in 1817, released from discipline as his literary 'partner', she wrote if anything twice as many letters. Exchanging news and ideas was essential to her being. As she wrote to her aunt in 1830, 'I really think if my thoughts or feelings were shut up completely within me, I should burst in a week – like a steam engine without a snifting-clack …'

Sending letters was expensive – Maria's later letters are full of grateful references to those who could provide her with free franks: officials, peers and MPs (one favourite much-exploited provider was the Earl of Rosse who served as Irish postmaster general from 1809 to 1831). Letters were paid by weight so it was often important to cram as much as possible onto each page. Mercifully for later readers, Maria seldom went in for the dreadful practice of overwriting at right angles to the original lines to save money, and her handwriting is nearly always legible.

Nearly all the letters I have chosen are to her immediate family, to whom she wrote most freely in a delightful conversational style. When she wrote to those outside it, she usually became more prolix and sometimes, when writing to men, rather heavily flirtatious. Her family was very large. Richard Lovell Edgeworth had provided Maria with three stepmothers in turn and twenty-one mostly much younger siblings. (Some of Maria's biographers have treated him as a kind of Irish Bluebeard but he appears to have become an affectionate husband except in his first marriage to Maria's unfortunate mother, which he described in his all-too-candid *Memoirs* as a folly he 'had brought upon himself'.) There were also several aunts and cousins: Maria's favourite correspondent was her father's younger sister, Margaret Ruxton, a sprightly, clever and highly sociable lady who had been one of the first to show Maria affection as a child. (It was she who encouraged Maria's stories and imitations of John Langan, the Edgeworths' steward, who was the original for

Honest Thady in *Castle Rackrent*.) Aunt Ruxton lived about forty miles away outside Navan in Co. Meath in a delightful cottage *orné* beside the Boyne, and there was much coming and going between there and Edgeworthstown. There were three Ruxton daughters and the middle one, Sophy, became Maria's particular friend. Maria used her as a sounding board for most of her novels and children's stories, and also as confidante in matters of the heart. (Maria was plain – or believed herself so – and seems to have had only one serious suitor, a Swedish diplomat, the Chevalier Edelcrantz whom she met in Paris in 1802. She turned him down, unable to bear the thought of leaving her father and living abroad, but she remained obsessed with him for many years after and painted an idealized version of him in one of her longest novels, *Patronage*.)

Frances Beaufort, Maria's last stepmother, became her chief confidante and correspondent after the death of Maria's father, whom she had married in 1798. Frances, two years younger than Maria, was highly intelligent and well read, and by her warmth and tact had earned all her stepchildren's devotion. Maria came to see her as her greatest friend and happily shared the task of bringing up Frances' own six children, the youngest of whom was forty-three years younger than herself and still only five years old when Richard Lovell Edgeworth died. After his death she took her young half-sisters at her own expense to London, France and Scotland to introduce them to a wider and more glamorous social circle than Edgeworthstown could provide. She wrote long bulletins of family news to Frances whenever they were apart, and after the collapse of Lovell Edgeworth, the oldest son, into debt and alcohol, worked closely in tandem with her for twenty years to keep the family home and Edgeworth estate afloat.

Two of Frances Edgeworth's daughters, Fanny and Harriet, also became Maria's main correspondents in her later life. Fanny, the oldest, born in 1799, was her adored favourite / quasi child. After Fanny herself married in 1837 and went to live in London, Maria wrote to her regularly every week. She shared Maria's interest in science and literature, and was serious and prudent, with a stockbroker husband who could advise Maria on financial affairs. Harriet, two years younger, was bright and funny and married one of Maria's favourite young men, Richard Butler, the clever bookish rector of Trim in Co. Meath. Unlike most of Maria's siblings, Harriet did not suffer from chronic ill health, and was able to cheer everyone with her high spirits. The threat of consumption runs like a black thread through Maria's letters. Her first two stepmothers, Honora and Elizabeth Sneyd, had died from it – and five of their children died in their teens or early twenties. Two more of Frances Edgeworth's children succumbed to it in the 1830s, though their mother lived to be ninety-five. Many of Maria's letters begin with a bulletin on the family's health. The damp cold winters of Co. Longford were a perpetual hazard and Maria's father would not allow his daughters to travel to healthier climates for lack of suitable chaperones. After his death, however, his widow Frances spent much of her time taking her daughters to English spas such as Cheltenham and Clifton. Numerous other ills of the flesh are recorded in Maria's letters, and treatment was usually worse than useless – calomel (or mercury) was a favourite prescription, as was Blue Pill (probably a purgative). Maria herself mainly enjoyed good health – apart from toothache and occasional bouts of erysipelas – thanks to a regimen of brisk early morning walks and reliance on her three favourite doctors, Dr Quiet, Dr Diet and Dr Merryman. In later years, she became a close friend of a famous Dublin surgeon, Dr Philip Crampton, and sought advice from him for all the family's ills.

Maria's letters show an extraordinary range of interests. Anyone going through them will be struck first by the sheer breadth of her reading. She was encouraged by her father to read everything from history and *belles lettres* to philosophy and political economy. Not many fathers would have pressed their teenage daughters to read Adam Smith's *The Wealth of Nations*. Novels were initially discouraged; the fifteen-year-old Maria describes them primly as 'acting on the constitution of the mind as Drams do on that of the body' but she could not resist Fanny Burney's *Evelina* (described later by Macaulay as 'the first novel a lady could admit to reading') and, like Jane Austen, adored Samuel Richardson's *Sir Charles Grandison*. The family assembled every evening in the library after dinner (at 6 pm) to read aloud and discuss the latest books sent from Dublin or London. 'In this house', reported Charles Kendal Bushe in 1810, 'literature is not a treat for Company upon Invitation days but is actually the daily bread of the family' – to which he attributed the excellence of their conversation. Maria's letters read like a rollcall of the most famous authors of the day. By the early 1800s she was already famous herself and in October 1814 had the gratification of finding herself referred to as the inspiration for Sir Walter Scott's first novel, *Waverley*, as the family read it around the library fire. (He later became a close friend and correspondent.)

Maria's letters are initially dismissive of another contemporary, Jane Austen (published anonymously at first). She found *Northanger Abbey* silly, approved of *Mansfield Park*, but gave up on *Emma*, which Jane Austen had sent her, as lacking a story. Jane Austen by contrast much admired Maria and wrote to her aunt half-jokingly in 1814, 'I have made up my mind to like no novels really but Miss Edgeworth's, yours and my own.' Jane's first love and dancing partner, Tom Lefroy, was later to make a fortune at the Dublin Bar and to buy an estate only five miles from Edgeworthstown and it is fascinating to speculate how she and Maria might have got on as neighbours.

Like all well-educated women of her class, Maria was also fluent in French. She devoured the latest French memoirs and novels and much admired Madame de Staël (whom she just missed meeting). She also was fascinated by Napoleon (whom she had briefly glimpsed, a pale figure on a white horse in Paris in 1802) and much moved by accounts of him in exile. By the 1830s she was reading De Tocqueville and Guizot, and by her seventies, was deep in Balzac's social realist novels, most of which shocked her by their content. She saw him as a moral Mephistopholes, though a superb writer. She never departed from her father's view that history and literature, even comedy, should inculcate good morals, and be 'of use'.

More unusual was Maria's fascination with science, again inculcated by her father. Richard Lovell Edgeworth had been a founder member of the Lunar Society with such luminaries as Dr Erasmus Darwin, Josiah Wedgwood, James Watt (pioneer of steam power) and James Keir (the famous chemist), and all his children were encouraged from an early age to undertake simple chemical experiments. In 1792 Maria's full sister Anna married Dr Thomas Beddoes who experimented with gases in his laboratory at Clifton (hoping they might prove cures for consumption – now known as tuberculosis), and Anna later carried on a prolonged flirtation with Beddoes' brilliant young Cornish apprentice, Humphrey Davy. They wrote poetry together and went for long moonlit walks. Davy came several times to stay at Edgeworthstown and the family attended his hugely popular lectures in Dublin. Through Davy Maria met the next generation of scientists or 'philosophers' as they were still known, John Herschel, Charles Babbage and Michael Faraday. Through Richard Butler, later her brother-in-law, she met and struck up a friendship with William Rowan Hamilton, a brilliant young Dublin mathematician who was the first to suggest there might be a third and fourth dimension. In her old age he made her an honorary member of the Royal Irish Academy and regularly sent her his learned articles for comment. (Aged seventy-eight, Maria admitted finding his one on Pure Time hard to comprehend.) In 1842, to Maria's joy, her youngest half-sister Lucy married another leading Irish scientist, Thomas Romney Robinson, head of the

Observatory at Armagh, who was able to gratify her insatiable appetite for scientific facts and discoveries at first hand.

Her practical interests were just as varied: her father had made her her own small garden below her bedroom window, and even in her late seventies she was still directing new planting schemes there and begging exotic cuttings from her botanist half-brother, Michael Pakenham Edgeworth, in India. Another was building: after her father's death, her letters record her making countless small improvements to the Edgeworthstown cottages and houses as she could afford them and few things gave her more pleasure than outdoor work, directing the laying of a new pavement or gutter or the lowering of the Edgeworthstown river bed. Unlike most Irish big houses, isolated in parks behind high stone walls, Edgeworthstown House was set at the very edge of the town. The house and farm were a busy hive of activities and her notes of conversations with servants, farm workers and tenants appear constantly in her letters: there was John Langan, her father's steward, Samuel Bristow, the coachman, and his wife Molly and Kitty Billamore, the devoted housekeeeper who looked after a succession of young Edgeworths in turn. Later letters have humorous accounts of the lumbering 'indoor man', Cassidy, known by Maria and her stepmother as 'the hippopotamus' and of Gahan, the Edgeworths' gardener, and his battles against invading pigs and turkeys.

Maria's letters are also full of visits to neighbouring country houses: initially, these were limited. Richard Lovell Edgeworth was too busy and too clever to find many of the Longford squirearchy congenial (they in turn suspected him of dangerously radical views) and to begin with only consorted regularly with two local families, the Granards of Castle Forbes and the Pakenhams of Pakenham Hall, including the rather disreputable Admiral Pakenham (who appears as a thinly disguised villain in two of Maria's best novels). But Frances, his fourth wife, encouraged him to expand his social circle, and by the early 1800s, after the family returned from Paris, they became in Maria's phrase 'great gadders'. There were regular visits to friends and relations in the surrounding counties, and to Dublin. One is struck, however, at how constricted Maria's movements were before her father's death. No gentlewoman could travel unaccompanied by public coach (hence her indignation at the General's treatment of Catherine Morland in *Northanger Abbey*). The advent of rail and steamboats transformed her later life. In her old age Maria made two daring expeditions to the west – to the Martins of Ballinahinch in Connemara (where she was inadvertently detained for several weeks) and the Catholic Moores of Moorehall in Co.

Mayo. Both families became her close friends and correspondents. There was also a constant stream of visitors from abroad. Edgeworthstown was seen as an oasis of cultured enlightenment in the boggy midlands, and as Maria's fame grew, it became almost a place of pilgrimage. In the 1820s Maria was also able to offer distinguished guests a visit to her brother Lovell's new school. Run on strictly non-denominational lines, it was much admired by visiting commissioners and politicians. Maria's stepmother Frances also contributed nobly to the ongoing hospitality at Edgeworthstown, summoning up excellent meals at the shortest notice and charming visitors with her sympathy. 'It is witchcraft, positive witchcraft,' reported a guest when Mrs Edgeworth made even Sir Walter Scott's shy son open up over the dinner table.

But outside the magic circle of warmth and culture at Edgeworthstown, there was always danger. However enlightened as landlords, the Edgeworths were part and parcel of the Protestant Ascendancy, seen as English settlers who had taken land from its rightful Catholic owners. Popular resentment, aggravated by acute poverty and lack of any subsistence except from the land, was always smouldering beneath the surface. In the 1790s, reignited by the French Revolution, agrarian violence flared up in secret societies known as the Whiteboys or Defenders who raided for arms, burnt houses and mutilated cattle. Maria's father, though he claimed never to have been threatened himself, helped raise a local militia to keep lawlessness at bay. Three years later in 1798, Ireland exploded into full-blown revolution and in September the Edgeworths found themselves in the direct path of an advancing army of French soldiers and Irish rebels. Though the Edgeworths' house was left untouched by the rebel army, thanks again to their reputation as benevolent landlords, Richard Lovell Edgeworth was nearly lynched by a mob of Protestant militia as a French spy and seriously considered selling his estate and moving to Wales. But he was persuaded by his father-in-law, Daniel Beaufort, that things would improve after the abolition of the ultra right-wing government in Dublin and Ireland's Union with England. Pitt had planned a bill for Catholic emancipation to follow the Union, but this was blocked by George III as contrary to his coronation oath – and was shelved for a generation. Richard Lovell Edgeworth erroneously believed the Union would bring trade and manufacturing skills to Ireland (he wrote a heavy preface to this effect in the second edition of *Castle Rackrent*). It failed to do so, and although the Napoleonic Wars kept agriculture prices high for most of his lifetime, on his deathbed he was prophesying famine and misery for Ireland in years to come.

During her father's lifetime, Maria's letters seldom offered political opinions of her own though they faithfully recorded his – to do otherwise would be 'far above [her] capacity and information'. But after his death she followed politics with breathless interest, fed by newspapers (including the *Irish Farmers' Journal*!) and letters from London. By 1818 she had got to know many of the leading Whig families, such as Lord Lansdowne and his Irish protégé, Thomas Spring Rice (later Lord Mounteagle) with whom she corresponded at length on Catholic Emancipation. When the bill was finally pushed through by the Duke of Wellington in 1829 after O'Connell's triumphant election in West Clare, she hailed it as the dawning of a new age of meritocracy in Ireland: 'Now everyman may educate his son with the hope he may go forward according to his merits.'[1] Maria had been brought up on eighteenth-century Enlightenment ideas and remained firmly agnostic all her life (she was almost equally scornful of Catholic 'superstition' and Methodist 'cant') but she and her family had many Catholic friends, and were proud of their connection with the Abbé Edgeworth, who had been Louis XVI's confessor and bravely accompanied him to the guillotine at the height of the Terror. However O'Connell's subsequent campaign for the Repeal of the Union and his recruitment of the newly nationalist Catholic priesthood to instruct their flock to vote against their landlords rapidly made him Maria's enemy. From the 1830s, her letters paint him as a dangerous demagogue condoning if not encouraging inflammatory speeches from the pulpit. She was never to give O'Connell credit for his control of his vast audiences and refusal to countenance civil violence. As she saw it, only the Union with England could now guarantee the rights of property in Ireland. Everything depended on good and wise government from Westminster. As she wrote to her stepmother in 1835: 'All our fate and future and domestic life hang upon this point. Will they [*Government*] be able to prevent those who have no property and no education from overturning by their numbers those who have some property & some education.'

There is an interesting exchange in her novel of the same period, *Helen*: the heroine is told 'Women are now so highly cultivated and political subjects of such high interest to all human creatures who live together in society … You cannot, I conceive, satisfy yourself with the common namby-pamby little

---

1   Quoting a reaction to the bill, told to her by Harriet Butler (see letter to Fanny Wilson, 14 February 1829).

missy phrase, "ladies have nothing to do with politics".' Maria certainly now did not – and did not hesitate to write to prime ministers such as Peel and Lord John Russell or to the Under-Secretary of State, Thomas Drummond, giving advice on cures for rural distress. However she strongly disapproved of Harriet Martineau's call for women's right to vote, which she considered almost as dangerous an idea as democracy itself.

In old age she claimed to belong to no party, but enlightened Conservatism as exemplified by Peel was probably nearest her ideal. And the Whig government's subsequent failure to deal with the Great Famine confirmed her view. At its onset, she was already a very old lady, and much bowed down by family tragedies at home. But she roused herself to use her fame and name to beg relief for Edgeworthstown and its surrounding districts. She had long before rejected from personal experience the principle preached by Harriet Martineau among others that charity was always wrong and that those 'who do not work shall not eat.' There were in Ireland 'such numbers who had no work – who could not work from extenuation, disease, etc. Humanity could not leave these to perish from hunger – or if humanity had been out of the question, fear could not have ventured it.'[2] The Irish peasant knew well enough how to retaliate. Maria had already lived through sixty years when landlords – or their agents – could be shot at from behind a hedge.

Generous and enlightened paternalism, such as her father had practised, was in Maria's view still the best insurance against social revolution – until education had percolated to the majority. She was not so far off the mark: Edgeworthstown was to survive as the family home for another three generations when many of the neighbouring big houses were burned out or abandoned and left to fall into ruin. The house itself is still immaculately kept, though now a nursing home, and so is the eighteenth-century walled garden where Maria once stamped on the garden frames as a neglected six-year-old and later happily planted her favourite 'everblowing' roses. And there is a fine new bronze statue of Maria herself, book in hand, looking down the main street of Edgeworthstown where she once walked briskly in her newly invented waterproof boots to oversee the paving of a footpath, or the building of the new market house …

---

2   Letter to Professor Jones, 14 June 1847.

ACKNOWLEDGMENTS

WHEN MARIA WAS ten, her father set her as a writing project an essay on Generosity. The result has not survived but it led to an Edgeworth family saying, 'Where is the generosity'.

This book has been made possible by generosity from many people.

First, I must thank Maria Edgeworth's great-great-nephew Professor Sir David Butler, who has allowed me to quote extensively from Maria's unpublished letters now held on loan in the New Bodleian. He has also most kindly allowed me to illustrate them with the drawings and sketches deposited there, mostly the work of Maria's stepmother Frances Beaufort Edgeworth and Maria's half-sisters, Charlotte and Honora Edgeworth. Charlotte in particular was a talented artist, dying tragically of consumption at the age of twenty-three.

The National Library of Ireland has also generously allowed me to quote from many of Maria's letters up to the end of 1817, which are held in their collection of Edgeworth manuscripts.

Dr Rolf Loeber also kindly offered the option of using pictures from two Edgeworth albums now belonging to him, which also consist mainly of sketches by Frances Edgeworth and Charlotte Edgeworth. He and his wife Magda have been hugely helpful over many years, sending me relevant articles, copies of Maria's letters held in American libraries, and driving me to see some outposts of the original Edgeworth estates.

Dr Edward McParland procured for me the splendid colour print of Trinity's Museum with its stuffed giraffe – or as Maria called it 'camelopardel'. Dr Anthony Malcomson arranged for Charlie Clements to send me the picture of Lord Oriel's temple at Collon. Brendan and Alison Rosse have lent me the magnificent picture of the 3rd Earl of Rosse climbing his telescope at Birr and also showed me Maria's correspondence with the 2nd Earl of Rosse. Trevor Fitzherbert kindly allowed my husband, Thomas, to photograph three miniatures of Maria's favourite Ruxton cousins, rescued from their family home at Black Castle (now burnt). Matt Farrell, the moving force behind the Edgeworth Society and the Edgeworth Museum, sent me the sketch of the main street of Edgeworthstown probably made in the 1820s, and the photographs of Edgeworthstown house, c.1880 with Maria's books still in place, as well as the photo of the Edgeworth vault at St John's Church. The Royal Irish Academy and the Irish Architectural Archive have both allowed me to reproduce pictures at minimum cost. Many of my other illustrations were photographed by my husband, Thomas, or Bartle Darcy, a helpful neighbour. The London Library staff kindly found me many nineteenth-century or early twentieth-century illustrated books.

For the letters themselves, my thanks go to the long-suffering librarians at the National Library of Ireland (NLI) and the Weston Library in the New Bodleian in Oxford, who brought me up successive folders of Edgeworth letters from the vaults over many months to read and copy. (I tried in vain to read Maria's letters on microfiche, but nothing can compare with the pleasure and comparative ease of reading the original manuscript letters.) The NLI librarians also kindly directed me to Maria's correspondence with Thomas Spring Rice, later Lord Mounteagle; with the famous Dublin mathematician Sir William Rowan Hamilton and with her favourite economist, the Reverend Richard Jones. I am also grateful to the librarians of the Special Collections in Trinity College, Dublin for allowing me to read through Maria's correspondence with Sir Philip Crampton. All four of these collections gave me valuable background information about the second half of Maria's life though in most cases I have not been able to quote from them directly for reasons of space.

Many other friends have also given me help and encouragement in my years of reading through and selecting from Maria's letters. My daughter Eliza, who first reignited my interest in Maria Edgeworth, lent me all her notes and, with Olda Fitzgerald and Barbara Fitzgerald, provided a bed in

Dublin while I was working at the National Library. Marianne and Tim Sheehy, and Jane Goddard provided me with many bednights in Oxford while I was reading through the even larger collection of Maria's letters in the Bodleian. John Fairleigh read through my typescripts at various stages and showered me with early nineteenth-century memoirs and letters, relating to Maria's life and times. Another Westmeath neighbour, Katharina Dedem-Laurens, lent me her brilliant thesis, 'Maria Edgeworth: A Sense of Place', which confirmed my view that Maria's letters from Ireland and her life as a 'domestic being' had not yet been properly explored. Robert O'Byrne, my husband Thomas, and my sister Linda Kelly have also all made hugely helpful suggestions as to narrative themes to follow and shared their much greater knowledge of Irish, English and European history.

Lastly, my thanks to my editor, Bridget Farrell at Lilliput, who has patiently helped with the highly complicated process of putting together letters and illustrations to create this book; and to Fred Krehbiel, whose generosity has made it possible to illustrate it as I had hoped.

ILLUSTRATIONS

The vast majority of black and white illustrations in this book are from the collection of Edgeworth drawings and watercolours in the Weston Library of the Bodleian, Eng Misc, Edgeworth MSS, Folders 901–903, which I have been allowed to reproduce by kind permission of Sir David Butler and his family. These appear on the following pages: 39, 41, 68, 71, 79, 94, 96, 104, 109, 115, 122, 163, 167, 174, 181, 195, 208, 226, 229, 283, 295, 315, 333, 370, 374, 383.

Maria's picture of herself falling off a ladder, p. 379 and the endpapers of the book can also be found in her letters MS Eng. Lett. Edgeworth in the Weston Library.

The famous portrait of the Edgeworth family by Adam Buck in 1787 is now on loan to the National Gallery of Ireland, but is also the property of Sir David Butler and his family, who have allowed me to reproduce it on the cover.

I am also grateful to the following institutions for allowing reproduction of the following pictures.

Title-pages for *Essay on Irish Bulls*, p. 74, and *Memoirs of Richard Lovell Edgeworth, Esq.*, p. 214, courtesy of The Lilliput Press.

The Edgeworth Museum for the sketch of Edgeworthstown main street, p. 237, and interiors of Edgeworthstown House photographed in the 1880s, p. 424.

The Irish Architectural Archive for the picture of Farnham House, Co. Cavan, p. 247 and the sketch of Maria Edgeworth's bedroom, p. 420.

The Paul Getty Library for the calotype of Michael Pakenham Edgeworth, p. 407.

The National Library of Ireland for the drawing by Arthur Young, p. 32 and the sketch by Harriet Beaufort of peasants queuing for food, p. 413.

The National Portrait Gallery in London for the mezzotint of Honora Sneyd, p. 27 and the calotype of Maria Edgeworth, p. 407.

The Royal Irish Academy for the frontispiece of Moore's *Irish Melodies*, p. 143.

A few other pictures have been kindly made available to me from private collections, *viz.* the satirical sketch by Caroline Hamilton, p.49 and the Temple at Oriel, p. 176. Pictures from our own family collection include the Gillray cartoon, p. 57, George IV's triumphal progress down Sackville St, p. 139 and the portraits of Kitty Pakenham and Sir Arthur Wellesley (later Duke of Wellington), p. 103 and Admiral Pakenham, p. 118.

Attributions for the colour pictures used in this book appear beside them.

NOTE ON TEXT

As far as possible, when copying Maria's letters, I kept to her original idiosyncratic spellings and punctuation, which largely consisted of dashes, with only an occasional full stop. I sometimes inserted extra commas or quotation marks where I felt sense required it. Indecipherable words I followed with a question mark in square brackets. In other cases I inserted an additional word (denoted by square brackets and italics) for clarification. Many of the original letters were cut for reasons of space and I marked these cuts in all cases by ellipses.

Like most writers of the period, Maria's use of capitals was more widespread and arbitrary than in the present day and I kept these as she wrote them. She used underlinings both for emphasis and to indicate French or Latin. For clarity, I used the greater freedom available in print to transpose her French phrases and book titles into italics. Titles of publications throughout have otherwise been reproduced in the form in which they originally appeared.

I

MARCH 1776 – MAY 1798

MARIA EDGEWORTH ALWAYS *claimed the rackety Irish squires of her famous novel,* Castle Rackrent, *were pure invention, but it is tempting to draw parallels with early generations of Edgeworths in Ireland. Two Edgeworth brothers had come to Ireland in the 1580s as part of a wave of late Elizabethan 'adventurers'. Both prospered – one, Edward, became a bishop; the other Francis, Maria's great-great-grandfather, became Chief Clerk to the Crown in Dublin. In 1619 James I awarded Francis 600 acres of land in Co. Longford, confiscated from a Catholic landowner, and Francis married a neighbouring heiress, Jane Tuite. But their descendants rapidly acquired all the traditional habits of the Anglo-Irish squire – hard drinking and gambling and extravagant hospitality, compounded in the Edgeworths' case by frequent absences at court in London. Near-bankruptcy was twice staved off by marriage to a rich widow. Maria's grandfather Richard Edgeworth, who chronicled the family history in* The Black Book of Edgeworthstown, *was the first to return to prudent ways, brought up by a sober Pakenham uncle. A shrewd lawyer, he fought off rival claimants to the estate and built up his rent roll, though with scant regard for his wretched tenants. He also married a clever well-educated woman, Jane Lovell, from Wales. Between them they carefully supervised their children's education. Richard Lovell, Maria's father, the only surviving son, was sent to Trinity College, Dublin, aged just sixteen, but quickly removed when it was clear he had joined a wild hard-drinking set. Instead he was enrolled at Oxford to study law.*

Unfortunately, Richard Edgeworth had introduced his son to an old legal acquaintance, Paul Elers, who lived within easy riding distance of Oxford. Richard Lovell, who was highly attractive to women, proceeded to flirt with (and possibly seduce) one of Elers' pretty daughters, Anna Maria.

Anna Maria Elers, Maria's mother. She had eloped with Richard Lovell Edgeworth aged seventeen.

Aged nineteen, he eloped with her to Gretna Green and almost immediately regretted it. Anna Maria was domesticated and prudent but barely literate. Richard was clever, restless and enthralled by Enlightenment ideas. He also had a distinct talent for mechanical invention. Soon after Maria, his second child, was born in 1768, he was introduced to the brilliant circle of writers, inventors and manufacturers headed by Dr Erasmus Darwin at Lichfield, which later formed the so-called Lunar Society (they met regularly at the full moon). At Dr Darwin's house, he met the beautiful intellectual eighteen-year-old Honora Sneyd, daughter of a local landowner, and fell passionately in love with her.

Unable to offer Honora marriage, he fled to France, taking his first child, Dick, with him and leaving his wife in England with two small girls. When Anna Maria died giving birth to a third daughter, Edgeworth almost immediately returned and declared his love to Honora. She accepted him and Maria found herself with a new stepmother at the age of five. Unlike poor Anna Maria, Honora shared fully in Richard's intellectual interests and together they set out to plan a new system for children's education – Richard Lovell Edgeworth had been an enthusiast for Rousseau's system of 'natural' education and had already tried it out on Dick with disastrous results: Dick, left to roam free without shoes or instruction until the age of seven, had proved quite ungovernable and finally had to be sent away to sea to serve under the Edgeworths' cousin, Captain Lord Longford. (He ran away from his ship and soon after emigrated to America.)

In 1775 Richard Lovell Edgeworth brought his children, now three small daughters and an infant son by Honora, back to the family estate at Edgeworthstown in Co. Longford. His father had died three years before and it was clear the place was going to rack and ruin under an agent's care. He threw himself into reclaiming

Engraved by Hopwood, from a Painting by Romney.

The beautiful Honora Sneyd, painted by Romney before her marriage.

it, remodelling house and gardens, clearing ditches, planting and draining. 'He has 40 men constantly employed and thinks of nothing but his duty,' wrote Honora admiringly. She and Richard were wholly absorbed in each other. Six-year-old Maria, largely ignored, remembered later her unhappiness, and trampling on the garden frames in the walled garden and the delightful sound of breaking glass.

But Honora was already showing symptoms of consumption, and the damp Irish climate was seen as a danger. In 1777 Richard Lovell Edgeworth brought her and the children back to England, and Maria was packed off to a boarding school at Derby, run by a Mrs Lataffiere. Maria's earliest surviving letter, written from school in careful copperplate to her stepmother, shows her pathetically eager for approval.

MARIA *(aged eight)* TO MRS HONORA EDGEWORTH
Derby, 30 March 1776

Dear Mamma,

It is with the greatest pleasure I write to you as I flatter myself it will make you happy to hear from me. I hope you and dear Papa are well. School now seems agreeable to me. I have begun French and dancing and intend to make [great – *crossed out*] improvement in everything I learn. I know it will give you great satisfaction to know I am a good girl. My cousin Clay sends her love; mine to my father and sisters who I hope are well. Pray give my duty to papa, and accept the same from, dear Mamma – your dutiful daughter.

> *Some of her stepmother's chilling responses to Maria survive, which cannot have given much comfort, and her father's are hardly better.*

Northchurch, 5 February 1778

Dear Maria,

Your father and I begin to think it long since we heard from you and beg you will write to us to inform us how you have gone on since your Father saw you at Derby. I hope Mr and Mrs Lataffiere will authorise you to inform us that your behaviour has merited their esteem [?] and that you have endeavoured to improve yourself in everything which you have an opportunity of learning – your being taught to dance may enable you to alter your common method of holding yourself if you pay attention to it & I must say you wanted improvement in this respect very much when you were here …

Great Berkhamsted, Herts, 1778

My dear Maria,

I have delayed answering your letter that some time might elapse to put your resolution of perseverance to a trial. I hope most sincerely that your answer to this will be accompanied with such an account from Mrs Lataffiere as will confirm me in my hopes of your becoming an amiable girl, a character which is of all others most desirable – With a benevolent heart, complying temper and obliging manners, I should make no doubt that by your mother's assistance you might become a very excellent and highly improved woman – Your person, my dear Maria, will be exactly in the middle ground between beauty and plainness – handsome enough to be upon a level with the generality of your sex, if accompanied by gentleness, Reserve & real good sense – Plain enough to be contemptible if unattended with the good qualities of the head and heart – These you have in your own power to attain and your behaviour this summer gave me hopes that your Ambition is excited towards the true perfection of the female character – ... What the French call Pretension can never please in any English woman – Perfect beauty cannot make it agreeable to people of sense & good taste; anything short of that species of personal perfection becomes the object of criticism to your sex if ... placed too forward in a female ... – Adieu, my Dr daughter, (write) to me in English and believe me to be your affectionate father, Richard Lovell Edgeworth.

[*Postscript by Honora*]

I cannot add anything, my dear Maria, to the advice of such a father as you are blessed with, except my most earnest wishes that you may be everything he approves & then I am sure your character will be such as (were you a stranger to me) would make me want you for the Friend of your affect. Mother, Honora Edgeworth.

You asked me many times to let you write to me; I am always glad to hear from you when you have inclination to write, but I wish you never to consider it a task.

By 1778 Honora's consumption had been confirmed, and she and Edgeworth were desperately moving from one location in England to another in search of any treatment that might delay her death.

RICHARD LOVELL EDGEWORTH TO MARIA
Sheffield, 2 November 1779

My dear Maria,

I am very sorry that I cannot give such an account as will please you of your mother's health. She still continues in a very dangerous situation but has her usual cheerfulness and serenity – Your last (letter) appeared to me more *en fille d'école* than your former letters. Indeed it is impossible to write without having something to say; at least it ought to be impossible. I send you part of an Arabian fable which I beg you to finish & am with great affection, your father, Richard Lovell Edgeworth

Subsequent letters to his younger sister Margaret, who had married a retired soldier, John Ruxton, gave anguished bulletins on Honora's decline and begged her frantically to come to England. She finally arrived too late. In the meantime, Maria became the immediate recipient of her father's grief – and another remarkable moralizing letter. There was at least a hint that relations had seen Honora's treatment of Maria as over-harsh.

RICHARD LOVELL EDGEWORTH TO MARIA
Bristol [?], 2 May 1780

My dearest daughter,

At six o'clock on Sunday morning your mother expired in my arms – She now lies dead beside me and I know I am doing what would give her pleasure … by writing to you at this time to fix her excellent image in your mind – As you grow older and become acquainted with more of my friends you will hear from every mouth the exalted character of your incomparable Mother.

You will be convinced by your own reflection that she fulfilled the part of a mother towards you & towards your sisters without partiality for her own or servile indulgence towards mine.

Though her timely restraint of you and steadiness of behaviour, yielding fondness towards you only by the exact measure of your conduct at first alarmed those who did not know her, yet now, my dearest daughter, every Person who has the least connection with my family is anxious to give sincere testimony of their admiration of those very circumstances which they too harshly associated with the idea of a second wife –

Continue, my dear daughter, the desire you feel of becoming amiable, prudent and of Use. The ornamental parts of a Character with an understanding such as yours … necessarily ensues. But true judgement and sagacity in the choice of friends and the regulation of your behaviour is to be had only from reflection and from being thoroughly convinced of what Experience teaches in general too late, that to be happy, we must be Good – God bless you and make you ambitious of the valuable praise which the amiable character of your dear Mother forces from the virtuous & the wise.

My writing to you in my present situation will, my dearest daughter, be remembered by you as the strongest proof of the love of your approving and affectionate father, Richard Lovell Edgeworth

Honora on her deathbed had urged Richard Lovell Edgeworth to marry her younger sister Elizabeth Sneyd – rather to his surprise and to Elizabeth's, who was not at all in love with him. However, when he proposed a few months later, she accepted him. The engagement, though legal (the bill banning marrying a 'Deceased Wife's Sister' only became law later), shocked both her family and Richard's sister, Margaret Ruxton. The Sneyds forbade the bans and the couple were eventually forced to find a clergyman in a London parish to marry them. But Elizabeth was to be a far kinder and more congenial stepmother to Maria than the 'incomparable Honora'. And Richard's letters began to show more open affection for his eldest daughter.

Shortly afterwards he decided to send Maria to a fashionable boarding school in London to give her polish – a vain attempt as Maria showed no aptitude for music or drawing or dancing and remained painfully shy. But she entertained her fellow pupils with ghost stories at night and made one close friend, Fanny Robinson, daughter of a Northamptonshire baronet. Fanny teased her for her sedateness and bookishness (Maria was already showing strong bluestocking tastes encouraged by her father), but gave her the affection she craved.

By 1782 Richard Lovell Edgeworth was already a father of eight children. It was clear from his intermittent visits to Ireland that his estates in Edgeworthstown were being hopelessly mismanaged by an agent, and he had already decided before Honora's death that he must return to Edgeworthstown himself fulltime, not only as his duty but from financial necessity. Maria, aged fourteen, was removed at short notice from her finishing school to return to Ireland, much to her delight. Nothing could have been better than to be allowed to live with her beloved father again.

The family reached Dublin in early April. Maria's first impressions of the extraordinary mixture of squalor and grandeur of the city and the dilapidated state of Edgeworthstown House and its swarming retainers were to be brilliantly recalled in her later novel, The Absentee.

Maria's earliest surviving letters from Ireland are to her old school friend Fanny Robinson. They begin, not surprisingly, with school gossip and Maria's admiration for Fanny Burney (whose romantic novel Evelina had been published three years before to huge acclaim), but they also show her interest in letter writing as an art – she cites two famous English models – and her first literary endeavour, given to her by her father, translating from French Madame de Genlis' letters on education (Madame de Genlis was governess to the French Royal family). Unfortunately this came to nothing as a rival translation appeared when Maria's was half done.

TO FANNY ROBINSON
Edgeworthstown, 15 April 1782

… So there have been wonderful revolutions in Wimpole Street, the rebel Angel is "fallen, fallen, fallen from the blest abode." But seriously how does Miss Denis, Miss Masin and Miss E. Dent do? All x-x-x w I hope.

This present day is one of the hottest we have had this summer, but I defy the sun and all its wicked works for I am seated in a shady arbour on the stump of an old tree – Do you envy me? – But perhaps you are insensible to the heat. I am sure you must be if you could sit baking in a playhouse to see Miss <u>Siddons</u>.

It is the utmost I would do to see Miss Burney for I am not, as you seem to be, Siddons mad, having only a likeness of her in a Review … You are acquainted with Miss Burney, pray tell me all you know of her … I read Evelina over twice, once with a malicious view of discovering a fault, but alas before I had read it half through, I forgot my intentions. Lord Orville is a man after my own heart – his character did not want a title to give it dignity; it is saying a great deal for the Hero but when I say the Heroine thought so too perhaps I say still more for her. It was the character of the man and not the lord she loved – Why then did Miss Burney give him a title – was it to recommend it to titled Readers? If so she did their taste or her Book great injustice … And I may be so bold to say of her young Plebiean admirers some injury … It is preparing for them Disappointment and Ennui at least … Evelina had not title & but small fortune and she married an Earl! Will no conclusion be drawn from this? Will no hopes be raised?[3]

… As for the Book you are so kind as to enquire about – Alas, it is only a humble translation of Madame de Genlis' letters. I had just finished the third volume when a rival translation appeared in all its Glory – one volume however is printed and my father thinks of compressing the other two into one & publishing them in Dublin.

… What easy sprightly letters Grey's are (published by Mason) – I dare say you have read them – They are not the stiff performance of an author written under the rod of criticism and of a Presentment that they would be published as authors' letters usually are – All that I have seen of Pope's give me that idea, the style is too correct to be free … Don't you think so? You hear I am asking

---

3   In Fanny Burney's novel, which was to be the model for respectable romantic fiction, Lord Orville
     is the high-minded hero who falls in love with the seventeen-year-old heroine and marries her after
     numerous vicissitudes.

trifling questions across the British channel with as little ceremony as if you were in the same room with me. I hope you will transport me, or at least my ideas, on return to Crawford ... If I should meet Miss Burney there – I should be completely happy – If there is any resemblance between her own character & her amiable Evelina, I should not only be desirous but ambitious of her friendship[4]...

Maria's subsequent letters to Fanny Robinson show her becoming happily absorbed in her new life at Edgeworthstown, though still devouring a formidable number of books. Her father, impressed by Maria's intelligence and willingness to learn, decided to make her his bookkeeper and secretary for estate business and she rode out daily with him on her pony Dapple to inspect fields and outlying tenant farms. It was also a time of intense political excitement in Ireland: the Volunteer movement had sprung up ostensibly to 'defend' Ireland against a French invasion in the wake of the American revolution but in fact to put pressure on England to grant the Irish Parliament more political independence. Shortly afterwards it fizzled out, dissolved by its leader Lord Charlemont as it became apparent it could lead to more dangerous strains of insurrection.

TO FANNY ROBINSON
Edgeworthstown, 15 September 1783

... You desire me to read <u>Julia de Roubigne</u>[5] ... I won't promise you I will, though I am as fond of <u>Novels</u> as you can be I am afraid they act on the constitution of the Mind as Drams do on that of the body ... But your recommendation will induce me to read any other species of books – Have you finished Rollins' Ancient History yet and how did you like it? I am reading the History of the only conqueror I will ever like – Peter justly called the Great. I shall read the life of Charles the Twelfth as soon as I have finished but I am afraid all Voltaire's Eloquence will not prevent my wishing his hero to lose every Battle ... I have finished Moliere's and begun Marivaux's Theatre ... – You see I read several Books on different subjects at a time ...

---

4   Maria in fact wrote to Fanny Burney asking if she would accept a correspondent from Ireland but received no response.
5   Romantic epistolary novel by Henry Mackenzie, published 1777. Its opening words were 'The friendship of your Maria, misfortune can never deprive you of ...', which may be why Fanny had recommended it.

Now indulge me in talking to you of a subject which … fills my whole mind (except when it is empty) – the present state of Politics here. What should you think of a Civil War? Upon my word there is danger – The people are in a state of universal fermentation. The Counties, Corps, Provinces are all sending Delegates and making what they call <u>Spirited</u> <u>Resolutions</u> – a free Parliament is the cry – a free Parliament they will have or none at all – There is to be one of the greatest and most respectable meetings held on Monday next (to decide on some plan to be supported by the united exertions of the Volunteers of Ireland) that was ever seen in this … Country. My father went up to Town this morning to speak at it … They say your Ministry in England means to oppose with all their strength & the Catholics here hint that if they are not allowed the right of voting they will join them – But I cannot believe it, the ministers of England must be too well informed to think the Volunteer army nothing but a name, or to venture to trifle with several 1000 men in arms with a Charlemont, an Ogle and a Flood at their head – I tell you what, my dear Fanny, I am not too proud to be vain & so let me praise my father … His speech to the Leinster delegates was received with the greatest applause … Pray look sometimes at our Irish papers to see what's doing here … Cast your eye over a map of Ireland now and then that you mayn't be frightened when I talk of Drogheda & Dungannon & Tipperary & Carrickfergus & a few other such names …

It is unlikely that Fanny Robinson, fresh from a London season, responded to Maria's interest in Irish politics. Meanwhile, Maria, remote from balls in rural Co. Longford, convinced herself that Fanny's social life in London would not have suited her and offered a further long lecture on Ireland, reflecting her father's views.

TO FANNY ROBINSON
Edgeworthstown, Autumn 1783

… You have mentioned in several letters that you are going to Balls. I have an odd opinion to ask you – are you <u>happier</u> at a Ball than anywhere else? You will laugh & say to be sure I am; or perhaps you will ask me why I make such a curious enquiry? I will tell you why – because I am inclined to believe that it is all the preparations, the Music, the dress, the praise & the bustle which constitute the charms of a Ball … Our tastes do not in these aspects

I believe agree but I see the obvious cause for their disagreeing – you have a very agreeable person, agreeable manners & many external accomplishments which I want – You are active, nimble & dance well. I am awkward & dance very ill, it is not therefore the least surprising that you should be happy in a ballroom where you are praised … or that I on the contrary with every personal disadvantage … should feel myself much less at my ease in company than amongst friends who set little comparative value on such qualifications … I know their value for I know the want of them, and the pain arising from that want is certainly the most exact measure of that worth …

I promised you my dear Miss Robinson that I would give you some account of the manners of the people I live amongst and that I would communicate all the observations I have an opportunity of making on the peculiarities of … the climate etc.

The Irish are perhaps the laziest civilised nation on the face of the Earth. To avoid a moment's present trouble they will bring on themselves real misfortunes. When urged by necessity (for without that spur they would never exert themselves) they work with excessive violence for a short space of time and then sink again into a species of torpid inaction – for this indolence peculiar to the Irish peasantry several reasons may be assigned … the most powerful is low wages of labour, 6d a day in winter and 8d in the summer … every day labourer has about 3 acres of land sown with potatoes enough to afford a subsistence to him and his wretched family. He does not covet or even seem to relish the luxuries and conveniences of life – they live in a hut whose mud built walls can scarcely support their weather beaten roofs, you may see the children playing before the *abris sans* shoes, *sans* stockings, *sans* everything – the father of the family on a fine summer's day standing in the sunshine at his door, while his house is ready to fall upon his head … You go up to him and tell him he had much better set about repairing his house – he would answer you Oh faith Honey, when it falls it will be time enough to think of picking it up …

… To conclude their character, the Irish are remarkably hospitable to strangers, friendly and charitable to each other; *à propos* about charity I must observe to you that the charity of the higher class of people is one of the greatest checks to industry. It encourages idleness amongst the Poor and increases the number or rather the swarms of Beggars, which invest the streets of Dublin. Let the rich raise the wages of labour, the rewards of industry, that would be true charity … The lower class of Irish are extremely

An Irish family outside their cabin, drawn by Arthur Young in 1776 to illustrate his Tour of Ireland, *though not used. Maria would have read Young's book and her letter to Fanny Robinson echoes Young's descriptions.*

eloquent, they have a volubility, a fluency and a facility of delivery which is really surprising ... and they are good lawyers ... necessity obliges them to exercise their abilities for fraud and artifices. The Irish language is now almost gone into disuse ... except in their quarrels with each other. It is a remarkably harmonious language ... the Irish claim their origin from the Phoenicians.

There are finer lakes in this country ... than you could have any idea of; the face of the country is disfigured by large tracks of bog. It is supposed that these bogs were originally formed by the leaf and bark of immense forests of trees. A peasant who was working in bog owned by my Father found several feet below the surface a coat, a basket full of arms and a wooden bowl ... the coat was neither knit or woven – it was of a manufacture quite unknown – my father has sent it over to the Royal Society ...

You think my dear Fanny that I change my employments, my tastes, my pursuits every four months – I must tell you what I am about in my own defence; well I'm writing a book – a Book – yes a book and in six volumes, I began it a month ago and I have written two volumes, but I will tell you neither the title or the subject until it is published ...

The book mentioned was probably Maria's first attempt at a novel. But her father encouraged her instead to apply her storytelling talents to the project begun with him and his second wife Honora – providing simple moral tales for children to replace the usual diet of fairy stories and nursery rhymes. All his children were now to be educated at home without governesses or tutors, and he allotted each of his younger children in turn to the care of an older one. Maria was made responsible for Henry, her stepmother Elizabeth's second child, born in 1782. Her next surviving letter is to her stepmother's sister, Charlotte Sneyd. Charlotte and another sister, Mary Sneyd, had taken over the care of the younger Edgeworth children in the aftermath of Honora's death and were soon to come to live permanently at Edgeworthstown to help with Richard Lovell Edgeworth's ever-expanding family.

TO CHARLOTTE SNEYD
Edgeworthstown, 9 December 1787

… I think, my dear Aunt Charlotte, I did not know till Henry returned to us after his six weeks absence how very agreeable even a child of his age can make himself … His journey has been productive of so much pleasure to me from the kindness and approbation you have shown and has left my mind so full a conviction of your skill in the art of education that I should part with Henry again with infinitely more security and satisfaction than I did two months ago. I was really surprised to see with what ease and alacrity little Henry returned to all his former habits and occupations … nothing seemed strange to him in anything or anybody about him. When he spoke of you to us, he seemed to think that we were all necessarily connected in all our commands and wishes, that we were all one <u>whole</u> – One great polypus soul …

The 'great polypus soul' at Edgeworthstown was subject to frequent deaths as well as births – two of Elizabeth's children had died in infancy – and in 1790 Richard Lovell Edgeworth's beautiful fifteen-year-old daughter by Honora, also named Honora, died, like her mother, of consumption. This is Maria's first surviving letter to her Aunt Ruxton, her father's sister Margaret, who was to become her favourite correspondent. The Ruxtons lived at Black Castle outside Navan in Co. Meath in a delightful large cottage orné *and there was constant coming and going between there and Edgeworthstown.*

TO AUNT RUXTON
Edgeworthstown, 11 February 1790

Your friendship, my dear Aunt Ruxton, has I am sure considerably alleviated the anguish of mind my father has had to feel, and your letter and well deserved praise of my dear mother's [*stepmother*] fortitude and exertion were a real pleasure to her. She has indeed had a great deal to bear … In my father's absence, she ordered everything, did everything, felt everything herself. Unless, my dear aunt, you had been present during the last week of dear Honora's sufferings, I think you could not form an idea of anything so terrible, so touching – such extreme fortitude, such affection, such attention to the smallest feelings of others, as she showed on her death-bed!

My father has carefully kept his mind occupied ever since his return, but we cannot help seeing his feelings at intervals. He has not slept for two or three nights and is, I think, far from well today …

He said the other day, speaking of Honora, "My dear daughters, I promise you one thing, I will never reproach any of you with Honora. I will never reproach you with any of her virtues." There could not have been a kinder … promise, but I could not help fearing that my father should refrain from speaking of her too much, and that it would hurt his mind …

Maria's second stepmother, Elizabeth, weakened by almost yearly pregnancies, and Honora's fourteen-year-old brother Lovell were also showing consumptive symptoms and in the following year, Richard Lovell Edgeworth decided to take them both to Clifton to seek doctors' advice. Maria, aged twenty-three, was left in charge of her remaining seven siblings, much to her alarm.

TO AUNT RUXTON
Edgeworthstown, September 1791

Now that my father and mother are gone [*to England*] you cannot imagine with what pleasure I reflect that we have so good and kind a friend as you, my dear Aunt Ruxton, so near us … For though the unbounded kindness and confidence my father and my dear mother expressed towards me when we parted was enough to reassure a disposition more timid than mine naturally is, yet I cannot help feeling unusual timidity when I look round me and think I am trusted with so valuable a charge.

*Maria's favourite aunt, Margaret
Ruxton, Richard Lovell Edgeworth's
younger sister.*

*Richard Lovell Edgeworth and the
memorial to his daughter Honora,
painted by Adam Buck, 1790.*

We had the pleasure of hearing last night that they landed safely at
Holyhead after a sixteen hour passage [*which*] ... was my father says,
remarkably rough. He says he was sick enough for two, my mother for four ...
They proposed being absent only till the first week in October; but allowing
for the usual chances of travelling, we may think ourselves exceedingly happy
if we see them in the middle of October. – You, my dear aunt, who know the
excessive kindness with which they treat me more as a friend and equal than
as a daughter, can imagine how I miss the pleasures I have been <u>spoiled</u> with.
But yet I feel much more cheerful than I had any idea I should ... because
my sisters and Lovell are so kind to me and all the children go on so well
... Emmeline has the care of Charlotte and I think, there cannot be a more
sweet-tempered child.

My sister and I hope you will not forget to give all our loves, one by one,
to Letty and Sophy. If Margaret will do me the favour to accept of them, I will
soon send her some wee-wee stories which she commissioned me to write if
I could ...

A month later, Richard Lovell Edgeworth, delighted with Clifton, wrote to instruct Maria to bring the entire family to join him there, where they would see the world and she and her older sisters would find husbands. The youngest child, two-year-old Thomas Day, was to be entrusted to Sophy Ruxton at Black Castle. Sophy, nine years younger than Maria but clever and bookish, was to become her most intimate friend.

TO AUNT RUXTON
Edgeworthstown, October 1791

My dear mother is safe and well, and a fine new sister, I suppose you have heard. [*To be called Honora.*] My very dear aunt, since the moment I came home till this instant my hands have trembled and my head whirled with business but the delightful hope of seeing my dear father and mother at Bristol is in a fine perspective at the end. My father has written the kindest possible letter and Emmeline is transcribing his directions … We are to set off as soon as we can … I write by this night's post to Mr Hanna, to take lodgings for us at Dublin and we are, as you will see, to go by Holyhead …

And now, my dear Sophy for your <u>roaring</u> <u>blade,</u> Thomas Day, Esq. He is in readiness to wait upon you – whenever you can have the charity to receive him? Name the day, my dear aunt which will be the least inconvenient if you can – and Molly⁶ or John Langan⁷ shall bring him the old or new chaise to your door … I will send Hume unopened in Thomas' lap …

TO SOPHY RUXTON
Edgeworthstown, October 1791

I must and I will find time to write one line to you, my dear Sophy, to tell you not that I like you, not that your conversation interested me extremely and that the ease and openness of your manners particularly suited my taste – for if <u>thou</u> hast not found out all this, I shall not trouble to tell it <u>thee</u> … I hope Tomboy will deliver this with his own hand. How very good you are to take charge of him. He has orders to lay, if he can lift it – a clumsy writing desk of Sister Maria's to lay at your ladyship's feet. Don't let your pride prick up

---

6   Wife of the Edgeworths' English coachman, Samuel Bristow.

7   The Edgeworths' Irish steward, who was to be the original of Honest Thady in Maria's novel, *Castle Rackrent*.

your ears, I am not going to give it to you ... only to beseech you to take care of it in my absence and if you will, my dear Sophy, it will be very agreeable to me to think it may sometimes bring me to your thoughts. I have but few friends in the world, but those few I hope I shall never lose. Wherever I am ... a very great proportion of the happiness of my life must depend upon the approbation and affection of the friends I love. I send the story I began for Margaret[8] merely to prove to you I had actually begun – it is very badly done and for my own credit I would not send it, only on the faith that you will not show it to anybody, and return it by Molly ...

Maria, in charge of six children, arrived at Holyhead after an exhausting 33-hour passage, then took the long coach journey to Clifton, arriving early November 1791. The family did not return to Edgeworthstown until November 1793. Anna (Maria's younger sister) meanwhile had become engaged to Dr Thomas Beddoes, described by her father as 'a little fat democrat of considerable abilities, of a great name in the scientific world'. Poor little Thomas Day Edgeworth, who had been left with the Ruxtons, had died while they were away.

By New Year 1794, England was at war with France in the wake of the French Revolution, and the recruiting officers were out in Ireland. Maria's father had invented a new telegraph system to give early warning of a French invasion and was endeavouring (without success) to persuade the government to install it.

TO SOPHY RUXTON
Edgeworthstown, 22 January 1794

... Mr Fox[9] and Lady Anne were here last Sunday and are returning immediately to Kilkenny. Mr Fox, I believe, got but one recruit out of John Langan and to all our enquiries for men for "my uncle", John Langan shakes his head, puts up his shoulder or changes from leg to leg which are all in him sad tokens of his distress ...

Give my love to Letty[10] and tell her that her rose is in good preservation and is along with the quaking grass blooming on my bureau ...

---

8   Sophy's younger sister.
9   Richard Lovell Edgeworth's uncle and commander of the Longford Militia.
10 Sophy's older sister, Letty.

TO SOPHY RUXTON
Edgeworthstown, 23 February 1794

... The latest telegraph news arrived here last night in a letter from Lovell to my father. The Speaker behaved like himself in everything except in unluckily having lost the Memorial. My father wrote a new one, approved of in flattering terms by Colonel Doyle; in still more flattering terms by Lord Charlemont. My father went to see the Longfords all warm and alive – Mr Edward Pakenham just came over with a Mr Clements – the Mr Clements who erected signal-posts along the coast of England and who was said to be coming over to establish similar posts – but he has come only to take possession of a good estate. Observe, ladies and gentlemen, that the word "telegraph" and "telegraphy" have been carefully avoided in this new Memorial because both party spirit and national pride dislike the sound of the French telegraph.

Thank my aunt and thank yourself for kind enquiries after "Letters for Literary Ladies".[11]

I am sorry to say they are not quite as well as can be expected ... when they are fit to be seen – if that happy time arrives – their first visit shall be to Black Castle. They are now disfigured by all manner of crooked marks of Papa's critical indignation which I would not have you see ...

My mother is better this evening,[12] but she is so very cheerful when she has a moment's respite that it deceives us. She calls Lovell the Minute Philosopher at this instant because he is drawing with the assistance of a magnifying glass ... a beautifully small drawing of the new front of the house.[13]

TO AUNT RUXTON
Edgeworthstown, 8 May 1794

My father has just had a letter from Anna[14] who is safely landed in England. She says she suffered less than she ever did and "luckily escaped a watery

---

11   This was the draft of Maria's first book, an exchange of letters about the proper education of women, published in 1795. The last section, a witty essay on the Noble Science of Self-Justification – on feminine methods for conducting an argument – was later expanded into her comic novel, *The Modern Griselda*, in which an over-argumentative wife finally drives her husband to leave her.

12   Elizabeth Edgeworth had just given birth to her last child, William.

13   Richard Lovell Edgeworth had just begun a new round of 'improvements' to the rambling old family house.

14   Anna had married Dr Beddoes at Edgeworthstown three weeks before.

Anna Edgeworth, drawn after her marriage to Dr Thomas Beddoes. Pretty and vivacious, she attracted many admirers, including Humphrey Davy, Beddoes' young assistant.

Dr Thomas Beddoes, described by Anna's father as a 'little fat democrat of considerable abilities'. He founded the Pneumatic Institute in Bristol, which experimented with medical cures by gases.

grave". A boatful of passengers was rowed by such a set of drunken Charons that it was half filled with water and nearly lost …

My father is perfectly well and very busy out of doors and indoors – The snail of the banisters of the new staircase has just crawled into the hall and certain beauteous pillars have appeared, whose future place of destination no one will tell me … Your hated triangular hatbox of a passage is going to be destroyed and an entrance *dans tous les règles* made into the hall – so that hereafter no one shall complain of having lost their way …

My father brought back certain books from Black Castle, amongst which I was glad to see the Fairy Tales … We are reading a new book for children Evenings at Home by Mrs Barbauld and Dr Aikin [*which*] we admire extremely.[15] Has Sophy seen them? And has she seen the fine Aurora Borealis which was to be seen last week and which my father and Lovell saw with ecstasies. The candles were all put out in the library and a wonderful bustle was made, before I rightly comprehended what was going on …

---

15 Pioneering teacher and writer on children's education and also a talented poet. Maria had met and much liked her in London and Clifton. Dr Aikin was her brother.

TO AUNT RUXTON
Edgeworthstown, June 1794

How melancholy the advertisement of Black Castle looks in the newspapers!.[16] The pretty Drawing-room, the Bats wing Turret which I love and all the happy days I have spent with you [*are*] full in my recollection. Will the cheerful bookcases be left empty shelves? – And who will sit upon the sofa when you are gone? I know you will think more about the trees and shrubs you have planted with your own hands but for these I do not pretend to have such a near interest ... The blue sugar-chest is the only thing in the house I hate and I hate it because it always sat upon the sofa beside you, just where I wanted to sit – and always made more noise with its padlock than I with my tongue. Sugar-chest, I hate you!

... I like to read as well as talk with you, my dear aunt, because you mix the grave and gay together and put your long finger upon the very passages which my short stumpy one was just starting forward to point out ...

You are very good indeed to wish for "Toys and Tasks"[17] but I think it would be most unreasonable to send them to you now ...

TO SOPHY RUXTON
2 July 1794

Having the honour to be the fair day of Edgeworthstown as is well proclaimed to the neighbourhood by the noise of pigs squeaking, men bawling, women brawling and children squealing etc

... I am glad you are still at Black Castle – while you are there, there is hope you may come here. Consider that Rostrevor[18] is in the air, and Kinsale nobody knows where and summer goes and winter comes and life goes – what then? A Picture of a Skeleton which to Sneyd's unprejudiced imagination looks very droll! ...

There are, an't please you, ma'am a great many good things here – There is a Balloon hanging up and another going to be put on the stocks: there is soap made and making from a receipt in Nicholson's "Chemistry" – there is

---

16   The Ruxtons were planning to let their house and move to England, probably after the murder of the local rector at Navan.

17   The first chapter on a book on Practical Education that Maria was now writing with her father.

18   A seaside resort in Co. Down where the Ruxtons rented a house.

Fairday at Edgeworthstown: a sketch by Charlotte Edgeworth.

excellent ink made by the same book – there is a cake of roses just squeezed in a vice by my father according to the advice of Madame de Lagaraye, the woman in black cloak and ruffles who weighs with unwearied scales in the frontispiece of a book, which perhaps my aunt remembers, entitled *Chimie de goût et de l'odorat.* – There is a set of accurate weights, just completed by the ingenious Messrs Lovell and Henry Edgeworth, partners – for Henry is now a junior partner and grown an inch and a half upon the strength of it in two months. The use and ingenuity of these weights I do or did understand; it is great, but I am afraid of puzzling you and disgracing myself attempting to explain it ...

My father bought a great many books at Mr Dean's sale. Six volumes, I believe, of *Machines Approuvés*, full of prints of paper mills, gunpowder mills, machines *pour ramonter les bateaux* ... – a great many things which you would like to see, I am sure, over my father's shoulder. And my aunt would like to see the new staircase – and see a kit-cat view of a robin redbreast sitting on her nest in a sawpit, discovered by Lovell – and you would both like to pick Emmeline's fine strawberries round the crowded oval table after dinner – and to see my mother look so much better in the midst of us – Adieu, dear Sophy.

But peace at Edgeworthstown was under a growing threat. Ireland had suffered chronic agrarian 'troubles' for most of the century. Now, emboldened by events in revolutionary France, secret societies of armed peasants known as Defenders had re-emerged – attacking landlords or anyone suspected of taking land after an eviction. Though Richard Lovell Edgeworth claimed that there were no Defenders on his own estates, he played a leading role in setting up a local militia, partly to prevent more extremist Protestant elements taking control.

TO AUNT RUXTON
Edgeworthstown, 11 August 1794

… There have been lately several flying reports of Defenders, but we never thought the danger <u>near</u> till today. Last night a party of forty men attacked the house of one Hoxey about half-a-mile from us and took, as usual, the arms. They have also been at Ringowny where there was only one servant left to take care of the house – they took the arms and broke all the windows. Today Mr Bond, our high sheriff, paid us a <u>pale</u> visit – thought it proper something should be done for the internal defence of the town of Edgeworthstown and the County of Longford and wished my father would apply to him for a meeting of the county. My father first rode over to the scene of action to inquire into the truth of the reports – found them true and on his return to dinner found Mr Thompson of Clonfin and Captain Doyle, nephew to the general and the wounded colonel who is now at Granard. Captain Doyle will send a sergeant and eleven men tomorrow over to my father – tonight a watch is to be set up, but it is supposed that the sight of two redcoats riding across the country together will keep the evil-minded sprites from appearing to mortal eyes "this watch".

My father has spoken to some and caused many of the people of the lower class to be spoken to and he imagines they will come here to a meeting tomorrow to consider how best they can defend their land and tenements – they bring their arms to my father to take care of. You will be surprised at our making such a mighty matter of a visit from the Defenders – you, who have had soldiers sitting up in your kitchen for weeks – but you will consider this is our first visit.

The arts of peace are going on prosperously – the new room is almost built and the staircase is completed – Long may we live to run up and down it.

TO AUNT RUXTON
Edgeworthstown, 20 September 1794

Do you remember the old shoemaker who used to wear a broad black collar round his neck and who always looked as if he was going to be hanged? This man, known by the name of Old Moor, has a son called by the name of Young Moor … He has just made himself a sergeant and in this character with all his red, blue, green and yellow <u>un</u>blushing military honours, he made his appearance in a conspicuous seat at Church on Sunday to the admiration and amusement of a most respectable and devout congregation. This morning my father came down to breakfast early with the intention of being at Longford early to attend a secret committee and he was drinking his chocolate and talking to Lovell … when Samuel came in with "Sir, here are some soldiers, a whole parcel of 'em, sir, who have had a brawl, if you'd please to see 'em, sir, I believe they have enlisted my lord's painter" – "My lord's painter!" said my father – "What is his name?" "My lord's painter – he as painted Lord Granard's house – he is at the door."

Upon enquiry my father found that "my lord's painter" was an old grey haired man, who was made drunk by one Matt Farrell, … who had first forced a guinea into his pocket and then robbed him of it and then insisted upon his being duly enlisted in his Majesty's service. The soldier who presented the poor painter and his bundle of brushes tied up in a handkerchief was little Mackin who, not many weeks ago, was a car-driver in his honour's service; but he drew on his gloves with fine an air, called my father "my dear" and talked so confidently … of "military service" that none could dare to see the cardriver through the regimentals. In spite of little Mackin, the quondam cardriver's knowledge of military affairs, my father could not be persuaded that the painter was duly enlisted – he discharged him.

A few minutes after … Samuel re-entered with poached eyes. "Sir, they have seized my lord's painter again and are forcing him into a house in the town". My father was wroth at this piece of tyranny and went to enforce justice. Now the person who had seized the painter … was Sergeant Harry Moor. He made his appearance with a constable, half yellow wig, half black hair – Charlie Monaghan, the husband of the celebrated washerwoman – they stood opposite the library window. My father at the door of the new hall was reading to the painter his examination, the ladies crowding the bow window, when lo!

they saw young Moor draw and "brandish high th'-Hibernian sword". Charlie Monaghan, with a stick in his hand, beat or seemed to beat his coat but Charlie Monaghan was not a hero and young Moor ran off to fight another day ...

A warrant was immediately made out to conduct the hero to gaol for contempt of his Majesty's justices. The constable and John Langan and Mr Lovell Edgeworth went to seize Harry at his castle whither he had taken refuge, ... My father got into his chaise which was waiting for him to go to Longford and meant to do himself the honour of receiving Sergeant Moor as he went through the town. In the middle of the street stood the undaunted hero – My father confident that his emissaries were at the back premises, thought he had the gentleman safe, but at the moment he heard my father give orders to seize him, he darted into his house – Monaghan was not ready at the back door and Moor escaped. My father, however, knowing that a sergeant was a man of too much consequence to be entirely lost, determined to send kind enquiries after him to his commanding office, and pursued his way to Longford with "Turner on Crimes and Punishments" in the chaise with him.

About half past five, my father returned looking extremely tired, and to our surprise quite hoarse. "After I have eaten something for I have eaten nothing since morning" said he "I will tell you my adventures".

Dinner was soon over and we drew round the sofa to hear. "I was reading in the chaise when the stagecoach passed me full drive, a chaise following, driver drunk as usual ... I saw one of the wheels was just coming off – I called to the coachman but he did not heed. As we came up, the coachman whipped his horses into a gallop and I called and called till I was so hoarse I could call no more, in vain till a jolt came and crash ..." [*rest of letter missing*]

TO MRS ELIZABETH EDGEWORTH
Edgeworthstown, November 1794

Maria's father and stepmother had gone to visit the Ruxtons at Black Castle to allow Maria's increasingly frail stepmother a rest from domestic cares.

My dear Mother,

All's well at home – the chickens are all good and thriving and there is plenty of provender and of everything we could want or wish for – therefore we all hope that you will fully enjoy the pleasures of Black Castle without being anxious for your bairns. Darcy [*the local carrier*] goes to Dublin tomorrow – I send again for candles lest there should be no light in the hall or in my lady's bower. Emmeline [*Maria's sister*] does not send for tea, because I told her you would bring some from Mrs Armstrong. I hope my zeal has not been, as it sometimes is, too officious. I have told Kitty that no fruit, alias raisins, are to be had in Dublin and she says "Very well, ma'am".

Your girth-web is safely lodged in your dressingroom and my aunt Charlotte's parcel is safely lodged in her drawer – and thank her for the sweet legacy she left me – we eat it today after dinner. It was sugar candy and it gave rise to some observations on chrystalisation which will not be forgotten. Honora's little cheeks are very rosy and she looks to use Kitty's expression "as fresh as a rose in June".[19] There is a little basket in the chaise which I some time ago gave to Henry and; if it is agreeable to you, he wishes you would give it to Miss Margaret Ruxton, who wants a work-basket more than he does. The key to the chaise seat is inside it and Stewart and Animadversions on the School for Scandal …

Pray tell my dear aunt that … it rejoiced my heart to hear her say when she took leave of me that she did not love me less for knowing me better.

Kitty wakened me this morning saying "Dear ma'am, how charming you smell of coals! Quite charming!" – and she sniffed the ambient air thrice …

Kitty Billamore, the Edgeworth's devoted housekeeper, had come with them from England where coal was used in fires, unlike the peat used at Edgeworthstown.

TO LETTY RUXTON
Edgeworthstown, n.d. 1794

… You will look very blank when you come back from the sea and find what doings there have been at Black Castle in your absence. Anna [*Beddoes*] was extremely sorry that she would not see you again before she left Ireland, but you will soon be in the same kingdom … I daresay you will not leave Black Castle again without many a long lingering look. I wish you would gather a nosegay of quaking grass for me. I love it much and I have never seen it in Ireland except in your drawing room, till Anna brought a bunch of it with her from Black Castle.

I am not nearly so lazy as I was when you were obliged to exhort me to leave my butterfly of immortal memory – Give my love to dear Sophy and

---

19   This was the second of Maria's half-sisters to be christened Honora, born 1791.

thank her for Marianne.[20] I think the story very interesting and Marianne a very good girl – she makes, however, too many reflections and too long … I don't like M. Clemal's patched-up deathbed repentance – the legacy he leaves to Marianne makes him quite a good boy again in her eyes … Do you approve of the catastrophe being brought about by sending the hero to the Bastille to cure him of inconstancy? I think Marianne is in rather an awkward situation when she goes to let her prisoner out upon condition that he should ask pardon of her and her mama. Nothing but a temporary convenient fit of frenzy and desperate fevers in both hero and heroine could have brought up the dignity of their characters again after all this …

TO AUNT RUXTON
Edgeworthstown, 11 April 1795

My father and Lovell have been out almost everyday when there are no robbers to be committed to jail at the Logograph – This is the new name instead of the Telegraph because of its allusion to the logographic printing press which prints words instead of letters[21] … My father will allow me to manufacture an essay on the logograph, he furnishing the materials and I spinning them. I am now looking over for this purpose Wilkins' Real Character or an Essay towards a Universal Philosophical Language. It is a scarce and very ingenious book – some of the phraseology is so much out of fashion that it would make you smile – such as the synonym for a little man, a Dandiprat. Likewise two prints, one of them a long sheet of men with their throats cut so as to show the windpipe while working out the different letters of the alphabet. Another being a view of all the birds and beasts packed ready to go into Noah's ark.

Sir Walter James has written a very kind and sensible letter to my father promising all his influence with his Viceregal brother-in-law. My father means to get a letter from him to Lord Camden[22] and present it himself though he rather doubts whether, all things taken together, it is prudent to tie himself to Government. The raising of the militia has occasioned disturbances in this county. Lord Granard's coach was pelted at Athlone and his Lordship compelled to take an oath … He billeted however at Athlone having met 500 men who scattered instantly at the sight of his military force.

---

20   French novel by Marivaux.
21   The name was afterwards changed back to Telegraph.
22   The Irish Viceroy.

The poor people are robbed every night. Last night a poor old woman was considerably roasted – the man who called himself Captain Roast is committed to jail, he was positively sworn to here this morning. Do you know what they mean by the White Tooths? Men who stick two bits of broken tobacco pipes in each corner of face and mouth to disguise the face and voice[23] ...

TO AUNT RUXTON
Edgeworthstown, 20 April 1795

There is a whirlwind in our county, my dear Aunt, and no angel to direct it though many booted and spurred desire no better than to ride in it – There is indeed an old woman in Ballymahon who has been the guardian angel of General Cosby – she has averted a terrible storm which was just ready to burst over his head. The General by mistake went into the town of Ballymahon <u>before</u> his troops came up and while he was in the inn, a mob of five hundred people gathered in the street. The landlady of the inn called General Cosby aside and told him that if the people found him they would certainly tear him to pieces. The General hesitated but the abler general, the landlady sallied forth and called aloud ... "Bring round the chaise-and-four for the gentleman <u>from</u> Lanesborough who is going <u>to</u> Athlone". The General got into his coach incog. and returning towards Athlone met his troops and thus effected a most admirable retreat ...

Monday Night

Richard [*Ruxton*] and Lovell are at the Bracket Gate. I hope you know the Bracket Gate – it is near Mr Whitney's and so called, as tradition informs me, from being painted red and white like a bracket cow. I am not sure what a bracket cow is but I suppose it is something not unlike a dun cow and a gate joined together. They have got a nice tent and a clock and white lights and are trying nocturnal telegraphs which are now brought to satisfactory perfection ...

Sneyd with sparkling eyes returns you his sincere thanks and my mother with her love sends you the following lines which she composed today for him

---

23   The Whitetooths or Whiteboys were another of the secret societies that sprang up in Ireland in the wake of the French Revolution.

"To give me all that art can give
My aunt and mother try
One teaches me the way to live
The other how to <u>dye</u>"

My mother, though she makes epigrams, is far from well …

TO AUNT RUXTON
Edgeworthstown, January 1796

… My father is gone to Longford where he will, I suppose, hear many dreadful Defender stories: he came home yesterday fully persuaded that a poor man in this neighbourhood had been murdered, but he found he was only <u>kilt</u> and was "as well as could be expected" after being twice robbed and twice cut with a bayonet. You, my dear aunt, who were so brave when the County of Meath was the seat of war, must know that we emulate your courage – and I assure you in your own words "that while our terrified neighbours see nightly visions of Massacres, we sleep with our doors and windows unbarred."

I must observe, though, that it is only those doors and windows which have neither bolts or bars that we leave unbarred and these are more at present than we wish, even for the reputation of our valour. All that I crave for my own part is, that if I am to have my throat cut, it may not be by a man with his face blackened with charcoal. I shall look at every person that comes here very closely to see if there be any marks of charcoal upon their visages, Old wrinkled offenders I should suppose would never be able to wash out their stains – but in other a <u>very</u> clean face will in my mind be a strong symptom of guilt – clean hands proof positive – and clean nails ought to hang a man …

TO SOPHY RUXTON
Edgeworthstown, 27 February 1796

… I have a great deal bottled or rather bundled up for you – Though I most earnestly wish that my father was in that situation which Sir T. Fetherstone now graces[24] and though my father had done me the honour to let me copy his

---

24 Richard Lovell Edgeworth had stood for election as an independent for Co. Longford but had been narrowly defeated. He was elected with the support of Lord Granard two years later.

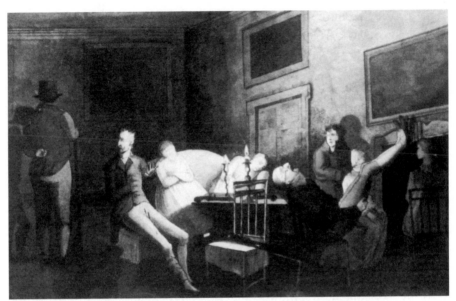

An Irish country house barricaded against an attack. Painting by Caroline Hamilton.

Election letters for him, I am not in the least infected with electioneering rage. Whilst the Election lasted we saw him only a few minutes in the course of the day – then indeed he entertained us to our heart's content. Now his mind seems relieved from a disagreeable load and we have more of his company.

You do not mention Madame Roland,[25] therefore I am not sure you have read her ... We think some of her memoirs beautifully written and like Rousseau – she was a great woman and died heroically, but I do not think she became more *aimable* and certainly not more happy by meddling with politics – <u>for</u> her head is cut off and her husband has shot himself. I think if I had been Monsieur Roland I should not have shot myself for her sake and I question whether he would not have undrawn the trigger if he could have seen all she intended to say of him to posterity ...

I do not know whether you have ever heard of a Mr Pallas who lives at Grouse Hall. He lately received information that a certain Defender was to be found in a lone house which was described by him – he took a party of men with him in the night and got to the house very early in the morning – it was scarcely light. The soldiers searched the house but no man was to be found. Mr

---

25 Muse and *salonnière* to the leading Girondins, she helped her husband escape during the Terror, but
    was guillotined herself in November 1793. Her three-volume memoir written in prison was entitled
    Appel a l'impartiale postérité and upheld sacrifice as the supreme feminine virtue.

Pallas ordered them to search again ... they searched again in vain. They gave up the point and were preparing to mount their horses when one man who had stayed a little behind his companions, saw something moving at the end of the garden behind the house – he looked again and beheld a man's arm come out of the ground. He ran towards the spot and called his companions but the arm had disappeared – they searched but nothing was to be seen ... "Come" said one of the party "Don't waste your time here looking for an apparition among these cabbage stalks – come back once more to the house". They went to the house and there stood the man they were in search of in the middle of the kitchen.

Upon examination it was found that there had been provided a secret passage from the kitchen to the garden opening under an old meal chest with a false bottom which he could push up and down at pleasure. He had returned one moment too soon ...

I beg, dear Sophy, that you will not call my little stories by the sublime title of "my works" – I shall else be ashamed when the little mouse comes forth. The stories are printed and bound the same size as Evenings at Home but I am afraid you will dislike the title. My father had sent the "Parent's Friend" but Mr Johnson has degraded it into the "Parent's Assistant".

This was the first instalment of Maria's stories for children. Richard Lovell Edgeworth had chosen as publisher Joseph Johnson, a well-known English radical, who had already published Mrs Barbauld's Evenings at Home. *The book proved an instant success and Johnson proposed that later editions should be published on finer paper with illustrations. Sophy Ruxton suggested as illustrator her friend Frances Beaufort. Frances was the eldest daughter of the Reverend Daniel Beaufort of Collon, Co. Louth, a gifted travel writer and amateur architect whom Richard Lovell Edgeworth already knew and liked.*

TO SOPHY RUXTON
Edgeworthstown, Spring 1797

... I am really obliged to Miss Beauforth for all she has done for me, and we long to see the drawings; but yet we had rather be good and patient than run the chance of their travelling by any but the best mode of conveyance. Perhaps when my father returns, he may be trusted with them ...

TO SOPHY RUXTON
Edgeworthstown, October 1797

I do not like to pour out the gratitude I feel for your unremitting kindness to me, my dear Sophy, in vain thanks but I may as well pour it out in words as I shall probably never be able to return the many good turns you have done me. I am not nearly ready for your "Irish Bulls"[26] – I am going directly to the "Parent's Assistant". Any good anecdotes from the age of five to fifteen (good latitude and longitude) will suit me and, if you can tell me any pleasing misfortunes of emigrants, so much the better for I want to represent the effects of good and bad education in the conduct of two different forms of *émigrés*. I have a great desire to draw a picture of an anti-Mademoiselle Panache, a well informed, wellbred, French governess, an emigrant lately settled at Bath to introduce young ladies into company ...

By the blind bookseller my father will send you some books and I hope we shall soon have finished Godwin[27] that he may set out for Black Castle. There are some parts of his book [*Essays*] that I think you will like much – "On Frankness" and "Self-taught Genius" but you will find much to blame in his style and you will be surprised that he should have written a dissertation upon English style. I think his essay on Avarice and Profusion will please you, even after Adam Smith – he has gone a step further ...

When we showed Miss Beaufort's beautiful drawing to little William, he asked immediately if those little boys were blowing bubbles ...

TO AUNT RUXTON
n.d. November 1797

... I rejoice very heartily that your favourable opinion of Practical Education does not change with its change of dress. The prophecies of so good a judge as Dr Beaufort are most comfortable words ...

I wish I could continue to give you good news of my mother. These days of bettering only make her relapses more melancholy – when she has a moment's respite, she is as ready to converse with us all as if she forgot her illness ...

---

26 This was to be a book of Irish stories or sayings – proposed by her father to show an English audience the natural wit and intelligence of the Irish. See page 74.

27 William Godwin, who had married Mary Wollstonecraft, was a well-known radical and also published by Joseph Johnson.

Maria's second stepmother, Mrs Elizabeth Edgeworth, died of consumption in November 1797.

Maria's father had already been struck by the very pretty 27-year-old Frances Beaufort, who had been commissioned to provide the illustrations for Maria's books. He had met her several times at her father's rectory in Co. Louth and been impressed by the good nature with which she had taken his criticisms. In the spring of 1798, aged fifty-four, with seven children still at home, he proposed to her and was accepted. Maria was initially devastated by the prospect of a third stepmother, this time two years younger than herself, but was persuaded by Sophy Ruxton – and by Frances' intelligence and tact – that her father had chosen well. Her last stepmother was to become her best and closest friend for the rest of her life.

TO FANNY BEAUFORT
Edgeworthstown, 16 May 1798

Whilst you, my dear Miss Beaufort have been toiling in Dublin, my father has been delighting himself in preparations for June. The little boudoir looks as if it intends to be pretty. This is the only room in the house which my father allows to be finished as he wishes your taste should finish the rest. Like the man who prayed for the eclipse put off, we have been here praying to have the spring put off as this place never looks so pretty as when the lilacs and laburnums are in full flower. I fear, not withstanding all our prayers that their purple and yellow honours will be gone before your arrival. There is one other flower which I am sure will not be in blow for you, a little western flower called "love in idleness". Amongst the many kindnesses my father has shown me, the greatest, I think, has been in his permitting me to see his heart *à decouverte* – and I have been convinced by your kind sincerity and his that in good and cultivated minds, love is no <u>idle</u> passion but one that inspires useful and generous energy …

You call myself, dear Miss Beaufort, my friend and companion – I hope you will never have reason to repent beginning in this style towards me. I think you will not find me encroach upon you. The overflowings of your kindness … will fertilise the land, but will not destroy the landmarks. I do not know whether I most hate or despise the temper that takes an ell where an inch is given.

… Many foolish people make fine plantations and forget to fence them; so the young trees are destroyed by the young cattle … You need not, dear Miss

Beaufort, fence yourself round with very strong palings in this family where all have been early accustomed to mind their boundaries. As for me, you see my intentions, or at least my theories, are good enough – but if my practice be but half as good, you will be content, will you not? But Theory was born in Brobdignag and Practice in Lilliput. So much the better for <u>me</u>! I have often considered since my return home, as I have seen all this family pursuing their several occupations and amusements, how much you have it in your power to add to their happiness. In a stupid or indolent family your knowledge and talents would be thrown away or … worse still to be feared or hated – here, if it may be said without vanity, they will be the certain source of your daily happiness …

II

JUNE 1798 – AUGUST 1802

RICHARD LOVELL EDGEWORTH *married his fourth wife, Frances Beaufort, on 31 May 1798 in St Anne's Church in Dublin. It was a dangerous time for new married bliss. The 1798 Rising had already broken out in the counties surrounding Dublin and, as Frances recorded fifty years later in her* Memoir of Maria Edgeworth, *the journey back to Edgeworthstown through Meath was interrupted several times by reports of rebels hiding in the potato fields. At one point Edgeworth had to shield his new bride from the sight of a dead man hanging in the shafts of a farm cart. But the large extended family awaiting her at Edgeworthstown gave her the warmest of welcomes and Maria's, she recorded, was exceptional. Maria's letter to Sophy two weeks later overflows with the happiness brought by Frances to the whole family.*

TO SOPHY RUXTON
Edgeworthstown, 20 June 1798

… Hitherto all has been quiet in our county and we know nothing of the dreadful disturbances in other parts of the country but what we see in the newspapers. The priests are very active and seem to have great power over the people and a religious war in Ireland must be worse than any other – It is scarcely credible that in these days the priests could make the people believe that they would render them invulnerable by sprinkling them with holy water. I am sorry that my uncle and Richard were obliged to leave you and my dear aunt as I know the continual state of suspense and anxiety in which you must live while they are away.

I fear we may soon know by experience what you feel for my father sees that Lord Cornwallis is coming over here as Lord Lieutenant – and he thinks it will be his duty to offer his services in any manner in which they can be advantageous – Why cannot we be left in peace to enjoy our happiness? We are indeed happy – the more I see of my friend and mother – the more I love and esteem her and the more I feel the truth of what I have heard you say in her praise … I never saw my father at any period appear as happy as he does, and has done for this month past – and you know that he <u>tastes</u> happiness as much as any human being can … So little change has been made in our way of living by the arrival of a new mistress that you would feel as if you were going on with your usual occupations … amongst us. We laugh and talk and enjoy the good of every day … How long this may last, we cannot tell. I am going on in the old way – writing stories. I cannot be a captain of dragoons and sitting with my hands before me would not make any of us one degree safer … I have finished a volume of wee-wee stories – about the size of the Purple Jar all about Rosamund. Simple Susan went to Foxhall a few days ago, for Lady Anne Fox to carry to England … Mr Fox did not think it safe that she should remain here any longer, but last post she received encouragement from Lord Farnham to stay.

My father has made all our little rooms so nice for us – they are all fresh painted and papered, Oh rebels! Oh French! Spare them! We never injured you and all we wish is to see everybody as happy as ourselves …

On 22 August the long-awaited French finally landed at Killala in Co. Mayo. 800 French troops under General Humbert disembarked unopposed and then routed the first instalment of local yeomanry who fled back eastwards in the so-called Races of Castlebar. Co. Longford was directly in the line of the French advance towards Dublin.

TO SOPHY RUXTON
Edgeworthstown, 29 August 1798

We have this moment learned from the sheriff of this county, Mr Wilder, that the French have got to Castlebar – They changed clothes with some peasants and so deceived our troops. They have almost cut off the carabineers, the

'United Irishmen in Training under the sign of the "Tree of Liberty"', by the English cartoonist James Gillray, published June 1798.

Longford Militia and a large party of yeomanry who opposed them. Another gentleman, who returned from Athlone a little after the Sheriff, says that the French have got to Tuam –

The Lord Lieutenant is now at Athlone – and it is supposed that it will be the next object of their attack.

My father's corps of yeomanry are extremely attached to him and seem fully in earnest – but, alas! by some strange negligence their arms have not yet arrived from Dublin – My father this morning sent a letter by an officer going to Athlone offering his services to convey intelligence or reconnoitre, for having no arms for his men, he feels himself in a most terrible situation with no power of being serviceable to his country in any other capacity. We who are so near the scene of action cannot by any means discover what <u>number</u> of the French actually landed – some say 800, some 1,800, some 18,000, some 4,000 – The troops march and countermarch, as they say themselves, without knowing where they are going or for what.

Poor Lady Anne Fox! She is in a dreadful situation – so near her confinement she is unable to move from Foxhall to any place of greater safety and exposed every moment to hear the most alarming reports – She shows admirable calmness and strength of mind. Francis and Barry set out tomorrow morning to England …

We have nothing to wish for but peace. We have plenty and happiness to our heart's content. You would scarcely believe perhaps that [*my father*] goes on regularly every morning in lessons in algebra ... God send that the French may soon go and you may soon come ...

TO AUNT RUXTON
From Mrs Fallon's Inn, Longford, 5 September 1798

We are all safe and well and have had two most fortunate escapes – from the rebels and from the explosion of an ammunition cart. Yesterday we heard about ten o'clock in the morning that a large body of rebels armed with pikes were within a few miles of Edgeworthstown. My father's yeomanry were at this moment gone to Longford for their arms which Government had delayed sending. We were ordered to decamp each with a small bundle – the two chaises full and my mother and Aunt Charlotte on horseback ... We were all ready to move when the report was contradicted – only 20 or 30 men were now, it was said, in arms and my father hoped we might still hold fast to our dear home. Two officers and six dragoons happened at this moment to be on their way through Edgeworthstown escorting an ammunition cart from Mullingar to Longford – they promised to take us under their protection ...

My father most fortunately detained us ... they set off without us. Half an hour afterwards as we were quietly sitting in the portico we hear – as we thought close to us – the report of a pistol or a clap of thunder which shook the house. The officer soon afterwards returned, almost speechless ... The ammunition cart, containing nearly three barrels of gunpowder packed in tin cases, took fire and burst half way on the road to Longford. The man who drove the cart was blown to atoms – nothing of him could be found – two of the horses were killed, others were blown to pieces and their limbs scattered to a distance – the head and body of a man were found a hundred and twenty yards from the spot ... Mr Rochfort was thrown from his horse, one side of his face terribly burnt ... and was carried into a cabin ... My mother went to the spot and had Mr R brought home in the carriage ... I have not time or room, my dear aunt to dilate or tell you half I have to say. If we had gone on with this ammunition cart, we must have been killed.

An hour or two afterwards, however, we were obliged to flee from Edgeworthstown – The pikemen, 300 in number, ... were within a mile of the town. My mother, Aunt Charlotte and I rode – passed the trunk of the dead man, bloody limbs of horses and two dead horses by the help of men who pulled on our steeds – all safely lodged now in Mrs Fallon's inn ...

TO SOPHY RUXTON
Edgeworthstown, 9 September 1798

You will rejoice ... my dear Sophy to see ... we are safe back at Edgeworthstown. The scenes we have gone through for some days past have succeeded one another like pictures from a magic lantern and have scarcely left the impression of reality upon the mind. It all seems like a dream ... "Oh ho!" says my aunt "things cannot be very bad with my brother, if Maria begins her letters with magic lantern and reflections on dreams ..."

When we got into the town this morning we saw the picture of a deserted, or rather a shattered village – many joyful greeted us at the doors of the houses – none of the windows of the new houses in Charlotte row were broken – the mob declared they would not meddle with them because they were built by the two good ladies, meaning my aunts.

Last night my father was alarmed at finding that both Samuel [*Bristow*] and John [*Jenkins*] who had stood by him with the utmost fidelity through the whole Longford business were at length panic struck and wished to leave him. Samuel said "Sir, I would stay with you to the last gasp if you were not so foolhardy" and here he cried bitterly "... but Sir ... I have heard about 200 men in Longford swear they would have your life". All the town were ... last night under a similar panic – they were certain the violent Longford yeoman would come and cut them to pieces ...

The house had been spared, it turned out, mainly because the Edgeworths' housekeeper, Mrs Billamore, had done a kindness to the family of one of the local 'rebels' who forebade his men to sack it. Meanwhile Richard Lovell Edgeworth, long suspected by his Protestant neighbours as a dangerous radical, had been falsely accused by an excitable sergeant of aiding and abetting the rebels – and had been very nearly murdered by a mob of Longford yeomanry a few days before.

TO SOPHY RUXTON
Edgeworthstown, 19 September 1798

... I forgot to tell you of a remarkable event in the history of our return –
all the cats, even those who belong to the stable and who had never been
admitted to the honours of sitting in the kichen, all crowded round Kitty
with congratulatory faces, crawling up her gown, insisting on caressing and
being caressed when she re-appeared in the lower regions. Mr Gilpin's slander
against cats as selfish unfeeling animals is thus refuted by stubborn facts ...

When Colonel Handfield told the whole story of the Longford mob
to Lord Cornwallis he said he never saw a man so much astonished. Lord
Longford, Mr Pakenham and Major Edward Pakenham have shewn much
warmth of friendship on this occasion.

Enclosed I send you a little sketch which I traced from one my mother
drew ... of ... the field of battle at Ballinamuck ... about four miles from the
Hills. My father, mother and I rode to look at the camp – perhaps you recollect
a pretty turn in the road where there is a stream with a three arched bridge.
In the fields ... on the right hand side of this stream about sixty bell tents
were pitched, the arms all ranged on the grass – before the tents, poles with
little streamers flying here and there – groups of men leading their horses to
water – others filling kettles and black pots – some cooking under the hedges –
the various uniforms looked pretty – Highlanders gathering blackberries. My
father took us to the tent of Lord Henry Seymour, who is an old friend of his
– he breakfasted here today and his plain English civility and quiet good sense
was a fine contrast to the mob etc. Dapple, your old acquaintance, did not like
all the sights as well as I did ... [*The sketch has since disappeared.*]

TO SOPHY RUXTON
Edgeworthstown, 2 October 1798

My father went to Dublin to see Lord Cornwallis about the Court of Enquiry
on the sergeant who harangued the mob. About 1 o'clock today Lovell returned
from the Assizes with the news, met on the road, that expresses had come an
hour before from Granard to Longford for the Reay Fencibles and all the
troops – that there was another <u>rising</u> and an attack upon Granard, 4,000 men
the first report said, 700 the second. What the truth may be it is impossible
to tell – it is certain the troops are gone to Granard and it is yet more certain

General Humbert, leader of the French invading force, surrenders after the Battle of Ballinamuck.

The Surrender of the French General Humbert To General Lake at Ballinamuck: September 8th 1798.

that all the windows of this house are built halfway up – guns and bayonets dispersed by Captain Lovell in every room. The yeomanry guard paraded today, all steady – guard sitting up in the house and in the town tonight.

Thursday morning

All alive and well. A letter from my father – stays to see Lord Cornwallis on Friday. Deficient arms for corps given by Lord Castlereagh …

> *The sergeant who had incited the Longford mob that nearly murdered Maria's father was to be tried at the next sessions, but was now ashamed and penitent so Richard Lovell Edgeworth did not press the trial. Knowing the man we terrified of ghosts, he said to him as he came out of the courthouse, 'I believe, of all, you had rather see me alive than have my ghost haunting you!'*

TO SOPHY RUXTON

Edgeworthstown, 19 November 1798

You have, I suppose ... or ought to have, whitlows upon your thumb and all your four fingers for not writing to me! Tell me what you are saying and doing and above all where you are going.

My father has taken me into a new partnership – we are writing a comedy – will you come and see it acted? My father has made a charming theatre in the room over his study – it will be twice as large as old Poz's little theatre in the diningroom. My aunt's woollen wig for old Poz is in high estimation in the memory of man, woman and child here. I believe the play will be acted in January – I hope the Pakenhams, Mr Fox and Lady Anne – Dr and Mrs Beaufort will be here to see it. Oh! How much you all are wished for – I give you the playbill:

Mrs Fangle (a rich but learned lady ... coquettish) ---- Emmeline

Caroline (a lady of large fortune, sprightly, witty and whimsical) ---- Charlotte

Jemima (acting maid to Mrs Fangle, the daughter of a distressed gentleman, arch – but affecting simplicity) ---- Bessy

Sir Mordaunt Idem (a wellbred gentleman in love with Mrs Fangle – fond of family and blazonry – an enemy to anything new) ---- Henry

Opal (nephew to Sir Mordaunt and hating everything <u>old</u>, in love with Caroline and wild for illumination ---- Sneyd

Count Babelhausen (a noble of German extraction, an illuminatus, very clever and artful, makes love to both Mrs Fangle and Caroline) ---- Lovell

Heliodorus and Christina (Mrs Fangle's children on whom he tries strange experiments) ---- William and Honora ...

My father's court martial we expect will soon come on ... Lovell has bought a fine apparatus and materials for a course of chemical lectures which he is going to give us. The study is to be the laboratory – I wish you were <u>in it</u> ...

The play, Whim for Whim, *was acted twice, a month later, to neighbours to great applause – Richard Lovell Edgeworth designed ingenious experiments for the children; Frances Edgeworth painted the scenery and arranged the dresses. The script was sent to Sheridan who rejected it. The day after the second performance, Richard Lovell Edgeworth, his wife and Maria left for Dublin. Edgeworth was now an MP and wished to attend the Irish Parliament, now*

engaged in furious debate over the proposed Act of Union, which would abolish
it. From there he planned to take the boat to England for a delayed honeymoon
with his new wife, bringing Maria with them. The two Sneyd aunts were left
in charge of the remaining children. It was to be Maria's first visit to Dublin
since her arrival in Ireland sixteen years before.

TO SNEYD EDGEWORTH [*Maria's thirteen-year-old brother*]
Dublin, March 1799

… I will give you a journal of the day … the pleasantest day I have passed since
I left home …

11.00 Breakfast – [*fingers*] – good – muffins etc – unpacked a parcel for
Johnson – Letters for Literary ladies, second edition, … [*Maria's satirical essay*
on education] letter from Johnson very pathetic – account of his going to prison
– like Mr Freeman in Newgate[28] …

12.30 Chaise at the door. Papa said he would go with us … – glad boots
not dirty – clean gowns – went to see Lady Longford – saw her and Caroline
– Miss Caroline Pakenham, I mean … like Bessy. Father liked her very much,
had some conversation – a rare thing in Dublin.

3.00 Went to see Lord Charlemont – Lady C not at home – Lord C
had been very ill but he let us in – walked through a hall which was nothing
extraordinary – through a massive passage which felt cold – came suddenly
upon a beautiful little statue of Venus in a window – passage – passage –
passage – until we found ourselves in a beautiful little ante chamber – a large
statue of Venus in a recess – was just turning my eyes to contemplate her
beauties when opposite to her a door opens. I forget Venus and fixed my eyes
upon a little old man, bent with age, who advanced towards us with trembling
steps from a far end of a most magnificent room – this little old man was
Lord Charlemont – It was difficult for him, old and infirm as he is, to appear
with dignity in the midst of such magnificence – and yet he did – and all the
statues and all splendid books in his vast library and the library itself vanished
from our eyes … whilst we listened to his conversation – He is as polite as
his letters – and though when he attempts to move, he seems to us as if he
would fall to pieces, yet once he is seated in his armchair and when he speaks,

---

28   Joseph Johnson, Maria's publisher, had been convicted for 'seditious libel' for printing a pamphlet by
the Unitarian Gilbert Wakefield attacking the Prince of Wales. Maria and her father later went to
see him in prison.

Lord Charlemont in old age.
Richard Lovell Edgeworth had
been his aide-de-camp during the
Volunteer campaign in the 1780s.

his countenance is illuminated by sense and benevolence. He said when we came into the room as he seated himself, "I sit down ladies for two excellent reasons because I am not well enough to stand – and because I may treat you with the familiarity for old acquaintance – you are my old acquaintance." Lord Charlemont took us into a little little room which is his sanctum, as retired as if it had been 100 miles from any room – venetian blinds half let down – showed us what he said was the [*object?*] he most prized – an onyx about 4 inches long upon which the head and half the body of Queen Elizabeth was exquisitely carved. The floor of Lord C's library is so finely polished that it is with the up most difficulty I could keep upon my legs, and how he managed I cannot conceive, but I skated through it without disgracing myself. In one of his rooms there are busts of all the Roman Emperors and Empresses – you would know them all, I dare say, but I found myself in shameful perplexity … I saw the famous Faustina's head who had the bath of milk of 700 asses – and likewise Poppae who powdered with gold dust[29] …

---

29   The rooms described by Maria were removed when the house was converted to be the Dublin Municipal Gallery in the 1930s.

4 o'clock. Tell Lovell the band, the Warwickshire band was playing in the gardens when we came out of Charlemont's house <u>and</u> the troops looked beautiful amongst the trees & upon the unequal ground. The horses neither liked the drums … nor the music. They reared and kicked and I was right glad to give up the music and get clear off with my precious life …

Adieu, I am sent to dress – we are going to the circus to see Astley's horsemanship … love to dear Henry and everybody for indeed I love you all, sincerely and the more for comparing you with others …

TO CHARLOTTE SNEYD
Dublin, 2 April 1799

Here we are waiting for a wind and likely to wait some time, according to Mr Kirwan the monarch of the clouds … In the paper of tonight you will see my father's farewell speech on the Education bill. He keeps his temper about a thousand times better than I should in his situation …

Some time ago amongst some hints to the Chairman of the Committee of Education, you sent one which I have pursued – you said that the early lessons for the poor should speak with detestation of the spirit of revenge – I have just finished a little story called "Forgive and Forget" upon this idea … I am very much obliged to Bessy and Charlotte for copying the Errata of "Practical Education" for me and should be <u>extremely</u> obliged to the whole Committee of Education and Criticism at Edgeworthstown if they would send corrections to me from their own brains – the same eye (if I may judge by my own) can only see the same things in looking over the book twenty times …

Will you give my love to Henry and thank him for his kindness in sending me the two nice toothpicks. Tell Sneyd there is a political print just come out of a woman, meant for Hibernia, dressed in orange and green, and holding a pistol in her hand to oppose the Union …

Adieu, my dear Aunt Charlotte … my love to everyone in the library, the hall, the dressingroom and all the bedchambers.

After a tour of Richard Lovell Edgeworth's old friends in the industrial north of England, the family party spent two months in Clifton, where Maria's new stepmother gave birth to her first child, Fanny. Maria later recorded her terror at carrying the newborn baby down the stairs to show her father, but Fanny was to become her favourite sister. They returned to Edgeworthstown in September

1799 so that Richard Lovell Edgeworth could take part in the final stages of the Act of Union debate. In typical quixotic fashion, he had decided to vote against the bill, although he firmly believed the Union with England would bring English capital and industry to save Ireland from rural poverty.

The return from England coincided with the anonymous publication of Castle Rackrent. *Maria had largely written it several years before, encouraged by her Aunt Ruxton's amusement at her comic imitations of John Langan, her father's steward and by her grandfather's stories of earlier Edgeworths in his* Black Book of Edgeworthstown.

TO LETTY RUXTON
Edgeworthstown, 29 January 1800

… I am sorry that Arundel[30] affords so little society … but you are better off in Arundel than we are in the county of Longford, for you have a beautiful country around you to make amends for the want of good neighborhood but we have only black bogs and dirty roads – you see dear Letty, that my ideas have been so much enlarged by my Travels that I do not, as once you may remember hearing me as we were rambling along the gravel walk near the mount, circumscribe my vision of perfect felicity to a ride on the Foxhall or Mullingar Road – I am now so liberal minded that I would allow a longer and larger furlough! …

Some time ago we took a walk to see the old castle of Cranalagh,[31] from which in the last rebellion (but one) Lady Edgeworth was turned out naked, I should say – without any clothes to a Lady with your delicacy – God send that we may never be turned out in the same way – as especially as this is very raw weather for Lady Godivas and Peeping Toms. Part of the castle, just enough to swear by, remains to this day, and with a venerable wig of ivy at top cuts a very respectable figure …

Before this reaches you my father will be in Dublin, he goes on Saturday next to the call of the House for the grand Union business. Tell my aunt that he means to speak on the subject on Monday. His sentiments are unchanged: that the Union would be advantageous to all the parties concerned, but that England has not the right to do to Ireland <u>good</u> <u>against</u> <u>her</u> <u>will.</u>

---

30   The Ruxtons had rented a house in Sussex.

31   The Edgeworths' ancestral home. It was burnt down in the rising of 1641. The infant Edgeworth heir, Maria's great-grandfather, escaped death by being hidden in a basket of provisions and brought to Dublin by a loyal retainer; Maria would have read the story in *The Black Book of Edgeworthstown*.

Will you tell me what means you have of getting parcels from London to Arundel? Because I wish to send to my aunt a few Popular Tales which I have finished as they cannot be wanted for some months by Mr Johnson [*her publisher*] ... We have begged Johnson to send Castle Rackrent – I hope it has reached you – Do not mention to anyone that it is ours ...

Although Maria described it as 'ours', Castle Rackrent had been written almost entirely independently of her father, and was published anonymously. But the authorship soon leaked out and added hugely to Maria's growing fame as a writer of delightful realistic stories for children and co-author with her father of Practical Education *published two years before. Richard Lovell Edgeworth reported to Daniel Beaufort that even the king had read it and had 'rubbed his hands and said "What, what – Now I know something of my Irish subjects".' It was quickly republished in Maria's name. Her father added a heavy preface stressing that this was a portrait of the unreformed Irish squirearchy of a bygone age, and that the union with Great Britain would complete their reformation and herald a new age of Irish industry and prosperity for all.*

To Maria's pleasure, her father, now deprived of political employment in Dublin, was at home and disposed to look for social and intellectual interests nearer to home. A neighbour, Mrs Tuite of Sonna, six miles away, proved to be the sister of Richard Chenevix, well known for his chemical experiments with metals and a fellow of the Royal Society.

TO SOPHY RUXTON
Edgeworthstown, 20 October 1800

This morning dear Henry took leave of home and set out for Edinburgh. "God prosper him" as in the language of a fond old nurse, I keep continually saying to myself [32]...

Mr Chenevix, a famous chemist, was so good as to come here lately to see my father upon the faith of Mr Kirwan's assurance that he would "like Mr Edgeworth". I often wished for you, my dear Sophy, whilst this gentleman was here, because you would have been so much entertained with his conversation about bogs and minds and airs and acids etc etc – His history of his imprisonment during the French Revolution in Paris I found more to my taste. When he was thrown into prison, the first thing he did was to purchase

---

32 Henry was to train as a doctor.

Boy Driver at Castle Saunderson
1801

A shivering boy driver waits outside Castle Saunderson, sketch by Frances Edgeworth.

Chaptal's and Lavoisier's Chemistry and to study them with all his might – then he represented himself as an English gentleman come over to study chemistry in France. M. Chaptal got him released and employed him and he got acquainted.

About three weeks ago we went to Castle Saunderson[33] where we spent several most agreeable days. Mr and Mrs Saunderson spent a fortnight with us and were very agreeable but they have both the misfortune to be deaf as posts …

TO SOPHY RUXTON
Edgeworthstown, 2 December 1800

… You are so near Johnson[34] that you must of course know more of Maria's sublime works than Maria knows of them herself – and besides, Lovell who

---

33 In Co. Cavan.
34 Maria's publisher.

thinks of them ten times more than Johnson has not let you burst in ignorance. An octavo edition of Practical Education is to come out at Christmas – we have seen a volume which looks as well as can be expected. The first two parts of Early Lessons containing Harry and Lucy ... have just come to us! Frank and Rosamund will, I suppose come after with all convenient speed. How "Moral Tales" are arranged or in what size they are to appear I do not know ... Some weeks ago we received four engravings for frontispieces – they are beautifully engraved by Neagle and do justice to the designs, two of which are by my mother, and two by Charlotte ... There are three stories which will be new to you, The Knapsack, The Prussian Vase and Angelina.

Now, my dear friend, you cannot say that I do not tell you what I am doing. My father is employed in making out Charts of History and Chronology such as mentioned in Practical Education. He has just finished a little volume containing Explanations of Poetry for children – it explains "The Elegy in a Country Churchyard", "L'Allegro", "Il Penseroso" and "The Ode to Fear". It will be a very useful schoolbook – It goes over to-night to Johnson ...

TO SNEYD EDGEWORTH
Edgeworthstown, Spring 1801

Sneyd, now aged fifteen, had gone to Dublin with his father to enrol at Trinity.

My dear Tormentor,
I am surprised to find that I have been able to live so long without you, and I dare say, so are you. You know you thought I should grow as dead as dead small bees when I have neither you nor my father to torment me into spirits ... as to our adventures – in the first place you have been told that Lady Longford, Lady Elizabeth and 2 Miss P[akenham]'s spent a morning with us and you need not be told that they are each in their turn as agreeable as agreeable can be – Lady Elizabeth has sent a bottle of Essence of Mustard to rub poor little William's knees and spindle shanks and the Essence of Mustard and the Essence of Time has so far recovered him that he is no longer a cripple – he cannot yet "mount the Alps", that is the stairs ... but he can walk on level boards like a child just out of leading strings and he has ridden on the rocking horse and he has ridden a pick-a-pack on my back ...

We – that is my father, Mrs E, Charlotte and Maria are just returned from Foxhall where we have been dining and making merry with excellent raisin wine and walking and seeing the monument and statue recumbent of that valiant knight Sir Nat Fox who has one foot upon a globe and the other upon a skull[35] – Mr Fox was in good spirits and very talkative alias agreeable – the children are wonderfully improved – your charmer Selina is really a pretty soft skinned puss with large eyes – not cat's eyes – but Fanniken for my money all the world over …

Maria had been encouraged by her father and stepmother to think of Fanny as her own child.

Be it known to you that I have not neglected to sow your spinach – now for misfortunes – arm yourself with Philosophy – the snails have eaten every leaf and leaflet of your peas – I could not help it please your honour – upon my word and conscience – Sorrow take me if I could! I had the peas stuck with good sticks after they were dead in hopes they might come to life again and crawl up the sticks – so, I pulled up sticks and peas and snails – and I was going to sow a fresh crop for you of my own peas when my father was so good as to let me take Gaynor out of the garden to help me – and Gaynor dug and I dug … and at last the whole garden was dug and three new drills are sowed and will please the snails! … your columbine is in purple beauty – your manure in good condition – Lady Ann Fox has beautiful avenues and a pretty little hot house well furnished with grapes which I hope we shall taste if they and we live …

TO HARRIET BEAUFORT [*Frances Edgeworth's sister*]
Edgeworthstown, n.d. 1801

I rejoice, my dear Harriet, that you are no longer an invalid. Pray become as fat as our own little Fanny and as rosy – she becomes every day more entertaining and engaging – she knows all her words and some of her consonants and is never at a loss in conversation though she has but a few words in command …

I've just received six parts of Early Lessons and Frank and Rosamund which William reads with an eagerness which flatters me much. They will now I suppose soon be published … I forget whether I mentioned that we have just sent Errata for a new addition of Belinda which Johnson desired …

---

35 The late seventeenth-century monument and its little chapel are still extant beside the ruins of Foxhall, though the knight has lost his head.

Little Fanny
Edgeworth, aged two,
a sketch by her mother.

Belinda, *Maria's second novel, was published later that year, very much modelled on Fanny Burney's* Evelina *(the story of a young girl's entry into society). Maria tore out the title-page with her name and gave it to her Aunt Ruxton to read; Mrs Ruxton exclaimed at the good writing and commended it to Maria as showing a proper knowledge of 'high life which people have who live in the world'. When Maria failed to respond, she accused her of being envious of a rival author, whereon Maria burst into tears and showed her the torn-out title-page. Her aunt was cross at the deception and took a dislike to* Belinda *ever afterwards. (Maria herself came to dislike the priggish heroine – see her letter to her Aunt Ruxton of 26 December 1809.)*

TO SOPHY RUXTON
Edgeworthstown, 18 June 1802

... Tell my mother that the bodies of all here are in perfect preservation and that Fanny is as patient as Job or Griselda, William's eye not inflamed – Sneyd's nose snuffling but very little – Maria writing – neither too much nor too little in her own opinion – and well and good in her own opinion. Tell my father that Sneyd and I and my Aunt Mary (who ought to have come first) spend half an hour every day after breakfast trying to understand the book which professes to explain to the meanest capacity the use of all the criss-cross lines on the rulers and sectors in a case of mathematical instruments – and we get on pretty well but I see at a distance that alarms my imagination precociously.

How to find the solidity of a pig?

… I am writing at present the history of a young lady, who, when she gets into high life and fashionable company, forgets her best friends – and is at last punished as she deserves – as you and my aunt must have seen a great deal of this world, perhaps you can supply me with some anecdotes or hints …

You will rejoice to see that my father's telegraph has been presented to the National Institute and that its superiority is acknowledged, but what shabby saviours! – to claim it as their own!

TO LETTY RUXTON
Edgeworthstown, 1 August 1802

… This being the first of August we may expect soon to see Richard Coeur de Lion[36] coming over here in a barrister's wig and whether with or without a wig we shall be most happy to see him …

I have been much interested by the Letters from Lausanne,[37] I think them in some parts highly pathetic and eloquent, but as to the moral tendency of the book, I cannot find it, turn it which way I will … The Savage of Aveyron[38] is a thousand times more interesting to me … I have not read anything for years that interested me more. Mr Chevenix will be here in a few days when we will cross question him about this savage upon whom the eyes of civilised Europe are fixed …

Richard Chenevix brought over with him from Sonna a M. Pictet from Geneva who had translated Maria's books on education and stories for children into French. Richard Lovell Edgeworth was intrigued with Pictet's description of society in Paris – now newly reopened to English travellers for the first time

---

36   Richard Ruxton, Letty's older brother.
37   By Isabelle de Charrière, published 1799. Originally from Holland, she had settled in Switzerland and attracted much attention with her beauty and intellect. Boswell had proposed to her as a young man while studying law at Utrecht.
38   The famous *enfant sauvage* found in the woods in France.

in ten years following the Peace of Amiens in March – and decided to go to France. He set off in September with his wife and three older daughters, Maria, Emmeline and Charlotte. Emmeline was left at Clifton after her marriage to a Swiss surgeon, John King, a colleague of Dr Thomas Beddoes, a match of which her father rather disapproved.

Richard Lovell Edgeworth bought a large comfortable coach in London, and the family party of four travelled on first to Brussels, then Paris. They found themselves rapidly accepted in the best circles, thanks to their reputation as educationalists, and Maria, to her surprise, received her first serious proposal – from a 46-year-old Swedish diplomat with scientific tastes, the Chevalier Nicolas Edelcrantz.

Despite encouragement from her father to accept, she turned him down, unable to contemplate life away from home and family. In her Memoir, her stepmother recorded the pain this caused Maria as she had been seriously in love with him, and Maria's letters to Sophy Ruxton show her avid for news of him for years after. They never met again.

For her father, post-revolutionary French society proved so attractive that he briefly contemplated bringing over the rest of his large family to live in France. But this vision was brought abruptly to an end in spring 1803 by the threat of renewed war with England. Forewarned by friends at Napoleon's court, the family left Paris and caught a boat to England in the nick of time from Calais. But Lovell, Richard Lovell Edgeworth's 28-year-old son, was caught in France on his way back from Switzerland and was to be miserably interned there as a prisoner of war for the next twelve years. Maria and he had never been close, but his internment was to have serious consequences for the family and Edgeworthstown after her father's death.

ESSAY

ON

IRISH BULLS.

BY

RICHARD LOVELL EDGEWORTH,

AND

MARIA EDGEWORTH,

AUTHOR OF CASTLE RACKRENT, &c.

Summos posse viros, & magna exempla daturos,
Vervecum in patria, crassoque sub aëre nasci!

JUVENAL.

LONDON:

PRINTED FOR J. JOHNSON, 72, ST. PAUL'S CHURCHYARD.

1802.

III

AUGUST 1803 – OCTOBER 1807

THE EDGEWORTHS' COACH *did not head immediately back to Ireland. Instead it headed north to Edinburgh, where Henry, who was studying medicine, had been reported ill. Reassured by his kindly mentors, the Scottish philosopher Professor Dugald Steward and his wife, that they would watch over him, the party returned to Edgeworthstown in early summer 1803. They found Ireland in a disturbed state once more and faced with the threat of a French invasion. Richard Lovell Edgeworth again offered his telegraph to the authorities as an early warning system and this time it was accepted.*

TO SOPHY RUXTON
Edgeworthstown, [?] August 1803

My father has really been harassed to death lately for he has had this house to fortify – walls to build up before the library window, thick doors and bastions etc as of yore – Then he has had to do the whole duty of his corps on permanent pay ... and besides he has been tormented with Justice of the Peace business – a whole nest of little villains ... have been discovered in Edgeworthstown, who get together to drink unlawful toasts such as "Here's to the star which was lit in America, which shined in France and quenched in Ireland ..." Five or six boys of 12 and 14 were all found yesterday morning lying and perfuming themselves in the library – Charlotte has drawn most excellent likenesses of two of them – little miscreants ... what hopes for such a rising generation.

TO AUNT RUXTON
Edgeworthstown, August 1803

… The gentlemen of this county are enrolling as fast as they can, but that is very slowly – 900 people assembled before this hall door and were ready and eager to enroll themselves the day the news came from Dublin of the disturbances.[39] Since that time they have all hung back – not a man yet enrolled! Everything seems however perfectly quiet. As to our manner of going on … it is much the same as usual; except a mixture of military and literary affairs – interludes of calling muster roles – trying on sachets – Order arms – Stand at ease! – 'ttention. Books in reading – Maria reading Lambert's *Oeuvres Philosophiques* – likes them much – Charlotte – Ditto? – Mrs E – likes him much. Aunt C and M – reading *Tableaux de Famille*, like it but think it too long …

TO SOPHY RUXTON
Edgeworthstown, 16 December 1803

I think my father and Francis[40] will leave us in a few days and then God speed them! And keep Bonaparte away until the giant Isosceles is ready on the coast to meet him. I presume you have read the laws of the triangle and are appointed with this famous giant – Poor Lovell – it is a pity that he should not see the establishment of the telegraph in its prosperous days when he was such a steady and useful friend in adversity …

TO SOPHY RUXTON
Edgeworthstown, November 1803

… After you went, my dear friend, and after I had recovered strength of mind enough to do anything without feeling you at my elbow, I determined to set about Leonora [*her new novel*] and to read The Sorrows of Werther[41] in their black binding by way of preparation for the genuine sentimental style – but lo!

---

39 Robert Emmett's abortive rising on 23 July, which resulted in the murder of an elderly judge, Lord Kilwarden.

40 Francis Beaufort – Maria's stepmother's brother, a naval officer, was on leave after being wounded, and was helping to set up the telegraph.

41 *The Sorrows of Young Werther*, famous tragi-romantic novel by Goethe, first published in 1774, said to have driven young men to 'copycat suicide'.

Just as I was opening the book, Papa called to know how many acres there were in Paddy Somebody's lease and a rent roll which I had for six months put off every day copying until tomorrow. And my head was filled for three days with three lives renewable for ever or alienation fines, Breaking up fines, fines upon renewal, … When these were <u>ousted</u>, came the telegraphic vocabularies – and then a pair of sleeves for Fanny's trousers … wherefore Leonora is put to sleep for the present. And I am going to do another modern sketch – title – "The Modern Griselda". I think it may be made very entertaining and mean to allow my modern Griselda three husbands, a moderate allowance, for the full exercise of her talents – I shall work hard with the hopes of having something to read to my father – This has always been one of my greatest delights and strongest motives for writing – Lazy Lawrence – The Bracelets and the Limerick Gloves and the Purple Vase were all written whilst my father was out somewhere or other on purpose to be read to him on return …

> *These were some of Maria's stories for older children. Her father attached a heavily bombastic preface to the collection, which, as a later biographer of Maria wrote, 'could only have had the effect of repelling readers' but the stories were praised by the* Edinburgh Review *as near to perfection.*

The post is just come and has brought two letters, one from Francis [*Beaufort*] and one from my father – substance of said letters – the gentlemen and their four yeomen in hackney chaises arrived at the Duke of Leinster's, who had offered his tower as a station – his grace very civil – Francis remained – Papa went on to Castleknock – conversed with telegraphs from Castleknock to Maynooth for half an hour – Mr E then proceeded to Dublin – went to the Castle, found nobody at home left a note … that's all I know …

My head has been these days in Lady Mary Montagu's Turkish Letters – and I see nothing but visions of beauteous Fatimas and palaces wainscotted with mother of pearl by nails of emerald etc – pray look at the description she gives of a camel and a buffalo and tell me whether you think them a good resemblance[42] …

---

[42]   Lady Mary Wortley Montagu had spent two years in Turkey from 1716 to 1718. Her letters, published after her death, caused great scandal by their descriptions of nude oriental beauties – and inspired painters such as Ingres. She had also been the first to first to preach the Turkish practice of variolation to prevent smallpox, later modified by Edward Jenner to vaccination.

TO MRS EDGEWORTH
Black Castle, Summer 1803

… We have been great gadders since we came – one morning we went to the cottage at Swinnerton – very very hot walk, I was literally melted into silence, … but cold veal and resting five minutes in the pretty cottage parlour restored the powers of both mind and body. It was so ordered that Margaret and I walked home by the high road – do you smell an adventure coming? If you do not, you have no sagacity – Whilst we damsels were pacing the <u>lonely</u> way a very stout ill looking man with a very stout ill looking stick in hand came up very close to us and said "Ladies, I am a distressed person – be pleased to give me some money" – he spoke more in the imperative mood and he had not the air of a beggar – or as I hear the London beggars generally denominate themselves, an "asker". – "I would recommend it to you, Maria", whispered Margaret keeping her head stock still … "I recommend it to you, Maria, to give him something indeed" – I was determined to have some diversion out of him first for I saw some cabins not far off and knew he would not knock me down. I asked him sundry questions about his way of life etc – "Madam, I have been a person of distinction in my time – In what time, Sir? – Madam, I have kept three hands at work – At what work, Sir – Madam, I was by profession a master tailor" – (the rest of his history was more incoherent than interesting) – I had a guinea at the bottom of my pocket which I left snug there. I drew out a purse – in which there was a solitary shilling – turning the purse inside out, I said to the man of distinction "You see, Sir this is the only shilling I have in the world"; he marched off one way and we the other – quite satisfied and thus bought me a reputation for courage – very cheaply – in Margaret's mind …

We dined one day at Mr Everard's of which dinner you have heard the history from my Aunt's. There was a Mrs Charles Dallas there and her husband Captain D who has travelled all over the Carnatic, four thousand miles in eleven months and had the conveying of Tippoo Sahib's four sons and 600 wives – and after all that, looks much like another man – only thin and sallow … Polite 74 year old Lord Laidlow was also there – he is an old courtier of the King's … We missed seeing my Lady Kenmare freshly arrived from Paris with all the Parisian fashions full upon her – her head *à l'Egyptienne* – her body in brown muslin with a drapery of fine lace put the Lord knows how over it – this is the newest wonder of the County of Meath – I humbly cited a lace drapery of Lady G–'s of which I had lately heard, but was laughed to scorn.

An encounter in the woods – sketch by Charlotte Edgeworth.

What do you think of lobsters dressed with peas? – a new dish which Mr Cusack affirms to be all the fortune in England. My dear little Fannykin, how can you be such a goose as to think your bed full of snails – it is well she never saw a lobster alive or else she would dream of them crawling over her ...

TO SOPHY RUXTON
Edgeworthstown, 3 January 1804

... We are not certain at the present of my father's return. Mrs E had a letter from him this morning dated Glenties, near Galway January 4th. He says that he has fixed all his stations but ... after having been much delayed by fog – one whole day in particular in which as he says Captain Beaufort and he from morning to night could see nothing but one another's faces.

Various <u>movements</u> (I hope you are initiated in diplomatic language) have been made to him by government during his absence ... they seem indeed to be in a desperate hurry and that is not surprising but they little know the man if they think it possible to be more zealous and more expeditious. You know that I am no politician by profession but in moments like the present I prophecy that Bonaparte, if he does not accompany his troops, will perish in France and if he does will perish in Great Britain. He has continued to place himself with upstart folly in such a perilous situation that fall he must … I am heartily glad that poor Lovell finds Montpelier as agreeable as any place can be to a prisoner. The accounts in the morning papers of Bonaparte's treatment of the foolish prisoners of Valenciennes is horrible![43] …

Politics goodbye and good morning to you – I am going to Gaybrook … we, that is Mrs E, Miss W[aller] Aunt M, C and M.E. – a joyful coachful … On our journey nothing remarkable happened except that the old grey horses did not tumble down and the hired pair that took the lead did not turn around every 10 mins as they had done on a late expedition to Sonna – Mrs E read, to my great delight, Florian's beautiful little piece "Le Bon Mariage". C and I all the while sat niched up in a corner of the coach enveloped in a fur tippet, a muff upon my hands, a muff under my feet, Charlotte wedging me up with all her warmth … We came to the lake of (something or other) near Mullingar then adieu to "Le Bon Mariage", and out popped every head but mine to say – Very pretty – Really pretty – Oh how pretty – … I never stirred from my corner … till presently I heard of a sunset that looked like Mount Vesuvius and I really could not help seeing Miss Waller's face and my Aunt Mary's all illuminated and rosy as if they had been sitting with Lady Clementine to receive Mr Charles Grandison.[44] I came out of my fur tippet, put my nose out of the window and would not have missed the sight of the volcanic sunset for … We forgot all time until Miss Waller perceived that George [Bristow, the coachman] in his customary ignorance of geography or location was passing Mrs Smyth's gate; we stopped him by making such noise as we could make and now we are at Mrs Smyth's very handsome, very convivial, very warm mansion …

I wish, my dear Sophy, that when you build another house you will build it on the plan of Mrs Smyth's schoolhouse … you must imagine a pretty neat garden – hollyhocks and peonies in full blow in the middle of the snow. We saw about a dozen healthy children of various ages carrying on their straw manufacture; last year the profits of this infant manufacture were £170. This is not playing at working … Mrs Smyth has the good sense to make these children mix active with sedentary employments – they are taught to wash and

43   English travellers caught in France when war resumed were known as 'détenus' and treated well especially if they had money. Sailors and troops taken off English ships were confined in brutal conditions, as were low-ranking French prisoners of war in England.

44   Hero of the hugely popular eighteenth-century novel by Samuel Richardson.

do all manner of household work so they can never want bread because they will be fit for useful servants or helper-wives upon Dr Atkins plan. They are also accustomed to work in their garden and will know a sheep's head from a carrot etc. Lest the straw manufacture should go suddenly out of fashion, Mrs S means to provide them with other means of providing their bread. She thinks of small tape looms – as tape must always be useful ... Perhaps you, who have seen so many straw schools may have seen the little tool for cutting the straw but it was new to me. Suppose a handle of a screwdriver ... and in it ... make a hole about the size of a quill and when this hole is made insert a wire: gyrate like a spiders web ... divide your spider's web into as many compartments as you wish your straw to be cut into – then thrust your straw endways through it and it will be cut or split into even strips as quick as thought ...

TO SOPHY RUXTON
Edgeworthstown, 1 February 1804

I wish I had a telescope that could see to Dublin that I might have a glimpse of you in your court dress[45] ... I am glad that my father and Sneyd had the pleasure of a peek at you.

My mother begs that you will give the enclosed half note to Miss Byrne's, the mantua maker, and will you buy for me a quarter of a yard of white plush to line a hat. Henry and Sneyd are very busy working at geometric telegraphic accounts and Charlotte who is really the best of sisters is helping them from morning to night. You will rejoice to hear that Henry who has been brought into action recently, appears so well and his powers have evolved so magically to fill the occasion that my father has been [*lost*] in admiration and affection, and admiration and affection are more nearly connected in my father's mind than in most people!

TO AUNT RUXTON
Edgeworthstown, April 1803

... I wrote to Louisa last post giving her an account of my father's first words and thoughts on seeing Griselda;[46] I shall go on where I take it for granted she left off – Telegraph, accounts and bits of wood and litigious tenants

---

45   Sophy had just been presented to the Viceroy at Dublin Castle.

46   *The Modern Griselda* – a brilliant satire on a discontented wife – had been written unknown to her father. It was much admired by Byron among others.

absorbed my father's attention completely from 9 to 10 last night. I being upstairs "mending an old rag in my closet", my aunt Mary with pertinacious kindness placed the book before him for the 20th time and he began to read it – he exclaimed continually at the likeness of the writing and of the allusions to Maria's – then he said it must be written by one of the family – he did not think it could have been by Maria because she could not have done it without his knowledge. He guessed Anna – Emmeline – Sneyd – Charlotte, and Lady Spencer; when I came into the room he attacked me with "Upon my word, Maria, upon my word I never saw a book so like your writing as here" – I went on ruling a sheet of paper and being as hypocritical as I conveniently could – He then gravely and with a look of puzzled vexation said "Do put me out of pain and tell me if it is yours".

"My dear father, you have often told me you would know my writing anywhere – now will you give me a decided opinion if this is my work or not and I will then tell you if you are right."

"Judging from the writing I should decidedly say that it is yours, from the improbability that you deceive me, I should judge that it is not yours!"

I then told him and the moment the words had crossed my lips he repented and of course I did the same. He wished he could have read it all the way through without being told whose it was. I will not tell you anything more of what he thinks until you have read it – As I always err in telling too much instead than too little …

TO SOPHY RUXTON
Edgeworthstown, June 1804

… How like you Miss Williams as editor of Louis 16th's letters, and how like you the letters? Lady G[*ranard*] lent us a book which I think deserves to be burnt on a dung pile – *Anecdotes de la Cour de France sous Louis 15 et Madame de Pompadour* – if it comes your way don't read it – it is vile trash or rather scandalous trash. Madame Pompadour's favourite maxim is *après nous le déluge* – So, acting upon it, she in fact prepared the scaffold for Louis 16th by exciting the indignation of the people by the horrid debaucheries of her king – I only wish he had been the victim, not that excellent-hearted Louis 16th whose only fault was too much humanity and immoveable aversion to shed the blood of those who had raised their arms to shed his with butcher-like impunity[47] …

---

47 The Edgeworths' cousin the Abbé Edgeworth had attended Louis XVI to the scaffold and written a moving account of his last days.

Louis XVI awaits his execution with the Abbé Edgeworth (left) attending him. The Edgeworths were immensely proud of their connection with the famous Abbé.

DEATH of LOUIS XVI. King of FRANCE.
who was beheaded Jan.ʳ 21. 1793.
When on the scaffold he did say – Wringing his hands with upcast eyes.
Receive my Soul O God I pray – And Oh forgive my Enemies
Publish'd June 12.1798. by C. Sheppard Nᵒ 25 St Peters Hill Doctors Commons.

TO MRS EDGEWORTH
Black Castle, 21 August 1804

I have been so sick & headachy these last two days that I have not been able to read, mark, learn or … digest any of the good things by which I am surrounded, but this morning I am myself again …

On our journey, Fanny was much entertained by a description Henry gave her of the process of tanning and he showed her the oaks stripped of their bark & the heaps of bark piled on the ground … She will have many wonders to tell you – She enjoyed at Castletown, Delvin a new pleasure – Breaking an egg for herself! I never saw a child so much like a little gentlewoman … I am convinced that children who are not restrained about eating are never disgusting gourmands – you know the anecdote of the woman who said to the child "Miss, you would not eat all these things if we were at home – I know that, said the child, that is the very reason that I eat them now I am abroad."

Dear mother, Fanny has given me a great deal of pleasure and if you had invented for ever, you could not have thought of anything that would have delighted me more than to bring her here … Fanny ate a bit of lobster yesterday at my request with prodigious heroism – she is now working at Sneyd's patch waistcoat beside me like the good girl on the cover of the new spelling book. My Aunt's trellis is very pretty and her blush roses, jessamine etc here are flowers enough for me or Madame de Genlis …

TO MRS EDGEWORTH
Black Castle, 4 September 1804

Sophy & Margaret & I & Letty Corry[48] and Richard and a Mr Upton went yesterday in a boat – Before I proceed any further I should warn my father, lest his imagination take fright that Mr Upton is a married man who has been given over for the gout, the palsy and the dropsy (but he is now in ruddy health/aside) – I wished for you 20 times as we were seeing the beautiful wooded banks of the Boyne and I wished for William 40 times as we were going over the locks on the canal … We went through ten locks in the space of about 8 miles – what an immense expense! – and I had full leisure to understand their mechanism – … there is something sublime in the opening and shutting of the river doors of the river gods – Some of the double doors begin to have a little of the sublime of antiquity. In some, the racks and pinnions and hinges were so rusty that it was not until after a considerable waste of time that the woman whose business … it was could accomplish pulling, pushing & hauling them open and after we were shut in, we found that the sluices at the upper gates which were intended to be closed leaked so much that almost as much water came in one end as came out the other … this was a sort of Castle Rackrent on the waters … One woman attends four locks at 4 miles distance and she runs continuously to get before the boats – hard duty! … When I saw this masculine woman with her bare brawny red shapeless legs and muscular arms tugging and striving at her work regardless of how much of her person she exposed … – my imagination went from mechanics and hydraulics to morality & metaphysics and I said to Sophy – "Would you rather have a woman without modesty or without chastity?" Sophy said she would rather have a woman without chastity than without

48   The Ruxtons' first cousin.

modesty but she would rather <u>be</u> a woman without modesty than chastity – I doubt it – I am afraid you might think me profligate for doubting but I represented that one virtue loses ... half its virtue when separated from the other ...

I was pondering upon these matters when a gentleman who looked like a dried officer galloped towards us on the narrow road under the rocks ... Richard exclaimed "That's Lord Hardwicke!"[49] Seconds after him came galloping Mr Foster, Colonel Foster, two scarlet and gold figures, aides de camp & Mr Keating in the rear. Scarlet and Gold galloped back to a chaise and four in which were 2 ladies in white bonnets much like other ladies. Lady Hardwicke and her daughter – Mr Foster came back towards our boat and bowed and spoke to us but I did not like his looks. I thought he looked right glad that Edgeworth was not in the boat as well as his daughter – I thought he will do nothing – perhaps it is better to say and think that he can do nothing.[50]

The galloping figures and the chaise and four passed over like figures in William's camera obscura and all vanished at a turn in the rocks which led to Beaupark – all but poor fat good natured Mr Keating who is not so fond of galloping and stayed behind to talk to Richard and Sophy ...

I have been much entertained and instructed by Tookes' Life of Catherine [*the Great*] – it is Mr Fox's book, I will bring it home with me – but there are really bad things in this book which I think ought to have been in Latin or omitted – I do not see how the female public is to be benefited by learning the detail of all the gross vices of an empress who was as brutally profligate as the worst of the Roman emperors.

TO AUNT RUXTON
Edgeworthstown, 20 September 1804

Our bodies arrived here in excellent plight yesterday to a seven o'clock dinner. We had an extremely pleasant journey, my uncle is indeed a most agreeable and kind travelling companion – we carved and ate our cold chicken very much to our satisfaction and gave the body and bones and crumbs that fell from the rich man's table to a little child we met on the road who was carrying her infant sister on her back ... Your horses performed amazingly well even

---

49   The Viceroy.
50   J.L. Foster, Lord Oriel's nephew, was part of the administration at Dublin Castle that had turned down Edgeworth's earlier offer of his telegraph system.

when they came to the soft boggy road going down to the Float.[51] … We found chaise and horses waiting for us and were carried over on a great tray full of water, for the upper deck of the float had decayed and … nothing but a sort of tray remained. The Irish Charon cried "Never fear! The Bishop of Killala always comes this way and his coach and horses too"! He did all he can to persuade my uncle to carry his carriage and horses over, … but my uncle was civilly incredulous and professed a prejudice for his horses going by dry land. So John, your John, drove them back to Castlepollard to feed them and came back by Camlin bridge towards night.

… Dear little Fanny was the first we saw hurrying to the steps and all joyful, then my father with maturer joy and my mother rosy and smiling – my father says that he has quite accustomed himself to live without me but he will now try if he can accustom himself to live with me.

TO AUNT RUXTON
Edgeworthstown, September 1804

… I have been very prudent not bringing forward in conversation the joys of Black Castle – I was very near it once or twice but checked myself in time … – all things considered, I believe I have not lost my considerable portion of my father's affection by my six week's absence … [*He*] continues to think Olivia & Leonora[52] flat & spiritless & stuffed with morality – but he says it will be recommended by governesses and read by Misses – my uncle is now finishing it & I long to hear what he thinks – I shall correct it with all possible care – partly I suppose from the female spirit of opposition …

TO SNEYD EDGEWORTH,
Edgeworthstown, 13 November 1804

Dear Sneyde Weedie – I am afraid now you are in college[53] it is too great a liberty to call you by so familiar a name but old habits cannot be taken off as easily as boots.

"Now <u>you</u> <u>are</u> <u>up</u>, my dear brother" perhaps you will be so good to bring me down a gown – for further particulars inquire of Miss Nangle at whose feet

---

51   This was the raft used to cross the Inny River between Castlepollard and Edgeworthstown.
52   The heroines of her new novel, *Leonora*.
53   Sneyd was now reading law at Trinity College in Dublin.

you are accustomed to lie – or at Miss Byrne's, mantua-maker, Hume Street South, or if it be inconvenient, do not make any enquiries at all for the gown is by no means near my heart ... three new coats for the girls [*her half-sisters*] are much nearer my heart ...

TO SOPHY RUXTON
Edgeworthstown, Christmas 1804

A merry Christmas to you and a happy new year, my dear Sophy, and I don't know any of my friends who are more likely to have a happy new year for I know none whose means of happiness are more in their own power ...

... I am not doing anything at present for I am between having finished Leonora and beginning something else – I have not decided what. I wonder how a spider feels when it has finished one web & has not begun another. I have been reading Washington's life or rather trying to read it for it is so dry & so full of American politics it sticks in my throat ...

We spent (Papa, Mama & me) a few pleasant days at Castle Forbes whereof I gave my aunt a history but I forget it all now – I only remember that Lady G[*ranard*] and her excellent mother were very kind to me – Lord Longford who has been here as you may see by the frank has told me a great many anecdotes of gaming, eating & extravagant men which will all tell in Ennui[54] ...

The net, dear Sophy, the pretty brown net you gave me with all its complement of bows proved of sovereign use to me at Castle Forbes & I would not exchange it for Bonaparte's crown or Madame Bonaparte's either ...

Poor Kitty has not been well & is not quite strong enough for the long labours of the toilette – so I supply her place and very happy I am bustling about ... making the fire & blowing the fire with a pair of bellows ... Then the water's to be boiled for shaving & the stockings to be put on the bed & the inexpressibles – two pairs, one flannel, one corduroy – and the flannel waistcoat and the calico d[*itto*] and the boots ... near the fire [*but*] not too near to be dried & the shirt to be aired & the hair to tied behind & the hearth to be swept & William & Ho[*nora*] to be brought to him for lessons & in such a bustle?"

Oh dear, the cravat – this morning I entirely forgot he must have a cravat ... because I had just sat down on the little stool by the fire to read Madame de Sevigné ...

---

54 Her latest novel in which the dissolute hero is transformed by a visit to his Irish estates.

I forgot to tell you that I smell the downfall of chemisettes[55] & beg you will work no more – for I observed at Castle Forbes *les élégantes* wore plain muslin kerchief crosses as in days of yore beneath their gowns every morning & another more certain omen! – we met women in dirty roads in red cloaks [*with*] worked chemisettes peeping from under them!! ...

TO SNEYD EDGEWORTH
Edgeworthstown, 9 February 1805

We all missed you very much on Mrs Beaufort's wedding day, January 29th, which we celebrated with a sort of masquerade without masks – a Twelfth Night such as we used to have, but we wanted gentlemen sadly. My father, Henry and you were terrible losses; nevertheless we were very merry and wonderful noisy –

Dramatis Personae

Miss H. Beaufort: Jennie the Romp in the Journey to London – a very decent romp.

Miss Louisa Beaufort: Mrs John Nettleby, admirably dressed with immense white feathers and French ringlets in her eyes – she looked and spoke quite like a dashing would-be woman of fashion and wanted nothing but a husband and Mrs Granby to torment.

Miss Charlotte E: Mrs Heidelberg – an excellent old lady with treble ruffles and black lace hood, a slow voice and prim manners, dignified sentiments and long winded morality – in fine contrast to the other characters.

Mrs Edgeworth: Mrs Candor, a full scandal-bag – she and Mrs John Nettleby had much conversation about the present anecdotes of the day, which shocked Mrs Heidelburg's delicacy much.

Miss E: Madame Duval, the old Frenchwoman in "Evelina" – hair drawn up to a prodigious height, powdered and surmounted with scarlet flowers, feathers and trumpery of all sorts, the whole holding by two pins which she was in dread all night should be pulled out by Squire Richard in the Journey to London, admirably played by William. He was at once noisy and countrified and as full of clownish schoolboy practical jokes as Captain Mirvan himself and once frightened "Madame French" nearly into fits by throwing a whole collared eel to her for supper ...

---

55   An embroidered or lace insert tucked into the neckline of a dress.

Miss Honora E: Miss Judy, the imaginary governess to Mrs John Nettleby's children, so well dressed and so well acted.

This morning arrived a very large packet for my Aunt Mary, franked by William Pitt!! Curiosity's eyes were all agaze. When opened, it proved to be an old book, a treatise on Exchange, a thick octavo. Upon further examination it was found there were divers snug cells cut in the leaves in which were bedded – spectacles for Aunt Mary, two cakes of white paint that will never change colour, a machine for mending pens for William, three yards of clog-springs for Maria – with a very entertaining letter from Francis Beaufort, chiefly giving an account of Betty, the young Roscius.[56] Francis says he is an imitator of Kemble and Siddons and has learnt from Cook to distort his eyes – he recites some tragic speeches well, but often rants. The public go mad about him – the Royal Dukes' carriages at his door! bulletins of his health pasted up! actors all subservient to his caprices! One night he refused to act till the manager had played at leapfrog over his back! If he is not spoiled it will be wonder indeed …

Maria was horrified to hear reports that her letters to her aunt at Black Castle were being passed on to other visitors; Sophy was repeatedly begged to stop the practice.

TO SOPHY RUXTON
Edgeworthstown, 26 February 1805

… The habit of shewing letters is a vile practice which I dare to reprobate though I know it to be my dear kind aunt who thinks "Such a letter will do my little niece Maria credit and I <u>will</u> show it" – but what is the consequence of this. Maria when she writes to Aunt Ruxton must look before she leaps which she does not like to do and she must consider whether such a thing is fit to be said to "Miss This & That" & Miss T'other as well as to Aunt Ruxton & whilst she is weighing consequences the genius of nonsense takes her flight and instead of that open-hearted laughter loving little fellow comes one, trim, spruce, full dressed with cautious and mincing gait, the genius of familiar epistles …

I hereby confirm to you Louisa's report of my continued health; I am fat & happy & have [*made*] my best worked muslin sleeves … And I have almost

---

56 A child prodigy actor who had become the rage in London.

finished working a pair of sleeves for Mrs Stewart,[57] the ditto of yours in shining cotton which I heartily repent, because shining cotton will not "wash and wear for ever, ma'am and make an underpetticoat afterwards".

Besides working unlawful houseworks [*word missing*] I have been reading a power of good books – *Montesquieu sur la Grandeur et Decadence des Romains* which I recommend to you as a book you will admire, because it furnishes so much food for thought; it shows how history may be studied for the advantage of mankind, not for the mere purpose of remembering facts and repeating them. I am laying myself out for wisdom, for my father has excited my ambition to write a useful essay upon professional education. He has pointed out to me that to be a mere writer of a number of pretty stories & novelettes would be unworthy of his partner, pupil & daughter & I have been so touched by his reason or his eloquence or his kindness or all together that I have thrown aside all thoughts of pretty stories & put myself in for a course of solid reading.

Sneyd has come home to spend a week of vacation with us. He is now full of logic and we perpetually hear the words syllogisms and predicates, majors and minors, universals and particulars, affirmatives and negatives, … – and we have learnt by logic that a stone is not an animal and conversely that an animal is not a stone. I really think a man talking logic on the stage might be made as diverting as a character in the Apprentice [*by Murphy*] who is arithmetically mad, pray read it – My father read it to us a few nights ago and though I had a most violent headache so that I was forced to hold my head on both sides whilst I laughed, yet I could not refrain …

Give my love to my uncle and Margaret and tell them I hear that the Float is sunk. It is well that we were not upon it! … The report changes as fast as the figure of a dragon in the clouds on a windy day. First it was "an ass laden with Spanish dollars belonging to one Tierney, of Drogheda, that sank entirely, only the man caught the rope and was saved". Then it was "nine cars loaded with yarn, please your honour, and Tierney of Drogheda along with them and they all went down and Tierney himself and the horses swam ashore". Then five minutes afterwards we hear that "the yarn was saved and nothing in life went down but the Float itself, though all the men and cars and yarn were upon it!" To gain any more correct information at this hour

---

57   Wife of Dugald Steward, Professor of Moral Philosophy at Edinburgh and Henry's mentor.

(ten) of the night … would be beyond the power of any "of woman born" for at this hour, of a fair day

> "Men, asses, dollars, yarn in gay confusion fall
> And one oblivious stream of whiskey covers all"

… Your little god daughter Sophy is one of the most engaging little creatures I ever saw and knows almost all the birds and beasts in Bewick from the tom-tit to the hip-po-pot-a-mus and names them all in such a sweet droll little voice …

TO HENRY EDGEWORTH [*in Edinburgh*]
Edgeworthstown, March 1805

My very dear Henry,

I think you were quite right in all your Union and anti-Union battle. It gives me the most sincere pleasure to see your letters to my father written just as if you were talking to a favourite friend of your own age … There is something in this perfect openness and in the courage of daring to be always yourself which attaches more than I can express, more than all the Chesterfieldian arts and graces that ever were practiced …

To business – I send you the Modern Griselda for a note for Mrs Stewart and my hearty love, not for yourself, but for her and a little bit of it, as much as she thinks proper for Mr Alison.[58]

The worked sleeves are for Mrs Stewart and you are to offer them to her – nobody can say I do not choose my ambassadors well! If Mrs Stewart should begin to say "O! It is a pity Miss Edgeworth should spend her time at such work!" please to interrupt her speech, though that is very rude, and tell her that I like work very much and that I have only done this at odd times, after breakfast, you know, when my father reads Homer or when there are long sittings when it is much more agreeable to move one's fingers than to have to sit with hands crossed or clasped immoveably. I by no means accede to the doctrine that ladies cannot attend to anything else when they are working – besides it is contrary, is it not, to all the theories of Zoonomia?[59] Does not Dr

---

58   Professor of History at Edinburgh.
59   Famous book on physiology by Erasmus Darwin, grandfather of Charles Darwin.

Darwin show that certain habitual motions go on without interrupting trains of thought? And do not commonsense and experience, whom I respect even above Dr Darwin show the same thing? ...

I am glad a son of Dr Darwin's is over your head [*in Henry's lodgings*] though I dare say he makes a thundering noise stamping about, for he is of a giant brood.

Upon my word, it is a fine thing to be an Edinburgh Reviewer – £200 a year and ten guineas a sheet![60]

Poor authors must hide their diminished heads. Besides it is always better diversion to tear, than to be torn to pieces. I should not however like to be one of the tearers, except it be the person who wrote the review of Dumont and Bentham. I envy that man whoever he is, but you never will tell me who he is. I assure you my envy would not prompt me to murder him.

Yes, pray consult Mr Stewart about your thesis, he is so benevolent I am sure he will spare you five minutes of his precious time and when you have his opinion you will be safe.

My father has written and mentioned your yeomanry corps and Charlotte will write to you her own pretty self ...

TO AUNT RUXTON
Edgeworthstown, 21 March 1805

Yesterday at almost half after 6 in the morning, little sister Lucy[61] came into this world. Do not be disappointed (if you can help it) that she is not a boy.

My mother is delightfully well this morning & at this moment in a sound sleep ... Lucy – for I think that seems to be her name, is a fine child with blue eyes – fair – & pretty hands. This morning as she lay beside her mother, all the children, Fanny, Harriet & Sophy came to be introduced to her – Their wonder seemed exactly in proportion to their ages – Sophy took to kissing her very cordially without asking by words or looks who or what she was or whence she came – Harriet after observing with some indifference the smallness of its hands suddenly exclaimed – I'll go & tell Charlotte ... Fanny watched with the conscious dignity of 5 almost 6 years old till she was summoned from the

60   Henry had joined the staff of the famous *Edinburgh Review* founded by Sydney Smith, Frances Horner, Henry Brougham and Francis Jeffrey in 1802.

61   The fourth daughter of Mrs Frances Edgeworth.

foot to the side of the bed; after examining "the poor little thing" joint by joint, feature by feature, she ended with kissing it most maternally & when her mother observed that she would be able to nurse Lucy a little, Fanny added with pride & joy in her eyes "Yes, I can teach her her letters too!"...

TO SOPHY RUXTON
Edgeworthstown, 25 March 1805

I am sitting with my dear little mother on a soft armchair at a decent distance from the fire writing on a little green desk on my knee ... she is very well & rosy & pretty & talkative – not feverish or any-ish that she ought not to be ... now my mother is going to dictate

"Tell Sophy in the first place that I am very much obliged to her, and you may put that in whatever words you please ..." (Memo: I cannot mind what I am writing, my mother and Harriet are so entertaining describing the dresses that they had when they were children)

"Oh Harriet, how pretty you used to look in your thin cambric frock with your pink slip under it."

"Yes, I remember holding it up going down the mahogany stairs at Headfort for I thought they were bloody."

"But then Harriet, you looked shockingly ugly in your arnotto rags and your sulphur stuff jacket & your old beaver hat that looked as though it had gone through a regiment." ...

Mama: "Maria, will you never be ready for me any more. Have you been all this time telling Sophy I am obliged to her --- the temptations of so many young men we have here in the house – footmen, I mean of course – no indeed, I don't know – for Henry thinks the present kitchen maid very pretty ..."

"I am afraid she is rather above the place that I want and would think the place too hard ..."

"Sophy did not mention whether she would milk cows or not; as we keep no dairymaid, the kitchen maid must milk ... I believe I'd better have nothing to with her – that is all I have to say to dear Sophy."

Tomorrow we all, viz. Mr Edgeworth, two Miss Sneyds and Miss Harriet Beaufort and Miss Fanny Brown and Miss Maria and Miss Charlotte and Miss Honora and Mr William Edgeworth go in one coach and one chaise to Castle Forbes to see a play acted by the ladies Elizabeth and Adelaide Forbes, Miss

The Edgeworth children listening to a story. Drawing by Charlotte Edgeworth.

Parkins, Lord Rancliffe, Lord Forbes and I don't know how many grandees with tufts on their heads, for every grandee man must now, you know, have a tuft or ridge of hair upon the middle of his pate ...

We have heard from Lovell, still at Verdun and in hopes of peace, poor fellow ...

TO SNEYD EDGEWORTH AT TRINITY COLLEGE, DUBLIN
Edgeworthstown, 4 May 1805

I am perfectly well, dear Sneyd, and rejoice every day that you did not come down here on my account or on any account, to lose your chance by imprudent good nature of another premium.[62] Believe me the will was as good, far better in my opinion than the deed. I thank you from the bottom of my heart – if that is better than the top – for the kindness you have shown me.

We are all very happy and tolerably merry with the assistance of William and the young tribe who are always at his heels and in full chorus with him ...

Charlotte <u>cordials</u> me twice a day with Cecilia[63] which she reads charmingly and which entertains me as much at the third reading as it did at the first ...

---

62   Maria had been severely sick after taking a small dose of opium for a violent toothache.

63   Fanny Burney's second novel.

We are a little, but very little afraid of being swallowed up by the French – they have so much to swallow and digest before they come to us! They did come once very near to be sure, but they got nothing by it …

TO AUNT RUXTON
Edgeworthstown, 31 May 1805

My father's birthday was kept yesterday much more agreeably than last year, for then we had company in the house. Yesterday Sneyd, now at home for his vacation, … contrived a pretty little *Fête Champêtre*, which surprised us all most agreeably. After dinner he persuaded me that it was indispensably necessary for my health that I should take an airing – accordingly the chaise came to the door and Anne Nangle and my mother, with little Lucy in her arms, and Maria were rolled off and after them in horseback came rosy Charlotte, all smiles, and Henry with eyes brilliant with pleasure – riding again with Charlotte after eight months absence. It was a delightful evening and we thought we were pleasing ourselves sufficiently by the airing so we came home <u>thinking of nothing at all</u>, when as we drove round our ears were suddenly struck with the sound of music and as if by enchantment a fairy festival appeared upon the green. In the midst of an amphitheatre of verdant festoons suspended from white staffs on which the scarlet streamers of the yeoman were flying, appeared a company of youths and maidens in white, their heads adorned with flowers, dancing – while the matrons, their mothers, and little children were seated on benches round the amphitheatre.

All this merry company consisted of the united family of the Bristows & Langans.[64] Old John has three sons – they have three wives and children innumerable – his eldest son's two daughters very genteel … all in white net – silk stockings too! & *coiffée* with only a well placed natural flower on their heads, were the belles of the evening – Sneyd & Henry danced with them & John Langan, the delighted father & grandfather sat upon the pier of the diningroom steps with little Harriet on one knee & Sophy on the other & Fanny beside him. Then cakes & syllabubs served in abundance by good Kitty – William who is at present in the heights of electrical enthusiasm proposed to the dancers a few electrical sparks to complete the joys of the day – All men, women & children flocked to the study to be <u>shocked</u> and their various gestures

---

64 The Edgeworths' retainers.

John Langan (the Edgeworths' steward) with Harriet and Sophy. Drawing by Charlotte Edgeworth.

& expressions of surprise & terror mixed with laughter were really diverting to my mother & Anne Nangle & I who had judiciously posted ourselves in the gallery. Charlotte and Sneyd as soon as it was dark came to summon us and we found the little amphitheatre ... illuminated, the lights mixed with green boughs and flowers ... and boys with flambeaux waving about ...

TO MARGARET RUXTON
Edgeworthstown, 21 June 1805

... I had a most pleasant long letter from my father today.[65] He has become acquainted with Mrs Crewe – "Buff and blue and Mrs Crewe"[66] – and gives an account of a *déjeuner* at which he <u>assisted</u> at her house at Hampstead, as

---

65   Richard Lovell Edgeworth had gone to London to appear as a witness for his neighbour, Judge Fox.

66   A celebrated Whig hostess. She had given a dinner in 1784 to celebrate Charles James Fox's election
     at which all the guests had come dressed in his colours.

quite delightful. Miss Crewe charmed him by praising "Tomorrow"[67] and he claimed remuneration on the spot – a song, which it is not easy to obtain: she sang and he thought her singing worthy of its celebrity. He was charmed with old Dr Burney, who at eighty-two was the most lively, wellbred, agreeable man in the room.[68] Lord Stanhope begged to be presented to him and he thought him the most wonderful man he had ever met.[69]

Tell my aunt that <u>Leonora</u> is in the press ...

TO AUNT RUXTON
Edgeworthstown, 6 September 1805

... I have been at Pakenham Hall and Castle Forbes – at Pakenham Hall, I was delighted with "that sweetest music," the praises of a friend from a person of judgement and taste. I do not know when I have felt so much pleasure as in hearing sweet Kitty Pakenham speak of your Sophy; I never saw her more animated or more pretty when she was speaking of her.

Lady Elizabeth Pakenham has sent me a little pony, as quiet and almost as small as a dog, on which I go trit trot, trit trot – but I hope it will never take it into its head to add

> "When we come to the stile,
> Skip we go over." ...

TO MRS EDGEWORTH
Black Castle, [?] November 1805

I have eaten so much goose that I have become almost a goose myself or rather a dormouse. I have been and am very well. But dearest mother, I do not give Black Castle credit for that health into which your unceasing kindness nursed me – I shall never forget it – nor Charlotte's – give my love to her ...

John the coachman was married yesterday – the day we arrived was to have been his wedding day but the priest refused to marry him without a note from his master – This threw John into an outrageous passion for it seems he is of

---

67   Short story by Maria.
68   Fanny Burney's father.
69   Lord Stanhope, Pitt's brother-in-law, but a convinced Whig, was a distinguished scientist and inventor.

an even more impatient temper than I am. Thumping his breast he came to "Richard" and swore that ever since he had determined to marry, everything in the world had gone wrong with him & the greatest misfortunes in life had happened to him.

"Which be they, John?"

"Why Sir, I am forced to wait for the note in the first place & then in the next, see you've exposed me to the whole world."

"How?"

"By asking me was not I married already!"

So much for an impatient bridegroom who it is said would fall into as great a fury if he was ordered to bring the horses to the door five minutes before his own time ...

TO AUNT MARY SNEYD
Black Castle, 17 November 1805

... We have (thank God) never had any stupid dinners & crowds of uninteresting people since we came here – Society I love but mere numbers I hate. We were at a large dinner at Lady Foulis, but there is good & amusement for those who please to be pleased. In winnowing and sifting characters, those who choose only to gather the chaff are much to be pitied, there are always grains of corn for whoever will take the trouble to pick them out – For instance, Sir Marcus Somerville tho' not brilliant told me something I never knew before that to keep steel grates bright you must rub them with oil when warm & then with lime ... I learned from Mrs Noble's son of 7 years old what I suppose everybody must know but myself that if you steep flax in a pond you poison the water – which poisons the fish – which poison the swans etc etc – There were swans on a pool at Mrs Noble's but Harriet did not seem to feel their superiority to geese.

... My father is hand & glove and hand and heart with the Bishop.[70] ... But what will surprise you the more he repeated the epigram to the Bishop ... with the best effect imaginable; he laughed & offered to provide for any of my

---

70   Thomas O'Beirne, Bishop of Meath. Working at Dublin Castle in the 1790s, he had blocked Richard Lovell Edgeworth's attempts to have his telegraph adopted but was now the Ruxtons' neighbour, installed in the Bishop's Palace at Ardbraccan just outside Navan. Maria distrusted him and later based the character of Commissioner Falconer in *Patronage* on him, but became a close friend and correspondent of his 'true as steel' wife, Mrs O'Beirne.

father's sons who would go into the church – the epigram was as follows on the bishop's turning his chapel into a diningroom

> "Why the kitchens turn'd chapel my friends I can tell ye
> The bishop 'tis plain makes a God of his belly"

We had a great dinner at the Bishop's – A large uncrowded table with elbow room enough for the cobbler who lived on the Combe – and good things enough for an <u>Epicure</u> – (venison excepted) – then such a dessert! Such grapes! I may wish they were now in your mouth – and such conversation ... The bishop is really a wellbred well informed man (when he is not in a passion) and from him I learned what I dare say Charlotte remembers from Caesar's Commentaries – that the Romans were first tempted to the conquest of the Gauls by the hopes of becoming masters of their delicious wines ...

TO FANNY EDGEWORTH [*aged six*]
Collon, 19 November 1805

Maria had moved on to stay with the Beauforts in Louth.

My dear good little Fanny,
I am very glad to hear from my aunts and Charlotte that you are growing every day more good humoured. I hope you will not be such a goose any more, or be afraid that William should eat you up; for unless you were a real goose he could not eat you up. He is as kind to you as my father used to be to my aunt Ruxton when they were children and if you were as good humoured as she was, he will love you always as well as papa loved, and loves sister Peg.
    ... Your letter to Harriet came this morning, it is well written for a little girl like you – Harriet has not read it yet ... She is walking in the garden with Mama and Louise. I have just been with her and grandmama to look at the greenhouse. Do you remember her laying the first stone of it? It is now a very neat house with glass windows and a glass frame for the roof like the hot bed in the garden and it is whitewashed within & filled with pretty geraniums, myrtles, roses and many other little plants which have too long names for you to read ...
    Harriet sends her love to you; Mama and Grandmama and Louisa are very glad to hear that you are good. Pray continue to grow better & better, my dear little Fanny, & that will please your friend & sister – Maria

[*Postscript from her mother.*]

My dear little Fanny,
I love you when you are good – pray forget how to cry and then you will always be loved by your affectionate mother, FE

TO SOPHY RUXTON
Edgeworthstown, 2 January 1806

I hope no cross post or other accident has prevented my aunt from receiving a note I wrote her the day we heard of poor Richard's terrible accident … For my part, I have been living away merrily with the state of health I brought here from Black Castle. Dr Kindness I prefer even to the three most skilful & least celebrated of their profession, Diet, Quiet and Merry-man – We have had one letter from Dr Henry Edgeworth since we came home, he seems in good spirits and quite intent upon his business. I am sure we shall see him this year with his diploma in his hand …

We have been for two days at Sonna where I heard his praises from Mrs Tuite with great delight. By <u>We</u> … I mean the *parti quarre* which of all other I like the best, papa, mama, Charlotte & I …

We have brought back from Sonna Ireland's "<u>Confessions</u>" – they are very entertaining – What happy times we live in when a man has a chance of making two fortunes, one by being a rogue & the other by confessing he is one – I think a farce might be made out of the antiquarians duped.[71]

In March Maria made another expedition to the Beauforts in Collon, then travelled on to stay with the Ruxtons at their seaside house at Rostrevor in Co. Down. It was the longest journey she had made so far in Ireland and the place brought out all her descriptive and storytelling talents.

TO MRS EDGEWORTH
Rostrevor, 21 March 1806

… The road from Newry to Rosstrevor is both sublime and beautiful – The inn at Rosstrevor is like the best sort of English breakfasting. But to proceed with

71   William Henry Ireland, son of a noted London antiquarian, had claimed in the 1790s to have found a cache of Shakespeare's letters and plays; his forgeries had deceived everyone including Dr Johnson. He afterwards claimed to have forged them as a joke against his father.

my journey ... I must go two miles and a half before I got to Fort Hamilton as my aunt's house is called ... You see a slated English or Welsh looking farmhouse amongst some stunted trees, apparently in the sea – you turn down a long avenue of firs, only three feet high, but old-looking, six rows deep on each side. The two former proprietors of this mansion had opposite tastes – one all for straight and the other all for serpentine lines – and there was a war between snug and picturesque of which traces appear every step you precede ... The house is bare and ugly in front ... two storeys high. Before the door, the bay of Carlingford ... vessels under sail, near and distant – little islands, sea-birds, and landmarks standing in the sea. Behind the house, immediately sheltering its back, the mountains of Morne – sublime ... In the parlour is a surprising chimney piece ... with wonderful wooden ornaments and a tablet representing Alexander's progress through India, he looking very pert, driving four lions.

After dinner I was so tired that in spite of all my desire to see and hear, I was obliged to lie down on my aunt's bed to refit. After resting but not sleeping, I groped my way down the broad old staircase, felt my road ... and arrived in the parlour where I was glad to see candles and tea and my dear aunt and Sophy and Margaret's illuminated affectionate faces. Tea – "Come now" says my aunt "let us show Maria the wonderful passage – it looks best by candlelight."

I followed my guide through a place that looks like a description of Mrs Radcliffe in lower life – passage after passage, very low roofed and full of strange lumber – came to a den of a bedchamber, then another, and a study like the hold of a ship and fusty – but in this study were mahogany bookcases ... and wellbound excellent books. All kinds of tables, broken and stowed on top of each other and parts of looking glasses, looking as if they had been there a hundred years and jelly glasses on a glass stand as if somebody had supped there the night before. Turn from the study and see a staircase more like a stepladder, very narrow – but one could squeeze up at a time ... two chambers – if chambers they could be called – quite remote from the rest of the house, low ceilings, strange scraps of many-coloured paper on the walls, an old camp bed, a feather bed with half the feathers out – one window, low but wide.

"Out of that window" said my aunt "as Isabella told us, the corpse was carried for it could not get down the narrow staircase".

"Who is Isabella?" cried I – but before my aunt could answer I was struck with new wonder at the sight of two French looking glasses in gilt frames, side by side, reaching from the ceiling to the floor – and placed exactly opposite the bed.

"Isabella" said my aunt "is the gardener's wife and you shall see her tomorrow – she told us all the strange histories of the house." ...

Back at Edgeworthstown there was news, which, as Maria's stepmother wrote was 'one of those tales of real life in which romance is far superior to the generality of fiction ...' A letter had just come from Lady Longford announcing Kitty Pakenham's engagement to General Sir Arthur Wellesley. He had proposed to her ten years before when he was an impoverished young officer in Dublin and had been turned down as an unsuitable match by her family. Now returned from a series of brilliantly successful campaigns in India (where his brother Lord Wellesley was viceroy) he had discovered she was still unmarried and proposed again without having seen her. Sophy Ruxton, Kitty's close friend, was to attend the small private wedding in the Longfords' family house in Dublin.

MRS EDGEWORTH TO SOPHY RUXTON
Edgeworthstown, 13 April 1806

... Pray tell dear good Lady Elizabeth we are so delighted with the news and so engrossed by it that, waking or sleeping, the image of Miss Pakenham swims before our eyes. To make the romance perfect we want two material documents – a description of the person of Sir Arthur and a knowledge of the time when the interview after his return took place ...

Continued by Maria.

How glad I am that you will have the delightful pleasure of being with Miss Pakenham! I love her most sincerely and I cannot tell you how grateful I feel to Lady Longford for writing such a warm kind letter to my father.

Have you received – but I know you can think of nothing now but Kitty Pakenham ...

TO MRS EDGEWORTH
Navan, 1 May 1806

My dear nurse of my body & my mind – both are at this instant in very good plight and of all my sixpennyworth of complaints I have none left worth speaking of. The rats of horses did much better than we expected & <u>pounded</u>

Kitty Pakenham/Wellesley – sketch from her portrait by Sir Thomas Lawrence.

General Sir Arthur Wellesley – painting by Robert Hone, 1804.

on most finely to Castlepollard – met Stevens there, his nose less pimpled & purple than formerly – met also Admiral Pakenham who looked much handsomer and more like a gentleman than formerly – even had a clean coat & combed beard – walked half a mile with my father[72] …

At Clonmellon my father met Sir Benjamin Chapman[73] who pressed him much to dine with him – Here's a lady try if you can persuade <u>her</u>, you are a Bachelor etc – how would you not, dear mother, give sixpence to have seen the scene – Up bowled the Baronet, no, not bowled for nothing could be less round – but up came a lath of a man with a great deal of sharp practice in a disagreeable wizzened countenance – out came a profusion of compliments on Rackrent, Griselda etc etc – then a modest request to dine & sleep – Impossible etc. But wld accept of his obliging offer to drive through his grounds – Away trotted his agent to open the gates … The demesne of Sir Ben I believe pretty but I was tired & anxious to get to Allenstown. Nevertheless the Baronet wld not be content till he had walked me through the whole house, drawingroom,

---

72   Uncle of the 2nd Earl of Longford, Admiral Pakenham had served in the navy and then in Dublin Castle. He had married Louisa Staples, niece and heir to Thomas Conolly of Castletown in Co. Kildare, but was considered by Louisa's relations – and the Edgeworths – to have coarse naval manners.

73   Owner of Killua, a large estate outside Clonmellon, Co. Westmeath. His late-nineteenth-century descendant ran away with the family governess and became the father of Lawrence of Arabia.

*Peasant girl met on
the road, sketch by
Charlotte Edgeworth.*

library, bedchamber not excepting his own – Some pictures I believe were good
especially two Wouvemans with the white horse that is so often mentioned in
Gesner's letters[74] – & there was Oliver Cromwell & Susanna & the Elders &
more than I could admire … and Sir Benjamin's breath smelt so of garlic … all
the time he talked which he did without stop or stay – I went to the brink of a
fib to avoid his invitation to dine with him as we came back – said we were to
dine with Lady E[*lizabeth*] P[*akenham*]

Tell good Kitty that the joy I felt when I found the bottle of lemonade
in the carriage can only be conceived by a very thirsty or very feverish person
and the biscuits & cakes were so <u>very</u> very good. My father and I blessed her a
100 times … A girl on the road who saw me with the lemonade bottle at my

---

74   Highly valued and prolific seventeenth-century Dutch painter, noted for his equestrian scenes.

mouth grinned from ear to ear & looked with such delighted sympathy that I can be sure she thought it was whiskey.

5 o'clock – At Allenstown found Major Waller & Belinda & Jane[75] … In the evening Miss Jane Waller sang & played delightfully … But she is so affected & looked so much at her elbow & makes such incessant drapery work when sitting or standing that she put my father out of patience …

Dr Beaufort saw Sir Arthur Wellesley at the Castle – Tell Charlotte he says Sir Arthur is a gentleman like <u>handsome</u> man – very brown & quite bald – with a hooked nose – looks like a Roman. – He did not travel with Lady Wellesley – could not wait – went in the mail – was a day past his leave of absence, a whole day – Lady W followed with his brother, the clergyman – Anne Nangle said last night what a charming thing it would be if this brother would take a fancy to Sophy – But the salt sea is between them now …

TO MARGARET RUXTON
Edgeworthstown, 23 May 1806

… My only scrap of news, I fear Sophy has told you already – Lady E … Pakenham told it to us. When Lady A. Wellesley was presented to the Queen, her Majesty said "I am happy to see at my court so bright an example of constancy – If anybody in this world deserves to be happy you do."

Then her Majesty enquired "But did you really never write one letter to Sir Arthur Wellesley during his long absence? "– "Never Madam:" "And did you never think of him?:" "Yes, very often, Madam."

I think the Wellesley Budget is now exhausted – I am glad that virtue & constancy are sometimes approved at court & hope the bright example may be followed.

… I hope your house is going on bravely and that you cultivate <u>your</u> <u>garden</u> better than I do my mount – I went on my return yesterday to visit it & to make out a list of the killed & wounded, 6 officers & innumerable common men – Captain Pyracanthus among the wounded – Lieutenant Hawthorn dead – Col. Provence Rose severely wounded but have hopes of his recovery. Pray tell my aunt … that Major Periwinkle such as we admired at Fanny's railing by the new chicken house will climb if allowed a stick …

---

75 Cousins of the Beauforts.

TO SOPHY RUXTON
Edgeworthstown, 12 July 1806

This is the third sheet of paper in the smallest hand I could write I have had the honour within these three days to spoil in your service – stuffed full of geological and chemical facts which we learned from our two philosophical travellers, Davy and Greenough – but when finished I persuaded myself they were not worth sending[76] …

Our travellers have just left us and my head is in great danger of bursting from the multifarious treasures that have been stowed and crammed into it in the course of one week. God grant I may keep a tenth part for you. As memoranda for future questions … You have I suppose read in Nicholson various papers of a Mr Knight on trees & saps & leaf buds etc – Put me in mind to tell you of an exp[*eriment*] not yet published about sowing plants on a wheel – very ingenious. Also, do not fail, for my dear aunt's sake to tell you how any tree may be made to live 4 or 500 or a thousand years certain.

This Mr Andrew Knight … is brother to your Payne's picturesque Knight – Equal or superior in the land of science to his brother in the land of taste. Payne Knight has a beautiful place: put me in mind to tell you how his house, Downtown Castle is built – mixture of Grecian & gothic architecture. And don't forget to ask me about the water in pillars of giant's causeway & the description of a toad the size of a dog with a bushy tail – Also ask about waiter at Killarney & a duel – Also about English volunteer peasants in their new clothes & their opinion of Bonaparte … And what Sir J. Banks gives to his porter & don't forget to ask me about soot ink in Herculaneum manuscripts … And the lazzarati at Naples & Prince Julio Romano & the medieval flag – And the King of Naples selling his own fish with his shirtsleeves tucked up – and the Queen forging a letter from her brother of Austria … and the Prince Borghese making a bonfire of the golden book – And the manner in which they lately made the modern Romans light the street …

From this list you may guess the confusion of good things in my pate. Mr Davy is wonderfully improved since you saw him at Bristol. He really has an amazing fund of knowledge upon all subjects & a great deal of genius; and

---

[76]   The Edgeworths had first met the young scientist Humphrey Davy at Bristol where he had been a pupil and protégé of Dr Beddoes, Anna's husband. Now a rising star of the scientific world, he had moved to London and had just been on an extensive tour of Europe. George Greenough, his companion, was a distinguished mineralogist, who later founded the Royal Geological Society.

what surprises me most is the improvement in his manners ... Mr Greenough, his travelling companion, has a very disagreeable voice and at first sight not a very intelligent countenance – yet he is very intelligent and ... has a taste for wit & humour ... They are gone to complete their tour, the principal object of which is mineralogy ...

Dr Beddoes is much better but my father does not think his health safe. Anna[77] is pretty well. I am very well, but shamefully idle – indeed I have done nothing but hear and if I had had a dozen pair of extraordinary ears and as many heads, I do not think I could have heard or held all that was said.

TO HONORA EDGEWORTH
Rostrevor, September 1806

Maria was staying once again at the seaside in Co. Down with the Ruxtons.

... We have at last accomplished our visit to Tullamore [*Tollymore*] Park – Twelve precious souls and all agog to dash through thick and thin! We were fortunate enough to have two of the finest days I have seen this summer, no rain, no wind & neither more nor less of the sun than we liked ... The views of the park more than answered my raised expectation, I never saw or could have imagined anything equal to [*them*] ... We rambled on for some time amongst the woods – resting from time to time to enjoy the most beautiful views of cascades, trees & mountains. I think the great error in all plantations is leaving the trees too close together. Even at Tullamore ... the fault appears and was the principal mark of distinction between artificial & natural woods ... One whole mountain was covered with larch, & I was informed that I ought to admire it because it was planted in imitation of the Alps. Nevertheless I thought the uniform multitude of green spires neither subtle nor beautiful ...

Near Tullamore there are beautiful cottages with pyracanthus in full red berry on their walls – nothing so pretty or effective, tell Sneyd, to hide an ugly gable end as a pyracanthus – We met in the park the proprietor of the place, Lord Roden & his son Jocelyn, a fat Bob Darwin of a youth of 18 – They showed us a number of cottages they were building, on a pretty green near their grand gate. It was very agreeable to see they were so eager in improving the country – & not absorbed in their own selfish magnificence ...

---

77 Anna had caused much family disapproval by leaving her husband for Davies Giddy, Humphrey Davy's original patron, but had returned home to look after Dr Beddoes when he became ill.

A woodland arbour at Tollymore Park.

TO SOPHY RUXTON
Edgeworthstown, February 1807

... We paid a long promised visit to Coolure[78] & spent a few pleasant days there ... Admiral Pakenham is very entertaining & appears very amiable in the midst of his children who dote upon him but not half as much as he dotes upon them – two of them on his knees sometimes & everything in their hands & mouths the moment they signify their will and pleasure. Yet notwithstanding all the coaxing & all the strange jumble of things they hear from him, the children are not spoiled but as goodnatured, happy, unpolished but as agreeable urchins as ever you saw – Much of this must be attributed to their amiable mother who with <u>the infinite power of gentleness</u> is constantly watching over their good – I am confirmed in my opinion that to excite strong affection in the minds of children for their parents is most wise – as well as most pleasant an early education.

... We were fortunate in seeing something of the mirror of Colonels whilst we were at Coolure. Col. Edward P[*akenham*][79] burnt his instep by falling asleep before the fire out of which a turf fell; so he was luckily detained in the country a few days longer than he had intended & dined, breakfasted etc with us – He is very unaffected & agreeable – wonderfully modest considering all

78   Admiral Pakenham's house beside Lough Derravaragh.
79   Lord Longford's younger brother, on leave from the army.

Edgeworthstown House drawn by Francis Beaufort showing the new bow window (left) added to Maria's bedroom, and her garden below.

the flattery he has met with – He says the women of rank & *ton* in England are growing abominably [*like*] Frenchwomen in their morals …

… This moment we have the following *billet* from good Lady Elizabeth Pakenham "Our Edgeworth friends will rejoice that dear Kitty is well & had a stout boy the 3rd of this month"! I am sure I am very glad of it …

In April 1807 Charlotte, one of Maria's favourite sisters, succumbed to consumption. She had been ailing for over a year and a plan to send her to Madeira for the winter had been vetoed by her father for lack of a suitable chaperone, much to the indignation of her great friend Louisa Beaufort who wrote to her sister, Frances Edgeworth, 'My beloved Charlotte was a sacrifice on the altar of prejudice offered to cowardice & fear …'

Perhaps because of this, her death left Richard Lovell Edgeworth and Frances devastated. Maria persuaded them to take refuge away from home at Black Castle, leaving herself and the Sneyd aunts in charge of the younger children. When her father returned, he occupied himself by enlarging the library, which entailed breaking through the old outer wall of the house, leaving two square pillars to support the opening and building out beyond it. He also laid out a new garden for Maria at the west end of the house visible from her bedroom window, which gave her immense pleasure.

TO AUNT RUXTON
Edgeworthstown, September 1807

My beloved Aunt and friend – friend to my least fancies as well as my largest interests – thank you for the six fine rose-trees and thank you for the little darling double-flowering almond tree. Sneyd asked if there was nothing for him? – so I very generously gave him the polyanthuses and planted them with my own hands at the border of his garden pincushions …

Enclosed I send a copy of an epitaph written by Louis XVIII on the Abbé Edgeworth – I am sure the intention does honour to H[*is*] M[*ajesty's*] Heart and the critics here say the Latin does honour to H[*is*] M[*ajesty's*] Head …

William Beaufort who sent it to my father says the epigram was communicated to him by a physician at Cork, who being a Roman Catholic of learning and foreign education, maintains a considerable correspondence in foreign parts …

TO AUNT RUXTON
Edgeworthstown, 13 October 1807

I am seated at this moment in the middle window of the recessed library, Sneyd & Honora kneeling in the next window, laughing *à gorge déployée* over Sterne's Maria, which they are reading aloud & which they say should be called Sterne's pocket handkerchief – and while they are criticising Sterne's dirty sentimentality, here is Harriet between the windows, putting the map of the world together & groaning over the impossibility of finding the place of the Pacific Ocean and in the middle of the room is Fanny jumping over the skipping rope with all her might – & behind my mother's back who is working at the table, lolls Sophy reading from Jenny Wren or Mother Hubbard

> "The pig he was stubborn, the pig he was strong
> He squeaked & he struggled the whole way along"

And here comes William with a new lock & key in his hand, turning the key & making the tumbler jump & click for the public entertainment – and here comes my aunt Mary talking of Henry's prescription, or of the woman at Rostrevor's repository for an antispasmodic for a cough …

TO HENRY EDGEWORTH [in London]
Pakenham Hall, Christmas Day 1807

A merry Christmas to you, my dear Henry and Sneyd! I wish you were here at this instant and you would be sure of one – for this is really the most agreeable family and the pleasantest and most comfortable castle I ever was in.

We came here yesterday – the <u>we</u> being Mr and Mrs Edgeworth, Honora and M.E. A few minutes after we came arrived Hercules Pakenham – the first time he had met his family since his return from Copenhagen ... My father has scarcely ever quitted his elbow since he came, and has been all ear and no tongue.

Hercules has given a full account of all their proceedings in that piratical expedition.[80] The town would not have been bombarded at all if Colonel Edward Pakenham's advice had been taken – the Colonel viewed the town carefully and discovered a pass through a range of gardens, by which he could have <u>filed</u> in all the troops by night and there would have been no resistance. Was this not enough to excite indignation? <u>But</u> as Lady Longford says, the Colonel might have lost his life if he had conducted the attack.

The Danish General Peyman, a gallant old man, came and sat in his chair at the works – he could not stand, having been wounded in the leg. One fine church and <u>one</u> of the fine libraries were destroyed but (in spite of the newspapers) the National Library and the Observatory escaped ...

The yards and magazines Captain Pakenham describes as orderly and magnificent in their treasures beyond imagination – for ten days our troop employed five hundred horses and eight thousand men every day in carrying away the shipping, rigging, sea stores and ammunition of all kinds. I write the numbers in words lest you think I mistook a nought in the numeration. The noise of the seaman and troops shouting and hallooing at everything they found – the blows of the men taking to pieces some finished vessels to bring them back to England – the horses trampling, the ammunition carts rolling ... Captain Pakenham said it was impossible to conceive it without hearing it. In the immense dockyard everything was found in the most precise order – every rope, every sail, even the minutest article numbered and labelled for the ship to which it belonged – the cartridges made up, to every gun its charge.

---

80   The English government had ordered the capture of the Danish fleet to prevent it being commandeered by Napoleon, although Denmark was neutral.

This labelling Captain P. says he is sure will be imitated in our navy – good in everything.

But with what indignation the Danes must have beheld this scene! And how they must hate the English for ever and ever and ever! Yet strange to tell … these people either concealed their hatred so well – from fear – or felt so little – from stupidity – that in a country town where Captain Pakenham gave a ball to the inhabitants, all that could be stowed into the room flocked to it – and some of our men who were taken prisoners were paid a shilling a day and allowed to pleasure themselves all over Copenhagen! …

Captain Pakenham went with Sir Arthur Wellesley on the expedition up the country: saw much of the people – long-haired, sulky, comfortably clothed and housed, coarsely fed on black and <u>blue</u> bread, corn and milk – some potatoes … Such abundance of horses and carts that all his regiment was carried. Put in requisition fifteen hundred thousand rations of oats – gave tickets of receipt to the peasants, all paid for by Lord Cathcart. The first peasant whose oats were seized took the receipt which was to entitle him to payment with sulky incredulity – but when he found that he actually got the money, the country people flocked in with their oats in astonishing quantities …

Lady Wellesley was prevented by engagements from joining the party at Pakenham Hall – both the Duke and Duchess of Richmond are so fond of her as no tongue can tell. The Duke must have a real friendship for Sir Arthur – for while he was at Copenhagen his grace did all the business of his office for him[81] …

---

81   Sir Arthur Wellesley held the post of Chief Secretary to the Viceroy in Dublin.

IV

JANUARY 1808 – MARCH 1813

BY 1808 MARIA *was a highly successful fiction writer with four novels and a series of children's stories in print but her father had decided that his 'partner', as he termed Maria, must now reapply herself to more serious writing. He proposed, much to her alarm, a sequel to their book* Practical Education, *designed as guidance for older students, to be entitled 'Professional Education'. It was to cause Maria much anguish and anxious consultation with family, and successive chapters were dispatched to suitable advisers.*

TO SOPHY RUXTON
Edgeworthstown, 29 January 1808

I cannot ... let this frank go without a line to you. I will tell you how "Professional Education" goes on which, as it is the object of my waking and sleeping thoughts, I know by sympathy must be interesting to you.

"Clergymen" has been entirely re -written and I hope, as papa and mamma both think so, it has been improved – I have about seventeen pages ... to copy.

"Country Gentlemen" – done. I think tolerable, nothing brilliant – gone to Lord Selkirk, who begged to keep it a fortnight that he might first get a pamphlet of his own out of his head, which ... must be published before the meeting of Parliament. Besides this chapter, Lord Selkirk has that on "Statesmen, diplomatists" etc. This, I think, is *"ce que j'ai fait de moins mal"* as Madame de Genlis said.

"Education of Princes" has been with Mr Keir and has his approbation strongly, except in one point which we shall alter – it will take me three days to make that alteration.

"Lawyers" – totally re-written. It has been with Judge Fox and has received his unqualified approbation. I wish Richard [*Sophy's brother*] could read it before it goes to press; and there is one reason I wished to go to Gaybrook[82] for I would have taken it with me and would have got him to sit up half a night to read it – I know he would do that and more for his old friend Maria.

"Military Education" – corrected since its return from Mr Keir – story of Captain Spike taken out in consequence of Mr Keir's objections to it as too softening, and a better story from the Life of Bertrand du Guesclin, which I read to you on the sofa, put in its stead.

"Physician" – still to be done. This is the only one we have to do except the preliminary chapter which is a mass of heterogenous stuff – must be entirely new formed – will be at least seventy pages. I shall have the whole time the rest of the book is printing to do this – because, though the preliminary chapter must come first, it may be printed last by the common ingenious contrivance of paging it separately in Roman figures.

I never thought this book would come so near to a conclusion. I am still well repaid for all the labor it has cost me by seeing my father is pleased with it & thinks it a proof of affection. I cannot help however looking forward to its departure.

TO AUNT RUXTON
Edgeworthstown, 9 June 1808

My father and mother have gone to the Hills[83] this day to settle a whole clan of tenants whose leases are out and who expect that because they have all lived under his Honour, they and theirs these hundred years, that his Honour shall and will contrive to divide the land that supported ten people amongst their sons and sons' sons to the number of a hundred. And there is Cormac with the reverend locks, and Bryan with the flaxen wig, and Brady with the long brogue and Paddy with the short and Terry with the butchers-blue coat and Dennis with no coat at all and Eneas Hosey's widow and all the Devines pleading and

---

82   A neighbouring country house in Westmeath, demolished in the 1960s.
83   An outlying part of the Edgeworth estate. Maria later used the name in her novel *Patronage* for the house in which the impoverished Percy family took refuge.

Edgeworthstown tenants, sketch by Charlotte Edgeworth.

quarrelling about boundaries and bits of bog. I wish Lord Selkirk was in the midst of them with his hands crossed before him – I should like to know if he could make them understand his Essay on Emigration – or his last "Essay on the defence of the country" – Some of these descendants of the kings of Ireland, some of this race of mountaineers who insist upon living & dying in the spot of land where they were born, must serve his Majesty or beg – sooner or later ...

My father wrote to Sir Joseph Banks[84] to apply through the French institute for leave for Lovell to travel as a <u>literate</u> in Germany and I have frequently written about him to our French friends – and those passages in my letters were never answered.[85] All their letters are now written, as Sir Joseph Banks observed, under evident constraint and fear ...

---

84 President of the Royal Society since 1778.
85 Lovell was still a prisoner at Verdun in eastern France and reported in bad health.

TO MRS EDGEWORTH
Chantinee, 3 July 1808

Maria was staying with John Ruxton's eccentric brother-in-law, James Corry, father of Letty, in Co. Monaghan. She was afterwards to use him as the model for King Corny, the half-barbaric ruler of the Black Isles in her novel Ormond.

I must reserve the amusement of describing the humours of Chantinee till we meet, for folios of paper would not give you an adequate idea of their infinite variety. The house in which I now enjoy myself has stood, certainly, in spite of … all the efforts of man to throw it down or blow it up. Tell William and try if you can make him believe it, that after the house was built the owner quarried and blasted the rocks underneath till he made a kitchen twenty foot square and various subterranean offices. A gentleman who was breakfasting with him at the time … heard one of the explosions and starting, Mr Corry quietly said "It is only the blasting in the kitchen – finish your breakfast". But the visitor, not being so well trained as Charles the 12th's secretary, ran out of the house.

After all this was accomplished, and the house, contrary to the prophecies of all who saw or heard of it, still standing, the owner set to work on the roof which he fancied was too low. You may judge of the size and weight of the said roof when I tell you it covers a hall 42 feet long – two oblong rooms at each end of the hall 33 and 35 long, by above 20 broad and an oval room at the back of the hall seven and twenty by four and twenty. Undaunted by the ponderous magnitude of the "undertaking", this intrepid architect cut all the rafters of the roof clean off from the walls at all sides, propped it in the middle and fairly raised it altogether by men and levers to the height he wanted. There it stood propped in the air till he built the walls up to it, pieced the rafters and completed it to his satisfaction! But alas, he slated it so ill … that in rainy weather, torrents of water pour in and in winter it is scarcely habitable by man or brute. The walls and coved ceilings of the fine rooms and all the really beautiful cornices are so stained and spoiled with damp that it is lamentable and provoking to behold them. In the drawingroom … there is a fuschia sixteen feet high, trained to a dead stem of alder which is planted in its tub. The fuschia is six feet thick and as thick as matted honey-suckle on the garden wall – and you may shake it as you would a sheet of honey-suckle that you were pulling down. Geraniums 13 and 14 feet high all round the bow window of this room. Some in rich blossom, others ragged and wild, or as Mr C. says in *déshabillé*. He sacrifices the neatness of the room, to be sure, to his vegetable leaves, for he waters them every morning with soapsuds which stream about in uncontrolled meanders …

TO SNEYD EDGEWORTH
Edgeworthstown, 30 December 1808

How little we can tell from day to day what will happen to our friends. I promised you a merry frankful of nonsense this day and instead of that we must send you the melancholy account of poor Dr Beddoes' death. He died as easily, mind and body, as his best friends could desire … I enclose Emmeline's letter which will tell you all better than I can. Poor Anna! How it has been possible for her weak body to sustain her through such trials and such exertions GOD only knows. My father and mother have written most warm and pressing invitations to her to come here immediately and bring all her children. How fortunate it was that little Tom came here last summer and how still more fortunate that the little fellow returned with Henry to see his poor father before he died[86] …

Maria was now hard at work on a new collection of stories, Tales of Fashionable Life, *including a thinly disguised portrait of Admiral Pakenham as a devious naval officer in 'Manoeuvring'. She was horrified to find once again her private letters to Sophy Ruxton were being read aloud and might broadcast the connection.*

TO SOPHY RUXTON
Edgeworthstown, 5 January 1809

My dear friend … I am going to give you as good a scolding as ever you had in your life. And for what? – Rummage, scan your conscience … – You sent my letter to you to Anne Nangle & she read it at Allenstown[87] – She says she scanned it over carefully before she read it, but no part of it as I recollect was fit for anybody but you – And how <u>could</u> <u>you</u> serve me so – you who know what an utter horror I have of sharing letters – You with whom I thought myself so safe on this score that I could write any nonsense that came into my foolish

---

86   Tom was to grow up to be the romantic poet, Thomas Lovell Beddoes.
87   The Wallers' house in Co. Meath.

*Admiral Sir Thomas
Pakenham in formal dress.
He was to appear thinly
disguised in two of Maria's
best stories.*

head or heart. Very well – you will bring me only to write wise show letters
to you, and then you will see how you like them. – Other people perhaps may
not feel this as I do, but I absolutely cannot write at my ease when I think my
letters are to pass from one friend's hand to another – for what I say to <u>you</u> is
not always what I would say to <u>them</u> even if I did or could love them as well …
The degree of intimacy I have with you … puts in my power to convey to you
by a few words my meaning … which words would be totally unintelligible &
convey false ideas to others – You know all this as well as I do & yet against
your judgement & your conscience & with your eyes wide open & all merely
for the pleasure of diverting people with my letters – I am willing, <u>if</u> <u>I</u> <u>can,</u> to
divert the public with my books, but my letters are solely for those to whom
they are directed …

    Now I must tell you further that I am excessively vexed at the thoughts
of that paragraph about my Admiral's blackguardism etc to the little Stewarts
– I feel as if I was a treacherous tell tale – a vile double dealer, pretending to
defend & betraying a friend's private conversation that passed perhaps when

he was warm with wine. Oh Sophy I cannot tell you how much I am vexed with myself, 1,000,000,000,000 times more than with you –

My father, who is a thousand times better & a better friend than I am, says that upon thinking over Captain Dashleigh's character in Walsingham's history and seeing how like it is to Adm P [&] how all who read it are struck with that likeness – so my dear I will take out every trace of resemblance and put another character in its place …

TO AUNT RUXTON
Edgeworthstown, 11 January 1809

I wish you had heard what old John Langan said when we told him of your accident [*Mrs Ruxton had broken her arm*] – After he had lamented for some moments he grew angry & exclaimed "But what business had she there to be getting that way up on them o' of the way places – But that's the way with <u>yees</u> all … And I'll be engaged it was to do a civility any how to somebody of us – Well blessed be God it's no worse – for troth Mistress Ruxton is a good & kindhearted lady – none better – "

… On Friday we went to Pakenham Hall upon the faith of a note from Lord L setting forth that no company was expected there until Monday. So we sat down only 32 to dinner! Our party Papa, Mama, Aunt Mary & Maria – found there Lord L – Lady E P, Caroline P, Henry P, Mrs P, Admiral P, two Miss Pakenhams, Mrs Tuite, Mr Tuite, Mr H. Tuite – Lady Levinge – 3 Miss Levinges (fine girls), Mr Dease, Mrs Dease, Mr William Stewart / 3 children out of the room – I can't recall the rest – In the evening a party of twenty went from P. Hall to a grand ball at Mrs Pollards … Lord Longford acted his part as Earl Marshall in the Great Hall sending off carriage after carriage in due precedence & with its proper <u>complement</u> of beaux & belles – I was much entertained & very well – had Mrs Tuite & Mama & Mrs P & the Admiral to talk & laugh with – saw abundance of comedy. There were three Miss—s from the County of Tipperary, three degrees of comparison, the positive, the comparative and the superlative – excellent figures with white feathers as long as my two arms joined together, stuck in front of what were meant for Spanish hats. How they towered above their sex, divinely vulgar with brogues of the true Milesian race … handing cakes and cider etc to my Lord! …

We stayed till between three and four in the morning. Lord Longford had to save our horses which had come a journey, put a pair of his horses and one of his postillions to our coach – the postillion had, it seems, amused himself at a <u>club</u> in Castlepollard while we were at the ball and he had amused himself so much that he did not know the ditch from the road – he was ambitious of passing Mr Dease's carriage – passed it – attempted to pass Mr Tuite's – ran the wheels on a drift of snow which overhung the ditch – and laid the coach fairly down on its side in the ditch. We were none of us hurt. The <u>us</u> were my mother, Mr Henry Pakenham and myself. My mother fell undermost – I never fell at all for I clung like a bat to the handstring at my side, determined that I should not fall on my mother and break her arm … None of us were even bruised. Luckily Mrs Tuite's carriage was within a few yards of us and stopped and the gentlemen handed us out immediately. Admiral Pakenham lifted me out and carried me in his arms as if I had been a little doll and set me actually on the step of Mrs Tuite's carriage, so that I never wet foot or shoe. And now, my dear aunt, I have established a character for courage … for the rest of my life! The postillion was not in the least hurt, nor the horses – if they had not been the quietest animals in the world, we should have been undone – one of them was found with his feet level with the other's head. The coach could not be got out of the ditch that night, but Lord Longford sent a man to sleep in it that … no one might steal the glasses. It came out safe and sound in the morning, not a glass broken.

Miss Fortescue, Caroline and Mr Henry Pakenham went up, just as we left … to town or to the Park to Lady Wellesley who gives a parting ball on Monday night and then follows her husband to England.

Poor Mrs Stewart has been waiting for the crowd to abate – All the Gosfords, Lady Olivia Sparrow[88] & many other fine birds were to come after we left … Monday next we go to the Tuites for a few days. – So I think we are become quite dissipated …

TO SOPHY RUXTON
Edgeworthstown, January 1809

… Mr Fox & his precious lady passed this gate today without calling to see us or writing to thank my father & Mrs E for a kind invitation … Mrs E happened to be in the kitchen at the time. Old John Langan came in and

---

88   Lady Olivia Sparrow had acted as the main go-between for the ill-fated marriage between Kitty Pakenham and Sir Arthur Wellesley.

told us this fact with high indignation – "Mrs F nodded her head to me from her carriage as she passed – Sorrow take her and her nod too! A pretty lady isn't she and a fine wife! – I hate her for she has spoiled as good a man as ever breathed – Sorrow! Take her!" added he growing very red & going right shoulder forward out of the kitchen "I wouldn't be sorry if her neck was broken going to Dublin!"[89] ...

TO SOPHY RUXTON
Edgeworthstown, 5 February 1809

Three of the most agreeable days I have ever spent we have enjoyed in this visit of our Pakenham Hall friends to us ... There is something quite captivating in Lady Longford's voice and manners and the extreme vivacity of her countenance – ... I never saw a woman so little spoiled by the world. As for Miss Pakenham, I <u>love her</u> ... Upon reflection I might have been more prudent in some of our midnight conferences at the delightful curling-hair time, but upon the whole it is in vain to strive against nature & as prudence is not my forte at 40 I feel it never will be – & so let it go! ...

My father, I dare say, pleased Mr Fortescue because Mrs Fortescue pleased him much – & I have often observed that the verb to please is in human life, whatever the grammar may say, a reciprocal verb ...

I have sent my <u>head</u> to my aunt by Mrs Fortescue ...

This, according to her stepmother's Memoir *was a print of a large buxom lady entitled 'Miss Maria Edgeworth' done as a frontispiece for a magazine. Maria wrote under it,*
    'O, says the little woman, this is none of I.'

TO MARGARET RUXTON
Edgeworthstown, 18 March 1809

I have been busier than any working bee you ever saw or heard – three volumes of Tales, viz. I vol. Ennui, – 2nd vol. Mde de Fleury ... 3rd vol Manoeuvring ... have all been corrected within this last month – revised by my father, Mrs E & Aunt Mary Sneyd & myself & have been actually sent to Johnson who has

---

89 Judge Fox had remarried after Lady Anne Fox's death, beneath him, in the Edgeworths' view.

Mrs Maria Edgeworth

*'This is None of I' –
fanciful engraving of
Maria published in a
journal in 1807. In real life
she refused to allow herself
to be drawn or painted.*

made a promise to have them printed & out in 6 weeks … Three more volumes are to come out by the time the public has digested these – so announced in the preface … The collecting & sending of these stories so suddenly was Papa's thought, & the reason he did was that he wishes to meet their coming out in London – Mama wrote to my aunt last week to open to her this London scheme – As far as anything is certain in this life I believe it is fixed. My aunts & Hon. go to Byrkely Lodge – My father, Mrs E, William & I to London – stay, I fancy, 6 weeks or two months – travel in the old coach & I hear sell it when we get to London town & buying a <u>secondhand</u> (never tell!) barouche. "Why" says I "is not the coach good enough?" "No" quoth Papa "for we shall spend next winter in Dublin & must have a decent carriage." "Ho, Ho is it so!" quoth I – "many things between the cup & the lip" – But I see preparations making and old coach boxes being dragged into the yard for the journey to London – Well if it turns into a comedy it will do very cleverly – and Drury Lane may be rebuilding whilst I am looking high & low for good characters – never so hard to find as in these days! – vide Mrs Clarke[90] ...

TO SOPHY RUXTON [*who had been ill*]
Edgeworthstown, 28 April 1809

... I shd like your Dr Patience better if he had others to assist him & you may call in ... my favourite Doctors, Diet, Quiet & Merryman – Merryman above all I have a great opinion of for persons of our constitution – Dr Diet perhaps takes into his consideration external as well as internal applications (for all these Doctors love to catalogue their sphere of practice) and I shd humbly suggest to him that stripes of camomile have been found very servicable in cases similar to yours ...

TO SOPHY RUXTON
Edgeworthstown, 6 June 1809

... My father tore a note I wrote to you in the last frank to my aunt, having the impudence to read it whilst I was out of the room; he found I had told you that Col. Barry who was here, was very affected & so full of fine people who all were particularly fond of him that he made me sick – My father said it was very imprudent to write this, for that it would be repeated. I replied it was as safe with you & safer than with him, for you would as soon as cut your tongue out as to repeat any of my private opinions that could hurt me & that you had prudence enough to know what shd not be repeated. – To all that he acceded – yet would tear the note – A Mr Holland, a grandson of Wedgewoods & a surgeon at Nutsford, Cheshire & intended for a Physician called here in the course of a pedestrian tour – spent two days – very well informed and with unpresuming manners[91] ...

---

90   The notorious mistress of the Duke of York, discovered to have sold commissions for the army.

91   Henry Holland was to become one of Maria's greatest friends and correspondents. He travelled around Europe as physician to the Prince Regent's exiled wife, Princess Caroline of Brunswick, and later, as Sir Henry Holland, became physician to Queen Victoria. He was to marry the daughter of Sydney Smith.

TO MARGARET RUXTON
Edgeworthstown, July 1809

… I am very glad that you like the end of Ennui [*her new novel*] – I was afraid you would have thought it stupid – How dare you say I have no character for patriotism to love? I am remarkable for patriotism out of my own country & if you doubt it you may look in the Edinburgh & Monthly & Annual Review where if I remember right, I am stiled an amiable patriot – My aunt Mary, I believe, intends to copy for you part of a letter … which came just opportunely to tell us that Lady Geraldine is admired in foreign parts … But I have never meant Lady Geraldine as a perfect character, I am quite content if you think her new – And as to the old nurse if you will but allow her to be natural. I am satisfied that you should think her a vile hag …

TO SOPHY RUXTON
Edgeworthstown, July 1809

… I have just been reading Captain Carleton's Memoirs of Spain and am in love with both the Captain & his general Lord Petersborough – How Lady Wellesley would delight in this book! – The present times seem to be acting those times in Spain exactly over again – the character of Lord P <u>attempted</u> by Sir A.W.,[92] I have also been reading one of the worst written books in the language yet one that has both entertained & instructed me, in spite of the author … and all his thereofs and thereons & all his platitudes – Sir John Hawkins' life of Dr Johnson – he has thrown a heap of rubbish of his own over poor Johnson which would have stifled a less gigantic genius … I have learned more from this book than from many an elegant & well arranged performance[93] – What a miserable wretch was Johnson at the end of his life without a home, without a friend and with, I fear, an insane mind … As to Mrs Piozzi, she was not worthy of such a friend as Johnson – she wanted only to make a show of that mammoth of literature[94] … In this book of Sir John Hawkins I find a Latin epigram of Johnson's on a Mrs Molly Aston who used

92   Sir Arthur Wellesley had left the previous July to take command of the Peninsular army.
93   Sir John Hawkins, one of Samuel Johnson's executors, had published the first biography of Johnson in 1787 but it was much criticized for its malice and mass of irrelevant material.
94   Mrs Piozzi, formerly Mrs Thrale, had published her memoir of Dr Johnson in 1796 and his letters to her two years later.

to be, it seems, a great declaimer in favour of liberty – My father, Honora, Sneyd & William made some impromptu translations of it sitting round the table after dinner – Here they are, Which is best!

I copy the Latin for my uncle and if I write it wrong he must not be angry as my father always is, as if I could write or paint Latin correctly by instinct.

> *Liber ut esse velu, suariste pulchra Maria*
> *Ut maneam liberta – pulchra Maria, vale!*

> Why on the love of freedom should you dwell
> When he who loves it must bid you farewell

Another: To please Maria freedom I pursue
          To keep my freedom, I bid her adieu

Another: Does fair Maria bid me to be free?
          To keep my freedom, I must fly from thee
          Maria, freedom bids me love – oh why?
          For following her I must Maria fly. ...

Early in September Richard Lovell Edgeworth was seized with acute stomach pains that lasted for several weeks and caused Maria huge anxiety.

TO SOPHY RUXTON
Edgeworthstown, September 1809

My dear friend – My father has (in his own words) had a much better night tho' wakened every hour & not a fiftieth part of the pain he has had for six nights past –

Yesterday was a most trying day for him as Mrs Tuite with Mr Chevenix ... came in the morning and he had a long letter to dictate to me about surveying bogs – All this was done & he rode & walked a little afterwards – Then Mr & Mrs Jephson & Mrs Burleigh dined here & he talked a great deal & with much eloquence as he lay on his sofa in the evening & wrote a long letter of his case, 5 pages, to Hartegan – And after all this fatigue instead of being the worse for it ... he slept better ...

TO MARGARET RUXTON
Edgeworthstown, 1 October 1809

[*I write*] to give you the delightful assurance that my father is now convalescent
& getting every day & night better & better – That he is still much emaciated
& altered in his appearance I cannot deny but everyone tells me that this is
so much the better … I suppose it is with health as with riches "Light come,
Light go" – I am now sufficiently at ease my dear Meg to be merry & talkative
again as my dearest aunt Ruxton knows – I sleep in the room with her – such
fine talking at night! What a delight her company has been to us & what a
cordial to my father …

She has been in some degree rewarded by finding Mr John Foster here who
has much entertained her with his conversation – especially with his account
of the eleven thousand virgins who suffered martyrdom at Cologne whose
skeletons or skulls he saw all stuck round a great church there in niches with
St Ursula at their head whose skull was distinguished by a red riband round it.
The man who showed them used to fish the skulls out of their niches when he
wanted strangers to have a nearer view of them by sticking a kind of hook at
the end of a rod into the holes of their eyes … St Ursula who was treated with
the greatest respect was hooked down by her red topknot –

Mr JF happened to travel through Bonne at the time when the French
had just sent commissioners to turn all the monks out of their convents,
and he gave us an excellent description of a well dressed venerable monk of
above 65 years of age who came into the inn where he was – said he was just
turned out of his convent, had no means of living and besought Mr Foster
to take him as a servant – At a fine convent near Bonne Mr Foster saw an
ass standing at the door just laden with the ancient books of the convent –
two monks standing in mute despair, whilst they were loading the *paniers* …
Mr F went inside the convent for there was such confusion nobody minded
him – perhaps took him for one of the French commissioners – soldiers &
monks mixed, going up & down the great stairs and through the cloisters –
the library, chapel & refectory most magnificent – all tearing down! All that
the holy men most reverenced profaned … over the fine marbled walls of the
chapel scrawled in red chalk by the French – "*Paix aux carbonniers! – Guerre
aux palais!*" …

TO SOPHY RUXTON
Edgeworthstown, 8 October 1809

Frances Edgeworth had just given birth to a son.

… My mother is already wonderfully well & up … The little Francis is a fine little boy – blue eyes and dark hair – I am told the upper part of his face is like Dr Beaufort & the underpart like my father but I fear I cannot see any likeness in such young things.

The Bog Commissioners whom William has named the gentlemen of the Irish Turf have accepted graciously of my father's services but the pay is not yet settled and Mr Joseph Banks is written to and "begged to state what should be the pay of a member of the society of civil engineers …" Mr Foster called here on his return from Ballinasloe and brought Admiral P with him – I could not help being diverted by the idea of two such different gentlemen journeying together …

P.S Monday morning – My mother is admirably well and her little son sucking in health & strength & every virtue from her and my father slept well last night.

TO HARRIET BEAUFORT
Edgeworthstown, 20 October 1809

… I have the pleasure to tell you that [*Mrs E*] is now going on as well as possible except that she suffers much pain from one of her breasts to which the little hero has never yet taken kindly. He and she too are excessively tired with his efforts to suck it and to bite some milk out of it – The nipple is sadly wounded and nobody but she whom my father says was born to be the mother of heroes could bear this torture with so much fortitude …

My father … is almost restored to his usual health … He dined at Sonna with me the day before yesterday and … was not in the least tired with going 18 miles … Mr Chevenix whom we saw at Sonna was very entertaining and told us a number of Parisian anecdotes, some too horrid & some too long for repetition … One of the celebrated Madame de Staël I can find time & room for – You know Bonaparte has forbidden her to come to Paris but she had a great desire to see Talma the famous tragic actor and she obtained permission to go to Lyons ... to see him. In the midst of the play one night she started up & stretching her arms ... far out of the box towards the stage exclaimed in a voice that all the house could hear *"Toute la puissance de mon ame est dans la sienne!"* Fine stage effect! *A la Corinne*

The anecdote in the papers some 3 or 4 years ago ... of our friend, young Ségur,[95] the translator of "Belinda" is quite true – He did fight a duel with one of Bonaparte's generals ... and was never heard of afterwards by anyone for several years – Just before Mr Chevenix left Paris, young Segur's friends heard he was safe in America – He was too good & noble spirited a youth to live safely amongst Bonaparte's Generals – Mr C says that the Parisians are now as eager to go to the new Court as ever they were to go to that of Louis 14th – that it is magnificent to Eastern profusion but ill-bred as you may guess when officers make no scruple of allowing and pushing ladies to get into the magic circle – 7 Queens sit all in a row with more diamonds than are to be found anywhere but in the Persian or Arabian Tales – The Queen of Spain – The Queen of Holland – The Queen of Naples – The Queen of Etruria (?) – The Queen of Westphalia – The Queen etc – Poor creatures! [96]–

TO MARGARET RUXTON
Edgeworthstown, 10 November 1809

... Give my love to yourself & to Letty Corry and say that I am much obliged by your kindness in thinking and writing to me at such a time & be assured that if I hear the three Counties talking of it in both my ears I will be as secret as the dead till I am allowed to speak – In the meantime it is a great comfort to me that I may talk of it to Mrs E – We are both much provoked with you for not saying the happy man is Tom Rothwell – How can you be so provoking as to say a <u>Mr Rothwell</u>? Now if it is not Tom Rothwell I shall break my heart ... And if it is ... I most heartily rejoice & congratulate Letty – for I think it is the very happiest *dénouement* of all her troubles ... She will be free from the tyranny of a more than ¾ mad father and she will have an affectionate good humoured husband ... who will think himself honoured ... & raised in his own eyes ... As for the rest it is not given to all the world to have the happiness or the misery for marrying for love & as you wisely say it would be all the

---

95 Joseph-Alexandre, Vicomte de Ségur; he had escaped execution by an escape from prison during the Terror, and fled to America where he died in 1805.

96 These were the assorted wives of Napoleon's brothers.

same at the end of a calendar year – Whereas the pleasures of hot houses &
greenhouses and coaches & horses & barouches & good houses & land are of
long and increasing duration ...

To all this, many & many an honest plain spoken body would ... answer
"true for you" – and I should reply – not true for me, but true for many & wiser
persons – And all have not the same mean of happiness in their power – But
I have so good an opinion of Letty Corry that in good earnest I depend for
her happiness ... by the affection her father will show her and I have no doubt
that she will love him [*Tom Rothwell*] better at the end of a year than many a
miss who has jumped out of a two pair of stairs window in a mad love fit ...

I have this morning seen the Ed[*inburgh*] Review of Prof. Ed[*ucation*] –
which we all think the most stupid insufficient review of a book we ever read –
in fact it is no review of the book but an essay on two or three pages in the work
on classical literature – and in this essay of theirs they have repeated a dozen
times all that my father has said & without reference or acknowledgement
almost in his very words – They say they will not decide the two questions
whether Miss E's book is worth buying or whether it is worth borrowing – But
they have shown sufficiently that they think it worth borrowing for they have
borrowed from it unconsciously[97] ...

TO HONORA EDGEWORTH
Edgeworthstown, 9 November 1809

> *Honora, aged eighteen, had been sent with her two Sneyd aunts to her uncle's
> house, Byrkely Lodge in Staffordshire, for the winter – both for her health – the
> family feared she too might be consumptive – and for social life. Richard Lovell
> Edgeworth was well aware that Edgeworthstown offered few opportunities for
> his daughters to meet suitable young men.*

... Your account of your ball, my dear Honora, was voted by all who heard
it to be the best account of a first ball that was read or written in this family
and I thank you for addressing it to me – for indeed I was much interested
in hearing all your feelings as well as all your adventures – I quite love Mr
Mundy from your description of him; he must be a charming old man, almost
as charming as our dear Abbé Morollet ...

---

97 The *Edinburgh Review* had attacked the book, mainly for its omission of any reference to religious
instruction.

We are at this moment in great eagerness to hear of Sneyd's having been called to the Bar – He left us on Friday on the canal coach and when he reached Mullingar he could not get a place on the mailcoach and the canal frozen – he was consequently delayed a night – <u>walked</u> the next morning to Sonna 5 miles – had an agreeable conversation with Mrs Tuite who walked a mile back with him – all this he told us in a note per coach yesterday – But we are all in anxiety to learn whether he reached Dublin in time to be called to the bar this term – he had not a day scarcely to spare –

We have had a bevy of wits here – Mr Chevenix, Mr Henry Hamilton, Leslie Foster and his particular friend, Mr Fitzgerald, Lord Fingal and Lord Norbury … It was a most extraordinary thing in this house yesterday to see at dinner 7 gentlemen everyday and only 3 ladies – Mrs Tuite, Mrs E & myself. On the whole they were very agreeable & gave much entertainment … Lord Norbury is this moment a Lord of the Treasury and Privy Counsellor[98] … Besides all this, two days before we saw him, the Lord Lieutenant … after a drunken bout had thrown him over his head. This is a feat at which the Duke of R[ichmond] is said to excel all his contemporaries – a glorious accompaniment for the representative of Royalty! – Mr Fitzgerald is very witty and so as he is John Foster's friend I am bound to take it for granted he has amiable and estimable qualities … At present, I hold my judgement in most charitable suspense – I like John Foster more & more the more I see of him – his solid good qualities, excellent understanding and steady friendship of my father make me quite blind to that little solemnity of manner which some people dislike in him.

… I am glad to tell you for dear Caroline Hamilton's sake[99] that she seems perfectly happy in her marriage – and all who know her speak in the highest terms of Mr Hamilton's head and heart. His manners are much improved since his marriage and the intercourse with Lord Longford's family has taught him to bring out his knowledge & talents with a much better grace than formerly – he does not snuffle half as much as he did, and I like his conversation much better; for more of his knowledge now comes through his mouth and less through his nose.

I think I have gone through three of our four beaux but have not yet told you that Mr Chevenix appears to me wonderfully improved since we saw him in Paris …

<hr>

[98] Notorious as a Hanging Judge and virulent anti-Catholic, it is surprising that he should have been welcome at Edgeworthstown.

[99] Previously Caroline Pakenham.

Bonaparte over the gates of the Louvre has erected a triumphant car brought from Italy. The wits have written under it

> *"Qui doit entrer la-dedans?*
> *C'est Bonaparte, le char-la-tan"*
> *"le char l'attend"*

I don't at present recollect another scrap of wit except a bit of droll nonsense of Lord Norbury's – Somebody asked if Miss Whyte were not a blue stocking – "Oh yes", said a gentleman "She is blue! blue! b<u>luer</u> than anything you ever saw, I can't tell you how blue – what is bluer than blue?" *"Morbleu!"* exclaimed Lord Norbury.

 … Goodbye – my father is better than I have seen him for years and I have this morning walked with him in mud to far <u>far</u> beyond Barny Farrell's or Batchelor's Walk and never did you see such mud figures as we all returned!

Maria's father had begun an official report on the bogs of Ireland and how they might be used. The commission brought a miraculous improvement in his health, and an opportunity to employ his fifteen-year-old son, William, who was to be trained as an engineer.

TO AUNT CHARLOTTE SNEYD
Edgeworthstown, 3 December 1809

… [*My father*] is much interested in this bog business … The belief that he is both improving William and providing for his future establishment as an engineer makes the business particularly interesting and William every day improves in the <u>art of managing his talents.</u>

 Mrs Edgeworth is returned to the library [*after her illness*] and I cannot describe the difference she makes in our happiness … I am delighted that you have turned the scales against Dublin for this year[100] – as I agree with you that Ho[*nora*] is better situated in England … Dublin society may be, I am told by good judges, … much improved since I was there 10 years ago – but I certainly do not retain an agreeable impression of it …

Maria was later to change her opinion and much enjoy visits to Dublin.

---

100 Richard Lovell Edgeworth had proposed renting a house there for the season.

Edgeworthstown, 11 December 1809

Your letter, my dear Honora, gave me a great deal of pleasure and received a great deal of praise from my father which would have given you some satisfaction. We all wish we were acquainted with Mr Greeves whom you describe so well and long to have a peep at the model of the Edistone [*sic*] lighthouse.

My father has received a letter from Captain Beaufort dated Nov. 29th conveying a very civil & kind message from that Mr Wilson[101] whom I believe you saw in London some years ago: he offers to purchase instruments for this Bog surveying business etc – Francis says he was at last adapted my father's telegraph to nautical purposes and he has sent the Admiralty lately an index to the naval instruments for which they graciously thanked him …

… The bog surveying goes on most gallantly and my father seems much interested in the business – We had dinner yesterday with a new surveyor recommended by Dr Beaufort, who has come down for a guinea a day and has taken a room at Mrs Liddy's where he lodges and does all his work …

Sophy has been all morning endeavouring to write a note to her dear Honora, but … the pencil is not propitious and she now by her mother's advice gives it up and commissions me to give her best compliments to her aunts and her greatest love to Honora and them – The other day she asked me some foolish question and I said "Use your own understanding and don't come to consult me always as if I was "an old witch" – To which she politely & poetically replied "My dear! I never come to consult you as an old witch but only as a good fairy." –

Lucy continues as droll & as like Admiral Pakenham as ever – yesterday at dinner I was considering which of the children I would begin with if I was to play a hungry ogress and I said I would eat little Francis for supper & Sophy for breakfast & Harriet in between breakfast and dinner and Fanny for dinner … "And" interrupted Lucy "you would keep me to snuff out the candles for you at night." …

Edgeworthstown, 26 December 1809

… I have just been reading for the fourth time, I believe The Simple Story which I intended this time to read as critic, that I might write to Mrs Inchbald

---

101 Francis Beaufort's father-in-law.

about it – but I was so carried away by it that I was totally incapable of thinking of Mrs Inchbald or anything but Miss Milner and Doriforth who appeared to me [*such*] real persons whom I saw and heard ... that I cried my eyes almost out before I came to the end of the story – I think it the most pathetic and the most powerfully interesting tale I ever read. I was obliged to go from it to correct Belinda for Mrs Barbauld who is going to insert it in her collection of novels with a preface – and I was really so provoked with the cold tameness of that stick of stone, Belinda that I could have torn the pages to pieces. And really I have not the heart or the patience to <u>correct</u> her – As the hackney coachman said "Mend <u>you!</u> – better make a new one.".

TO SNEYD EDGEWORTH [*fragment*]
Edgeworthstown, n.d 1809

I am sorry I cannot give Miles[102] the permit he desires to go on with reprinting Rackrent – But my father wishes to have some <u>additions</u> made to it – and I fear in this instance <u>additions</u> will not according to the Irish usage of the word be synonymous with <u>improvements</u> ...

I am inclined to think that I could say better all my father wishes to have said about the modern manners of Irish McQuirke in the story I am writing of Patronage and I think the points might there be introduced and that plan would give more time for arguing them properly. – All this I have stated and will restate and re-urge – but in the last event of things you know that I must do what my acting and most kind literary partner decides and in the meantime can say nothing to poor Mr Miles than <u>stay a bit</u> ...

Richard Lovell Edgeworth had proposed that a new edition of Castle Rackrent *should be heavily annotated with notes on Irish manners. This was one of the rare times Maria dissented from his views and her comic masterpiece was left in its original form.*

TO AUNTS CHARLOTTE AND MARY SNEYD
Edgeworthstown, 9 March 1810

... We all rejoice that the time approaches for your return to us but I fear that Byrkley Lodge will not echo this sentiment!

---

102 Her new publisher, Myles Hunter.

And on their side of the question therefore I will say you are quite right, I think, not to travel till the weather is fine both on your account and on Honora's – very sorry indeed should we be that, after laying in a stock of health and being so well she should catch cold on her way home – I fear that Edgeworthstown must at all events appear very chill to her, and to you when you arrive – I assure you all our fine rounds of company have finished long ago and we have been reduced to the society of 3 plebeian surveyors – one of them Sally's abomination! for reasons best known to her – another so desperate a squinter and stutterer that it is a mercy … or rather the best possible proof of their good nature and good education that none of the children have laughed at him at dinner … Sophy looks upon him with such grave and dignified commiseration! I fancy that surveyors, engineers, Bog-Board and all however will soon be at an end for I think Ministry are going … going … gone! …

What a sad prevaricating figure Lord Chatham[103] has made in his Exn! – The reason I know so much about it is that I read the papers every day to save (my father's) eyes and if the Star does not get new types soon I believe mine will not stand it for long – for the ink is now, like George Falkeners', whiter than the paper – I fear Lord Wellington will not come home a popular hero[104] – but he has his good £2000 per annum secure and I don't believe he has heroism enough to be sorry for that – Poor Lady Wellesley! – The price of victory, the price of marrying a hero is terrible!

I think Mrs H. Hamilton [*Lady Wellesley's sister*] is a thousand times more happily tho' less grandly married – And she is as gay as a lark and plump as a partridge …

Lady Longford has been so kind to take Miss Louisa Pakenham, Admiral P's eldest daughter to Dublin with her this winter and to introduce her as if she was her own daughter and she has given one and will give three balls for her – Caroline … calls them Louisa's benefits – There are 4 Miss Gunns in Dublin on whom the envy and scandal and wit of Dublin now runs very high and loud – perhaps you have heard of them? They were, it is said, walking and flirting one day on the terrace at Windsor with the Duke of Cumberland and the King asked who they were – and on hearing they were the Miss Gunns his Maj. exclaimed "What! What! Brass Ordnance Hey?" So they go by the name

---

103 Pitt's elder brother had just disgraced himself by his indecision while leading a large expeditionary force to destroy the French navy at Walcheren, and was forced to resign soon after.

104 Wellesley had become highly unpopular after his retreat to Portugal but it was in fact a carefully planned strategic retreat to his newly fortified Torres Vedras.

of the King's <u>brass</u> <u>ordnance</u>. The wits of Dublin say that the D. of Richmond appears always like Robinson Crusoe with a Gun on each shoulder and that Sir Charles Saxton, his aide de camp is like <u>Friday</u> following with a spare Gun … balls naturally lead to dress – will you, my dear aunts, hold with Mrs & Miss Sneyd a cabinet council on the following delicate point:

Are long sleeves & long lace sleeves still essential to a gentlewoman's existence? – I have a sarsnet gown with short sleeves and I should like to buy some sort of sleeves to wear with it … If they <u>are</u> necessary, will you tell me what a pair of <u>real</u> lace sleeves would cost – I should like plain mignonette lace I think better than any other … I cannot decide my own mind till I hear the result of your cabinet council – I have a pair of patinette sleeves which cost me a horrible sum, £2.10 but I am told by Mrs Tuite that patinette is an abomination in the eye of fashion …

In March there was the first direct news of Lovell for many months. Richard Lovell Edgeworth had tried repeatedly to arrange his release from Verdun through French contacts, without success.

TO AUNT RUXTON
Edgeworthstown, 19 March 1810

… The other day, we had a visit from a Mrs Coffey … no relation she says of your Mrs Coffey.[105] She looked exactly like one of the pictures of the old London Cries. She came to tell us she had been at Verdun and had seen Lovell. She had been taken by a French privateer as she was going to see her sons in Jersey and left Verdun at a quarter of an hour's notice as the women were allowed home – and had not time to tell this to Lovell or get a letter to him from his friends … From her description of the place and of him, we had no doubt she had actually seen him. She came over to Ireland to prove some man who is a prisoner at Verdun … is not dead but "all alive O" … She knew nothing of Lovell but that he was well and fat – and a very merry gentleman two years ago … She told the story of a French wet nurse at Verdun with no milk which horrified the good Kitty … She hates the French – and Bonaparte the more vehemently <u>and</u> blesses her stars that little Francis is safe in her arms.

---

105 Molly Coffey, the Ruxtons' housekeeper.

The Sneyd aunts and Honora were to return to Edgeworthstown bringing a
carriage with them. Maria passed on minute instructions to Sneyd in London
to arrange its purchase; and soothe her half-brother, who had already had some
battles of will with his father.

TO SNEYD EDGEWORTH
21 March 1810

My dear Brother of the half blood and the whole heart … your note gave me
a great deal of pleasure and delighted my father "Pray tell Sneyd that I am
more anxious … about him than any lover is about his young mistress" … Pray,
my dear sir, keep this in mind whenever he gives you proof of his solicitude
which vex or plague you at the moment – for men – even fathers and authors
of Practical & Professional Education – are not perfect … and I do not think
it is possible for a father to be fonder of a son than he is of you … Now let me
brush up my wits and go to business and give you <u>verbatim</u> what my father has
just dictated to me about the carriage that is to be bought. "Tell Sneyd that
the barouche seat to Mr Wakefield's chariot is an insuperable objection – I beg
he will go to Holditch … Holditch is the second coachmaker in wealth and I
believe in credit in London – He lives in Long Acre … – Let Sneyd apply to
him and beg from me the favour of his assistance in choosing a second hand
chaise – I do not restrict it as to price – … What I want is a light travelling
chaise … If the whole be upon springs so much the better, but I do not, as
Captain Holditch knows, think that <u>essential</u> … As soon as he has completed
the bargain, Sneyd will also have his aunts' arms painted on the chaise and visit
Byrkley Lodge … and say I wish them to have the convenience of travelling
home in it. He will enquire … from his acquaintance in town for some safe
mode of conveying it to Lichfield … Your aunts write that they are ready to
return in it as soon as the equinoctial winds are over …"

So much, my dear Sneyd, for the affairs of the carriage … my father has
another <u>little</u> commission – begs you will buy for him in a shop, which he
thinks may be found on the left hand of Fleet Street or else in some shop in
Foster Lane, 4 dozen drills – some of the smallest size …

Your letter to William has arrived and was forwarded to him at Coole
where he has been bogging all week – he has just sent it by a little gossoon
to us …

William tells me from Coole that Mrs Apreece is going to be married to Playfair – This we all expected but how William heard of it at Coole we can't guess – Unless from Lord Longford who, we hear, is just returned to P. Hall ...

Mrs Apreece was a very rich, very pretty widow whose conquests and social progress in Edinburgh were avidly followed by Maria and a source of much amusement. She had called unexpectedly at Edgeworthstown in summer 1808 and stayed several days. Her latest reported suitor, John Playfair, an elderly professor of natural philosophy and mathematics at Edinburgh, had been spotted kneeling at her feet to tie her shoelaces.

TO SOPHY RUXTON
Edgeworthstown, early April 1810

... Sneyd & William returned this morning and have been so entertaining that I have done nought but listen to them from 9 till 4 ... I think Sneyd looks very thin, but I hope we shall fatten him up – He has a horse that he likes and means to ride the circuit. The Sol[*icitor*] ... General goes this circuit and we shall have the pleasure of a day of his company ...

This was Charles Kendal Bushe, famous as 'silver-tongued Bushe' and later Lord Chief Justice of Ireland. His shrewd pen portrait of the Edgeworth family at this time was published by his granddaughter Edith Somerville in Irish Memories *(1917). He described Richard Lovell Edgeworth as a 'very clever fellow of much talent ... [who] talks a great deal ...' but was far more taken with Maria whom he found 'remarkable for the total absence of vanity ... No pretensions, not a bit of blue stocking to be discover'd ... I think her very good looking and can suppose she was once pretty ... it is impossible to be an hour in her Company without recognizing her Talent, benevolence and worth.'*

TO SNEYD EDGEWORTH
Edgeworthstown, May 1810

... My father is gone to Dublin at last after a week's putting off the day – Fanny and he got into the mailcoach at the gate this day and very happy Fanny looked though she is going to have her jutting tooth drawn – But she will have ample compensation for this as she will be for some days with her aunt Waller and ... go to a play – and to hear the cathedral service she longs to hear etc.

My aunts & Ho[*nora*] actually set out from Byrkley Lodge last Thursday and I suppose will be in Dublin on Wednesday and will be here about Saturday or Monday or the day that was between ... I am sure their new chaise must have been a great comfort to them in travelling ...

I do not like Lord Byron's English Bards and Scotch Reviewers though as my father says, the lines are very strong and worthy of Pope and the Dunciad. But I was so much prejudiced against the whole by the first lines I opened about the "paralytic muse" of the man who had been his guardian and is his relation and to whom he had dedicated his first poems that I could not relish his wit – He may have great talents but I am sure he has neither a great nor good mind and I feel dislike and disgust for his Lordship & his book ...

TO SOPHY RUXTON
Edgeworthstown, May 1810

Now I have to announce the safe arrival, good looks and good spirits of our friends. – They had a very pleasant journey from Dublin on a delightful day and they took root again in the old soil so completely in one night and a day that it is difficult to believe they have been transplanted for so many months – ... Honora seems perfectly well – has no appearance of fever ... Her manner, I think, improved ... and she is as perfectly free from all affectation as ever she was ... I believe she has also improved in music, but of this, you know I am no judge. My aunt has bought for her a new piano forte which, I hope, will not be spoiled by its voyage & journey.

Fanny, my own dear Fan, justifies all I ever thought or hoped of her, ... she ... soberly enjoyed everything she saw during her few days in Dublin ... One day when she dined at Mrs Foster's, John Leslie F offered her a ticket for Higgins' lectures – she had heard one of his lectures – Mrs F. seeing her hesitate ... asked if she would wish to go again – and Fanny said "Yes, I daresay I should be entertained but I think Mr Higgins shows a great many experiments in one lecture and if I do not understand what they are all meant to prove, I should have a confusion of things in my head which would do me more harm than good" – Mrs Foster exclaimed that she was the most judicious girl of her age she ever saw ...

... My father was pleased with Harriet Foster and that pleases me for I quite love her – The very last words I said to Harriet F when she came into my room to help me ... the morning she left us were "Now Harriet, never let ANYONE ... not even your mother, persuade you to marry for brooches or coaches for remember, it would not be safe for you" – She promised me with tears that she never would – When the Count proposed ... she wrote to assure me that she did not like him for brooches or coaches – and she added "When you know him, you will perceive that he would have utterly despised a <u>brooch</u> & <u>coach</u> <u>woman</u>"[106] ...

TO SNEYD EDGEWORTH
Edgeworthstown, 16 June 1810

... A diminutive note brought to England by Mrs Mount[107] arrived here yesterday – dated 25th May 1810 – it is written with superlative caution for he says that even ladies are searched for letters from France. He says "I am in tolerable health and this situation suits me in every respect – I have written 6 or 7 letters this year and I have not had a letter from England or Ireland since the last week in May, 1809!!!" He desires that we should write a letter to Mrs Mount, not to carry over to him, but to tell her whatsoever we wish him to know ... But he says that Mrs M will not return till next spring – Now I think before that time, Lovell will be here, as we see by the papers that an exchange of prisoners including all those detained since the commencement of the war is nearly adjusted with the French government ...

My father and William are still happily busy in the bogs – my father will soon make a <u>report</u> and thinks most of the bogs improveable and at no great expense – The bog boots arrived from Dublin this morning and were unpacked at breakfast and give universal satisfaction ... My father is not only pleased with them for their solid utility, but for their being a mark of Mr Wakefield's attention & kindness – Pray be so good as to tell this to Mr W. and to thank him in my name for having remembered and executed so well my commission – Will you also do the needful of paying him for them – I suppose they will come to 4 or 5 guineas carriage included ...

---

106 John Leslie Foster's sister and a beauty, judging by her portrait. She is said to have met, and rejected a proposal from, the young Count Mastai Ferrari, who then took orders and rose to become Pope Pius IX. She had just become engaged to the twice-widowed much older Count de Salis who had inherited large estates in Co. Antrim. She settled at Rokeby Hall in Co. Louth and remained a close friend and confidante of Maria's.

107 Lovell had arranged for her to be his emissary from Verdun.

Besides my father and William's delight with the boots, they made another person in the family supremely happy – little Francis who was stuffed bodily into one as Gulliver was with the Marrowbone ... Francis is a darling little fellow with more than a double portion of his father's constitutional joy and you will delight in him ... He will be able to say Sneyd before you come, I am sure – He already makes a good hand of <u>Maria</u> – ...

TO AUNT RUXTON
Edgeworthstown, 21 June 1810

When shall we two meet again? This is a question which occurs to me much oftener than even you think ... when I am in any society I peculiarly like or when I am reading a book peculiarly suited to my taste and feelings ... By great good fortune and by the good nature of Lady Charlotte Rawdon, who is the least <u>wordy</u> and most <u>deedy</u> of her family, we had the "Lady of the Lake" to read just when the O'Beirnes were with us. A most delightful reading we had – my father, the Bishop and Mr Jephson reading it aloud alternately ... It is a charming poem – a most interesting story, generous, finely drawn characters and in many parts the finest poetry. But for an old prepossesion ... in favour of the old minstrels, I think I should prefer this to either the "Lay of the Last Minstrel" or "Marmion".

Our pleasure in reading it was increased by the sympathy and enthusiasm in our guests. We were very sorry when the O'Beirnes left us this morning – Mrs O'Beirne is true steel to the backbone. They are gone to Temple Michael and we shall go tomorrow (very civilly) to pay a long-awaited, long-owed visit to Lady Kilkenny and Mrs Bourke but not to beg a dinner, ma'am! We have the note of invitation snug in our pockets ...

Under what description of Christian do you think Mlle de L'Espinasse[108] comes – have you read or tried to read her 3 volumes of letters to poor Gilbert! – I have desired Sneyd to ask Dumont whether Mme de L'Espinasse's Gilbert is also Mme De Staël's M. Guilbert – Surely no man ... deserved so hard a fate as to be haunted by two such heroines. Some of the letters in Madame du Deffand's collection are very entertaining – for instance those of the Duchesse de Choiseul and the Comte de Broglie ... the others *fade* ... tiresome & trifling

---

108 Jeanne Julie Éléonore' de Lespinasse, originally companion to the blind Madame du Deffand, had later set up a rival salon in Paris. She fell hopelessly in love with the Comte de Guibert who married another woman, and died in misery at the age of forty-three. Her letters were published by Mme de Guibert in 1809.

– but all together curious as a picture of that profligate, heartless, brilliant and *ennuyed* society …

TO AUNT RUXTON
Edgeworthstown, 2 August 1810

I have been hard, very hard writing notes for Mrs Leadbeater – 50 pages – and in spite of your difficulties in getting through the cottage dialogues, my dear aunt, I must say … I have fallen absolutely in love with the <u>text</u> and begin to think there is no such author to be found as my author …

> *Mrs Leadbeater, a Quaker from Ballitore, Co. Kildare, had written to Maria for advice on her book of 'Cottage Dialogues'. Maria wrote an introduction to the book and took endless trouble to find her a publisher.*

TO AUNT RUXTON
Edgeworthstown, August 1810

… Sir Thomas & Lady Ackland spent a day here and seem very goodnatured but as to the rest, no great matter … He can talk of all the Edinburgh Revs and quote bits of fine writing and fine speaking … But for all this, when my father was not hearing or looking [*he spoke*] in such a low rapid voice that I was at my wit's end to hear what he said … He was so awkward & bashful that till very late in the battle, he could not get out to me that he is nephew to my friend Mrs Charles Hoare and that his aunt when he was coming to Ireland desired him to introduce himself … Just at the door when he was going away … he pressed me much to send my love to his aunt … and to promise I would go to see her whenever I went to England – My love I sent her, that is as much as she wants – but no promise to trust myself again in the fine lady's den … There is no occasion for quitting my happy home a second time to go to see one who could not find out that I was a good friend till the public told her I was an AUTHORESS[109] …

    … Lady A is rather pretty when she does not poke out her chin and close her eyes when spoken to. This, I suspect, is a new fashioned English grace as I have seen it affected by more than her Ladyship – my father mimicked it once

109 This was Maria's old schoolfriend Fanny Robinson, who had married a banker. Maria had stayed briefly and unhappily with her in London in 1792 at her father's insistence.

(by mistake) in answering her and she colored all over and kept her chin in better order thenceforward ... She altogether put me in mind of Miss Pennel in "Cecilia"[110] who wanted to be married that she might order minced veal & mashed potatoes every day for dinner ...

TO SOPHY RUXTON
Edgeworthstown, October 1810

... Will you by return of post without fail, send me <u>the length of my aunt's foot</u> – as you know I have been trying all my life to get it – But, seriously, draw her foot exactly upon a large sheet of paper and half her leg [*as high*] as a pair of half boots reach and say nothing to her, good, bad or indifferent ... for I have a charming opportunity of getting from England a new and divine kind of boot for her that shall keep her feet dry in spite of her ... in all weather ...

You saw, I suppose, that Francis Beaufort was regularly posted – Captain E Pakenham, the Admiral's eldest son, was here for a day or two this week – I like him – and recollect all they told me of Mrs H[*amilton*]'s fears of his being spoiled – [*he is*] not in the least spoiled yet – he told my father he had an insatiable desire to acquire information – and indeed he [*shewed*] that whilst he was here – I particularly was pleased with his respectful manners towards my father – He has some of his father's quickness of repartee, but with his <u>own</u> manner ... gentle and wellbred without slang of any kind[111] ...

We were talking of a Mrs— and I said "What, is she alive still; the last time I saw her she seemed as if she had lived that one day longer by particular desire" – "I am sure then" said he very gently in a slow voice "I cannot tell by <u>whose</u> <u>desire</u> ..."

TO SOPHY RUXTON
Edgeworthstown, November 1810

Maria's father had just taken his wife and Maria to Kilkenny for a few days of theatre-going and social life. The plays were acted by a mixture of professionals and aristocratic amateurs.

---

110   Novel by Fanny Burney, published 1782.
111   Edward Pakenham was the heir through his mother to her uncle Thomas Conolly and his huge Palladian mansion, Castletown, in Celbridge, Co. Kildare. He was later to change his name to Conolly.

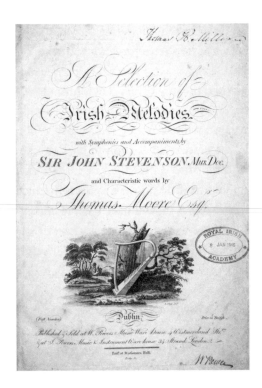

Title-page of Moore's famous Irish
Melodies, *first published in 1808.*
Maria met him in Kilkenny.

… We certainly set out on Tuesday and shall be in Dublin on Wednesday and
shall stay neither more nor less than a fortnight …

As to all the fine ladies and gentlemen at Kilkenny, they are all gone from
my mind like a dream – I am to my mother's admiration fully mistress of all
the intimate histories of the Bushes and Powers' marriages etc and know their
faces asunder.

Mrs Gervais Bushe charmed me – I did not like her sister Mrs Latham
nearly so well … Her brother Mr Latham talked to me a great deal and I
thought him a clever man and I fancy he thinks so too –

I heard nothing from gentlemen or ladies like double-entendres – Indeed
I detest that sort of conversation and if a woman had all the charms and
accomplishments upon earth I should think her odious and disgusting whilst
she talked in that way.

I thought Moore[112] recited well – but I don't like his looks altogether – and
I think he lets himself down – Have you seen his Love & Reason – and his
Melologue – If you wish it I will copy and send it to you –

---

112 Thomas Moore, Irish poet, also known as Anacreon Moore, was one of the star performers at the
Kilkenny theatricals, and was just beginning to make his name from his songs.

TO SOPHY RUXTON
Edgeworthstown, early November 1810

Contrary to my belief, it is actually determined that we set out for Dublin on the 13th to hear Davy's lectures[113] – six tickets are bought for Mr and Mrs E – Miss H – F and ME – and for Mr William E. Mrs Billamore is now rumbling in the garrets for a trunk to pack our heavy possessions which is to go before us tomorrow … lest the old coach should go crack crack and leave us in the middle of the [?] bog – Now my dear Sophy, tell me whether we may hope to see you there? Consider we shall stay but one fortnight – Lord Fingal was so kind as to come here yesterday with Lady T. Dease and he told me that my uncle is gone to Dublin. Tell me everything about it clearly – Honora, Fanny and William go with us …

Maria's stepmother recorded in her Memoir *that during this short stay in Dublin, the Edgeworths made several new friends in the scientific world who became pillars of Maria's later life, including the young doctor, Philip Crampton, later Surgeon-General of Ireland and brother-in-law of Charles Kendal Bushe, and the very young astronomer, Thomas Romney Robinson (later head of the Observatory in Armagh).*

TO HONORA EDGEWORTH
Black Castle, 13 February 1811

Now, my dear sister, a letter of odds and ends which I promised you yesterday which I must make haste and pour out of my mind before the Knoxes come – They did not come yesterday because the roads were impracticable – So scribble and scribble-scratch goes my pen and you must take the things just as I can recollect them … elegance is out of the question, post haste is the order of the day.

First for yourself, my dear teamaker, I <u>have</u> a story for you of which if I did unfold it would charm your attention so that the tea would remain unpoured out till dinner time … For the moment I shall only announce it to you under the title of the story of Mrs Moutray's "Fair Unknown", or as Sophy would

---

113 Humphrey Davy was now a huge celebrity whose lectures drew packed crowds: Maria afterwards described them in a letter to her friend Mrs O'Beirne as 'as eloquent and beautiful as those of the old minstrel in the last lay.'

call it Mrs Moutray's *L'Amanounze* ... Now I must turn to Aunt Charlotte and do you stand in for me to say to her "My dear Aunt Charlotte, when my uncle was ill I took in for him a flannel waistcoat of which the 9th part of a man had made 9 times too large for him and in gratitude for this small service he told me the following excellent find – That when he was abroad in the neighbourhood of the monastery of Grand Chartreuse in Dauphiny, he found that in all the adjacent country, the people were subject to rheumatism and consumptions but that the inhabitants of the Chartreuse ... never had any of these diseases from generation to generation and an intelligent superior of the order told my uncle that he attributed the exemption entirely to their dress – a flannel shirt or wrap worn next to the skin ... Tell Aunt Mary that ...

Tell my aunts that aunt Ruxton has just cleaned the paper in her diningroom which was black as soot by the following simple method imparted to her by one of Mr Boylan's veteran paper cleaners – First rubbed the paper with bran on a cloth lightly – then put whiting on a cloth and rub it over the paper.

Tell Mrs Billamore that my aunt puts on every round of beetroot for salad a slice of hard egg – and that it looks very pretty and eats well – better than I have explained it ... My aunt puts a <u>leetle</u> anchovy in the cream sauce for this salad – which makes *un sauce avec lequel on mangerait son propre père* ...

TO SOPHY RUXTON
Edgeworthstown, late April 1811

... Hardy's Life of Lord Charlemont[114] is interesting and ... written in a beautiful style, but I do not think it gives a clear or <u>well</u> <u>proportioned</u> history of the times – There is a want of ... perspective in it. The man's pipe smoking out of the window is as high as the house. But Hardy is more a portrait than a history painter – I am as much in love as my aunt can be with both Lord Charlemont and Humphrey Burgh ...

If you have any curiosity to know the names of the writers of some of the articles in the "Edinburgh Review" I can tell you, having had from my literary intelligencer,[115] two huge sheets, very entertaining and sensible. Jeffrey wrote the article on Parliamentary Reform ... Sidney [*sic*] Smith on Toleration and Malthus that on the question of Bullion and ... I can also tell you those in

114 Maria's father had acted as Lord Charlemont's aide-de-camp during the Volunteer movement
     of the 1780s – and much admired him. See Maria's letter of March 1799 describing their visit to
     Charlemont House.
115 Probably her new friend, Henry Holland, who was studying medicine there.

the "Quarterly" among whom Canning is one. Thank my dear aunt for her information about Walter Scott ... My father will write immediately to ask him here. I wish we lived in an old castle and had millions of old legends for him. Have you seen Campbell's poem of O'Connor's Child? It is beautiful ... in many parts I think it is superior to Scott ...

TO SOPHY RUXTON
Edgeworthstown, 1 May 1811

My father is quite well & happy, eagerly working on the model of the spire of Edgeworthstown church – Oh will not my uncle come and see it put up? I believe the sight will have many spectators for the rumour that the spire is to rise ready slated through the tower of the church by means of machinery in the course of a few hours already has raised much curiousity among his friends and the general public.

I do not hear anything of a Board of Education and my father thinks there will not be any for some months – so there is no chance of his going to Dublin[116] – Sneyd is gone there and three vast packing cases of my grandfather's law books ... summoned into his service from every garret, every closet and every nook of this house, are following him in the boat to Dublin. – They will make a respectable figure in his lodgings and give him, I hope, the repute of hereditary law ...

This being May day, on the wettest I have ever seen, I have been regaled not with garlands and May flowers, but with the legal planning of the season – I have heard of nothing but <u>taking</u> <u>possession</u> – <u>ejectments</u> – <u>flittings</u> etc. What do you think of a tenant who took one of the nice new houses in this town and left it with every lock torn off the doors and with a large stone, such as John Langan could not lift, driven actually through the boarded floor of the parlour? The brute however is rich and if he does not die of whiskey before the law can get its hand into his pocket, he still will pay for this waste ...

My father has written to Walter Scott in consequence of your having sounded the news of his arrival in Ireland – My father has directed his letter to him at Smarmore Castle – which we understand is the name of the abode of Mr Taafe – what <u>style</u> of castle may it be?[117]

---

116 Richard Lovell Edgeworth had been appointed to serve on a new board enquiring into Irish education.

117 Original twelfth-century castle with later additions just outside Ardee in Co. Louth. It is now a hotel.

I have first hand another odd letter signed by three young ladies, Miss Clarissa Craven, Rachel Biddle and Eliza Finch. After sundry compliments in very pretty language and with all the appearance of seriousness they beg that I will do them the favour to satisfy the curiosity they feel about the wedding dresses of the Frankland family in the "Contrast". I have answered in a way that will stand for either jest or earnest – I have said that at a sale of Admiral Tipsey's smuggled goods, Mrs Hungerford bought French cambric muslin wedding gowns for the brides, the collars trimmed in the most becoming manner, as a Monmouth milliner assured me, with Valenciennes lace … I have given all the particulars of the bridegrooms' accoutrements and signed myself the young ladies' "most obedient servant" and perhaps their dupe.

I am going on with <u>Patronage</u> and wish I could show it to you to have your opinion of it.

TO SOPHY RUXTON
Edgeworthstown, June 1811

Huzza for the glorious Col Pakenham. But if anybody dares to think he is too good for you I will hate him or them – And you know it is impossible to hate Lady Longford – Therefore you know it is impossible she should think so"[118] …

TO AUNT RUXTON
[?] 3 July 1811

Never shall my beloved aunt <u>thirst</u> for a letter from her little niece while she has the power to pour forth … I do not know what beaux you regret for Ho[*nora*] … for except young Burke and Cousin Francis Fox and Captain Verner, sorrow beaux have we seen and young Burke is thinking of nothing but Euclid and four in hand, and Captain Verner only appeared and vanished and Francis Fox is to be seen for nothing at any time …

Now please to walk with me to the spire and see William perfectly well and in good spirits standing on the scaffolding round the top of the turret of the church which looks like the main mast of a man of war – Captain gives the signal and 4 men at the 2 corners upstairs begin to work the windlasses and in

---

118 Colonel Edward Pakenham had just become the hero of the Battle of Salamanca in the Peninsular Campaign. Maria's romantic hopes for Sophy came to naught – shortly afterwards, Colonel Pakenham proposed to the heiress Annabella Milbanke who refused him on grounds of hereditary madness in the Pakenham family. She was later to marry Lord Byron.

a few moments with a slow delightful motion the spire begins to ascend. The gilt ball & arrow glitters higher & higher in the sun and its iron skeleton rises by big beautiful degrees, till in 12 minutes and a half its whole transparent form is high in the air … Oh how I wished that you and my uncle had seen it … It goes up & down now at pleasure with the utmost ease …

But to go on with my sixteen morning visitors (almost as grand as the County of Meath!) – Next came Mrs Burke and her three daughters and in the midst of this crowd came Mrs O'Beirne just arrived from Newry … She brought with her her son, a boy of 8 years old, one of the finest & most handsome boys my eyes ever beheld, in a tartan plaid fit for Scott & the Duchess of Buccleugh …

Anna[119] I believe, is on her way here or just setting out and I hope she and her children will be happy here … I will do all in my power to make her so – I pity poor Emmeline if she is a little sore & irritable … I wish always to bear with her – as far as I know she sees and repents of her erroneous notions of me – However that may be I shall never think of anything but how I can serve or gratify her when it is in my power – which alas it is but very little[120] …

TO SOPHY RUXTON
30 August 1811

… Apropos of Anna I have wished for you 1000 times – She is far more agreeable to me and consequently would, I am sure, be better suited to you than she used to be. Sorrow has softened her manners and her vivacity … she feels now more the value of friends and less desire for acquaintance – and a great many more alterations all in my opinion for the better … especially some which arise from her being a mother … she seems as fond of me as any sister can be and confidential in conversation with me – she earnestly presses me to return to England with her – But that I cannot do …

Mrs Apreece has written me a very polite and flattering letter inviting me to England – to all this I have replied with due thanks etc etc but you know me – know the rest – that I would no more go to her than fly –

Mrs Clifford's entreaties go much nearer my heart for I like her and know she likes me, yet I cannot leave my father – I think, at his time of life … I could not be at ease or happy in another country with the sea between us …

---

119 Maria's widowed sister.

120 Emmeline had been jealous of Maria, partly because of the preferential treatment given to Maria by her father; Richard Lovell Edgeworth had always been prejudiced against his second-oldest daughter.

[*Postscript*] I have written a little play for our present large juvenile audience – to read for their amusement. I read it last night and it was liked which you know I ought not to say –

The scene is in Ireland – the title The Absentee. It is a mixture of comic and pathetic … I think I begin to understand the knack of dramatic writing better than when we hammered it flat, my dear Sophy, in the little dressingroom at Clifton – Then and always how kind you were[121] …

TO AUNT RUXTON
Edgeworthstown, 30 August 1811

… What book do you think Bonaparte was reading at the seige of Acre … Mme de Staël's book *Sur l'influence des passions*. His opinion of her and her works must have been wonderfully changed … She was charmed by him and exclaimed, you know, at a public dinner at Paris "How happy must that woman be who is married to Bonaparte". After that they quarreled and he had forbid her to come to Paris; she sent him word that she had heard and read of many heroes who loved women but he was the only hero she had heard of who was afraid of women. Bonaparte was certainly very afraid of her – for at her *soirées* he and his measures were spoken of with a freedom he could not endure and Mme de Staël used to utter many of those satirical *bons mots* which pass into general and rapid circulation among the Parisians – Bonaparte does not follow Mazarin's wise maxim "Let them talk, provided they let me act". He may yet find the recoil of the Press, which he meddled with so incautiously more dangerous than the common causerie [?] …

What do you think of our own poor king who goes 60 hours without sleep, then afterwards eats mutton and drinks chocolate! He has lived so long beyond the true calculation of probability that I begin to believe he will live forever and that your black gown which you so prudently bought will be of no more use to you – camphor it to secure it against the moths[122] …

I am very busy emulating you, my good aunt, and putting doors and windows to cottages – I am glad I have seen the cottages at Abbeyleix which show what can be done in Ireland with patience & money, but alas I have

---

121 Maria's father insisted on sending the play on to Richard Sheridan in London, much against her wishes. He refused it on the grounds that it would require too many Irish actors and would not appeal to an English audience and Maria shortly afterwards turned it into one of her most successful novels.

122 George III was now permanently confined as insane.

little of one and less of the other – The theatre at Kilkenny and all that it contained has passed away from my imagination but the images of these Abbeyleix cottages remain in my mind: Thady Conner, Barry Duffy and Barry Woods would never guess it, these cottages will raise laurels and pyracanthus to hedges round their gardens – My mother and the children and I have been as happy as possible cutting and pricking our fingers and digging and dirtying ourselves with the aid of little digging gossoons with patches of rags upon them working every evening lately at these gardens – I am glad to have some out of doors object and find it very advantageous to my health, never was better, nor able to eat more buttered cake at tea, except at Rostrevor! … "God bless you and spare you your health" as an old woman said to me the other day in the churchyard – "and grant that you may see that spire go up to your satisfaction and his Honour's great glory anyways" …

TO AUNT RUXTON
21 September 1811

I write by the express injunctions of my father three lines to tell you of the successful ascent of the spire on the 19th. A fine calm bright day – Sixty guests invited to a breakfast, more properly speaking a collation … All assembled in the library about 12 o'clock – the company including, according to John Langan's triumphant calculation five lords and one baronet … Some few who did not understand the nature of the thing had come out without breakfast – Mrs E, who has ever a provident eye to all things, had ordered chocolate, coffee etc to be in waiting and when these mistaken people had … swallowed comfortable cups we proceeded to the church.

Mr Keating politely offered the use of his garden [*the Vicarage beside the church*] where benches and chairs were arranged for the accommodation of the company … and the different groups, rich and poor, old and young, ugly and beautiful, were very picturesque, I believe, but I was too anxious but to see anything but one object at that moment. The bugle sounded – dead silence – and the spire ascended with an easy majestic motion that calmed all hearts and delighted all eyes. Not one word or syllable from the workmen who under William's command worked the windlasses … When it had reached its full height, fifty feet, painted and sanded to a perfect imitation of Bath stone, a red streamer which had been so contrived as to unfold itself … streamed in the wind and gave notice that all was finished and safe.

I never saw more judicious, friendly, affectionate [*manners*] than Lord
Longford's – he was as anxious that the day should go off well as if it had been
his brother's job, which is more than saying his own. And I must add in the teeth
of all your prejudice that Admiral P's conduct convinced me that where my
father's credit is seriously at stake, he knows how to show both friendship and
good breeding – Not a jest, not a sarcasm – but real earnest desire beforehand
that it should succeed and satisfaction afterwards in the complete success. But
now a truce with sentiment and home we walk if you please to breakfast.

You know my mother's talents for these things and aided by Anna and
poor good Mrs Billamore ... there was such a feast as gentles and simples
and nobles approved in the most flattering manner. In the middle of the two
long tables a winecooler full of flowers high raised – good effect – middle of
small table iced cake on a high glass jelly stand – prettily ornamented with
flowers ... all the best old china in the house – – Cold turkeys and chickens,
tarts, tartelettes that Molly Coffey need not have blushed to have owned,
blancmange and jellies etc ... abundance of fine peaches and grapes and Anna
had laid these out in great pyramids – A large dish of Italian salad at the head
of each table was both <u>pretty</u> <u>and</u> <u>useful,</u> and cold roast beef at the bottom
which, in the finest company of delicacies, I observe is never neglected. Each
table was nearly the same and all the <u>good</u> <u>things</u> were so divided ... that there
was no stretching or <u>troubling</u> <u>you</u> <u>Ma'am</u> or <u>begging</u> <u>your</u> <u>pardon</u> or <u>being</u> <u>so</u>
<u>good</u> ... in short all seemed pleased and at ease ...

A fiddler attended and Sneyd easily persuaded the ladies to think that
dancing on the green would be a pleasant thing – but the gentlemen did not
seem equally to like it – so <u>that</u> dropped through and people milled about and
diverted themselves as they liked –

We were fortunate indeed in having such a fine day – it began to rain
violently in the evening and today there has been a high gale of wind, but the
spire has been so thoroughly bolted down and built into its tower, we have no
fear that it can ever be stirred.[123]

TO SOPHY RUXTON
October 1811

... [*Humphrey*] Davy spent a day here last week and was as usual full of
entertainment and information of various kinds – he is gone to Connemara, I

---

123 Sadly the spire eventually rusted and had to be dismantled some sixty years later.

believe to fish, for he is a little mad about fishing – and very ungrateful it is of me to say so, for he sent us from Boyle the finest trout! – and a trout of Davy's catching is, I presume, worth ten trouts caught by vulgar mortals. Sneyd went with him to Boyle, saw Lord Lorton's fine place[124] and spent a pleasant day. Two of Mr Davy's fishing friends have since called on us – Mr Solly, a great mineralogist ... and Mr Children ... very handsome and a man of Kent ...

TO AUNT MARY SNEYD
Pakenham Hall [?], November 1811

... At Pakenham Hall we found to our great joy dear Lady Longford – and to our great surprise <u>dear</u> (yes <u>dear</u>) Lord Longford who had made an appearance an hour before – on one of his flying visits – he goes away again to England on Thursday – No one else except Mr Henry Pakenham and a whole tribe of merry children – Stewarts and Hamiltons – Kitty Hamilton is a delightful playful, wellbred, well taught, well tempered girl – Tell Fanny that the card playing passion rose to such an alarming pitch that the children were all found playing at cards before breakfast (Private ... in the watercloset) and Mrs Stewart with great good sense ... instead of immediate prohibitions turned the cards into a greater source of pleasure by cutting them into pattens which she painted and strung so well that they charmed the young folk ... Lady Longford ... gives an excellent account of Lady Wellesley and her children. She brought their picture – the children beautiful and they say very like – Lady W not the least like – Lady L was pleased with what my father said about this picture – "It is absurd of anyone to attempt to draw Lady Wellington's <u>face</u> because she has no <u>face</u>, she is all countenance."

Lord Longford was settling accounts in his study most of the evening and I the while was looking on at my father and Lady Elizabeth playing at cribbage – they counted so quickly, fifteen two, fifteen four that I was never able to keep up with them and made a sorry figure. Worse again at some genealogies and intermarriages which Lady Elizabeth undertook to explain to me till at last she threw her arms down flat on each side in indignant despair and exclaimed – "Well! You are the stupidest creature alive!"

When Lord Longford came in I escaped from cribbage and heard many entertaining things – one was of his meeting a man in the mailcoach who

---

124 Rockingham, now demolished, although the park survives as Lough Key Forest Park.

looked as if he was gouty and seemed as if he could not stir without great difficulty and never without the assistance of a companion ... At last Lord Longford discovered that this gentleman's gouty overalls covered fetters that he was a malefactor in irons and his companion a Bow Street officer who treated his prisoner with the greatest politeness. "Give me leave, sir – excuse me – one on your arm and one on mine and then we are sure we cannot leave one another".

A worse travelling companion this than the bear whom Lord Longford found one morning in the coach when day dawned opposite to him – the gentleman in the fur cloak as he had all night supposed him to be! ...

TO SNEYD EDGEWORTH
Edgeworthstown, February 1812

... All morning both my father and I were hard at work reading Mr Wakefield's MSS – Hard work indeed – such a scrawl! – such style – and so little in the 110 pages of description that I am in despair – and my father dumbfounded – What can we do? There is no possibility of publishing this – Mend this? – better make a new one – ten times over – But how can this be said to a poor author, who has been working hard – Yet said it must be, for it would be treacherous to a poor author, who consults us, much less for anyone for whom we have a regard to [*let him*] publish such a book[125] ...

To refresh us from our melancholy morning's drudgery we have been entertaining ourselves ever since tea with capping verses – William, Honora and Sophy – versus Maria, Fanny, Harriet and Mrs E – It is really surprising to hear Sophy, Harriet & Fanny – they have such a profusion of good lines by heart – William has made excellent use of the last month – has been laying in good poetry & literature – but battle is not decided – but ends (10 o'clock at night) by the entrance of sweetmeats for the combatants – Good night.

... Saturday morning –
All morning at Mr Wakefield's papers ... My father has told him the truth in the most friendly manner – that the descriptive parts of the book are below par

---

125 Edward Wakefield, philanthropist and authority on agriculture, had been commissioned by the government to write a survey of Ireland with a view 'to relieving chronic poverty and rural distress'. It was published later that year and generally applauded, thanks perhaps to Maria and her father's efforts to make it readable.

– that the statistical part is <u>impartial</u> and valuable but the whole style wants much revised …

Poor Father Tom continues ill – but Father RLE says he will do – a knock at the library door this morning and in walked Father Tom like a black and white ghost in his nightcap and hat – He revived after having a tumbler of excellent negus made by the neat-handed Kitty and a toast which de Fevre's son would not have outdone …

TO MRS BALLANTYNE [*an Edinburgh friend*]
Edgeworthstown, 4 June 1812

… Mrs Edgeworth is just come to chicken and asparagus after giving us another little brother – Pakenham Edgeworth he is to be and under the auspices of his godfather General Pakenham we hope he will become a hero – at all events he now does his first duty of sucking with admirable zeal and energy – he cost his mother but two hours pain … she was sitting in her chair in her dressingroom and had so little warning of pain that she continued reading … and at last … laid down her book and said – "I believe I must now go to bed" … She deserves to be the mother of heroes (as we all call Lady Longford) for I never saw anyone bear pain with so much fortitude as she always does …

This was to be Richard Lovell Edgeworth's twenty-second child and the last of Maria's siblings.

TO SOPHY RUXTON
Edgeworthstown, 16 June 1812 [first pages missing]

… I forget whether I mentioned in my last letter Mr Chevenix's marriage – Mrs Tuite is sadly vexed … the lady who, to use Mrs Tuite's expression, has ensnared him is a French widow, a Madame de Riault who has resided some years in England. Some say [*she*] had a <u>pension</u> from the Duke of Gloucester – some say from the Duke of Queensbury – at all events her character is doubtful – She is however very <u>fascinating</u> tho' near 50 – and among her other charms has £1000 a year certain in England and another perhaps receivable in France … where she and her bridegroom go … in August. I am very sorry for Mrs Tuite because this marriage overturns all her hopes of his settling in these counties and of her enjoying his society – As for him, I cannot say I am very sorry – I am rather glad when a man who loves to collect scandalous anecdotes of our sex ... is taken in, with all his boasted knowledge of the world.

... Have you seen the Ed[*inburgh*] Rev[*iew*] of Miss Bourke's last plays? It is very entertaining. One of her tragedies is founded upon a lady's love of ghost stories and fear of ghosts. The heroine goes mad from fear of a ghost in a black cloak and the curtain drops upon her in this condition ...

TO SOPHY RUXTON
Edgeworthstown, June [?] 1812

... My father has not read [*The Absentee*]¹²⁶ and is foaming for it! It is a great venture to send it off unknown to him – I pray you read it as fast as you can and send it under cover to E.B.L., Dublin Castle who will forward it down to me ...

TO MARGARET RUXTON
Edgeworthstown, 20 July 1812

I am heartily obliged to my dear Sophy – never mind, you need not turn to that direction, it <u>is</u> to Margaret, my dear, though it begins with thanks to Sophy – for having been in prodigious haste to relieve my mind from the agony ... I cannot by any form of words express how delighted I am that you are none of you angry with me and that my uncle and aunt are pleased with what they have read of the Absentee. I long to hear whether their favour continues to the end and extends to the catastrophe, that dangerous rock upon which poor authors ... are wrecked sometimes while their friends are even hauling them to the shore ...

Little Pakenham [*her youngest half-brother*] is going on bravely and sucks more than half the day – and his mother, praise be, thanks to Merrion Street and Mrs Brett the mantua maker, has four new gowns – and I am just <u>beginning</u> to write again and am <u>in</u> Patronage – and have corrected all the faults you pointed out to me and <u>Susan</u> who was a fool is now Rosamund and a wit – or at least only half a fool.

---

126 Maria's new novel, converted from an earlier play.

I suppose you have heard various *jeux d'esprit* on the marriage of Sir Humphrey Davy and Mrs Apreece?[127] I scarcely think any of them worth copying – the best is stolen from the *bon mot* on Sir John Carr "The Traveller beknighted" – "When Mr Davy concluded his last Lecture by saying we were in the <u>dawn</u> of science, he probably did not expect to be so soon beknighted."

I forget the lines – the following I recollect better –.

> "To the famed widow vainly bow
> Church, Army, Bar and Navy
> Says she, I dare not take a vow
> But I will take my Davy"

TO AUNT RUXTON
Edgeworthstown, 23 August 1812

> *Lovell, still a prisoner of war, was now in Paris but, despairing of ever returning to Ireland, had written to his father, offering to renounce his inheritance in favour of another son.*

I enclose a copy of a letter from Lovell which will give you exquisite pleasure – and who should see it as soon as you? You who have been always his steady friend [*and*] … known [*his*] warm affection for his father and family and … the solid foundation of his character – The weeds are killed – killed by the frost of adversity – the excellent soil remains and reproduces nobly – It is indeed a magnanimous and most touching letter … nothing for years has given [*my father*] so much pleasure … nor can anything be less probable than he should take the poor prisoner at his word and <u>will</u> away from him his birthright … We shall do all we can to get at Talleyrand by some friend. Can you do anything by means of good Sir R. George? – This glorious victory of Lord – I beg his pardon – Marquis Wellington's – those 22,000 prisoners – give good hope of being able to exchange our prisoner for some of the French <u>officers</u> – My father has written to Lady Wellington to ask if anything can be done by

---

127 As Lady Davy, Mrs Apreece became a noted political hostess in London, and Maria was to meet many celebrities at their house in Grosvenor Square, including Lord Byron. But the marriage did not prove a success in the long run. Humphrey Davy gave up his presidency of the Royal Society and other scientific bodies and spent much of his time escaping his hot-tempered and often ailing wife on prolonged fishing trips to Scotland and Europe.

her. How happy dear Lady Wellington must be! Had you in your papers the account of her running as fast as she could to Lord ... Bathurst's to hear the first news of her husband. *Vive l'enthusiasme!* ...

> *Meantime another festering family problem was coming to crisis point. Henry, aged thirty, whom Maria had had charge of as a child, was now qualified as a doctor but was showing increasing signs of mental instability – and consumption. He had been sent to Madeira two years earlier in the hopes of a cure, but his mental condition had worsened and his letters home had become incoherent. Maria's letter continues ...*

Alas, my dear aunt, poor Henry! In cons[*equence of*] letters from Dr Shuter and from other quarters representing the deplorable state of his mind and hinting, indeed distinctly saying, that all his friends there wished his removal from Madeira, my father wrote to order his return ... I must, in justice to Admiral Pakenham, send you a copy of the letters he wrote to Sir A. Gordon, a particular friend of his who is governor of Madeira ... My aunt has just received a letter from Henry – he has landed at Plymouth – is going to Bristol to Mr King's house who is prepared to receive him ... and willing to do him every possible kindness ... Mr K. [*Emmeline's husband*] has promised that it shall be as private as possible and that he will observe the utmost secrecy as to his situation. His two brothers and sisters have seen all that has been written – The truth, however painful, it is best should be known – for imagination may do more mischief than any reality – They were much shocked – They have still hopes that he may recover – Alas, neither Mrs E, nor his aunts nor I have any ... His letter to his aunt Mary saying "If I go home, I shall die because my family do not know the increase in my rank – It is impossible that they should!" At all events nothing could be more dreadful and dangerous than having him here. Poor, poor creature! ... It is however one blessing that he does not desire to come here for if he did ... how hard, how cruel, how almost impossible to refuse ...

> *Henry was to remain under Mr King's care at Bristol for the rest of his short life, dying the following year, 1813. Fortunately for Maria, there was an ample supply of younger siblings to cherish. Her stepmother's two oldest children, Fanny and Harriet, were now twelve and ten, old enough to be taken up to Dublin by*

their father to see a balloon ascent by James Sadler who was to attempt the first flight across the Irish Sea.

TO MRS EDGEWORTH
From Dublin, October 1812

... After a most delightful journey on the Castlepollard coach with Mrs Henry Hamilton – laughing, singing, talking – just as we came to the last stage Mr Henry Hamilton came from the top of the coach and changed places with my father on purpose to see Harriet's surprise or emotion at the first entrance to Dublin. However Harriet made no exclamation but observed with the most silent attention everything she saw ... Nothing could have been more good-natured than Mr HH – he continually placed Harriet where she could see best ... swaying her hand backwards and forwards and telling her the name of every remarkable building –

We dined altogether at Mrs H – Mrs Bella Hamilton and dear old Mr Sackville Hamilton dined with us fresh from London – intellectual and corporal dainties in abundance ... After dinner Richard Ruxton came in and said my aunt and uncle had thoughts of coming up to see the balloon ... In the evening we went to Astley's [*the circus*] – the second day to see the elephant – How I pitied this noble animal, cooped up under the command of a scarcely human creature who had not half as much reason himself ...

Thursday morning, to our inexpressible joy was fine – and the flag, the signal that Sadler would ascend, was to the joy of thousands, flying from the top of Nelson's pillar – Dressed quickly – breakfasted I don't know how – job coach punctual – crowds in motion even at 9 o'clock ... called at Sneyd's lodging in Anne Street – he and William gone – drove on till we came near Belvedere ... Most imprudently we ... got out of our carriage upon the raised footpath in hope of getting immediately to the garden door ... within 2 yards of us, but nothing I ever felt was equal to the pressure of the grasp! ... My father, quite pale calling with a stentor voice to the sentinels ...

The tide carried us to the door – An admirable Scotch officer who was mounting guard with a drawn sword, his face dripping with perspiration ... made a soldier put his musket across the door so as to force a place for [*Harriet*] to creep under – quick as lightning in she darted and Fanny and I and my father after her – All serene, uncrowded and fresh within the park ...

Instantly met Sneyd and William and the two Mr Foxes ... The balloon,

James Sadler, the famous balloonist, over Dublin Bay after his ascent from Belvedere Gardens in 1812. He nearly drowned in this attempt to cross the Irish Channel.

the beautiful many coloured balloon with painted eagles and garlands and arms of Ireland hung under the trees and filling fast from pipes and an apparatus which I leave for William's scientific description – terrace before Belvedere House – well dressed groups parading on it … mantles, scarfs and feathers floating – all the commonalty outside in fields at half price … We made our way behind the troopers' horses who guarded a sacred circle around the balloon – found my aunt & Sophy & Margaret – surprise and joy on both sides – got seats on the pedestal of some old statue …

The drum beats! The flag flies! Balloon full! It is moved from under the trees over the heads of the crowds … Mr Sadler, quite composed, this being his 26th aerial ascent, got into his car – a lady, the Duchess of Richmond I believe, presents him with a pretty flag – the balloon gave two majestic nods from side to side as the cords were cut … No one spoke while the balloon successfully rose, rapidly cleared the trees and floated above our heads – Loud shouts & huzzas – one man, close to us exclaiming … "Ah, musha, musha, God bless you! God be wid you!" – Mr Sadler, waving his flag and his hat and bowing to the world below, soon pierced a white cloud and disappeared – then emerging the balloon looked like a moon, black on one side, silver on the other – then like a dark bubble – then less and less and now only a speck … Never did I feel the full merit of Dr Darwin's description till then …

> "The calm Philosopher in ether sails,
>   Views broader stars and breathes in purer gales."[128]

In the event, Sadler's balloon was swept off course in a huge dogleg, first to the Isle of Man, then back to Anglesey, then north again until he finally had to ditch in the Irish Sea. His son Windham Sadler was to make the first successful crossing from Dublin four years later.

TO AUNT RUXTON
Edgeworthstown, 26 October 1812

Elections have been the order of the day with us as well as with you. I am glad to tell you that Lord Longford's troubles are over – he is now here and has just been telling us that his victory for Colonel Hercules was as complete as his heart could wish. Trouble – some <u>Tighe</u> supported or rather pushed by Sir Thomas Chapman has, I believe, cost Lord Longford two thousand pounds at least – Mr Tighe in a virulent speech abused poor old Mr Rochfort and there would have been a duel had not Admiral Pakenham prevented it by his presence of mind and well turned drollery.

Mr Tighe in his speech to the electors said "Mr Rochfort made his corps play "Protestant boys"."

Mr Rochfort who stood close beside Mr Tighe said "That's a lie" – Both gentlemen were proceeding to high words when the Admiral stepped between them and said, very gravely, "I did not know that this meeting was a music meeting but since you appeal to us to decide your cause by your musical merits – give us each of you a song and here's the sheriff who shall decide between you".

The idea of a song from two such faces and the Sheriff, Mr Pollard, being judge who has no more ear than a post, made everybody burst into laughter

---

128 From Part II of 'The Botanic Garden', a poem by Erasmus Darwin.

and the two angry gentlemen were obliged to laugh off their quarrel. After the elections were over, Sir T. Chapman said to Admiral P, "Do you know now – maybe you'd be surprised when I tell you I had once a great mind to stand myself. What would you have said to that" "That it was all a game of Brag and that as you were shuffling the pack there was no knowing what a knave might have turned up."

... I am sure you would have been pleased with Lord L's manner when looking at the library table this evening and expressing a wish to have such a one he added

"Ah, but Tighe has put it out of my power to have any of those for a twelve month at least!"

I had intended to remember at least 10 excellent anecdotes Lord L told us this evening ... of the cruelties of the French ... [*but*] I will only tell you one little one that refreshed us between the horrors.

Col. Hercules P[*akenham*] was walking with the civil engineer in the trenches of Badajoz, Col. P to visit his guard, the civil engineer to see that all was right at the depot. As they were passing a bomb came whizzing over their heads, lighted and burst amongst a party of soldiers of whom 500 were wounded and as they were carried off to hospital, the civil engineer, quite cool, moralised thus: "Major Pakenham, these are the accidents of war. – I wonder by this time you have not stealed your mind to these sights ...? – these fellows are carried off to Hospital and others supply their place – Such things happen – We must be prepared for them – Let us go to the Depot."

At the depot the civil engineer had his wheelbarrows piled in nice order and the spades and pickaxes in thousands laid out in stacks ... All was well but just as they were leaving ... a bomb fell and burnt [*the stacks?*].

"Oh heavenly Powers! my picks –" exclaimed the civil engineer clasping his hands in despair ...

TO SNEYD EDGEWORTH
Edgeworthstown, 27 November 1812

Sneyd had forwarded her letters from admirers.

... I am delighted with Mr Plunkett's [*?*] having quoted that passage from the Absentee – The whole of it, every word was written by my father.

You certainly do select and attach the best and most agreeable friends in the world – Nothing could be more amiable or agreeable than both Mr Smedley's and Mr Merton's letters … Mr Merton's is of a higher style and character … I think I scarcely ever heard praise more delicately and exquisitely expressed than his. The idea that when he and his bride were enjoying the springtime of domestic happiness they appreciated my writings is indeed gratifying … and touching to my heart – It reminded me of my father and Mrs E's sitting down together to read Letters for Lit. Ladies[129] the day after they married …

TO SNEYD EDGEWORTH
Edgeworthstown, February 1813

… Now for the stern, the vulgar realities of life – a carman, hight Farrelly, will call on you and you will perhaps curse him, but not on my account – for this time I have nothing to plague you about. Oh by-the-by I have … "Rokeby".[130] Said "Rokeby" is, in my opinion – and let every soul speak for themselves – most beautiful poetry – the four first cantos and half the fifth are all I have yet read. I think it higher and better because less Scotch, more universal style of poetry of any he has yet produced … Remorse is finely as drawn as in Shakespeare's Macbeth … I wish, however, there had not been so much murder – He gives us every variety of which the law takes cognizance. First murder with malice prepense – then simple murder or manslaughter or womans laughter at least – and I make no doubt that at the fire tonight I shall meet with accidental death … Heaven preserve us at least from <u>felo da se</u>!.

The character of Matilda is most beautiful, feminine, ingenuous and noble. The Irish O'Neil charming – but I regret he was barely born in Ireland, Wilfred, a Mr Arnott of a lover, as my aunt Mary would say – one most pathetic song "Weave no garland for me, Lady" made me really want to shoot him I was so sorry for him. All the rest of the songs I wish out of the book. What can be done with poor Wilfred – how can Scott and Matilda get rid of him – I verily believe he must be burnt tonight in the fire …

At the moment I am writing Patronage very hard against my father's return …

---

129 Maria's first published book for adults.
130 Walter Scott's latest ballad.

Silhouettes of Honora and Fanny Edgeworth.

TO SNEYD EDGEWORTH
Edgeworthstown, 13 March 1813

I hear that Honora looked very well and stepped back very smoothly at her presentation and that Mrs HH says she can give her a good character – But I wonder the Duchess could not contrive to find something to say to her – We have not yet heard of her shamrocks etc on St Patrick's day[131] …

I was quite sorry to part with your friend … Fox. He is very amiable and his manners are so wellbred and friendly that he won his easy way into the regard of all the family – We were much struck with the contrast in this respect between him and Mr G[*riffith*] – who tho' he seems an excellent young man and possessed of great activity, perseverance and talent is so circumscribed all in Self and maps etc – that he is like a dead man the moment any other subject is talked of.[132]

---

131   Honora had been presented to the Viceroy, the Duke of Richmond, at Dublin Castle.
132   The future author of the famous Griffith's Valuation was working as bog surveyor under Maria's father.

V

JULY 1813 – MAY 1817

ON 28 MARCH 1813 *Maria, her stepmother and her father set off once again in the family coach – this time for England. Having apparently fully recovered his health by his strenuous survey work on the Irish bogs, Maria's father, now aged nearly seventy, had decided to show off his brilliant elder daughter and still-pretty wife in London.*

For the first time Maria found herself feted in London society as a celebrity and her intelligence and modesty soon won praise in all circles. 'I had been the lion of 1812, Miss Edgeworth, Mme de Staël … were the exhibition of the succeeding year,' wrote Byron afterwards. He met her at breakfast with Lady Davy. He described her as a 'nice little unassuming Jennie Deans-looking body as we Scotch say and if not handsome, certainly not ill-looking … [whose] conversation was as quiet as herself.' Maria in turn was unimpressed with Byron's appearance. Byron, however was one of the few to comment favourably on her father, 'a fine old fellow … intelligent, vehement … and full of life.'

Edgeworth was generally judged as a red-faced, over-talkative and over-opiniated provincial bore. Maria must have been uncomfortably aware of his social failure in London, though she wrote bravely to her aunt of the 'honour and esteem' with which he had been met. The party left London for Clifton at the end of June just missing to Maria's regret the arrival of two of her literary heroines, Madame de Staël and Madame d'Arblay [Fanny Burney]. But she hastened to assure her aunt that her head had not been turned:

'*The brilliant panorama of London is over and I have enjoyed more pleasure and have had more amusement, infinitely more than I expected ... and received more attention, more kindness than I could have thought possible would be shewn to me ... now with the fullness of content I return home, loving all my friends and my own mode of life preferably to all others after comparison with all that is fine and gay and rich and rare.' (25 June 1813)*

Finally back at home, she wrote again.

TO AUNT RUXTON
Edgeworthstown, 26 July 1813

... I have begun a new series of "Early Lessons" which many mothers told me they wished. I feel that I return with fresh pleasure to literary work, from having been so long idle – and I have a famishing appetite for reading. For all that we saw in London ... I should be very sorry to live in that whirling vortex, and I find my taste and conviction confirmed on my return to my natural friends and dear home ...

The 'dear home' was now receiving, however, a stream of what Maria's sister Honora called 'Lordly and Literary' visitors met in London. Maria hastened to stress their simple virtues and sensible views to her aunt and cousin Sophy.

... Lord Carrington, a worthy domestic man is most amiable and benevolent without any species of pretension ... Mr Smith, his son whom we had not seen in London accompanies him and his tutor Mr Kaye, a Cambridge man, and Lord Gardner, who travels with them is Lord Carrington's son-in-law, but looks like his father-in-law, spindle shanked from the rheumatic gout ... [*but*] between the twitches of his suffering ... entertaining and agreeable ... [*They*] were at Farnham where they were most hospitably received. They had no letters of introduction or intention of going there; but finding a horrid inn at Cavan, they applied for charity to a gentleman for lodging [*who*] took them to walk in Lord Farnham's grounds. Lord and Lady Farnham saw them and invited them to the house ... They are so charmed by their hospitality, their goodness to the poor, their magnificent establishment, their neat cottages ... and as Lord Gardner sensibly said – "their judicious economy in the midst of magnificence"...

Charles Sneyd Edgeworth at the time of his engagement.

TO SOPHY RUXTON
Edgeworthstown, 19 August 1813

... Lord and Lady Lansdowne came to us on Tuesday and leave on Saturday – Lord Longford who as you know is not exuberant in praise truly says they are people to be esteemed the more they are known. My father asked Lord L. and Mr Jephson to meet them – Lord L ... extremely entertaining and agreeable – He says that Lord W was not at San Sebastien – that the loss for our army was not nearly as great as the papers stated ... Lord W is now in force and impatient for another engagement – Hercules P still suffers – another splinter I think which the surgeons cannot get out. What a hero he is ...

> *In late August there was much excitement. Sneyd, Maria's favourite brother, announced his engagement to Miss Henrietta Broadhurst, whom he had met in Staffordshire with his Sneyd relations. She was reported to be an heiress with an income of £800 a year! (Over £100,000 in today's money.) A combined letter of congratulations was sent to him from Edgeworthstown, ending with Maria's.*

... My dear brother – Smiles and joy were spread round the breakfast table by the paragraph read from the newspaper announcing the marriage of Charles Sneyd Edgeworth and Miss Broadhurst – It sounded well – it looked well and each could see it with their own eyes – In came John Bristow and John Langan and dear Kitty with their affectionate old and young faces wishing us joy ... And you have, my dear Sneyd, so much the wish and power of drawing family and friends closer together and of making them see and love each other's best qualities that I depend securely upon you for making me love your wife and for making her love me ...

To her aunt, however, Maria expressed some doubts.

TO AUNT RUXTON
5 September 1813

... The want of high birth and connection is undoubtedly an objection ... nothing is known of her but that she was Miss Broadhurst in Lyme – That objection is much lightened – She has <u>perfectly</u> the manners and appearance of a gentlewoman ... William who is a most independent umpire ... writes us word that he likes her much and that he agrees with Sneyd in thinking her like Anna ... My father has, as we all have, a strong aristocratic prepossession, and yet he never let this a moment interfere with Sneyd's wishes and happiness.

Come to us, my dear aunt, and I will read Patronage to you – I can promise this now as I know it is safe in his Majesty's stores and not gone to America as we had reason to fear – I have finished four little new volumes of Frank and Rosamund – humble as is the book I have executed it with pleasure in the hope that it may be useful ... Many mothers in England told us that they wished for more of these little books – my father has sprinkled them with seeds of science for me ...

I hope dear amiable little Francis will be as gay as a lark when he is with you – He looks gravely out only at first – and often when he is most pleased, he takes it soberly – His affection for Kitty and her affection for him is really romantic – I think if my mother had given her the Queen's wardrobe she could not have pleased her so much as she did by the letter she wrote to her about little Francis ... she deserves to have good friends and good servants for she knows how to value and reward them – I wish in the middle of all this sentiment that she had a good cook – Tell her that Sophy is looking for a word in the dictionary found "Fricassier – a paltry cook". She immediately exclaimed that the cook who had just left us was a <u>fricassier</u> – "Pray, Maria, tell Mamma so."

By the autumn, the stream of visitors and letters from London had abated and Maria was hard back at work at her father's insistence. She wrote defensively to her old friend Sophy to excuse a lack of recent letters.

TO SOPHY RUXTON
Edgeworthstown, 16 October 1813

… You might think my head full of Lords and Ladies and new acquaintance – of this you give me some hint – I believe foolishly I did write all about poor good natured Lord Carrington but I took care to say as little as possible about Lord Lansdowne and scarcely mentioned [*any others*] I have seen … I am now persuaded that I … have very foolishly given you the idea that I carry on an extensive <u>correspondence</u> of <u>new</u> <u>friends</u> <u>and</u> <u>admirers</u> – Quite the contrary – I have not since I returned from England added one single correspondent to my old established few – I have it is true been obliged to write and to answer many many letters … But do you think it is any pleasure to me to do this? If you knew how much I have written lately and how my days and hours are spent! My father has been very urgent with me to finish 4 volumes of Frank & Rosamund – These by hard labour – allowing myself only time for exercise in the mornings – I have finished – In the evenings reading aloud or hearing my mother read aloud to my father [*makes it*] scarcely possible to write a letter. In the morning before breakfast, Lucy's lessons … take a full hour … which I consider a positive duty as her mother entrusts her to me, but by getting up at half after seven, I do get time to write necessary letters – company of late frequently in the house. – After Frank & Rosamund came Patronage to be corrected which I completed but the day before my father went to Town – Then I had a preface of his to Early Lessons of 27 pages to <u>revise</u> – sixteen pages were written one day between Honora and me – Then about 101 pages of scientific matter was left to me by my father to make into a new volume of Harry & Lucy and this I have to do this moment – Guess in these circumstances whether writing long letters can be a <u>recreation</u> – and whether in such circumstances it must not give me some pain to find … that my best and oldest friends think I neglect them and have either shut up my mind to them or have filled it with quality [*?*] strangers …

But amusements and even London gossip could still be found in Co. Longford.

TO AUNT RUXTON
Edgeworthstown, 31 October 1813

Fine doings in the County of Longford, my dear Aunt ... Three days [*racing*] and a race ball! And to one of the day's racings and to the race ball ... Mrs E. – Ho. – Fan. – Maria – Lucy and Mr Griffiths ... I had never in my long life seen races – and as I have described races in Patronage I thought it as well to say that I had seen them –

But "*Mon siège est fine*" – I really think I describe things better, as my father says, that I have not seen ... for this reason that the number of particulars distract me from the general circumstances which characterise the whole – I am sure that if I was to re-write the whole of Patronage now that the Longford races are fresh in my memory I should make the description and the whole scene much worse than it now stands – There were indeed a few slight circumstances which marked the reality which I could not have invented without seeing them ... – for instance a row of trees from which the leaves had fallen [*which*] looked as if all the branches were blackened with crow's nests – but on more close observation these crows' nests move up and down and sideways ... and we found out that these trees were full of men and boys who had climbed branch above branch to the very top to view the races ... But in fine races in England it might be out of drawing ... to represent spectators parade in trees ...

As to the rest I was much amused tho' there was nothing I could use or write or use professionally ... a lady invited me into her open carriage and my mother begged me to accept so I might see all the humours of the scene much better than I could shut up in a coach – The varieties of squireens – buckeens and bits of jockeys who came to the barouche side to pay their compliments to the lady of the barouche and make their prophecies between the heats diverted me much ... – one thin lank mortified looking man ... whose horse had been the foremost rode up to receive the compliments of condolence upon his horse having <u>bolted</u> the second heat and thrown his rider ... "It all came of his not having minding the directions I <u>give</u> him." "What were they, Sir?" said I with great gravity. "Why ma'am not to give him his head at first as I know him to be but a three year old – and the danger of bolting!" – "And when he bolted he never put a second hand to him" said another man. "He's no more fit to ride a race <u>nor</u> a child!" ...

The ball was such a one I am glad to have seen but never wish to see again ... – the belle of the ball was a Miss Dowdall who came with a large Ballymahon faction – She was about Fanny's size, rather pretty, but dressed like a mad Flora ... in a bodice trimmed with full blown roses ... a head ... like the frontispiece of The Botanic Garden soused with roses with a bounteous hand ... She was attended by her grenadier brother, on the other side was a diminutive officer who carried her pocket handkerchief of prodigious size ... It is curious to observe how fashions work their way down. Fifteen years ago I remember hearing that Lady Edward Fitzgerald created universal astonishment at a ball at the Duchess of Leinster by making Lord Edward Fitzgerald carry her pocket handkerchief for her ...

You may imagine the contrast we saw in Honora and Fanny ... Honora and Fanny danced with Mr Griffiths, the Mr Foxes, John and Francis, and with Mr T. Edgeworth – Fanny was much admired ...

Lord Forbes had hurt his leg and could not dance ... I had a good deal of agreeable conversation with him especially at supper ... He told me two anecdotes of Lord Byron which should cover a multitude of affectations – He gave the copyright of Childe Harold to his tutor who was in distress – When Lord Falconer who was a friend of his died and his widow was left in distress, Lord B wrote to her and begged he might stand godfather to the child she was going to have – he gave the child at the christening five hundred pounds ...

TO AUNT RUXTON
Edgeworthstown, 9 November 1813

... We went last Monday to a play at Castle Forbes – or rather to three farces – "Bombastes Furioso" "Of Age To-morrow" and "The Village Lawyer" taken from Corneille's "Avocat Patelin" – the cunning servant boy admirably acted by Lord Rancliffe.

I have had a very entertaining account of Mme de Staël's ... reception at Blenheim – She calls it a magnificent limbo – splendour without, a deathlike silence of *ennui* within – she says she is very proud of having made the Duke speak – at the moment she was announced he was distinctly heard to utter these words – "Let me go away" ... Mme de Staël says she had the satisfaction of seeing his *table de conversation* on which was written in various scrawls – My horses – My carriage – The great chair – etc ...

Lord Byron's new poem – "The Bride of Abydos" – I hear is very beautiful and very short – it was wrote, it is said, in four days and he had for it a thousand pounds.

TO AUNT RUXTON
Edgeworthstown, 25 November 1813

… Sneyd has got into a very comfortable house in Baggot Street of which he has completed the purchase by both my father's assistance and by the generosity of my aunts – who made him a present on his marriage of a thousand pounds. They say they intended to leave him this sum and that they had rather <u>give</u> than <u>leave</u> as they enjoy the pleasure during their lifetime of being useful to their friends – you see there are good aunts in this world as well as Aunt Forde –

I enclose a letter from Lady Romilly … You will see that all agree Mme de Stael is frankness itself and that she has an excellent heart. Tell Sophy with my love that my father has now so softened towards Mme de Stael that he says he should like to see her, provided his younger daughters are out of the house …

Another friend … wrote me an account of the brilliant fortnight at Bowood when besides Mme de Staël, her Albertine, the Baron de Staël and Count Palmela, the Romillys and the Mackintoshes, there were Mr Ward, Mr Rogers and Mr Dumont. I hear that if it had not been for chess playing – music – and dancing between times, poor humans never could have borne the fatigue of attention and of admiration – I am glad I <u>was</u> <u>not</u> <u>there</u> …

I wanted to send you Mme de Staël's Zulma, Pauline and Adelaide etc – three books she wrote when she was 18 – prefixed to them is an *essai sur les fictions* which is excellent. I think Madame de Stael excels in criticism and it is wonderful that she should show so much judgement as a critic and so little as a writer. The fact is I believe that her passions do not interfere with the objects of which to judge on points of criticism … There is some fine eloquence in "Zulma" but altogether it is strange and absurd – "Adelaide & Theodore" is perhaps, without designing it, much in the style of Madame de Genlis … As to "Pauline", Mrs E and I are in astonishment at it!! and we do not know what surprises us most that it <u>could</u> be written by a girl of eighteen or that it should be published by a woman of forty – or indeed by a woman of any age – I do not think I am very fastidious, yet I really think it the most unfit story that could be put into the hands of a girl of 14 or 15 – As to reading it aloud, that is impossible ... Yet the <u>heroine</u> though she <u>falls</u> twice in the most indelicate and <u>motiveless</u> manner is at last made most interesting and engaging in her penitence ...

The first volume of Patronage is printed ... It will be out by Xmas ... Miles is in a hurry to bring out Patronage because Madame d'Arblay has a work in the press – But hers will not come out, her publisher says, till January or February – So that we shall not stand in competition with each other and of that I am right glad.

TO SOPHY RUXTON
Edgeworthstown, 25 January 1814

My father ... desires me to give his love to his dear niece Sophy – tell her ... her criticisms [*of* Patronage] are excellent – Tell her that as to the press gang I had hesitated at first but I determined to hazard it because I think it becomes us not to flatter public opinion ... but to dare to say what we think true and what may be useful – If we were now in the midst of a naval war it would be unsafe to touch on this subject but now that the war is chiefly by land and our navy is resting upon their arms it is time to speak out – the late Lord Longford actually wept after having executed his duty ... and he and all sensible and feeling soldiers I have ever spoken to ... abhor the practice and wish this disgrace to English justice and humanity abolished ...

Today about 2 o'clock it began to thaw and thawed so rapidly we were in danger of being flooded – rain pouring in at all points – and tubs and jugs and pails and mops running about in all directions! And voices calling and Lucy pale with her eyebrows up wondering if all the avalanches of snow thrown down by arms of men from gutters and roof and all sides, darkening windows and falling with thundering noise ...

Poor Robin Woods is very ill – I fear he will not recover. He has a little robin redbreast that sits on his foot and eats from his hand – he is or he was the most blameless of human creatures – his good old Margery is in great grief – They will never sit opposite to one another again with their dish of potatoes between them and their mug of milk – One day that I went in when they were at dinner I said "How happy you two look!" "Yes miss, we were that every day since we married" ...

Old Robin Woods,
drawing by Frances Edgeworth.

TO AUNT RUXTON
Edgeworthstown, 30 January 1814

... The dairy cook who yesterday was near destroying the kitchen maid by running at her with the spit has departed this day – When I see you, I will both frighten you and make you laugh at the description of this woman – One stroke I fear to forget and must tell you this day – during the late cold weather my mother sent an additional blanket to her room and next day said she hoped the blanket had kept her warm – "No, Ma'am, I never used it. Oh Ma'am it had been in the men's room – I would not lie, Ma'am under a blanket that a man had lain under!" ...

The snowdrops in my garden are just peeping out and their pretty white heads delight all the children and the peacocks – Poor old Robin Woods is better and ate a bit of roast pork today –

Postscript: Lovell wrote ... in high hopes of peace, his letter dated Dec. – He thought that peace was going to be signed with the allies on the left bank of the Rhine and that he should be immediately liberated – I think Peace will <u>be</u> sometime this summer – Don't you? Or do you?

The peace in fact was finally signed on 30 May 1814 and Lovell, released after twelve years as a prisoner of war, could begin to make his way home.

Meanwhile, Sneyd's new house in Dublin offered escape from the winter in Edgeworthstown.

TO AUNT RUXTON
Baggot Street, Dublin, March 1814

Here we are after a prosperous journey – Though the hackney chase did make a great noise, I made a noise and a greater noise too as long as I was able, reading the Marriage of Figaro which diverted my father very much. When I was hoarse past all endurance, your oranges, dear Aunt, were delicious and restored my voice nearly to its <u>natural</u> sweetness …

… Arrived here 3 o'clock – found Henrica quite well – and <u>looking very well</u> – Such a nice, pretty elegant house! And they have furnished it so neatly and comfortably – It is delightful to see my father here – he enjoys himself so much in his son's house – We found that we had been engaged to go yesterday to a great party at Mrs Richard Crampton's – … and as Sneyd seemed to wish it, I consented at first but after lying on the sofa for half an hour … I still felt tired and was so hoarse and coughed so much that I honestly told Henrica I was not able to go – My father better pleased – and Sneyd very goodnaturedly ditto …

Quite well today except croaking like a frog – Lady Longford has been here this morning and was most agreeably enthusiastic – told us that Sir E. Pakenham was so dreadfully fatigued after the battle [*of Vittoria*] (as he says by an uneasy horse) that he was not able to join again for four days … A buckle of Lord Wellington's swordbelt saved him – he wrote 4 times to Lady W in one week after the battle in high spirits but without ever mentioning his wound – He dispatched expresses in all directions to Lord Castlereagh immediately to break off the negotiations which in consequence are broken off – no peace.

Sophy and Miss Waller dine here – a party in the evening – the first Henrica has ever given – they were resolved to have open house this evening upon our arrival – She is so kind and wellbred and easy in her manner that I feel and felt ten minutes after I came here quite at home …

TO HENRICA EDGEWORTH
Edgeworthstown, March 1814

One line I must write tho' that cruel father will let me write but <u>one</u> line to tell you how happy I was with you [*and*] how glad I was to see you and dear

The temple in the woods at Collon built by John Foster, later Lord Oriel.

Sneyd in your own home, your comfortable, elegant and hospitable home. Your kindness made me happier than I could have been made for all the parties Dublin would have assembled ... I shall never forget either the kindness of your <u>Howd'ye do</u> or the far greater kindness of your <u>Goodby'ye</u> ... We read half a volume of O'Donnell and think it excellent – My father begs Sneyd will tell Lady Morgan so – But pledge him only for <u>as far as he has read</u> –

TO LUCY EDGEWORTH [*aged eight*]
Collon, March 1814

My dear Lucy, I thank you for your little note which was pretty well written and in which there was but one word ill-spelled. [*Picture of hand pointing*] <u>extremely</u> which you spelled <u>extremeley.</u>

I am glad you are happy and pray do not grow tired of being good before I come home. Whenever you want something to do I wish you would pull up some of the many weeds in my garden. If you should be kept in the house by rain, I wish you would dust my books which is a job I know you like – but do not let the books fall more than ten times.

... Honora and I had a very pleasant walk with my father to the Temple where Col. and Lady Harriet Foster lived – We walked through a wood in which the trees have grown up there 20 years ... Your mother remembers when they were all planted – So 20 years hence you may perhaps walk or sit under the shade of any tree which you now plant.

... My father has been very busy at your Grandmama's clock trying to prevent it from making a <u>whirring</u> disagreeable noise when it strikes. When my father had down the clock he wished that Francis was here to see it – Tell Francis this and tell him and Harriet and Sophy and Fanny that Grandmama and Grandpapa say they were very agreeable when they were here and they wish to see them again – I hope, my dear, that whenever you come to Collon you will make yourself as agreeable and improve as much as your sisters did ... Goodbye my dear Lucy – Give my love to everybody round the breakfast table – and a kiss to Pakenham – I am glad to hear that poor Kitty's cold is better.

TO AUNT RUXTON
Edgeworthstown, May 1814

My father would not let me write to you again till I could tell you that you may rejoice with us and hang sorrow and cast care aside for he is now out of all danger. The disease which for your satisfaction or dissatisfaction and for my own I have ... in Greek letters is called Podagra Nolhos – or misplaced <u>Gout</u> – I have it also in command that to add in due technical medical language that by proper treatment and regime, diet and quiet it is terminating happily by <u>discussion</u> instead of <u>translation</u> ...

No news yet of Lovell! – I am very glad that he did not come one of these last four days – in another week I shall be heartily glad to see him; for by that time I trust my father will be afoot again and able as he is anxious to be to receive him as such a long lost son should be received – joy truly into the midst of a happy family. Now the arrival of the Angel Gabriel (I hope it is not irreverend to mention his angelship?) would not make me feel happy or look happy when my father was ill and all my thoughts absorbed in the single question – Will he recover?

That question settled I can now think of anything you please – of all the wonderful events which have taken place in these last few weeks in France – So wonderful are they that wonder seems worn out and I have not the power of feeling surprise … A revolution without bloodshed! – Paris taken without being pillaged – the Bourbons after all hope and season for hope seemed passed for their race restored – re-entering their capital, their palaces – with what mixed sensations they must re-enter their palaces!

I dare say it has not escaped you, my dear aunt, that the Venus de Medicis and the Apollo Belvedere are both still missing – together! – I make no remarks – at least I am not quite so fond of it as the lady of whom it was said that she could not see the poker and tongs standing together beside the fireplace without suspecting something was going wrong …

I meant to have told you many things in this letter which I have omitted – and yet which are worthy of your hearing – for instance that Bonaparte asked to live in England and was much surprised that he was refused …

Lovell Edgeworth finally reached Edgeworthstown late on 10 May 1814 to an affectionate welcome from his family. Maria had been half dreading his return – he had been jealous of her twelve years earlier, referring to her in one letter as 'the serpent Maria'. Now he seemed gentle and undemanding – he refused to allow any public celebrations in Edgeworthstown, much to his father's approval, visited old servants and tenants, and behaved with suitable deference to his convalescent father. He himself was coughing and visibly in poor health and it was agreed that he should return to England to consult the leading doctors. He would call on Sneyd in Dublin on the way.

TO SNEYD EDGEWORTH
Edgeworthstown, 17 May 1814

Give me leave, my dear Sneyd, to introduce to your and Mrs E's acquaintance a friend and relative of mine, Mr Lovell Edgeworth. He sets off by the coach from this place this evening & will reach you I suppose about two o'clock tomorrow morning – I hope you will like him & find him an amiable & sympathising friend as well as an entertaining & agreeable companion.

Let me warn you not to be prejudiced against him by any little things in his manner which appear unfavourable. He has I believe caught a little of the French tone & air, which does not quite suit our English taste … His coat does not fit him, which is one of the circumstances most against him – His voice is not exactly what is agreeable to our ears – but these small impressions made by such trifling circumstances soon go off – and don't let them weigh with you above a few minutes – He goes prepared to find in you all the abilities which he feels he does not possess himself – and which your youthful genius promised. But don't let the fear of disappointing his expectations act upon your manners ... for if you show yourself such as you are, your natural generosity & excellence of heart are sure to please, perhaps more than the superiority of your understanding which cannot appear at first.

Everything I have seen of this gentleman – who you know is a new acquaintance to me as well as to you – interests me in his favour. – He shews a very affectionate heart and a great wish to do everything that is right & amiable & I think that he promises to be everything that will add to the happiness of his family ...

TO HARRIET BEAUFORT
31 May 1814

This day, my dear Harriet, my father's birthday, his 70th birthday, this day to which we have for the last six weeks looked forward alternatively with hope & fear is come at last – and hope prevails ... Yesterday his appetite returned and after eating an excellent dinner he suffered ... no return of fever or inflammation ... This morning at 6 o'clock Harriet brought me word – (and they were the pleasantest words I ever heard spoke) – he has had a delicious night – so we are all happy today ...

My father is now lying comfortably on the sofa in the library – in his crimson velvet cap which my aunt Charlotte made so expeditiously that it was ready to put on his head the moment he came out of his room ... His mind, you know is ever active, expanding in thought or in kindness for his friends – he is at this moment contriving how he can sit so as to write to your brother Francis with his own hand ...

Private: Lovell has been a source of great pleasure to my father – he finds him all he could wish his oldest son to be – I find him all I could wish my brother to be – His judgement has been exercised and strengthened – a mist seems with regard to myself to have been cleared from his usual orb – whether with [?] or rue or that best of medecines, time, I cannot tell – But I believe you know enough of me my dear Harriet to be quite certain that I think past unkindness good for nothing but to be forgotten – or rather to make us taste the more strongly present kindness ... But I beg this subject may never be recurred to ...

There was good news too from her publisher in London.

... Miles has written & behaved in the most handsome manner about Patronage – he says to me "I have this day placed to your credit for the copyright of Patronage subject of course to your approbation the sum of two thousand guineas" – Had I known what it [*the letter*] contained I would have kept it till today for my father's birthday ... we have resolved not to mention the sum out of our family ...

Understandably: the advance was over £200,000 in today's money.

TO AUNT RUXTON
May/June 1814

I will now give you a better account of our hospital than you have had, my dear aunt, for some time. My aunt Charlotte is come down to her usual pulse of heart ... and nothing but feebleness remains – Aunt Mary's cold which has confined her to her room is getting better – Sophy sitting up in the cabinet, drinking caudle at this present instant looking as delicate and clean and pretty as any little caudle-drinking lady you ever beheld – Harriet's cold gone – Francis & Pakenham's ditto ... Pakenham ... has been sitting for half an hour on my lap delighting himself with that inexhaustible fund of amusement – Bewicks Birds and Quadrupeds – a book which I never open without finding something new and entertaining. (Did you know that jackdaws so inclined live very comfortable in rabit burrows – Having just learned this I cannot forbear repeating it to you, my dear Aunt) ...

Friends' letters have flowed in to me in abundance. Lady Romilly has just written an entertaining note to enclose a letter from Madame Gautier ... *On dit que* London has been very dull this season for that everybody is poor – the P[*rince*] has been really ill – gout not coming out kindly – the expenses of his household so much exceeded all computation that Lord Liverpool has refused to advance more money and the consequence has been a violent quarrel between him & Lord Cholmondley in which the P[*rince*] took a warm interest so that he invited none of his ministers to Brighton except Lord Castlereagh and the moral is that if the P[*rince*] R[*egent*] did not hate the opposition ten times worse than he does these ministers they would not remain in power ten days longer – So it seems the

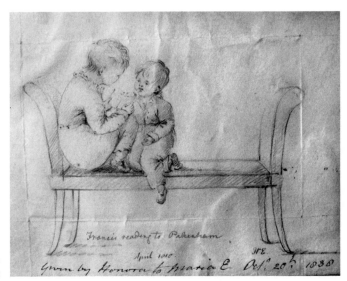

Francis Edgeworth, aged six, reading to his brother Pakenham. Sketch by their mother.

Prince remains suspended like Mahomet's coffin, equipoised but not by the force of opposite attractions but opposing repulsions ...

Do you care whether the English chancellor is or is not out of favour or whether the Princess Charlotte[133] is thinner or fatter – If you do my dear Aunt I am happy to inform you that she is thinner & much improved in her person & manners and that the chancellor is very much out of humour because he has not been consulted about her marriage – These great & rich people have all their mortifications of one kind or another – either they don't shoot birds enough or they don't make Royal matches enough. The D-----l mend them! ...

Her father was now working on a new book of technical improvements for wheeled carriages.

TO AUNT RUXTON
12 August 1814

... My father and the carriage both go on well – He was working too hard to get it finished ... by the 16th. But fortunately he is now relieved from the necessity or the ambition to do the impossible ...

---

133 The Prince Regent's daughter.

This morning I received a letter from a friend [*Dr Holland*] who begins by telling me that I should be surprised at its content – and so I was – The Princess of Wales[134] has invited Dr H[*olland*] to accompany her abroad – after consulting his friends he accepted ... The Princess is to proceed in the first instance to Brunswick where she will remain until her brother goes to the Congress of Vienna ...

Can you imagine anything equal to the impudence of those about the Princess Charlotte! They let her go out every evening for a week attended only by one footman – These evenings were spent to be sure with her mother at Connaught House ... They all heartily deserved to be dismissed – No wonder the young princess knew how to call a coach – and a waterman too ...

TO SOPHY RUXTON
Edgeworthstown, October 1814

... Mr O'Brien the dancing master has been here all day and old and young have been given up to him – old for <u>posts</u> and young for dances – He has done wonders – Honora and Fanny really dance well and he has taught them many pretty cotillions and country dances – Sophy & Lucy too have been brought forward wonderfully – and Harriet takes such pains that she will soon make up for the 4 days she lost when we were away from home – I cannot tell you how glad I am and for how many reasons that these young people have learnt to dance ...

Was Maria remembering her own failure to learn to dance gracefully at the same age and the cutting remarks on posture of her first stepmother Honora? The next letter to her aunt certainly implies it.

TO AUNT RUXTON
13 October 1814

You owe me kindness! Oh no, my dearest aunt, that is impossible – In a thousand, thousand ways from the time I was a blind child and a dumb child and an ill favoured child you have shewn me so much and such tender kindness

---

134 The estranged wife of the Prince Regent. She had invited Maria to call on her in London the year before, but Maria had refused on the grounds of her unsavoury reputation.

that the debt of love must ever be on my side. And I am not of Milton's devil's opinion that "Hell paying still to owe" gratitude is an irksome expenditure – quite the contrary ...

I had a letter the day before yesterday from the duchess of Wellington dated 5th October from Deal written just when she was going to embark for France – How very kind to think of us in such a moment of hurry and take the trouble of bidding us adieu – The whole of her letter was full of her children and of sorrow for quitting them – she says she has almost lived for the last 2 months at the school where they are now placed and has had the satisfaction of seeing that all the pupils are well taken care of, well taught and well fed – The last time she saw her little Douro, she says, she asked him what he advised her to do to make the time seem short to her while he and his brother should be absent – He answered "Get up early for that will make [you] strong to do things, read books of improvingness, and do your duty and that will make the time seem short". She adds "Here are my own lessons returned to bless me at Paris or at any other place".

How few ladies who were going ambassadresses to Paris would have their heads and hearts so full of their children or would think of taking such good advice.

Dr Holland's account of his progress through Germany with the Princess of Wales are very interesting. Nothing but balls, fetes, masquerades, acclamations wherever she appeared, especially at the Duke of Brunswick's court – Poor woman, what a change this must be for her – she is very good natured and attentive to Mr H ... The German courts he says are not like Madame de Bazetti's famous description "pomp without the common comforts & conveniences of life" and "dignity upon stilts with little support and dirty ground underneath". Jerome Bonaparte fortunately had a taste for building and decoration and intended to make Brunswick his residence – so he fitted up and furnished the palace delightfully and the Duke of B and the poor Princess of W have enjoyed all this – By what strange accidents are countries and the taste of nations improved! Who would have thought that the taste of a clumsy German count could be frenchified by the brother of a Corsican Emperor of France ...

Two days ago a young gentleman, Mr James Gordon, nephew of Mr Whitbread, came to us with a very polite introductory note from Lady Elizabeth Whitbread ... He has just returned from Paris where he spent 6 weeks and in a remarkably quiet drip by drip way of speaking he has given me a better account of Paris ... than I have heard or read from anyone else. Near Montmartre where the battle was fought previous to the entrance of the allies into Paris there is now a field in which the bodies of the dead have been so imperfectly buried that Mr Gordon actually saw elbows and limbs sticking up uncovered and the exhalation was so dreadful that ... he was obliged to hold a handkerchief to his nose. Over these bodies and the thin skin of earth that covers them was growing one of the finest crops of wheat that Mr Gordon says he ever saw.

He was present when the King entered Paris – so far from the general crying "*Vive Louis XVIII*" Mr Gordon says that he heard the troops by whom he stood repeatedly crying "*Vive l'Empereur*" – "*Vive Napoleon*". Berthier who rode before the King's carriage dared not look at the troops but passed on with his eyes cast down ...

The military are all attached to Bonaparte ... and the lowest and middle classes of the people, when they are not apprehensive of being heard by the friends of the Bourbons, express high admiration for Bonaparte with whom they think the glory of France rose and fell – They usually finish with "*Mais il avait trop d'ambition, c'est ça ...*"

Mr Gordon says that the circle about the Bourbons know little of what the sentiments of the people in general are ... – The King's processions and love of saints are not at all to the taste of the Parisian sinners – At the procession to Notre Dame and even at the elevation of the host Mr G says he saw the soldiers forcing the people down on their knees and there was considerable struggle ... The whole of what he hears of the state of Paris convinces me that the Bourbons have difficult cards to play and that if they keep their eyes only on the <u>court</u> cards as they were wont to do they will lose the game – They had better let Talleyrand play for them – no one plays better than he does ...

The common people of Paris were or fancied they were exceedingly fond of the little King of Rome and speak with pathos of the packing and packing off of his beautiful little barouche – his plaything carriage drawn by an ass – what a frivolous people!

But enough about them – and now we go to Scotland – Of course our young Gordon is enthusiastic about Scotland – but all in his cool way. His eyes did sparkle to be sure when he spoke of staying at Dun Robin – and still more they sparkled and he blushed a deeper dye when he talked of Lady Fredericka

Murray – Lord Mansfield's daughter – a young lady of fourteen or fifteen
with whom he acknowledges he is smitten – So much [*mathematical*] talent
he declares he never saw in any individual … But Lady Fredericka's talents are
not <u>only</u> for arithmetic, or else, my dear aunt, you would not give much for
them, – she has happy talents for conversation and most agreeable manners –
Mr G says he saw her in a company of one and twenty people, many of them
strangers to her, do the honours at table and say what was fit and polite to
each and that the way in which she afterwards went and played with her little
brothers and sisters delighted more than all the rest – By his account Lord &
Lady Mansfield & the whole family is charming & their castle or palace of
Scone the most agreeable in the world – And in the middle of all this, and at
the height of this panegyric on the Lady Fredericka, what do you think my
father said – To Mr Gordon's astonishment and dismay and … not much less
to mine, he turned suddenly round to us and cried

"<u>I prophecy</u> that <u>she</u> <u>will</u> <u>marry</u> a <u>blockhead</u>"

"A blockhead! How so Sir? – Why so Sir" cried Lady Fredericka's knight
– and a very animated droll conversation followed, which went off to my great
joy exceedingly well on all sides – My father argued that prodigies, especially
female prodigies, always do some silly thing sooner or later – Examples in
abundance alas! …

Now my dear aunt I have written all this to …[*divert*] you in Sophy's
absence … My father slept like a top last night and is quite well – but still he
is not so strong as I could wish and I cannot help now and then trembling for
the insecure tenure we have of all earthly happiness …

Friday evening

Here sits Pakenham at my feet playing with a pack of cards and suddenly
he screams amain

"Oh fie!" said I "Why do you scream so, Pakenham?"

"Because Lucy is taking all <u>my</u> kings" –

And never did Bonaparte frown more imperiously or lay a more powerful
accent upon <u>my</u> kings – As Mrs Barbauld says

" … so near approach
The sports of children & the toils of men" …

In her Memoir, *Maria's stepmother remembers that at this time the family were reading* Waverley *(published anonymously) and were enraptured by it. Richard Lovell Edgeworth immediately guessed the author as Walter Scott, exclaiming 'Aut diabolus, aut scotus' and encouraged Maria to write to him. She had almost finished her letter when her stepmother drew her attention to the postscript, which had a glowing tribute to her own novels as the author's model and inspiration. Scott had sent her an advance copy that had never arrived.*

TO THE AUTHOR OF WAVERLEY
Edgeworthstown, 23 October 1814

We have this minute finished reading Waverley. It is read aloud to this large family and I wish the author could have witnessed the impression it made – the strong hold it seized of the feelings of both young and old – the admiration raided by the beautiful descriptions of nature – by the new and bold delineations of character – the perfect manner in which every character is drawn from first to last, without effort, without that affectation of making the persons speak in character – the ingenuity with which each person introduced in the drama is made useful and necessary to the end – the admirable art with which the story is constructed and with which the author keeps his own secrets till the precise moment when they should be revealed, whilst in the meantime with the skill of Shakspear [*sic*], the mind is prepared by unseen degrees for all the changes of feeling and fortune, so that nothing, however extraordinary, shocks us as improbable; and the interest is kept up till the last moment. We were so possessed by the belief that the whole story and every character was real that we could not endure the occasional addresses to the reader. They are like Fielding: but for that reason we cannot bear them, we cannot bear that an author of such high powers and original genius should for a moment stoop to imitation …

After this criticism, the remainder of the letter is full of lavish praise in Maria's most prolix style, probably partly dictated by Richard Lovell Edgeworth. By contrast her next surviving letter to her adored father is written almost in shorthand. Edgeworth discouraged Maria's effusions. He had gone to Dublin to find a house to rent for the winter in order to give Honora, now nineteen, a social season.

TO RICHARD LOVELL EDGEWORTH
Edgeworthstown, 24 November 1814

Thankyou, my beloved father, for your good account of yourself – Wednesday, Thursday, Friday, whatever day you come we shall rejoice – but we do not grudge you to Sneyd and Henrica – glad you dined at Mr Knox's – Mrs H. Hamilton's – & Mr Taylors – and admire your toleration for the deficiencies of society.

The volume of Phil. Trans. for the year 1797 is not to be found here – Honora, the guardian of said volumes, says that she was aware that one of the parts of 97 was missing but she did not know the whole was wanting –

As to Early Lessons – I look forward with great pleasure to continuing them with the assistance of him who gave me Early and will I hope give me late lessons –

Francis is a good boy – And makes letters in sand with Fanny everyday ...

We rejoice that we have here the letters of Dr Holland's for your evenings at home, also Eugene & Guillaume – also Mansfield Park –

Your indulgent patience shall not be wasted – continue it – and I will continue to keep in mind that IOU a good story if my invention is not bankrupt – I will certainly in due time pay you – I think more of what IOU than what IO mankind ...

Adieu my dear father – all well here & all the foolish souls fond of fondness send that which must not be named to you.

I am your daughter – I suppose you prefer that to your affectionate daughter or your grateful daughter or any of these fudgeries – Maria Edgeworth

TO SOPHY RUXTON
December 1814

... This morning Fanny had a letter from Lovell dated the 10th – he writes in excellent spirits and tho' he has still flying pains, they seem to be all flying away fast – I hope never to return. The physicians and especially Dr Cleverly whom he thinks the cleverest says that all his remaining pains are owing to debility and nothing is wanting now but strength which air, exercise and food will give – They prescribe no drugs but hop pills ... for my part I am satisfied with hops in my beer ...

... Mrs Pollard, the bride & her groom have spent a day with us last Monday and brought with them Miss Napier who was so good as to wish to become acquainted with us ... She is very pretty and has a sweet voice which made all she told us of Holland still more agreeable. She has just been to Amsterdam with her aunt – Amsterdam she describes as a disagreeable place, the canals as green as green baize – She was told the Dutch ladies of Amsterdam were all intelligent & agreeable but the husbands sad eating and drinking money making brutes. The Prince and Princess of Orange too reserved to please the people ...

We did not talk of unfortunate daughters when Miss Napier was with us[135] – My father is charmed with her and in favour of her beauty, voice and manners ... and lays a scheme for half drowning her that Lovell might save her life and win her heart. We talked over Waverley with her – I am glad you all like it – ... We are just beginning Mansfield Park – the beginning is like real life and very entertaining[136] ...

Adieu, my dear Sophy – Shall I tell you what they are all doing around me at this moment in the library – they are all sprawling on the floor looking at a new rat trap which my father is showing Francis ... I never saw such a genius for mechanics – but there is no such thing as genius – Be that as it may, two pounds of butter vanished a few nights ago out of a shallow pan with water in it in the dairy – It is averred by all below that the rats ran away with said pounds of butter & Peggy Tuite the dairy maid, to make the story more credible, gives the following reason for the rats' conduct.

"Troth Ma'am, they were affronted because of the new trap that was set for them in the dairy – they only licked the milk but that occasioned 'em to run off wid the butter" Such revengeful rats! Zangas to the backbone! ...

TO SOPHY RUXTON
Edgeworthstown, 26 December 1814

A merry Christmas and a happy New Year to you my dear Sophy ... I am just risen from my bed where I had been pinned a day and a half with a violent headache and pains or as John Langan calls them, *pins* all over me ...

---

135 She was the daughter of Lady Sarah Napier, much disapproved of by Maria for eloping with a lover thirty years before.

136 The author, Jane Austen, was still anonymous. Maria had already read *Pride and Prejudice* with pleasure on the way to London in 1813 but had been shocked by the raciness of the plot.

I cannot, my dear Sophy, tell you anything about our plans for the spring, be assured I know nothing – nothing is settled – My father was near taking two or three houses [*in Dublin*] but [*is*] not a bit nearer taking any … All I hope & all which I think seemed positive is that Honora's to be the prime object in this instance & that whatever is most to her advantage will be decided upon – My mother on this occasion rises, if it is possible that one so high should rise higher, in my esteem by her courageous spirit of justice & simple plain dealing and plain speaking …

[*Postscript*] … I like Mansfield Park including all but the prosings of the conclusion.

In the end the problem of finding an affordable and suitable Dublin house for the winter was solved by Sneyd and his wife Henrica (now known as Harriette) offering their house in Baggot Street while they went to England in search of health. One of the rooms was adapted to provide a workshop for Richard Lovell Edgeworth, where he could try out some experiments on wheel carriages at the request of the Royal Dublin Society.

TO HARRIETTE EDGEWORTH
Baggot Street, Dublin, February 1815

… My father has been upon the whole much happier in Dublin than we expected … – and this we attribute chiefly to the comfort of your house which is a HOME – he never did have a home before in Dublin – Francis & the workbench have also been great pleasures – Francis has been very good & amused & amusing – Mrs E has given two nice dinners and nice evening parties which were much approved by all the people concerned. Dawson etc, who my father says is a model of a servant, performed their parts admirably – Armstrong is much better as a city than as a country servant – he is very alert, shopping & visiting & doing commissions.

About the stays I have only to say thankyou & bring them when you come. Pray tell me my dear what I am in your debt for my beauteous gown & I will send you a draft upon Hoares & for 16.0 which I owe Mrs Thomas Beaufort for said stays …

Maria found the social life of Dublin pleasurable but exhausting. She met Lady Morgan – a rival Irish authoress – and was 'agreeably surprised' by the

Sydney, Lady Morgan (née Owenson), Maria's literary rival. Maria had disliked any association with her until she met her in Dublin in 1815.

improvement in her. Lady Morgan, formerly a governess with the Fether-stonhaughs at Bracklyn House, Westmeath, had been married off by her employers, the Abercorns, to a respectable Dublin doctor and now had a salon. Then there was an added burden of redrafting Sneyd's biography of the Abbé Edgeworth.

TO SOPHY RUXTON
Baggot Street, Dublin, February 1815

My dear Sophy who I trust does not think Dublin has whirled her out of my head, much less my heart. The fact is I have scarcely had time to do all that it was deemed I should do, whether of duty or pleasure within the 24 hours – In the midst of all the engagements, drapers, dressings & dressmakers etc etc etc came the Abbé Edgeworth's life to be corrected – that is to say (Private) to be completely new written – the papers all in such dreadful confusion. But with my father's assistance they have been reduced to lucid order and … what it ought to be – <u>simplicity</u> – with the dedication to the K. of France written by my father – I think beautifully. Whether Sneyd will put his name to it or not is left to himself – my father advises NOT – I advise him to put his name along with my father's name.[137]

I beg you not to tell anybody – <u>not</u> <u>even</u> <u>my</u> <u>aunt</u> – that I have had anything to do with it.

Our time has been much more agreeably spent than I had any hopes it would be. My father has been pleased at some dinners, especially at Mr Knox's, Mr Leslie Foster's and at the Solicitor General's and he has been tired only at two or three levees & crowded evening parties where we indeed wished he would not have gone …

The Beauforts are at Mrs Wallers' – they came up in a hurry summoned by a Mrs Codd, an American who has come up to claim a considerable property and wishes to be identified … I will tell you when we meet of her *entrée* with Sir Simon Broadstreet – and I will tell you of Honora's treading on the parrot at Mrs Westby's party …

In March, Fanny, aged fifteen and Harriet, thirteen, were brought up to Dublin to join their parents, leaving only their two youngest sisters and three-year-old Pakenham at home. Maria's letters as usual were perfectly tailored to their young recipients.

TO LUCY EDGEWORTH [*aged eight*]
Baggot Street, Dublin, 18 March 1815

My dear Lucy,

I received your very well written and well spelled note this morning when Ferrilly the car man brought the box containing Honora's hat …

Thankyou for weeding my garden. Francis has written to thank you for what you have done in his garden. In the next frank, I will … send a little paper of seeds of <u>the</u> <u>rose</u> <u>of</u> <u>the</u> <u>alps</u>. These seeds were given me by a lady who has lately been in Switzerland and … who travelled for three days with Dr Holland. She says that Dr Holland is not at all spoiled by having been taken so much notice of by Princes & Princesses – But to return to the rose of the alps – I am told it is a dwarf or <u>low</u> kind of rhododendron. The seeds should be mixed with a little sand before they are sowed – they require no particular attention. I shall be much obliged to my aunt Charlotte if she will let you sow

---

137 The book finally appeared under Sneyd's name two years later.

them for me in any corner of the garden or in the place in the garden they call my rosary – where Kitty's bird is buried.

On Friday Dr and Mrs Buckley dined here and seemed very happy. While Dr Buckley was talking earnestly to the Bishop of Clogher and Dean Graves about Bonaparte, little Francis whose hour for going to bed was just then come, went up to the three tall men and squeezing himself between them pulled the skirt of the great Dr Buckley's court to make him hear him – Dr B did not feel the pull and went on talking – Francis pulled again & Dr B turned & looked down & stooped his large benevolent face to listen to Francis who with his head thrown back ... was looking up at him & saying "Dr Buckley, I wish you would take me to see the camelopardel".

"My dear, I will" said good Dr Buckley stroking Francis' head "I will take you to see the camelopardel tomorrow morning".

The next morning Dr Buckley called upon us to take us to the <u>College</u> where that animal is – It is not a camelopardel, but the skin of one stuffed & has been set up on its legs in the middle of the <u>museum</u> at the college. This museum is in a large room nearly half as long again as the library at Edgeworthstown – There are all round it presses with glass doors through which you can see the curiousities within –

The camelopardel is very like in shape to the print you have seen in Buffon & I believe in Bewick – but the print cannot give you an idea of its size. Its height from the top of its little horns ... to the bottom of its front foot is about 14 feet; Willie will show you how high that is ... Dr Buckley lifted Francis up on its back – but could not fix him there – Francis walked between its forelegs, completely under it and out between its hind legs without stooping. Its hair is short like that of Kitty's yellow & white hair trunk ... Francis ... asked how it was killed & Dr Buckley showed him the holes the bullets had made ...

Tell Sophy that we saw the rattlesnake and a snake called a whip snake twisted like the lash of a long whip – and we saw an armadillo and an ostrich egg which was rather large like your nine pin ball ... I will tell you more when we meet.

Last night we went to a ball at the castle where Honora danced with Captain Arabin. But of all this account shall be written another day ... I send this letter to you as you desired, directed to yourself and <u>sealed.</u> I am glad to do any little thing to oblige you when you do so many to oblige me – Thankyou for recollecting my fan – and thankyou 100,000 times more for being a good girl & attentive to all my aunts desire you to do – love to Sophy ...

Richard Lovell Edgeworth in early middle age, painted by John Comerford. *Courtesy of the National Gallery of Ireland.*

The Dublin Volunteers parade on College Green, 1781, painted by Francis Wheatley. Richard Lovell Edgeworth was to act as Lord Charlemont's aide-de-camp. *Courtesy of the National Gallery of Ireland.*

Sophy Ruxton, Maria's first cousin and favourite confidante. Highly intelligent and well read, she acted as Maria's sounding board for many of her stories. *Courtesy of Trevor Fitzherbert.*

Maria's half-sisters, Bessie and Charlotte Edgeworth, playing outside Edgeworthstown house in 1791, painted by Mrs Mary Powys, a family friend. The house had already been much altered and improved by Maria's father. *Private collection.*

United Irishmen looting a farmhouse, a savage contemporary cartoon by the English caricaturist James Gillray, 1798. Edgeworthstown House miraculously escaped damage by the rebel army, thanks to the family's reputation as benevolent landlords and an earlier kindness to a local 'rebel' by their housekeeper, Kitty Billamore. *Private collection.*

Henry Grattan declares the death of the Irish Nation at the last sitting of the Irish House of Commons in 1799. Richard Lovell Edgeworth voted against the Union on principle, although he believed it would bring much-needed capital and industry to Ireland. *Courtesy of Davison and Associates.*

Humphrey Davy demonstrates chemical experiments before a packed audience, cartoon by Thomas Rowlandson. Maria attended his lectures at the Royal Dublin Society in 1810 and found them as 'eloquent and beautiful' as the lay of an old minstrel. © *Trustees of the British Museum.*

The Museum at Trinity College, Dublin with its stuffed 'camelopardel' or giraffe, print by W.B. Taylor, 1819. Maria described a visit there with her six-year-old half-brother Francis in March 1815. *Courtesy of Trinity College, Dublin.*

George IV leaves Dunleary Harbour
(renamed Kingstown in his honour) after his
highly successful visit to Ireland in August
1821. Maria reported the scene in detail to
her invalid younger sister, Lucy, in a letter, 18
September 1821. *Private collection.*

Napoleon on St Helena: from the best-
selling account, *Napoleon in Exile*, by
his Irish surgeon, Barry O'Meara, first
published in 1822. Marie was fascinated by
this sympathetic memoir of Napoleon in
exile. *Courtesy of The London Library.*

Daniel O'Connell as 'The Liberator', lithograph by Alfred M. Hoffy, c.1847. Maria initially admired him during the struggle for Catholic Emancipation but later came to see him as a dangerous demagogue, threatening the Union with England and encouraging sectarian and anti-landlord agitation. *Courtesy of Wikimedia.*

Sir William Rowan Hamilton, president of the Royal Irish Academy. Maria met him when he was in his twenties and often invited him to Edgeworthstown. In 1842 he made her an honorary member of the Academy, a tribute to her passionate interest in science. *Courtesy of the Royal Irish Academy.*

Another precociously brilliant Irish scientist, Thomas Romney Robinson. He was appointed head of the Armagh Observatory at the age of thirty and remained director until his death in 1882. In 1843 he married Lucy Edgeworth, Maria's youngest half-sister, much to Maria's delight. *Courtesy of the Royal Irish Academy.*

The 3rd Earl of Rosse ascending his giant telescope at Birr, painted by his fellow astronomer, Charles Piazzi Smyth (later Astronomer Royal for Scotland). Maria was too old and frail to visit the telescope herself, but her young half-brothers, Frances and Pakenham, both called at Birr to admire it in 1843. *Courtesy of Lord and Lady Rosse.*

Maria writing her last story, *Orlandino*, at the age of eighty, to raise money for famine relief. The watercolour was made in secret by Louisa Beaufort, her stepmother's sister, hiding behind a pillar in the library at Edgeworthstown. Maria intensely disliked being drawn or painted. *Courtesy of the National Library of Ireland.*

Edgeworthstown House in the late 1850s, ten years after Maria's death. The bow window of her tiny bedroom is still in place (left) above the garden she planted. It was to fall off the wall several years later. The house has since been much altered to become a nursing home. *Courtesy of the Irish Architectural Archive.*

By April Maria's father was ill again and needed to return home.

TO SNEYD EDGEWORTH
Black Castle, 10 May 1815

... You probably by this time know that Mrs E – Ho – Fanny – Francis & William went home last Saturday by the Mullingar coach – I have heard of their safe arrival & of their finding my father much better ...

We, that is my father, mother, little Harriet, went on Sunday last to Castletown – the two days we spent there delightful. Lady Louisa Conolly is one of the most respectable, amiable and even at seventy, charming persons I ever saw or heard. Having known all the ... most celebrated people who have lived for the last fifty years [*she is*] full of characteristic anecdotes and fuller of that indulgence for human creatures which is consistent with a thorough knowledge of the world and a quick perception of all the foibles of honest human nature – with a high sense of religion without the slightest tincture of ostentation, asperity or bigotry[138] ...

I saw Lady Longford wonderfully well the day before we left – she gave with eyes lifted to heaven and streaming tears a most touching account of her son Edward and his sending her by his favourite servant the little bible which she had given him at parting and which he desired his servant to tell her he had read every day a portion as she had directed ...

The news had just come that General Sir Edward Pakenham, 'the mirror of colonels' who Maria had once hoped would marry her cousin Sophy Ruxton, had been killed in America. He had died in January leading an assault against Andrew Jackson's forces at the Battle of New Orleans, two weeks after peace had been signed between the two warring countries.

In July Maria was at Black Castle with her aunt, bringing her father to convalesce.

TO SNEYD EDGEWORTH
Black Castle, July 1815

... There arrived at Black Castle this morning a new party of ... visitors with quite a new budget of information – Mrs Airey and her two daughters &

138 Lady Louisa was the sister of the Duke of Richmond and widow of Thomas Conolly. Castletown had been left to Admiral Pakenham's eldest son, but Lady Louisa lived there until her death.

Mrs Everard. (Genrl Airey was not with them.) Mrs Airey … made a better defence for Lord Elgin carrying off the Grecian marbles than I thought could have been made for him. She says that Lord Elgin says that the French consul had actually prepared machinery & shipping to convey the whole of the Parthenon & various other of the buildings of the Acropolis to Paris where they had intended to erect the ruins precisely in the form they had found at Athens – To prevent these intentions and to prevent the Turks from using the finest marbles, as they were in the habit of doing, for making lime mortar, Lord Elgin interfered – At best, I think, it is but a bad defence now I have reduced it to writing. In conversation it passed, as many things pass, vastly well.

… I need not have troubled you with the 2 first pages of this letter full of marbles foreign to your business but I thought you would be on circuit & that it might entertain you in some dreary inn or at Omagh where of olden times you used to wish for a letter of any kind –

Success to your Honour! and as little sea-sickness as possible. Law is quite a sufficient plague …

TO LUCY EDGEWORTH *(aged nine)*
Black Castle, 17 July 1815

Your aunt Ruxton & Sophy & Margaret were pleased with the three copies you wrote of my father's "Address from the Butterfly" – I will give one copy to each … My father says he thinks you will write an excellent hand if you continue to take pains …

My father is better – and enjoys all the fine weather every day in the comfortable[139] – Pray tell Honora & Fanny that he scarcely ever gets in or out without thanking them for all the work they did to it …

Sophy is very happy, and very useful to my father – particularly in making his shaving rags … Yesterday General Airey came here & brought his two sons – one of them, a boy of 11 years old, is the boy who went with his mother and sister to see Ali Pacha's Harem – that is, the apartment in which his wives live –

… My mother asked this boy whether they gave him anything to eat – He said "Yes, they had a variety of dishes, almost all of them smothered with honey – in particular mutton or lamb stewed with honey"… My mother also asked

---

139 A specially adapted landau.

The Edgeworths' favourite retreat, Black Castle, the Ruxtons' house by the Boyne.

if they had knives and forks at this dinner in the harem – He said that knives were given to <u>them</u> being Europeans but that all the ladies and attendants eat with their fingers ... Please not to read or tell this to little Pakenham, who now, under the care of his 3 dinner guardians, eats so nicely ...

I am your affectionate friend & very old sister, Maria Edgeworth

TO SOPHY RUXTON
Edgeworthstown, September 1815

My dear friend, I have the pleasure to tell you that I think my father's health has been for a continuance improving – Sickness occasionally – but now ... [*his stomach*] has ceased to deprive him of the enjoyment of his days and nights – he sleep & eats – walks without pain and can stand out and endure more fatigue of body & mind than I can ... You who have so kind a heart must be like a bucket in a well – up and down – glad or sorry twenty times a week ...

... I am <u>at</u> <u>my</u> <u>backbone</u>[140] – Have not got the bone rightly laid down quite to my mind but am happily placing it in different positions of my fancy

---

140 She was working on a new novel, *Ormond.*

– Frequent interruption & being called eternally to something else, I believe much increases … my love for this bone – and if I am forced to drop it from my teeth continually I run back to it again with fresh ardour – and hurry off to a snug corner to be at it again in peace.

… I wished for you 50 times a day while Hutton & Griffith were with us – so many things continually occurred which would have suited peculiarly your tastes – and besides the study of the character of the two men would have interested you full as much as their geology – about which both were mad – God bless them![141]

And indeed a <u>little</u> madness as much as goes under the head <u>enthusiasm</u> is a blessing – gives zest to life, activity to talents. My father is as enthusiastic as is agreeable about experiments on wheel carriages – they will, I hope and believe, be as useful to the public as they are to his health …

Lovell has written a folio letter to Honora on various Bell & Lancaster schools he has seen in England – it is the very best letter of Lovell's I ever read – has charmed my father. I think Lovell will come over and establish a school at Edgeworthstown – he is enthusiastic about it. It is an object he likes of his own choosing – and in which my father will be delighted to assist him and allow him ample room and verge enough – His health seems better …

Tell my aunt I wish she could have seen the other day a vignette worthy of Bewick – Little Pakenham … had been dabbing with a brush at some drawing of his and when he could not get any amateur to admire it for him, he jumped down and ran for Tab, the little cat, and holding her by the back of the neck and fixing her forepaws on the table before his drawing, cried

"There, <u>Tab</u>! – There, <u>look</u> at that! Is that not pretty! Tab".

Tab was strangling all the time with her eyes half out …

TO AUNT RUXTON
Edgeworthstown, September 1815

… This morning's post has brought another more satisfactory letter from Lovell – the enthusiasm he feels about these schools seems to have quite cured his complaints and to have inspired him both with new body and new soul. He is full of the thoughts of coming here and establishing a school house & intent upon a wonder of a good boy of his, who is half footman, half schoolmaster –

---

141   Richard Griffith, who had worked earlier with Richard Lovell Edgeworth on the official enquiry into Irish bogs, was now making the first geological survey of Ireland. Maria reported him to Sneyd as 'very good humoured and easy'.

and the questions he puts to my father about him is "Whether to have or not to have a livery?"

To which my father will answer … most particularly

"Have a boy if you want one in a livery to brush your coat and clean your boots, and have a schoolmaster to teach your school but don't attempt to join the two in one or you will have neither good … "

TO HARRIETTE EDGEWORTH
Edgeworthstown, Autumn 1815

Harriette and Sneyd were both attending a series of spas in England and France.

Thankyou my dear heroine toothless Harriet for your note … I rejoice to hear that the dear duchess [*of Wellington*] was admired in Paris – That admiration will work well round to her husband's heart – of such stuff are men and heroes made – Men and Women and heroes very different …

I had a letter from Mrs Marcet today – She says that Madame de Staël was not popular in Geneva and that though she has a good society at Paris travellers write that she is not there so much admired as in London – The fact is that the Parisians are not such good listeners as the English and set more value upon art and less upon eloquence in conversation – Far from wishing to go, or to see others go, to the bottom of any subject in conversation, their motto universally is

"*Glissez mortels, n'appuyez pas*" …

TO HARRIETTE EDGEWORTH [*fragment*]
late November 1815

… I regret that Lord Longford is not to marry Lady A[*bdy*]'s sister, now Mrs Littleton, whose bright eyes at one time made such an impression upon him as to put Lady Elizabeth P[*akenham*] in mortal fear and to bring from her ejaculations about the drop of bad blood of which she ever had such a holy horror. It is remarkable that she was right also in offering up thanksgivings that he did not marry Lady Sarah Lennox – there was the drop too![142]

---

142 Probably a reference to Sarah Lennox's descent from Charles II's French mistress, Louise de la Kerouaille – Maria seems to have been fascinated by Sarah Lennox's scandalous early life.

But I am afraid Lord L will be so frightened with the dangers he has escaped that he will never venture to think of any wife bad or good – Do you meet him in Dublin? He has a drawing for me which Lady Lansdowne drew for me and gave to him 6 months ago – He is so good natured that I am sure however he will come and see my father as soon as ever he comes to P. Hall …

TO AUNT RUXTON
n.d. 1815?

… No letter yet from the Dublin Society[143] – My father very sick last night in his own words "I was as sick as a dog last night but I am as gay as a lark this morning."

We are reading "*Paris, Versailles et les Princes au dix huitième siecle*" – a book of anecdotes which Mr Forbes has lent us – in which there are some – pew! – pew! Some interesting and curious, some insufferably stupid. Like all books of anecdotes I ever read it leaves one in a mood after leading one on till tired to death from mere curiosity of seeing what will come next …

TO HARRIETTE AND SNEYD EDGEWORTH
Edgeworthstown, January 1816

… As I am with my pen at the grindstone here working out the 3rd act of a play for the 3rd time,[144] I have no means of paying my debts of entertainment in letter writing to either of you but by sending you other people's letters – I send you Lord Carringtons' – Lady Romillys' – Mrs Hollands' … Last not least I send you a letter from the Duchess of Wellington – Do not show it to anybody … Do not even tell the Merrions[145] the anecdote however tempting to tell of her children – But you may repeat to all manner of people her excellent answer about the hummingbird tippet and the diamonds.[146] … The book the Duchess of W mentions is your Abbé E's Memoirs … If she does not get that copy I will send her another – It is a great pity she left Paris before it reached her as she'd have done for it [?] with the Bourbons with a vengeance …

I like what I have read of <u>Rhoda</u> 50 per cent better than Emma[147] …

---

143 About her father's wheel experiments.

144 She was writing a series of comic dramas.

145 The Beaufort sisters who lived at 31 Merrion St.

146 *The Lady Magazine* had reported that the Duchess had dazzled Parisians by appearing at the Opera 'blazing with diamonds' with a tippet made of hummingbird feathers.

147 Published anonymously, *Rhoda* was a novel by Frances Jackson, a neighbour and connection of the Sneyd family.

TO HARRIETTE AND SNEYD EDGEWORTH
Edgeworthstown, January 1816

… Hunter [*her publisher*] writes me word that he sent by post under cover to Sir EB by 3 successive posts the 3 volumes of <u>Emma</u> – the 1st volume only reached me – the two others are I assumed sticking … somewhere in Sir EB's office.[148] If Mrs CJF can be so good as to rummage them out, Miss Waller may have them as long as she pleases. The first I cannot send back to her for reasons too long to explain, but there was no story except that Miss Emma found the man whom she designed for Harriet's lover was an admirer of her own – and he was affronted at being refused by Emma – and Harriet wore the willow – <u>and</u> <u>smooth</u> <u>thin</u> <u>water</u> <u>gruel</u> is according to Emma's father's opinion a very good thing & it is very difficult to make a cook understand what you mean by <u>smooth</u> <u>thin</u> <u>water</u> <u>gruel</u>! By the by since the influenza has reigned in this house and that water gruel has come into fashion this sentence has been oftener quoted and has occasioned more diversion than any one sentence from Fielding or Richardson, I believe, ever did …

> *Richard Lovell Edgeworth continued to be sick all through the winter and on 6 February he dictated instructions to Maria for his funeral, desiring to be 'buried in a private manner and at as little expense as possible' – and trusting 'entirely to my excellent son Lovell for the care of all the persons about me in proportion to their respective merits'. By May, he and Maria's stepmother were both back in Dublin consulting doctors. He wrote to Maria in a painfully shaky hand to try to reassure her.*

'Dear Partner, am sorry to tell you that my winter miseries have returned too regularly these later days … But it was not from anything that I eat. I rather suspect I caught cold in the street …

I cannot conclude my letter in a manner that can be more agreeable to you than by telling you how well Lucy repays your care of her – Her perfect simplicity & openness of mind, her quick & uncommon powers of observation, her knowledge & recollection of all common things & persons show that her understanding has been formed by natural growth and that she is not a clipped yew tree …'

---

148 These had been sent at the request of the still-anonymous Jane Austen who greatly admired Maria's novels.

TO LUCY EDGEWORTH [*in Dublin*]
Edgeworthstown, June 1816

... It has given me great pleasure to hear you have been so happy and so
useful ... William has arrived and ... has been entertaining us. We have
scarcely allowed him to breathe between one sentence and another. His
account of father and mother is very satisfactory considering all they have
been through – They will have leisure to re-fit at dear Black Castle. I
wonder how my father could support the fatigues and the crowds he had to
endure in Dublin. But all's well that ends well – and from William's account
of the experiments everything has succeeded and fully repaid my father for
his labour[149] ...

You are a woman of business, therefore remember to ask Mamma whether
any materials for porter should be written for to Dublin – Farrelly goes to
Dublin tomorrow – There is neither porter nor beer such as my father likes to
drink in the house.

... Francis & Pakenham send their loves to you. They are very good &
happy & merry all day long – and stick close together as usual ...

TO SOPHY RUXTON
Edgeworthstown, August 1816

... I have been ever since you were here mending up little plays – cobbling
work which takes a good deal of time and makes no show – I shall go back to
my jewish [*novel*] – with double pleasure[150] ...

My father has had only one sick day since you left us – as sick as he was
the day he took Dover's powders at Black Castle – He is better again now. I
cannot tell you ... how much he missed the stimulus of your company and that
of his dear sister. As for myself, I was so stupid the whole day after you went
that I could neither read, write, think nor talk – tho that can be done without
thinking ...

---

149 He had finally submitted his treatise on carriage wheels to the Royal Dublin Society.

150 This was *Harrington*, a novel with a Jewish hero, which Maria was writing as a corrective after an
American correspondent, Mrs Mordecai, had accused her of presenting the usual caricature of an
avaricious Jew in *The Absentee*. Mrs Mordecai became Maria's regular correspondent over the next
twenty years. See *The Education of the Heart*, ed. Edgar McDonald, 1977.

TO HARRIETTE EDGEWORTH [at Cheltenham]
August 1816

… You have great resolution in going over the England with only half of yourself – I hope you will be rewarded by health – next to love the greatest good below – I said <u>next</u> to love to please you – tho' quite out of character for an old maid and a philosopheress …

My dear Harriette, the moment I heard that the Duchess of W.[*ellington*] was at Cheltenham my first thought was to write a letter to her by you – but tho' this was my <u>first</u> thought … yet I believe it was best not to do it – for the Duke is so exceptionally afraid of having her relations and friends come upon him that Mrs Henry Hamilton would not go to London with her husband when the Duke was there lest she should "<u>embarrass</u> her sister Kitty" – those were her very words – and Lord L will not venture to introduce anybody or go near her <u>much</u> himself. Now they are just coming together again and drinking water at the well arm in arm I should be terribly afraid of throwing a straw across her path that might be of bad omen … She had a hard card to play and you who have with your husband … the whole pack in your own hands will make allowance for her and pity her …

Let me know as soon as you have decided to go to France and the how and when and I will pen letters to you to all our friends …

The Strutt visit went off to admiration and Mr H[*enry*] appeared much more agreeable than at Derby – he certainly is a clever man … Sneyd diverted us all by his description of the sudden change he saw in his countenance and manner from the moment that on the top of the coach he first saw the appearance of the house and place – I suppose he thought he was coming to some Irish shackamagarrick place.[151] Mr Strutt was particularly agreeable and well-bred in his manner of seeing things in Ireland from Dublin down to what he called <u>my</u> cottages – Dublin he thought a much prettier city than London and he said when he went into Rose's house – "This is really a house one would like to live in oneself, it is so clean and comfortable".

My father took him to see some of his bettermost tenants – Hugh Kelly … and James Allen and Miles – with all of which, especially with the footing on which my father is with his tenants, he seemed delighted – He is a truly

---

151 Maria and her father had stayed with the Strutts, rich industrialists and philanthropists in Derby in 1813, and Maria had described their house as 'quite a palace'.

*A 'bettermost tenant',
sketch by Charlotte
Edgeworth.*

benevolent man and benevolence is the true foundation of politeness – I think Edward Strutt much improved – he cannot help being too fat and speaking with a horrible provincial accent …

TO SNEYD EDGEWORTH
16 August 1816

… I have read or heard two volumes of <u>Glenarvon</u> but I cannot wade any further through blood and nonsense – I think it too absurd to do mischief.[152] There is one passage written by another hand – far superior – The account of the visit to the Princess of Madagascar – and her death … very like Sidney Smith's writing – Some of the poetry <u>beautiful</u> – like Moore's or Lord Byron's …

TO AUNT RUXTON
25 August 1816

My dearest aunt, I cannot lose a moment in communicating a piece of intelligence which I am sure will give you pleasure – Lord Longford is going to be married – not to Bess Pakenham – memorandum, I never gave credit

---

152 Lady Caroline Lamb's *roman-à-clef* about her affair with Byron was set in Ireland. Meanwhile Caroline Lamb had claimed in a letter to her publisher, John Murray, she had been unable to finish Maria's novel *Patronage* (set in England) because of its depiction of 'vulgar mediocre' life.

to that report – he is going to be married to Lady Georgina Lygon, <u>tenth</u> daughter of Lord Beauchamp – By the peerage we see that Lord B is 69 and having had but one wife, it seems probably that Lady Georgina, the tenth child, may not be a mere chicken – So much the better – Perhaps my dear aunt … you may have heard the news from some other friends but you will be glad to see the letter which Lord L wrote on the occasion to my father … [*Letter enclosed*]

This letter is like his own kindhearted unaffected self – and how perfectly polite as well as kind – God grant that all those I love may marry <u>well-bred</u> people – I am not quite so aristocratic as to add <u>well-born</u> – tho' in my secret soul I suspect there is a strong connection between these two things …

… Is it not odd that the name of <u>Beauchamp</u> should stare me out of countenance again … just when I had settled that it was not absolutely necessary to change the name of my reprobate young slasher <u>Beauchamp Courtington</u> … here comes another Beauchamp in Lord Longford's father-in-law – So there is a necessity to erase 529 Beauchamps. Heaven help my poor aunt Mary who must fall to <u>scratching</u> in the midst of the general rejoicing for Lord L's marriage – Now there is a melancholy drawback, a novel distress he never could have foreseen! …

Thankyou for the anecdote of the Duke of W – I wonder whether he will rejoice or whether he is too gloriously selfish to rejoice in his amiable brother-in-law's marriage and happiness – Heaven help his haughty mistaken soul – he has mistaken his road to happiness, I ween, after all the noise he has made in the world – he must go back to his duchess to ask the way sooner or later[153] …

TO AUNT RUXTON
Edgeworthstown, 18 September 1816

You know my dear aunt, it is a favourite opinion of my father's that <u>things come in bundles</u> – That people come in bundles, is, I think true as having lived without seeing a creature but our own family for months, a press of company comes all at once. The very day the Buckleys had come to us and filled every nook in the house the enclosed letter was brought to me … On opening the letter and seeing the signature of Ward I was in hopes it was the Mr Ward who … wrote the review of Patronage [*her new novel*] in the "Quarterly" …

---

153 Wellington's affairs in Paris were notorious.

of whom Madame de Staël said he was the only man in England who really understood the art of conversation. However upon re-examining the signature I found our gentleman was another Ward who is called the great R. Ward on whom Lady Holland wrote this epigram

"Ward has no heart they say – But I deny it.
He has a heart and gets his speeches by it"

How an epigram does prejudice us! I could never get this out of my head all the time he was in the house – He spent 2 days with us – and is just gone – He is a very gentle … courtierly agreeable man of the world, full of anecdotes & *bons mots* & compliments all of which he dishes out with a lavish hand … I am sure he thought we had heard Lady Holland's epigram and he exerted himself with superfluity of sentiment to convince us that he had a heart feeling alive …

Mr Ward was Under-Secetary of State during a great part of Pitt's administration and … is Clerk of the Ordnance and has been sent to Ireland to reform abuses in the ordnance dept … He told me he had heard in London that I had a sort of Memoria Technica by which I could remember everything that was said in conversation and by certain movements of my fingers could note down … all the ridiculous points!! When he first mentioned that he was determined to go to Edgeworthstown Mrs Ward exclaimed "Is it possible you will venture there when you know Miss E has the quickest eye for the ridiculous of anybody living and you know you are the most ridiculous man alive." …

Some of his stories at dinner were so entertaining that even old George [*Bristow*]'s face cut in wood could not stand it and … I thought the second course would never be on the table …

TO HARRIETTE EDGEWORTH
Edgeworthstown, 18 September 1816

… [*Mr Ward*] was much struck with Honora's beauty – said she so much resembled Lady Nugent that he was sure from the first moment he was introduced to her that he had seen her in a former state of existence as Lady Nugent – Pray enquire about Lady N. and look at her well if possible …

TO J.L. FOSTER
Edgeworthstown, 28 October 1816

> *John Leslie Foster had written asking Maria for a list of suitable books for*
> *children for the Kildare Place Society, which provided free schooling for the poor.*

I think your choice and your reasons for the choice of books you mention judicious –

For your first purpose to render reading easy and to make it agreeable to children the little stories from Mrs Barbauld's Lessons – Early Lessons & Parents Assistant – may as you propose be varied with <u>fables</u> with <u>cuts</u> [*woodcuts?*] & without morals – In spite of all Rousseau says, fables are easily understood & liked by children.

Pray remember <u>Bewicks</u> <u>Birds,</u> <u>Quadrupeds</u> <u>and</u> <u>Fishes</u> ... As to Fairy Tales I have no objection to a few of them for the purpose of luring the young reader on. We see how universally the Arabian Tales are liked by children of all ranks ... A selection from the Persian and Arabian Tales might be made – The Olive merchant beautiful! – Nine statues – Mahomet & his flying box (I forget the name of the story) – Aladdin's Cave etc. In reprinting these stories perhaps your literary gentleman might add touches of morality ... For example – instead of making Aladdin a worthless boy running around the streets ... let him be a remarkably industrious little fellow & much attached to his mother ... A few touches would make an honest boy of the little rogue and spendthrift in the Persian Tales who becomes possessed of the delightful flying box.

... Pray do not imagine I want to turn the Arabian & Persian Tales into moral tales ... Believe me, I am well aware by useful experience (vide Patronage) of the danger of making the morality of a fiction too prominent – I have repented – hope never to be <u>found</u> <u>out</u> in a moral again whilst I live. I am particularly aware that the Irish would be averse to dull morality – that Pat would say "True, your Honour – true for your Honour – too true" and the moment your back was turned would add "But I've no call for it."

From fables & fairy tales it will be easy to pass on to stories representing real life. Among those I wish you would recommend "The son of a genius" – a small volume worth many a large one. And here Sandford & Merton[154] immediately occurs as a book containing the active history of boys & therefore

---

154 By her father's old friend Thomas Day.

extremely interesting to boys – I know my father thinks this book would be dangerous to the lower Irish on account of the taunts ... at <u>gentlemen</u>. But I do not think there is in the book a <u>democratic</u> spirit – or spirit of insubordination to laws or the powers that be. The character of Sandford is so noble – the sympathy he excites for the great fundamental virtues – truth – courage – humanity – fidelity in friendship – independence & industry – is so powerful that I cannot relinquish the hope that Sandford & Merton may be received in the Irish Popular Library – Your literary gentleman may clear it of all which I am persuaded Mr Day himself would have wished to be retracted if he had lived to see the French revolution ...

To excite & to lead on gradually to the love of useful knowledge I know of no books equal to Evenings at Home. Atkins' Arts of Life useful but dry – Book of Trades – cuts [*woodcuts*] excellent – explanations ... often inadequate – My father is now writing lessons for Lovell's school which will accomplish in some measure what the Book of Trades has attempted ... You mention Leadbeater's Cottage Dialogues – they are excellent. I have seen them tried upon the class they were intended for with the best effect ...

Maria's list is followed by several more pages probably dictated by her father, recommending books for older boys, 'giving to the lower classes of Irish some food for their military spirit' – such as The Life of Nelson *or* The Seige of Serangapam – *yet 'discouraging revolution'. He recommended a recent penny life of Bonaparte as 'showing to what tyranny revolutionary government leads' and the* Memoirs of Madame de la Roche-Jacquelin *about La Vendée as 'showing the horrors of civil war'. In old age, his early radicalism had all but disappeared. But his enthusiasm for education for all classes had not. And he showed full support for his oldest son, Lovell, who had just set up his new model school at Edgeworthstown, ambitiously intended to bridge both class and religious barriers.*

TO SOPHY RUXTON
18 November 1816

... Lovell and his school go on admirably – Nothing can be more amiable and respectful (and I firmly believe sincere) than his behaviour to my father – and to myself everything that I could wish for, so perfectly at ease with me that I feel at ease quite with him – and as to the rest, I have, thank heaven the <u>worst</u>

of memories & the most convenient – It is a sieve through which all the bad slips and all the good remains …

TO MRS BILLAMORE
Edgeworthstown, December 1816

Their faithful housekeeper had gone to visit Black Castle for a rest.

My dear good Mrs Billamore, I write as I promised you … [*to*] tell you how all your children do and how all is going on in your absence – in one word the children are all <u>well</u> – and my father pretty <u>well</u> … and therefore enjoy yourself completely at dear Black Castle … I need not ask you whether you are happy – I know it is impossible for anyone so nearly connected with this family as you are to be anything but delighted at Black Castle. I hope you have walked all the pretty walks – and that you have not walked yourself off your legs.

I turned a pig away yesterday from your tree where he was routing with his snout & Prince was so cowardly that he did not dare to pull him by the ears; he only barked round and round and the pig despising him for a poltroon … So I roared at my window

"Is there anybody alive in the backyard" –

"Yes, Ma'am, Pat" –

"Then run and drive the pig that is routing at Mrs Billamore's tree."

It was raining very hard & Pat in his yellow waistcoat which you know he is scrupulous about wetting, but he ran out instantly & stoned the pig & when the pig ran & squeaked Prince grew wondrous brave & chased him <u>through</u> the gate in triumph …

Marianne has taken the jar into the flagged room to pound the pomatum – Lucy desires me to say that she is pounding away.

Fanny & Sophy desire me to tell you that they do the fruit for dessert <u>everyday</u> and Honora <u>generally</u> – So how it is I don't know – All that I know is that we have plenty every day & that it is a wonder in these hard times & Mrs Billamore away!

John Langan says that Mistress Billamore will be <u>fit</u> <u>to</u> <u>be</u> <u>tied</u> when she hears that the master gave Pat Connell four guineas a hundred for the butter instead of three pounds five for which Mrs Billamore bargained for it.

But Kitty, my dear, if you had seen how happy Pat Connell looked when he came to pay his rent & my father allowed him that unexpected price! – His

*Kitty Billamore, the
Edgeworths' faithful
English housekeeper.*

long chin became two inches shorter & tho' he looked before as if he had never
smiled since he was created, he smiled without power to help it & went away
with as sunshiny a face as ever you saw, <u>carrolling</u> his Honour's praises for the
best landlord in the 3 counties.

    Adieu, my dear good Kitty

*   By January 1817 Richard Lovell Edgeworth was clearly dying and he impressed
on Maria that his dearest wish was to see her latest novel,* Ormond, *published
before he died. He forbade her to waste time on writing letters – a promise that
Maria found almost impossible to keep. One way round it was to use Fanny as
her scribe.*

TO AUNT RUXTON [*in Fanny's writing*]
5 February 1817

My father has made it a serious point with me not to write any letters whatever
for a couple of months – But I shall certainly burst if I did not in that time
empty my mind to you – and fortunately I have a dear sister who is so entirely

a second self that I can empty my mind through her to you – … I cannot explain to you exactly why I am so earnest to finish what I am now doing, but you must take it on my word that it is essential to my happiness & to my going on well with my father – it is a new story and that is all I can say – But I cannot leave you groping in the dark …

If you recollect when we used to talk about Mr Corry[155] when you used to make me laugh by the hour, we agreed that I might introduce such a character provided I did not make it too like the original. Now I am attempting this … I am particularly anxious to know from you how I may go – and these are my questions – Do you think I may venture to use the handfuls of hemlock for the gout – The propping up of the roof while he builds up to it – The making of the postchaise … with his own hands. I shall not put in the blasting – tempting, almost irresistibly tempting as it is – The character upon the whole, I think, would rather flatter him if he read it, for my man is represented as a man of extraordinary genius, though but half civilised … "a mixture of the savage virtues & vices of the Csar Peter & of the shrewd humour of Sancho Panza". The man has a daughter but she is not in the least like Letty Corry – The chances are that Mr Corry himself would never read [*it*] unless he were put on the scent, but my uncle Ruxton & Letty R certainly would – So, my dear aunt, hold a bed of justice directly with Sophy & before I fall in love any further with my new born, send me word posthaste how far I may go. Pray give me your consent as I am already so far gone I cannot live without him …

There is the horn – we must go to breakfast – or we shall be found out …

But she could not resist exchanging literary and other gossip with Sneyd, who was now in Paris, or writing to her beloved Fanny who had gone up to Dublin for an operation on her eye.

TO SNEYD EDGEWORTH
Edgeworthstown, 29 March 1817

… I agree with you entirely in thinking the *Monument* [*de Saint Hélène*] a magnificent performance … I could not help sitting up to read it … My father is strongly of the opinion it is not written by Bonaparte and he grounds this opinion chiefly upon the passage relative to the Duke d'Enghien, he thinks no

---

155 The Ruxtons' brother-in-law – see Maria's letter in 1808 about her visit to his house.

man in writing, not even Nero, would in writing for posterity choose to say he had "committed a <u>crime</u> instead of a <u>fault</u>".

... Upon the whole I think that if it were not written, it was dictated by Bonaparte – His <u>mind</u> if not his <u>hand</u> is in it ... I know of but three people in Europe who could have written it – Madame de Staël, Talleyrand & Monsieur Dumont. Madame de Stael, though she has <u>abilities</u> enough, has not such habits of declamation ... she would never have got so plainly – shortly – & rapidly – through it. Talleyrand ... could not for the soul of him have refused himself a little more wit & wickedness – Dumont has not audacity of mind enough – [156]

... Henry Hamilton told us of the Duchess of Wellington when she was first ambassadress at Paris. Talleyrand called upon her – she was at first very unwilling to receive him, having a swelled face caused by a dreadful toothache. But when he came upstairs, notwithstanding <u>his</u> diseased, disgusting, frightful figure, his charming conversation, his wit & politeness made her forget <u>her</u> pain and she was quite <u>sorry</u> when he got up to go away ...

TO FANNY EDGEWORTH [*written by Harriet*]
Edgeworthstown, 2 April 1817

How kind & generous you are to write to one who cannot answer you

... If you do not buy yourself a pretty, an exceedingly pretty body [*bodice*], I will never forgive [*you*] and remember it is not yours but mine. And also buy for yourself a very pretty handsome comb for your hair ... Goodbye now, for I will not trouble you with my commissions until you have done your own ... I have 100 pages to write in this month & I shall go on upon them as long as I did upon the forty of The Absentee – My father hears my mother read over & corrects what I have written ... every night after I go to bed, which I do at eleven – and I walk every day & you will find me blooming like a rose ...

> *But Honora reported to Fanny life at Edgeworthstown as 'peculiarly unpleasant – my poor father so ill – my mother without sleep – Maria so miserable & yet working so hard all the time ... Harriet is reading a chapter of Maria's to my father in the morning as well as those my mother reads at night – so that he will sooner have done ...'*

---

156   The author was the Duc de las Casas who had accompanied Bonaparte into exile in St Helena.

By May, miraculously, Maria's book was finished and the first proofs arrived in time for her father's seventy-third birthday.

TO SOPHY RUXTON
Edgeworthstown, 31 May 1817

This day so anxiously expected has arrived – the only birthday of my father's for many, <u>many</u> years which does not bring with it feelings of <u>unmixed</u> pleasure – The first words I heard from Harriet were –"My father bids me tell you he is alive but that is all" – He had a terrible night – sick – sick – continuously with wracking pain in his head from the ineffectual effort – But when I went into his room and stood at the foot of his bed, his voice was strong & cheerful <u>as usual</u> and his face did not look so ill as I had expected. He said "Read the letter from Hunter, my dear". I did. It was a letter expressing the greatest delight at my father's reconcilement letter and saying that he feels proud and grateful that he is "connected with a man of such high honour & liberality etc etc". – Then I put into his hand 160 pages of Ormond which <u>kind</u>, yes I will say, <u>kindhearted</u> Hunter (God bless him for it!) had successfully managed to get ready for this day – How my dear father can in the midst of such suffering … feel so much pleasure as he does for such things is astonishing! Oh my dear Sophy, what must be the fund of warm affection from which this springs … It is wonderful (I cannot help reporting it while the feeling is still fresh in my mind) how my father's spirit lights up again phoenix like in an instant. His voice is <u>never</u> altered … [*it*] seems the voice of his incorrigible [?] mind, not his perishing body – "Call Sneyd to me directly."

My father swallowed some stirabout & cream & felt, he said, renovated – Sneyd was seated at the foot of his bed. "Now, Maria, <u>dip</u> in anywhere in Ormond – Read just there! Ha – at last I have brought you to obey me – Read on". I began "King Corny recovered" –

Then he said "I must tell Sneyd the story up to this."

And most eloquently & most beautifully did he tell the story – No mortal could have guessed that he was an invalid if they had <u>only</u> heard him <u>speak</u> …

I shall keep this letter open till the last moment that I may tell you how my father goes through the day – The children – Francis – Pakenham – Lucy & even the august Sophy are all running about this delicious day gathering all the flowers that can be found to celebrate this – Oh Sophy – last birthday – Poor Kitty has from her little spit of her garden produced a profusion of flowers – and she has been making cakes and preparing creams and the joy of the innocent unforseeing children is most touching – and melancholy –

Just as I had stopped writing, my father came into this room very weak & looking wretchedly, but ordered the carriage and said he would go to Longford to see Mr Fallon and settle about materials for William's bridge – ate a little broth – and we set out at once. He took with him his 3 sons & Maria to read Ormond – Great delight to me … and this wonderful father of mine went all the way through the tumult [?] of the most crowded market I ever saw … stayed near over an hour upon the bridge talking to Mr Fallon and was not at home till ½ after six … I do not tell you that he was not tired for he was so weak he could hardly stand when he got out of the carriage … He could not dine with us – Poor Kitty's trifle & all her good things in vain for him … After dinner he sent for us all into the library … father in his chair by the fireside – the champagne which he intended to drink with Aunt Charlotte on the table – We all sat there – Mama in the opposite armchair – Pakenham in the chair behind her – Francis on a stool at her feet. Maria beside them … Lucy – Sneyd … then on the sofa Honora – F – H & S – The two aunts next to my father & Lovell between them … I know you would like to see it all … In the midst of all the gaiety & talking and tasting champagne for the first time, my father in a feebler voice than I ever heard him speak said "<u>Yes – do my dear children – all be happy on your father's birthday – his last birthday</u>" – …

(Between dinner & tea) He is asleep now & I came up to my room where I have never written or sat since you were here with me … Adieu my dear friend – There is nobody in the world but you and my beloved aunt to whom I would & COULD have written so much.

Nine days later, Maria was called to her father's room – and in an extraordinary scene, he knelt in his nightshirt at her feet and begged her to promise never to squander the principal of her fortune. After his death, she would be rich and her many brothers and sisters would make claims upon her – which she must resist – quoting the example of Mrs Powys, an old family friend, once well off who now had to beg charity from her friends. Falling to her knees in turn Maria assured him that she was now quite cured of 'silly generosity'. He died five days later and she was to abide strictly by her promise for her remaining life. Far more important at the time were his last words for her: 'I did not know how much I loved Maria till I came to the parting with her.'

The last portrait of Richard Lovell Edgeworth, painted by Hugh Douglas Hamilton.

MEMOIRS

OF

RICHARD LOVELL EDGEWORTH, ESQ.

BEGUN BY HIMSELF

AND

CONCLUDED BY HIS DAUGHTER,

MARIA EDGEWORTH.

IN TWO VOLUMES.

VOL. I.

LONDON:

PRINTED FOR R. HUNTER,

Successor to Mr. Johnson,

NO. 72, ST. PAUL'S CHURCHYARD,

AND

BALDWIN, CRADOCK, AND JOY,

PATERNOSTER ROW.

1820.

VI

JUNE 1817 – OCTOBER 1825

RICHARD LOVELL EDGEWORTH *had worked out his will with great care. After thirty years of excellent estate management, helped by high agricultural prices generated by the wars with France, he was now a rich man and able to provide well for all his surviving children. His oldest son Lovell was to inherit a third of the estate immediately and the rest was to be put in trust to pay legacies to his widow, Maria and the younger children. Sneyd, Honora and William had already inherited Sneyd money from their mother. Maria was to have £500 a year, which with her substantial earnings from novels made her richer than she had ever expected.*

But there was the immediate problem of where the family would live. Frances, his widow, had six young children, of whom the two boys Francis and Pakenham were still only eight and five, and dreaded having to look for a new home. Much to her and Maria's great relief, Lovell behaved with 'the greatest kindness and generosity' and begged that they should share the house with him at least until he had found a wife. By pooling their financial resources, they could afford to live there much as they had before. The two Sneyd aunts, Charlotte and Mary, now in their late sixties, would return to their brother's house, Byrkley Lodge in England, as planned, taking their niece, Honora with them.

The main emotional burden for caring for all the Edgeworth children, old and young, now fell on Maria's stepmother. Deciding it was best for herself to remain at home with the younger children, she dispatched Maria and her oldest daughter

Fanny, 'who suffers most of all of us', to stay with Maria's adored Aunt Ruxton
at Black Castle. This would also give Maria time and space enough to begin the
project she dreaded but felt herself bound to accept – her father's dying wish was
that she should finish and publish his memoirs, parts of which he had written years
earlier and other sections dictated to her in his last weeks of life.

In the Memoirs, *Maria's stepmother wrote that Maria was unable to write*
letters in the months following her beloved father's death. In reality Maria's desire
to communicate by letter to those she loved was as strong as ever and burst out to
her stepmother almost as soon as she had left home.

TO MRS EDGEWORTH
Black Castle, late June 1817

My dearest friend, there is no employment so agreeable to me at this moment
as writing to you, and therefore I hope you will not be displeased at my
disobeying your injunction against writing letters – I write <u>no</u> others – except
a note to our good friend Mrs Fox & one to Harriet B[*eaufort*] …

Fanny this morning is gone with William in his gig to Collon [*the*
Beaufort's house] – The day not very promising – but she is well wrapped up in
a <u>box</u> coat of Bess Ruxton's – They will either stay to dinner or not according
to the weather – But Wm cannot stay all night as he must be off to his business
in the morning … Sunday is to him a day of rest but as he says an idle day at
present is to him most insupportable – He has worked very hard – yesterday
<u>too</u> hard as he walked 12 miles which but for some error … about the gig
might have been avoided … His face is so sunburned & blistered that all his
employers must admire him – He is very prudent & resolute in not answering
questions about his opinions as to the general expediency of the canal … He
thinks his out of door business cannot be finished in less than three days more
– This you know will bring our stay here to about ten days from the time we
left you – I should like to return home and so would Fanny … with William
– for though my aunt Ruxton's company & kindliness are delightful to me …
yet … I really wish to have more of my dear aunt Mary & Charlotte's society
before they leave … <u>Besides</u> for my own particular satisfaction of mind & body,
I <u>want</u> the interest, the <u>necessity</u> of occupation which I <u>can</u> find nowhere else
but at home.

... Murray[157] who goes on heaping coals of fire on my poor little bald (now literally <u>bald</u>) head has this day sent me a new poem "Paris" – but from the first look at it I know I cannot read it – Sneyd has taken Lord Byron's tragedy which Murray sent me to Dalkey but I shall desire him to send it here for my aunt ...

[*Postscript*] I am glad Lovell is going to act as a magistrate – quite right in all he has done.

TO MRS EDGEWORTH
Black Castle, [?] July 1817

... [*Francis Beaufort*] in his letter to Wm says that he has written various notes to people in London that I might not be plagued with literary letters ... He asked my general wishes as to the books[158] – I wrote in reply a request that he wd give & send them to whoever he pleased (accepting a copy for himself) and I told him my general, my <u>only</u> wish is not to hear of Harrington & Ormond till time has deadened the exquisitely painful & pleasurable associations that these names create ...

I shall be with you at home soon – And yet I am sure being here with my dear aunt who is kindness itself has been of great use to me – I eat – drink – sleep – like a natural animal – & am quite well – Fanny has a tinge of colour in her pale cheeks today – took a little row in the boat with Sophy – much the better for it ...

TO MRS EDGEWORTH [*fragment, n.d.*]

... The Bishop of M[*eath*] has urged to see me – But I declined & wrote as kindly as I felt to dear excellent Mrs O'Beirne who <u>luckily</u> was prevented from coming by a terribly swelled painful face. Wm went there ... The Bishop was kind to him ... and very talkative – But did not ask painful questions ... The Bishop ... <u>now</u> thinks this canal scheme unnecessary. How he does whiffle about! Wm says that every hope of employment has so raised the spirits of the poor people that he quite dreads the consequences ... if it should not go on – The people ... appear wonderfully and patient even under the pressure of famine[159] ... the

---

157 John Murray, the famous London publisher.

158 *Ormond* and *Harrington* (her 'Jewish' novel) had been published together.

159 There had been a second bad harvest and partial potato failure.

whole time of Sophy & Margaret is taken up with this soup shop – They do more than I could have thought possible – Since Richard came, conversation morning, noon & night about soup & various ways of preparing it with ricemeal etc – He changes his mind 5 times a day at least … What a blessing … I have still … for my best friend and guide a woman of a strong mind …

TO MRS EDGEWORTH
Black Castle, 9 July 1817

… Fanny bathed yesterday … for the first time – liked it much … I think it will do her good. – This is the first great inducement for me to stay a few days longer … Now be an honest woman, as I am – So help you – Let me know if there is any reason … or 1/100th part of a wish to the contrary.

I wrote a few days ago to Hunter to desire he would let me know & send me anything which has appeared in the papers about my father … also desire Hunter to send me any good pieces of biography he has heard of …

Oh my dear mother – what a great trust he has left me – Heaven grant that I may justify his opinion in this instance above all others and then I think I should die satisfied –

My aunt has given me all my father's delightful letters to her – I have read and re-read them and you shall have the pleasure – I have met many of yours too which made me love you – not <u>more</u> but the same as ever – There is a great pleasure is seeing in a long course of letters the consistency of a character and the consistency of affection – This I must say I have also seen with satisfaction (I will not call it <u>vanity</u> …) in my own letters both to my aunt & Sophy – immense bundles which they produced to my astonishment! Some of them will be of great value to me for my father's life – I mean to remind me of circumstances about Rebellion and Telegraph …

Without looking them over, I let Frannikin have the rummaging of 30 years exchanges with my most intimate friends … to whom I wrote all the nonsense that comes into head & heart …

Fanny is at this moment returned with my aunt from a visit to Ardbraccan … While they were [*there*] and I sitting alone in the bow window of this room scribbling to you, there drove dashing to the door a coach & 4 & two outriders in fine liveries – Now guess who – Ham Garnet & his sister! I scuffled out of the room – they left their names & messages to Miss E etc – My aunt's sudden imagination draws conclusion which I forbear to repeat because they would make you <u>smile</u> – and yet <u>that</u> is the very reason I should tell it you …

Recollect then that Ham said Miss Fanny is the most beautiful girl in Ireland – My aunt is now penning a <u>note</u> to Ham & invitation …

After a meeting in Navan Ld Fingal met my aunt's carriage in the street & coming up to the window whispered

"A piece of news you'll be glad to hear – I'm going to marry my daughter – well & happily – but I am so nervous about it – she will live in Wales away from us – a Catholic gentleman, a Mr Jones – He has ten thousand a year – lives in a most beautiful part of South Wales – Lady Harriet is to have £10,000 – and £10,000 hereafter & it is all delightful!"

And so the world goes on, some marrying! Some dying! Some dashing about in chaises & fours – and so the world <u>must</u> go while we live – and when we are dead and buried! …

Farewell dear mother, I am glad you have so many children and each of them objects of love and warm interest to me. Give my affectionate love to my dear aunts – Tell my dear aunt Mary I am not yet quite blunted to the sight of Harrington or Ormond – that poor orphan book …

Maria returned home a week later, and began the task of transcribing her father's unfinished manuscript, carefully consulting her family as to necessary omissions or alterations. She felt herself still incapable of writing or adding to it herself.

TO AUNT RUXTON
Edgeworthstown, 24 July 1817

My dearest aunt – <u>Why</u> I have not written to you I am sure you know – that I have been as busy as any working bee that ever existed – Literally have not had a moment's time except by candlelight … Now I am within sight of Finis – all the <u>readers</u> have been working as hard as myself to read one after another 600 pages of MS. – No easy task – All the house has been reading – thinking – copying for me with all their might … We have this day dispatched in a portfolio and carpetbag about 200 pages by the coach to Harriet Beaufort who will forward it by Saturday's mail coach to Dr Beaufort – I have written specially to Louisa to beg that if Dr Beaufort cannot immediately read it she directly send … it to you – but let me beg my dear friends that you will <u>fall to</u> reading it directly …

TO SNEYD AND HARRIETTE
Edgeworthstown, 8 August 1817

... Thankyou for the inestimable treasure you lent me of [*my father's*] letters to Dr Darwin.[160]

As my aunts & Honora are going from us I thought it both just & kind that they should know all that so much concerns those they have loved best, I proposed to read to them [*her father's manuscript*] – an hour every day – every morning in my room – I have read about 5 days and all are delighted & touched by the simplicity of the writing. I would never have had the courage to open the MS from that 10th June when I closed it at the page he last dictated to be inserted in the early part ...

I have employed myself only in reading letters – some of my father's incomparable – all showing wonderful consistency of character – It has been a melancholy yet soothing gratifying task. I have also begun to copy his dear MS that we may preserve his in his own hand in the family ...

TO SNEYD EDGEWORTH
Edgeworthstown, 21 August 1817

Thankyou, my polite as well as kind brother for the gift[161] & the manner of giving – the French proverb says who ever gives quickly gives doubly – I say who ever gives politely gives <u>cubically</u>.

I have been so long this morning rummaging over 400 letters to pick out some which I thought I <u>might</u> send you & Harriette that now I barely have time to write the needful.

I shall not send my father's letters to me till I have a safe private hand for they are such treasures & I am a miser!

I send you now several of my own in which your name & early history ... sometimes recur in little shining mica scraps – Harriette in these letters will see my mind without a rag to cover it or bless itself with – I hope she will not be shocked – There is a great deal of nonsense but I trust all to yours and her mercy – As far as I am concerned, I would rather my friends should know me to be just what I am ...

---

160 Dr Erasmus Darwin, founding member of the Lunar Society and one of Richard Lovell Edgeworth's oldest friends.

161 She had requested her father's copy of Bentham's legislature.

Maria's next letter to Sneyd gives a breathless account of an American lawyer's
arrival at Edgeworthstown to check out possible claims for her brother Richard's
claims to the Edgeworthstown estate. Richard, long dead, had two surviving
sons. Fortunately, after inspecting leases, the lawyer appeared satisfied with a
small final settlement of £500 and Honora was able to lend the money to pay
him off. A few weeks later, Honora and the Sneyd aunts set off for their journey
to Byrkley Lodge in Staffordshire, escorted by Lovell. Honora wrote sadly that
Lovell felt he was a jailer delivering his prisoners to a new keeper and how she
dreaded the monotonous luxurious life that lay ahead. Maria wrote to the three
exiles to pass on all the gleanings of news likely to be of interest.

TO THE SNEYD AUNTS AND HONORA
Black Castle, 27 November 1817

My very dear friends – How many times have you said in your hearts "Maria
has forgotten us" "Never! – never! – never" says Aunt Mary, Aunt Charlotte &
Honora – "Thankyou – thankyou – thankyou" – & I assure you all three jointly
& severally were never more decidedly right in all the days of your three lives
– The fact is that whenever I was going to write, either my mother, Sophy,
Fanny, Harriet, my aunt or Sophy Ruxton were just going to write or had
just written or had half written … and I as in duty or modesty or prudence
postponed my intended letter. But this morning … I am determined to write
and get my own frank …

We spent a very pleasant week at Ardbraccan … Mrs O'Beirne pronounced
such praise of Fanny as brought peony color to my mother's cheeks & tears to
her eyes – You know one word of praise from Mrs O'Beirne is as valuable as
<u>stern</u> sincerity can make it. Sophy sang the Scottish Mariners – & other hymns
for the bishop & he was charmed by her …

… I believe Sophy Ruxton told you that we have had the pleasure of the
conversation of Mr Talbot who has visited all the four quarters of the world and
who talks as familiarly of Cairo & Constantinople & the pyramids & Pompey's
pillar as we should of Dublin or Longford … All the entertaining & curious
things he told us which I wished to remember for you I have forgotten except
that his sister went up Pompey's pillar with the assistance of a ladder of ropes –
she had a British navy officer on each side & found it a very pleasant experience –

Mr T hurried us from Constantinople to Cairo & from Cairo to New
York & lake Ontario with the power of true genius – He spoke better of the

Americans than anyone I ever heard ... and seemed quite vexed at our having been prejudiced against them – You know he has a brother who left the British service ... & <u>returned</u> to the Lake Ontario where he purchased a great tract of land & is now living as an American chief – doing all <u>European</u> things for himself, even blacking his own shoes – How Mr Day would admire him –

We asked after our friend Lord Selkirk – Mr T said he does not comprehend the business that is now going on between him & the <u>Companies</u> – nobody does ... The settlement he attempted in Canada has totally failed ... He bought a vast swamp which he attempted to stock with sheep & of course the sheep all died of rot – He took over a colony of highlanders who had never been used to cutting trees as Dr Johnson would say because they had no trees in Scotland to cut down – These poor highlanders have perished & are perishing & I fear cannot be saved – Such are the consequences of obstinacy upon a large scale – even with a very benevolent disposition.[162]

... From America I will ship to Baggot Street – Sneyd has not yet set or heard of a tenant for his house in <u>Town</u> – but he has done with the house at Dalkey ... Meantime he gave ... a delightful dinner to Lady Dorothea Cuffe – now Campbell – They had a French cook for the day – at a guinea ... but all his fine dishes – *perdrix aux choux* – *tendrons de veau à la jardinière* and *poularde à la béchamel* were thrown away upon the company who devoted themselves to good white soup, fish, roast mutton & talking – Sneyd was called out after dinner & feared some disaster – But it was only for a bottle of wine for the French cook <u>who</u> <u>always</u> <u>expects</u> <u>it</u> .

Of books I have only to say that James' Travels in Sweden, Norway & Russia are delightful – and contain a <u>delightful</u> character of one who was once dear to me[163] & though he is now indifferent to me, I like to hear his praise – I rejoice that I did not marry him & that I did not leave my father – but I know it would have given that dear generous father pleasure to read his praises – There is an account of his inventions in mechanics & it is really gratifying to me to see how like his inventions & pursuits were to my father –

... I am now writing absolutely in the dark & Sophy snatches the pen from my hand – Enter <u>candles</u> ...

---

162 The 5th Earl of Selkirk had tried to set up a colony of poor Scottish farmers in the Red River Valley in Canada but clashed with the two companies who owned the fur trading rights. He bought part shares in one, the Hudson Bay Company, and made a deal with them, but serious conflict developed with the other, culminating in the Battle of Seven Oaks in which the local governor and twenty-one Scottish settlers were killed.

163 Her only suitor, the Chevalier Edelcrantz.

TO HARRIET BEAUFORT
Black Castle, 15 December 1817

> *Maria had been invited by Harriet to contribute to a literary review.*

I thought, my dear friend, that you had been aware that my thoughts are so
entirely intent on writing my father's life that I have it absolutely not in power
to engage in any other literary undertaking ... I cannot conceive any motive
upon earth that would induce me to let any other <u>literary</u> <u>employment</u> interfere
for one hour with so sacred a duty which I have promised to perform ...

Putting my present peculiar situation & duty & feelings out of the question
... writing for a review would be odious to me ... It would be utterly repugnant
to my taste & habits to criticize & cut & slash my fellow authors & <u>authoresses</u>
– and unless you cut & slash you are good for nought as a reviewer ...

Several years ago Mr Jeffrey wrote to me ... most particularly to request that
I would ... assist in the Edinburgh Review – assuring me of inviolable secrecy
(the old story!) my choice of any books & terms & time I chose ... I wrote my
answer ... it was a decided refusal – in what words I cannot recollect but for the
reasons I have just stated to you – adding what I admitted just now ... that there
is but one department of literature in which my knowledge & talents could
qualify me to be a critic – that is the line of belles lettres and works of fiction –
the very line in which I write myself – and in which I should therefore think it
<u>indelicate</u> if not absolutely dishonest to <u>review</u> – to deprecate my rivals – and to
<u>curry</u> <u>favour</u> – (odious expression! and odious action!) for myself ...

My very dear Harriet, believe me it is exceedingly painful to me to refuse
you ...

> *For the rest of the winter and spring Maria was working steadily to finish
> her father's* Memoirs, *diverting herself only by writing to Aunt Ruxton about
> the latest family reading – and a brief visit to Sneyd's newly rented house in
> Wicklow.*

TO AUNT RUXTON
Edgeworthstown, 21 February 1818

... I entirely agree with you, my dearest aunt, on one subject as indeed I
generally do on most subjects – but particularly about Northanger Abbey &

Persuasion – Northanger Abbey I feel to be one of the most stupid nonsensical fictions I ever read (excepting always the praises of myself & Lady Delacour). The behaviour of the General in packing off the young lady without a servant or the common civilities which any bear of a man not to say gentleman would have shown is quite outrageously out of nature – The whole I cd abuse with satisfaction for an hour but that it is not worth a moment's consideration – Yet many folks prefer it to Persuasion – None in this house, thank Heaven!

Persuasion, excepting always the tangled useless histories of the family in the first 50 pages, appears to me in all that relates to poor Anne & her loves to be exceedingly interesting & natural – The love & lover admirably well drawn so that we feel it is quite real – Don't you see Captain Wentworth or rather in her place, feel him taking the boisterous child off her back as she kneels by the sick boy on the sofa? And is not the first meeting after their long separation admirably well done? And the overheard conversation about the nut? And – But I must stop – We have got no further than the disaster of Miss Musgrove in jumping off the step.

… I am going on but very slowly & not to my own satisfaction with my work … But … you may be certain that I shall persevere in fulfilling the last duty of that partnership which nothing but the stroke of death could terminate on his side. Indeed while the hand of death was on him, he worked unceasingly & almost miraculously for me …

TO AUNT RUXTON
Spring Farm, Newtown Mount Kennedy, 20 May 1818

… This house [*rented by Sneyd*] is far beyond my expectations commodious & agreeable … Nine bedchambers besides 3 for men servants in the offices – a delightful library & agreeable sitting room – as to the number of doors, Edgeworthstown is nothing to this house! – It is said a carpenter who came to view it lay awake a whole night afterwards endeavouring in vain to count the doors …

The beauties of the County of Wicklow of which I am told I have as yet seen nothing astonish & delight me … I will only tell you what I have seen but not attempt description … !!!!

Drive from Dublin to Bray – Glen of the Downs – drive to Powerscourt church – Grattans [?] – Powerscourt etc seen only from the road – Lady Harriet Daly's seen only as we drove through to return a morning visit – Drive through Mr Gunn's [?] place, Mount Kennedy – Went to see Woodstock ... nothing remarkable – tho' we shd think it beautiful in our flat pancake Cty of Longford ... Met Lady Harriet Daly at Powerscourt church – very benevolent countenance ... and ... not ... so plain as I had been taught to expect – ... Lady Powerscourt beautiful –

Sneyd is so kind & as happy as possible – and Harriette so easy & so well bred that we feel ... completely at home ... The children are delighted from morning till night – I should observe that there is a pony here and an ass – both which make a great figure in the child's paradise – To say nothing of a barouche seat – a jaunting car & the sea! – shells on the seashore & boats inclusive ...

Farewell dearest aunt, I forgot to tell you that the first time I got up in the jaunting car – I thought I had seated myself very well – Pakenham on half my cloak between me and Mrs E – when lo! as the man whipped his horse & set off. I – standing up, I suppose – ... was as the carriage turned thrown off & out – flat I found myself on my back ... I was stunned but only for a moment – and my first thought was "Well, my dear father was right – a jaunting car as he always said is the most dangerous vehicle in the world" – I jumped up ... But when I was up I saw! ... Mrs E and Pakenham ... both down lying prostrate on their backs a yard from me ... Pakenham began to cry so I was sure he was not dead ... Mrs E could not stand at first – But sat on the edge of the grass – however she spoke & I saw there was no fractures of limbs ...

After this practical lesson in the nature of centrifugal force ... I have always sat still & held fast on a jaunting car ... but grandeur apart – I prefer our own dear carriage ...

By July Maria had finished the first draft of her father's Memoirs, *and submitted it to all the immediate family for approval. She now resolved to go to England to show it to two of her father's old friends, his brother-in-law Captain Francis Beaufort and the Swiss political economist Etienne Dumont. Dumont was due to stay at Lord Lansdowne's house, Bowood, in September where she was also invited.*[164] *She planned to bring her shy half-sister, Honora, who confessed to Sneyd her reluctance to travel in 'Maria's train ... picking up the crumbs.' To give her confidence, Maria took them both first to stay with her sister Anna and*

---

164 Dumont, originally from Geneva, had been the 2nd Lord Lansdowne's tutor and had become a close
     friend of all the leading Whigs. From hints in her letters to Sophy Ruxton and others, Maria had
     once fancied him as a suitable husband, but he remained firmly an intellectual mentor only.

Maria's dog, Foster, given her by Lord Oriel.

indulged in an orgy of shopping from the Bath dressmaker – she was feeling rich from her substantial earnings from Harrington *and* Ormond.

Much to Maria's relief, both Dumont and Francis Beaufort warmly approved the Memoirs. She went on with Honora and nineteen-year-old Fanny to spend the winter with the Sneyd relations at Byrkley Lodge in Staffordshire. They found the two Sneyd aunts sinking sadly into apathy with nothing to do, but for Honora and Fanny there were dancing lessons and parties and they were all invited to spend a dazzling week with the immensely rich Staffords at Trentham Hall – 'io livery servants', Maria reported to Fanny's mother – and 'a coach and four with two outriders' to drive them through the park.

Maria then took them back with her to London to stay with an old friend, Lady Elizabeth Whitbread in Kensington.[165] Her hopes were raised when Lady Elizabeth's handsome son took Fanny riding daily in Hyde Park. She was alarmed that her favourite half-sister would accept a proposal from Francis Beaufort's brother-in-law Lestock Wilson, a tongue-tied city broker whom Maria found painfully dull. They returned home sated with social life in early June to a house of invalids. Maria had been given a new pet dog by her father's old friend, Lord Oriel.

TO AUNT RUXTON
Edgeworthstown, 17 June 1819

"From six o'clock till breakfast time" … did my Foster lie, my dearest aunt … rolled up on my bed, at my feet, never stirs till I open my eyes and then he shakes himself and comes very modestly to lick my hand.

---

165 Widow of the radical MP Samuel Whitbread who had committed suicide in 1815.

Haymaking on the lawn at
Edgeworthstown.

He is the dearest, most amiable best bred dog of his noble and royal breed – and I thank you, my dear friends for his amiability – As you know I am pledged to believe that education does more than nature – He is as clean as a silken muff being washed regularly once a day besides all the washings in the rain and wet grass which he gives himself …

Now having spent 2 pages upon my dog it is time to think of some of my relations … My mother looks wonderfully well, considering all she has been through[166] – but I am certain that the sense of doing what is right and kind … is the best cosmetic …

Lucy is going on as well and better than Gardner expected … She has not lost flesh or colour or even her good-natured smile … She is raised a little in her bed with pillows so as to be able to write and read[167] …

Lovell's stomach has by its swelling … given us great alarm lately. He has yielded to our entreaties and goes up to town on Monday to take advice – It is a thousand pities that he should not have his health who really lives to do good to others – I cannot tell you how much [*Lovell*] has done here of all sorts of good within and without doors effectually within these last few months – At this moment he is out with his troops of 12 little happy workers from his school who are making hay on the lawn & never was hay better made. Each little troop under the command of its captain working with military order without military slavery – in busy not sullen silence …

---

166 She had taken her stepson William to England for three months to find him treatment for a nervous breakdown.

167 Lucy had developed a lesion on her spine and had been confined to bed for several months.

TO HARRIETTE EDGEWORTH
Edgeworthstown, 15 September 1819

Sneyd and his wife were still in France.

… Your letter gave me a great deal of pleasure from many causes – which if I divided into Ist, 2nd, 3rd etc my discourse might reach from here to Mullingar – I rejoice that you and Sneyd are now well enough to enjoy all the pleasures of Paris … Your visit to Mme Récamier amused us much – I do not know what Sneyd can have said to make her laugh – in my time she never went beyond the smile proscribed by Lord Chesterfield as graceful in a beauty … I think I would venture to lay a good sound wager that Mme Récamier will not go into a convent but it is a fine thing to talk of.

… Thus last week we have had the pleasure of having our kind friends Mrs & Miss Carr with us.[168] Mr Carr came over to Ireland on Excise business [*and*] was detained – Mrs E has taken advantage of the Sheriff's horses & two yellow jackets [*footmen*] to drive about – They went to Baronstown – Lady Sunderlin & Miss Catherine Malone did the joint honours of their house most amiably and gave us as fine a collection of grapes & peaches & nectarines etc as France could supply. Another morning we took them to see some of the tenants wh. Mr Curwen formerly met – Hugh Kelly's was as nice a house and parlor, gates, garden, all that should accompany a farm house as any that England could afford. James Allen – though grown very old & in a forlorn black shag wig – looked like a respectable yeoman – the country's pride – and at my instance brought out a fine group of grandchildren as ever graced a cottage lawn – indeed some of them were too nice for cottages as they were in white gowns & black lace pelerines [*capes*] it being Sunday – In driving home at the crossroads … we had the good fortune to come into the middle of an Irish dance – the audience on each of the opposite banks – picturesque youth, beauty, sunshine & variety of attitudes & expressions of enjoyment – the fiddler sitting & the dancers in all the vivacity & graces of an Irish jog delighted our English friends … It reminded me of Charlotte's drawing – by the by, some of her figures have been beautifully engraved.[169]

---

168 Friends from Hampstead. James Carr was Solicitor to the Treasury.
169 Maria had commissioned some of Charlotte's drawings to be engraved for use in her father's *Memoirs*.

'Dancing at the crossroads', Charlotte Edgeworth's original sketch of 1806.

Lord Longford luckily came here to breakfast while the Carrs were here – Miss Carr, you know, is Lady Byron's intimate friend & Lord L and all the Pakenhams are much attached to her though she had the misfortune to refuse Sir Edward – Miss Carr was so charmed with Lord L that she ended by thinking him very handsome ...

In September, to the family's joy, after a year at Byrkley Lodge, the two Sneyd aunts returned to Edgeworthstown, bringing Honora with them.

TO AUNT RUXTON
Edgeworthstown, September 1819

My dearest aunt, while my aunts Mary & Charlotte are happily lodged in their rooms taking off their bonnets, I write these few lines to joy your dear affectionate heart with the tidings of their arrival at their old home – From the moment they touched Irish ground, they have felt the worth of Irish hearts – I wish you could have seen & heard their arrival here – The poor people in the village & for many miles round had assembled; for a mile and a half from the town there was a line of children on each side of the road; from Lovell's school they met the carriage with bugles and bagpipes and all such music ... The crowd wanted to take the horses from the carriage but this was forbidden – Lovell had a few flambeaux which lighted the road completely and fortunately the horses were very steady – Good need they had of all their steadiness – Such popping of guns! Such huzzas – Such shouting – Such bonfires – Lovell walked to meet them & got in the barouche seat & came in with them.

... The whole village is illuminated to the poorest house – Every window has this day been cleaned! ...

After dinner – 9 o'clock – a fine moonlight night with clear high blue sky ... We have been walking through the village – Aunt Mary leaning on Lovell's arm & enjoying everything – not in the least tired. Every house ... most brilliantly illuminated – the arch above the town clock ... an arch of light ... ; fiddlers, pipers, horses – playing my great grandfather's march preceded us – and such perfect ... harmony prevailed as did the heart if not the ear good – Lovell opened a large school room which he had just finished and lighted it for the people that they might have a dance – All seemed happy and we enjoyed seeing my aunts so received by the people to whom they have been so many years so kind – They felt it much ...

The health of Maria's favourite half-sister, Fanny, meanwhile was causing anxiety, and she was sent to consult Dr Philip Crampton in Dublin, who had treated the dying Richard Lovell Edgeworth and become a close family friend. He reported no serious illness and recommended riding and fresh air. Maria, who believed firmly in the rule of mind over matter, hastened to feed Fanny's intellectual interests.

TO FANNY EDGEWORTH
Edgeworthstown, 20 December 1819

My dearest Fan – dearer to me than sandalwood, tortoiseshell or ivory –, Thankyou for your most kind words which repay all I have felt – for there was such a blank in my room & such a silence when I went to bed the first night you went away that I was quite melancholy ... – I am rather angry with Foster for daring to lie as he does with his head on your pillow – I stretch an old carpet over your end of the bed & there he lies ... My dear, I feel inexpressible pleasure (and therefore I try to express it) on reading Crampton's opinion of you – and of Sophy – I shall end by adoring that man.

In Brand's last number fifteen there are two or three curious facts which I am sure Crampton could not have had time to read – mention them to him – They say that Mr Zamboni [?] has made a new voltaic pole – see page 177 – Page 100 … a Dr Hutna [?](probably some fabulist) avers that he can at pleasure draw sparks from his little finger or any part of his body – I wish he could have seen my mother's exhibition of the electrical petticoat.

Page 102 look at effects of cinchona – a man cured of fever by sleeping in a room with a great quantity of fresh bark – simply by the effluvia …

I asked Lovell to send you the old newspapers – better old than none – the smell of a newspaper I know will do you good – Don't be in a hurry to come home – I can live without you …

[*Fragment*]

Enter Pakenham [*Fanny's seven-year-old brother*] one corner of handkerchief at eye & in great rage – Those impudent sheep – What do you think, Maria – Just now I went to drive them away from Honora's plot & bed & the moment I had driven 'em off when I turned my back, one came up & set his great head against my behind & knocked me down – I never saw such a sheep in my life – and he ran after me to the steps – almost …

TO FANNY EDGEWORTH

31 Merrion Street, Dublin, February 1820

(Sunday morning before breakfast)

Maria was now herself in Dublin staying with the Beaufort sisters at their aunt's house, known as La Maison des Amitiés.

… I have this day read Mrs More's Moral Sketches[170] – some chapters admirably written – lively & strong & eloquent, wonderfully so for a woman of 80. Pray get it for your reading society – the chapter on English opinion of French society & Madame de Staël etc – But one point I think she has missed – the ambition Madame de S's book will raise among English women to become leaders in politics – "England's best hope" – "Pious ladies" & the chapters on higher professions & negligent practice are excellent – and the beginning of a chapter called "The Borderers" I liked very much – She takes a world of pains

170 Hannah More, novelist, playwright and philanthropist: she had set up schools for poor children and had been much admired by Maria and her father.

to prove she is not a methodist & to please all parties – Labour in vain ... the latter half of the book is long & tiresome & too much! Too much!
Private

My dear Fanny & Harriet, I see that Marmontel's life is one of the books which Mrs More prescribes particularly & I read & I recollect that there were some pages in which Dr Beaufort said were unfit & therefore pray read only the history of the revolution in the last vol. which Mary was reading to me & his early life till he gets to Paris – for your innocent minds would not understand the evil parts yet you might be put to the blush or to the lie for having read the book – Consult your mother ...

Richard Lovell Edgeworth's Memoirs *were due to be published later that spring. Maria, who had been alarmed by the candour of her father's writing about his early life and dreaded hostile reviews, was already planning to be 'far, far away' when the* Memoirs *appeared – she had decided to take two of her half-sisters, Fanny and Harriet, to Paris. New dresses would be required for them all – but the French government was reported to have imposed heavy tariffs on foreign clothes.*

TO FANNY EDGEWORTH
Black Castle, 24 February 1820

... By a note from H[*arriet*] B[*eaufort*] this morning I find the ginghams are bought – so pray with your usual kindness to me contrive to like them – Pray do not neglect to have the petticoats so made & worn for a Miss Everard has told me of the ban [?] of things only put on & not really worn.
... Such crowds of morning visitors came yesterday – the Bishop of M. & two daughters and a Captain Stewart (Scotch Greys, cousin of Mrs O'Beirne's) – handsome & agreeable – the bishop entertaining all with anecdotes of Tom Grenville, little thinking how tender a subject it was[171] ...
Before the Bishop & train had departed came a coach full of Everards – Then a curricle with beautiful grey horses which you would have admired – Col. Plunkett, Lord Dunsany's son – shot through the jaw after the Battle of the Nile – but very talkative & entertaining nevertheless and he has been 7 years in Italy & knows every bit of marble etc – And all the society – and

---

171   Thomas Grenville, a well-known Whig politician and bibliophile, had offended her by describing the diplomatic scenes in her novel *Patronage* as unconvincing.

he talked to me with foreign politeness & English & Irish deediness who to write to serve me & gave me directions about travelling & has promised me letters – especially to Italy – and it was in vain to answer I don't intend to go to Italy ...

TO FANNY EDGEWORTH
Black Castle, 3 March 1820

... The news of Miss Tuite's marriage comes from Sonna ... – to a Mr Lyons – good old family, Co. Westmeath & he amiable but fond of inferior company – Mrs T took her abroad to break it off – but her heart nearly breaking, old Mrs Arabin has got Mrs Tuite to consent – I hear it has been a long attachment ...

... Now for the important subject of dress & smuggling – From all the enquiries I have made I am convinced that there is no danger in taking over apparel that has already been actually worn & that is bonafide for our own use, but it is necessary that I should be able to take my oath to this point. The only thing we intend to take as a present is a tabinet gown for Madame Gautier which present I give up & shall keep it for myself & then I shall swear with a clear conscience – Make four pairs of sheets, let them be marked & washed & make yourself, Harriet & myself all large sleeves – make the skirts without gores & put a breadth extraordinary in each & put three or four tucks of half an ell [?] each in each skirt so as to allow for cutting of flounces afterwards – whatever muslin remains, make into a shirt? – even if the bodice is wasted, as the muslin is cheap it will be no great loss.

Let your workmanship be as slight as possible but let your gowns be worn by Harriet & you before I come home – My own I will wear – Manage the brown net gowns after the same fashion – I have written to Mrs O'Beirne about the stockings – wear your Sutton boots, I rejoice that they fit ...

Maria with her two young half-sisters reached Paris in early May where she had rented a flat in the Faubourg St Germain. For someone who had seldom travelled abroad except under the protection of her father, she proved extraordinarily resilient as chaperone. As in London, she found herself immediately besieged by old and new acquaintances. Several Irish friends had houses there – the Granards, her neighbours from Castle Forbes in Longford, Harriet Foster, niece of her father's old friend Lord Oriel, who had married the Count de Salis, and Mr Chenevix, brother of Mrs Tuite of Sonna, who had married a rich French countess. Harriet and Fanny made their debut at Lady Granard's where Maria reported with joy that they and their dresses were much admired – Harriet in turn reported to Honora Maria's ability to turn from dazzling exchanges with French intellectuals to rolling with laughter in the privacy of their flat. From Paris they went on to stay with old Birmingham friends, the Moilliets, at their beautiful chateau outside Geneva and paid a visit to Coppet, the home of Maria's heroine, Mme de Staël (who had died three years before). After another two months in Paris, they returned to London and then by stages through England to reach Edgeworthstown in early spring. Damp Edgeworthstown was full of invalids after the winter, and Maria's youngest half-sister Lucy was still confined to bed on Crampton's orders.

TO AUNT RUXTON
Edgeworthstown, 3 March 1821

… I have nothing new to tell you of ourselves – I hope warm weather will restore Aunt Charlotte's strength … William continues perfectly well – Fanny is pretty well and rides every fine day – Lucy going on well – Honora … much thinner and weaker than she ought to be – such is our bill of health. I forgot to say that I am perfect – All but my eyes which are painful whenever I use them for more than an hour at a time … Harriet comes to read to me every morning before breakfast for an hour, sometimes two hours – This is my feast. – First she reads Orlando Furioso – a page or two which she and Fanny have translated the preceding day – then Hooker's "Essay on the means of improving Natural Philosophy" – an old essay written in Charles 2nd's time which contains more than I ever read on the same subject except Lord Bacon's – After half an hour of this solid essay which is written in the most old fashioned tiresome style imaginable, we get to Madame de Sevigné's Letters –

Tell Sophy that Peggy Tuite who turned into Peggy Mulhern has just produced a dead child – It was impossible to save both … When my mother said to Peggy's brother "Do not let people in to crowd around and heat her room" he answered "Oh ma'am sure I am standing here at the door continual to keep them out since three in the morning" – the tears dripping from his eyes fast on the ground as he spoke – He then set off to Longford in search of a physician for her … and all the time, the ould mother Tuite … was sitting rocking herself and crying under the big laurel near the gate that Peggy might not hear her …

Our excellent boy, who is a match in every … virtue for your boy John, has been ill these ten days past with erysipelas … which has ended in spitting blood … [*He*] is now out of danger and his father Brian Duffy relieved from an agony of heart which few English manufacturers would be able to comprehend – I don't think man grows in the scale of created beings by being turned into a machine – or into part of a machine – most manufacturers are only parts of machines – …

Though Maria's father had believed strongly that Ireland needed its own industrial revolution and had taken Maria on numerous visits to factories in northern England, she had remained unconvinced.

TO AUNT RUXTON
Edgeworthstown, 4 May 1821

… I beg you will obtain for me the newspapers in which the death of M. Edelcrantz is mentioned. As I am not of Margaret's opinion concerning the happiest state in the world, I rejoice that it did not fall to my lot. How unhappy I should be at this moment in Sweden, away from all my friends! Thank God & my father I have escaped this wretchedness[172] …

As Sophy is so much interested in poor Peggy Mulhern I must mention that she is getting well. I have just been to pay her a visit. When we asked her why her husband was not with her she said "Oh Ma'am, we have but the one room for all & till I am well he'd be too delicate to be coming; Barney Woods gives him a bed below."

"*Où la délicatesse va t'elle se nicher.*"

Our kitchen maid – I beg your pardon for descending to such low personages … our kitchen maid walked ten miles yesterday to see her father after she had finished her day's work. Now this father of hers is nearly a fool & quite a brute – He has constant employment as a labourer with a good gentleman but he wants to go through the world to make a beggar of himself – And his daughter went to persuade him not to make a beggar of himself – He was not at home – But he met on her way back & he beat her as he could stand over her because she advised him not to turn beggar and walk the world – And she sat down by the side of the ditch & cried – not for the beating – but

---

172 Maria had still not forgotten her only suitor who had proposed to her in Paris eighteen years before.

because he said he might as well have no daughter "Yet I send him home half of every penny I get – & can't do more & not go naked!"

The Irish are a most interesting people – What different objects of interest filled my mind and my letters this time last year & now – But I do not find that the Prince de Croen or the Princesse Galitzene etc etc etc have dilated or exalted my mind so that it cannot contrast & fasten with delight upon these low concerns.

… Margaret will agree to this and smile – smile – perhaps smile in scorn at human nature. But we, my dear aunt settle things otherwise. We do not attribute this to the want of feeling in the human heart but in its wonderful power of adapting itself to circumstance & seizing & changing to fresh objects of interest that spring from those that have been destroyed – The cuckoo is singing – Our trees, horse chestnut & beech leaf out beautifully – so I hope are yours. I have just planted two rose acacia & I hope that an ass will not eat these as he did the last I possessed –

TO AUNT RUXTON
Edgeworthstown, 8 July 1821

….. So Buonaparte is dead!¹⁷³ And no change will be made in any country by the death of a man who once made such a figure in the world! He who commanded empires and sovereigns dies a prisoner in an obscure island disputing [?] for a bottle of wine, subject to the petty tyranny of one Sir Hudson Lowe – His desiring that he should be opened & an account of the disease of which he died should be sent to his son shows that his affection for that son was real – What does his Empress think or feel – for him or for herself? And what are the chances for the little King of Rome¹⁷⁴ – or Duke of Ischia or intended Bishop?

TO AUNT RUXTON
Edgeworthstown, 3 August 1821

What do you think is my employment out of doors at this moment – and what has it been this week past – my garden – No such elegant thing – But making a gutter – a shore & a pathway in the street of Edgeworthstown & I

173 He had died on St Helena on 5 March.
174 Napoleon's son.

Edgeworthstown main street before Maria's improvements.

do declare I am as much interested about it as I ever was in writing anything in my life – We have never yet found it necessary to give some assistance to the poor labouring classes who have no work – and I find that making said gutter & pathway will employ twenty men for a fortnight or 3 weeks and feed them well with meal – with Mrs E's assistance ...

> *Queen Caroline, the estranged wife of George IV, had unexpectedly died two weeks after she had attempted to attend her husband's coronation. Maria viewed her with sympathy, fed by regular bulletins from the Queen's physician Dr Holland, although she had refused an invitation to call on her while in London. Meanwhile George IV was making a State visit to Ireland to much apparent loyal enthusiasm. When informed that 'his greatest enemy' (Napoleon) was dead, he is reported to have reacted with joy, believing they were referring to his wife.*

TO FANNY EDGEWORTH
Edgeworthstown, 13 August 1821

... The poor Queen's entrance was upon the raised platform ... destined for the K[*ing*] & nobles – she was preceded by a fisherwoman who had her cap in one hand roaring out Queen! Queen! ... The Queen passed to the Commons door of entrance which was shut in her face. Now, as our dear little Francis says with his father's true spirit of a gentleman, this was too much for, vile as she is, she is a woman & Queen of England. And now that she is neither Queen nor woman, now that she is no more, everybody must feel this more strongly. The account of her death in the Farmers' Journal is admirably done – I think Dr Holland must have written the description of her appearance at the last – I am glad he was steady to her and staid the night after all was over … Her faults lie buried with her.

So now to black crepe for the living – such is human life (Lord Byron in a parenthesis understands this & is a devil of a man for genius) …

TO LUCY EDGEWORTH [*still confined to bed by a spinal complaint*]
Black Castle, 18 September 1821

I always keep one ear open to collect amusing things for you, my dear Lucy, but sometimes nothing of the right sort comes for hours together and at another times so much pours in at once … that it goes out of my other ear before I have time to stop it … However when Richard [*Ruxton*] came from Dublin on Saturday I was determined that I would stop some of the many pretty nothings from going out of my head and you should have them …

Richard took his uncle Fitzherbert[175] on a party of pleasure to Dunleary to see the King's departure – The tent with crimson silk drapery was in excellent taste and the view of the frigate & the harbour beautiful, but of this you have heard enough from the newspapers and the Sol. Gen [*Charles Kendal Bushe*]. But Mr F was looking through a good little telescope with which Richard had provided him – he saw a man on board the King's ship sitting down upon a sofa and all the spectators had settled that this must be his Majesty and … were exclaiming "I see his shoulder! I see his head! I see his face, God bless him". But Mr Fitzherbert said "It is not the king at all – It is my old friend, Admiral Sir Thomas Nagle" … and he wrote a note and sent a boat – and the man on the sofa read the note and started up and got into the boat and came to shore & recognised Mr Fitzherbert standing on the beach and embraced him with joy – and there I take leave of them to enjoy talking over past times …

This Sir Ed. [*sic*] Nagle was one of the men who really was so drunk when he first landed that he cd not stand – The Sol. Gen has ably cleared Lord Londonderry & his Majesty of having been in the same happy state … The

175 Mr Fitzherbert owned a large estate near Navan and eventually made Richard Ruxton his heir.

George IV's triumphal progress down Sackville Street, now O'Connell Street, Dublin. Painted by John Rushington Reilly.

King had been singing German songs for them and told Sir Ed. Nagle he had never been so happy as during his visit to Ireland – But to go on with Richard's view of the departure from Dunleary – He saw the two gentlemen mentioned in the papers who swam to the side of the King's ship (geese that they were) for the pleasure of shaking hands with his Majesty – and his Majesty stooped over and did shake hands – the least he could do ...

I have much more sympathy with the poor woman who swam with her petition in her hand to the king – Richard saw her & the petition held above the water – she was taken on board the king's vessel and I <u>hope</u> her petition granted ... I admire the woman ...

Several of the English nobility who were with the King ... in London & at Oxford declare that the Dublin dinners and entertainments were far more handsome and better managed ... I am sorry his Maj[*esty*] went away without seeing the waterfall at Powerscourt which had been prepared at such cost to him.[176] It was well judged of Lord P. to invite Lord Fingall.[177] In this country

---

176 A special dam had been built to make the waterfall more spectacular and had burst its banks: luckily the King dined too well at Powerscourt and had never got to it.

177 A Catholic peer and old friend of Maria's father.

it is now the fashion to be all liberality & Cat[*holic*]s are now much in favour with all loyally disposed persons. At least this good remains from the royal visit and it is a notable result …

Now free from serious writing and estate duties at home, Maria decided to take Fanny and Harriet back to England for another winter. Starting in late October, she brought them on a dazzling whirl of Whig country houses, staying in turn with the Carringtons at Wycombe Abbey (where she unkindly described Lady Carrington as resembling Lady Bertram in Mansfield Park*), the economist Thomas Malthus at Gatcombe Park and ending with the Lansdownes at Bowood. She reported jubilantly to her stepmother that the girls had thus seen and been seen by more good company than in a full London season. In January they stayed again with Lady Elizabeth Whitbread but Maria was disappointed to find their hostess' son, who she had earlier hoped for as a suitor for Fanny, now showed no interest. Maria then rented a house in Holles Street, and was delighted to find how cheaply she could live there. The three sisters returned to Edgeworthstown in late June. Ireland was once again suffering from a potato blight and famine.*

TO AUNT RUXTON
Edgeworthstown, 23 July 1822

… The famine seems to have been as capricious as the malaria in passing over some spots & lighting upon others – We go on in our parish without having recourse to public works – the poor near here did not depend entirely upon the potatoes – they were accustomed to buy meal and often meat – and though they have spent all their money and have to look for rent, they are not starving – How we shall look or do without the rent I do not know – But Lovell is better paid than almost any other landlord in this county.

He is now a magistrate … So much the better – the more he mixes with the gentlemen of the county – He is really so good-tempered & takes with such kindness remonstrances against his daily pursuits … that it is almost impossible to find fault with him – I wrote him a strong remonstrance & he seems to like me the better for it …

Maria decamped to Black Castle for much of the winter to enjoy the company of her beloved aunt.

TO MRS EDGEWORTH
Black Castle, 6 December 1822

How do you all do after last night's hurricane. Have any trees blown down? Has the roof of the greenhouse been blown down? Has the spire stood?[178] Is Madgy Woods alive? How many roofs of houses in the town have been blown away and how many hundred slates & panes of glass to be replaced?

The glass dome over the staircase at Ardbraccan has been blown away – two of the saloon windows blown in – Mr Everard's porter's lodge has been blown down – the steeple & church of Virginia on the road to Fargestown [?] has been blown down – *on dit* – that is, the mailcoach man …

When I came down to breakfast, I mean to prayers, the first object I beheld were the two large elms opposite the breakfast room window lying prostrate upon their uptorn roots! – My aunt & uncle & Bess & Mrs Fitzherbert all with uplifted hands deploring – One of these trees is a real loss, the other … next to the house is better away & as nobody here wd ever have had the courage to cut it down t'is well that it has blown down …

Mem. – the two great elms who were blown down last night were English elms – never plant them – only lateral roots …

TO MRS EDGEWORTH
Black Castle, 9 December 1822

I am exceedingly sorry for your trees, my dear mother – Not only for the irreparable loss to the place – irreparable at least in our time – but I am most sorry on your account who will feel for the trees and for the place more than anybody else – ten times more than Lovell himself – I grieve for the beautiful beech … I assure you that I had not power to recover my spirits the whole day yesterday after I read your letter. But I always found you were at the bottom under the trees in my mind – no-one in the world loves them as you do. – As to the skylight – it was very bad at the moment but a carpenter & a glazier can repair that – But who can replace the beech & the elms & the chestnuts! Twenty or fifty years must pass & we must pass away first …

I am as much tired as you can be of the hurricane – [*but*] I must tell you that when Barry, sitting with his wife in Richard's dining room at Merrion

---

178 Her father's telescopic spire.

Sq, heard the fall of the chimneys & the crash of the glass in front & rear of the house, he started up shouting "It's beginning, Kitty! The massacre of the Protestants!" and out he ran to the hall for blunderbuss & sword.

His wife as wise as himself told this & Richard & all of us rolled with laughing …

Mrs General D[*illon*] was here yesterday … was agreeable – knew formerly Sir Hudson Lowe when he was not a knight – described him – a high cheekboned Scotch looking man – with fair complexion – yellow hair – large yellow overhanging eyebrows … never looked up in anyone's face & seemed to dislike to be looked at … when invited to dinners & expected to tell of his Italian travels etc he would never talk – Mrs Dillon could never bear him … The second volume of O'Meara … in some points tiresome – very injudicious to introduce the history of the Italian spies bamboozling Sir Hudson Lowe.[179]

… It is curious to see the different points of view in which the same work appears to different people – My aunt R much shocked by the vulgarity of Bonaparte's abuse of Sir H[*udson*] L[*owe*] – and by his want of dignity in adversity that she has scarcely time to feel indignation against his oppressor or pity for his sufferings – She repeats "But he was not a gentleman … my dear Maria, you may say what you please. He was a great conqueror I grant you & made roads – but he was not a gentleman."

My uncle & Bess for some time thought Sir H.L could not be too strict.

But Bess when she herself had the toothache last night pitied him for his carious teeth and said "Oh now Sir Hudson is growing too bad –"

TO FANNY EDGEWORTH
Black Castle, 12 December 1822

Fanny was staying with the Stricklands, land agents for Lord Dillon's estates at Lough Glynn in Co. Roscommon, who had recently become great friends.

… It is a great addition to the happiness I enjoy here to be certain you are with friends who I believe as you say are as fond of you as even I could desire and as you have a horse also & Mr S[*trickland*] to ride with you I am satisfied

---

179 Barry O'Meara, an Irish surgeon, had attended Napoleon as his personal physician on St Helena. His sympathetic account of the emperor in exile became a huge bestseller. Sir Hudson Lowe, the governor of St Helena, had forced him to leave the island two years before Napoleon's death.

that both your body & mind are happy. For my part I cannot be better and am as happy as the day is long chatting with my dear aunt who after all the varieties I have seen appears to me independently of the partialities of friendship & relationship the likeness of the person I have most loved in the world ... In reading O'M[*eara*]'s account of Bonaparte that which has pleased me most has been the conviction that he had heart ... & that he loved his wife & child. The next point that interested me was his answers to the question which was the happiest time of his life & the next happiest? I believe in the truth of his answers – What a triumph of literature is the description of Bonaparte with the hammer in his hand opening the box of new books & how all his hope of posthumous fame rested upon his code of laws & public works ...

My dear, my head is so filled by this man & this book at this moment that if I don't care I shall fill my whole letter with O'Meara – But with you I suppose the O'Meara or the Bonaparte fever has subsided by this time ...

TO FANNY EDGEWORTH
Black Castle, 3 January 1823

... There is a mason at work on the kitchen chimney here who talks so much finer than Locke or I can that I must put down a sentence of his –

"Ma'am, there are five ways of entering this chimney, Heaven grant us the luck of taking the right! And that the smoke may not retaliate."

He knew what he meant by retaliate for he explained –

"See! Don't you see, Ma'am. I have been seeing it myself – The smoke when it leaves the chimney top blows against them trees and then retaliates down the chimney."

We have been enchanted by <u>Peverill.</u>[180] But I must not touch upon such enchanted & enchanting ground for I am under promise only to write a short letter ...

Meanwhile Lovell was already having trouble running the Edgeworthstown farm and had begged his stepmother to take over the management so he could devote more time to his school.

---

180 *Peverill of the Peak*, Walter Scott's latest novel.

TO MRS EDGEWORTH
Black Castle, 10 January 1823

… Your [*letter*] reached me this morning before breakfast and the moment I had swallowed and while the church bell was ringing in my ears …

If any carman from E'town come within my reach 1 cwt of meal which as you say is excellent shall be sent to you … In reply to my questions about the quantity of mangel-wurzels to be given to one cow daily [*my uncle*] declares he does not know in the least, that he never did anything in his life by rule or rote – he believes that straw is always given at same time or hay which puzzles him (& me) – he believes a small bucket of mangel-wurzel – whether once or twice a day he cannot tell though – And I cannot ask Sophy at this moment because she is not well …

I hate not to answer your questions punctually so I have been routing for cowman & cowboy to cross question about mangel-wurzel – Cowman not to be had because he did not come on Sunday – Cowboy gone home with a thorn in his foot – Nevertheless by plaguing I have got all I want without tormenting Sophy – Peggy Flood, who is dairy maid & sees the cows fed, answers all & says – that a can full of mangel-wurzel is given every night & morning to each cow – and said can contain about 20 quarts – A bundle of hay weighing suppose one quarter of a hundred is also given each night & each day to each cow – & upon this they thrive & give good milk. The mangel-wurzel sliced to about the thickness of "my hand" – I mean Peggy Flood's.

I suppose you know what my uncle has just told me & one of the few things of which he is sure that if turnips be given along with mangel-wurzel, it is death to the cows – several having died in the neighbourhood in consequence of eating turnips & mangel-wurzels same time –

Mr White came in while I was writing & he being a farmer I cross questioned him … I will tell you that he opened his eyes to saucer size when I mentioned 1 cwt of mangel-w – for 3 cows! He said it was preposterous, But then my aunt says he is stingy & starves cow, sheep, man & beast – stick to Peggy Flood's evidence …

Meanwhile, Francis, aged twelve, had been sent to Charterhouse in England rather than Lovell's school after much family consultation. Anna Beddoes' two sons were already boarders there. Francis, who had been educated hitherto at home, was showing signs of precocious brilliance, especially in Latin, which had been taught him by his father.

TO FRANCIS EDGEWORTH
Edgeworthstown, Spring 1823

I asked for this frank from Lord F[*orbes*] on purpose to tell you how much I like your letter to Pakenham [*his younger brother*] about Latin prosody[181] – Not that I understood one syllable of it but I feel that it was kind of you to think of it for Pakenham and am assured by good judges that it was well done. [*Richard*] and Bess have been here this last week – they brought little Tommy [*Rothwell*] with them – Pakenham likes him very well though he says "he would be the better for the discipline of a school" (his words).

Richard has been every day to Lovell's school and has been very much pleased with it. He says he does not think that one individual could "in any other way have created such a mass of information, ability and happiness at the same time."

One thing however he found wanting – Latin prosody – As he was speaking to me on this subject – and his wish to have little Tommy understand it before he goes to school, I recollected your note to Pakenham and borrowed it from him. Richard sat down … at the library table and studied it for a quarter of an hour, pen in hand, at the end of which time he construed a Latin line which he put in order – Your letter had made him for the first time understand the business clearly.

… Richard R is, I believe, forty years of age! Dr Johnson says nobody ever learns a new language after forty or even materially adds to their stock of knowledge – The dogmatic doctor would not have believed that a man <u>could</u> much less would of his own accord learn Latin prosody after 40 – and learn it from the advice and prescription of a youngster such as you, Sir – …

I cannot agree with you in admiring Tom Beddoes' play[182] – But I am glad you have picked out the two best thoughts in it and even these are only conceits – bordering upon nonsense. I do not think that an idea or an expression being quite <u>new</u> is always a proof of it being quite good. Many young writers are run away with & misled by this idea of ORIGINALITY – unless a thing be good it is not valuable – and therefore not admirable for being <u>original</u> – Do not give up your own good sense and taste formed or forming on the best classical models – I should be very sorry that you were "caught" by this jingling of a

---

181 Lord Forbes as an MP was entitled to free franking for his mail.

182 Anna's oldest son, the future romantic poet, had made a name for himself at Oxford with a play, *The Bride's Tragedy*. He had earlier nearly been dismissed from Charterhouse for wild behaviour and Maria disapproved of him as Francis' mentor.

name – very sorry that you were to catch the vile ambition of imbibing Tom Beddoes or imitating anybody in writing rhodomontade – wild, odd, strange things above & below criticism.

Receive from me, my dear Frances, in remembrance of these exhortations, Middleton's Life of Cicero – and Cicero's work on republics which I believe is just published …

Visits to neighbouring country houses continued apace; Maria was making every effort to create a wider social circle for her younger sisters.

TO AUNT RUXTON
Farnham, Co. Cavan, 17 March 1823

… Our week here has been pleasant & my companions have enjoyed more than I expected riding and boating. We had three delightful days as fine as spring of which we took advantage … Yesterday we were out almost all morning boating on the lake – we rowed all round the wooded islands & up to Bishop Bedel's ivy matted tower … I wish ivy would grow on your old castle as it grows here – & I wish that Sir Walter Scott would come to Ireland & make this, Bedel's tower, the scene of a story – I was much pleased by many of the cottages here and the woodmen and labourers' houses – They are all sensibly built and comfortable – with nothing for ostentation and whatever there is of the picturesque arises naturally … The people are all busily employed, cheerful and industrious – Several of them were spinning – and the men and boys weaving. In one room we saw a nice bedstead built of plaited bullrushes – It was like a fourposter bed with one side against the wall – mats instead of curtains … The gardens and potato fields and little shrubberies about the woodmen's houses are all neatly kept. There were so many comfortable happy looking men, women & children in all the cottages we visited and they seemed so glad to see Lady Farnham & spoke to her so naturally of all their concerns without any servility or flattery that she rose many many degrees in our esteem … She has done a great deal of good and this neighbourhood shows the advantages of great proprietors residing on their estates. Henrietta and Selina [*Lady Farnham's daughters*] speak of the great pleasure they feel in living here & knowing the families of all the poor people round them. They say they are much happier at home than in London …

Farnham House in Co. Cavan, c. 1820.

We saw the servants assembled for evening prayers last night [*Sunday*] for the first time – I was struck by the number & afterwards asked Lady F how many – She counted 34 house and stable servants regularly fed – "But then their families, their wives & children are a great drain" said she. I should not like to have the care of such an establishment & of the happiness of so many people. I do not wonder that poor rich Lady Farnham's eyebrows have fixed into the strained arch of care. I only wonder that the arch does not give way. Lord F is in remarkably good health – she manages him admirably – people no more see the wires that move him than in the best puppet show – How wonderful that he manages his stables & money affairs so well!! ... How few would have done so much good & made so many people happy – I don't know any woman of shining talents, certainly any Bas Bleu, in England or Ireland who would have done so well as Lady F – Mrs E [*her stepmother*] could have done it all & more, but she would not have done it for such a Lord & master – I shd have been seen with a face a yard long the first week or been found drowned in my jug the first month ...

TO SOPHY RUXTON
Edgeworthstown, 26 April 1823

… We had a wedding here last night – & who do you think was the bride, our housemaid Elizabeth Mulloy and the bridegroom was a very handsome young man seven years younger than herself – but no matter that is his affair – He has been faithfully attached to her these 3 years & when she represented to him that she was much older than he, he replied "But that's no fault of yours, Miss Mulloy – it only shows that you would not be easily pleased for no doubt you had offers enough."

Could the court of St James have suggested a more polite answer.

But the bridegroom, besides being polite and handsome, has an excellent character & a good trade – is a good carpenter & a good son – And what is very curious is like Elizabeth Mulloy of a decayed gentry family – his parents have an estate … in this neighbourhood on which there was, when they were obliged to sell it, a mortgage of £30,000 … So the descendant of the two unfortunate families have intermarried like the unfortunate families of the Stuarts and the Sobieskis.[183] … Lovell cleared out one of the large rooms of the school & prepared tables and tea and cakes etc … – & desired the bride to invite whoever she wished to tea & a dance – he and the young gentlemen boarders acted as stewards …

TO FANNY EDGEWORTH
Black Castle, 19 May 1823

… We found Mr Butler here whom my aunt had engaged sometime [*ago*] and he has found himself so comfortable that he has consented to stay this day in spite of his conscience which tells him he ought to be marrying someone in his parish.

My aunt took [*him*] to herself this morning and after her fashion prodded and plagued till she made him tell her which of her two nieces he prefers. He shook & flushed in every limb & stammered out "I know I should not say [*this*] – according to the general opinion – Honora & Miss Sophy would be generally thought the prettiest but I own Miss Harriet pleases me most." Now is this not odd? – Harriet, I am pretty sure, would not have him if he was [?] to the Ally Kosher [?] – and the others would. If he finds out this, he will be most

---

183   The Sobieski Stuarts claimed to be the heirs of Bonnie Prince Charlie; two of them settled in
    Scotland where they were paid a small royal pension.

pleased in the end with the person who best likes him – I have pinned him to a time for going to Edgeworthstown & he has promised to go there Tuesday in the second week in June …

By June, however, Maria had set off again with Harriet and Sophy for a long-planned tour of Scotland, primarily to meet her literary hero, Sir Walter Scott, with whom she had been exchanging letters for some time. They spent a blissful fortnight in Edinburgh being shown its beauties by Scott himself and then went on to stay with him a few weeks later at Abbotsford by the River Tweed, which he was busy transforming into a Gothic castle. Maria much admired Scott's taste in building and the walks and plantations he had made, only wondering how he had produced his vast output of novels as well.

'All day long from the moment he sits down to breakfast (at which by the by he sits a comfortable time) till night when unwillingly we take our candles, he is conversing or walking or reading with us – WHEN has he time to write – He says "Oh I have plenty of time – people always have time enough if they would but use all they have – I rise early – Early, how early – Only at 7 o'clock. And in the 3 hours from 7 till 10 he gets all this monstrous quantity of writing done. – Lady Scott says that sometimes when they are alone on a rainy day he gets a quarter of a volume written off at once."'

Enchanted by Scott's conversation, the warmth of his family circle, romantic picnics by waterfalls and lakes with Sophy singing them Scotch ballads, the visit was perhaps the highlight in Maria's long life and she broke down in tears as she said goodbye, promising to return with Fanny the following year.

Back in Ireland, she reported to Fanny that thirteen-year-old Francis had had a brief encounter with a colossus of a different sort.

TO FANNY EDGEWORTH
Edgeworthstown, 6 October 1823

… Your Francis wrote a most entertaining letter to his mother containing not only the history of his journey but his arrival at the Charterhouse & his walking up the tremendously long room with Pakenham after him & the voices in each side calling out "Here's old Pad & young Pad – where have you been, old Pad?" "Where did you find young Pad."[184]

---

[184] Maria's youngest half-brother, aged eleven, had just joined his brother at Charterhouse school.

... I forget whether it was in your letter or mamma's that he gave an account of his meeting with Mr O'Connell (whom he calls O'Connor) in the stage coach – I am too lazy to go to hunt for the letters – Besides, Mamma is gone to Fox Hall to bring home young Em & old Em.[185]

But he met O'Connell in the coach who recited Grey's Bard.[186] When he travels with his own children they always make him repeat verses – I hear he is a very amiable family man. He pumped hard at Francis & Pakenham to find out who they were & the different shades of caution & discretion in Pakenham & Francis' letters are well marked & very amusing. Mr O'C said "From what part of Ireland are you? The north or south –" "Towards the middle, Sir". "The county of Longford perhaps – Maybe you know Mr O'Ferrally – he is a kindhearted offhand good fellow" – "Yes, Sir" – Maybe you know Major Edgeworth" – "Yes, Sir" – "The Edgeworths of Edgeworthstown are not far from Longford".

"Miss E is – at home now, Sir". There was a break as you see left in the dialogue which F[rancis] understands the passion of curiosity & the figure of suspense too well to fill up – till we see him ... –

TO SOPHY RUXTON
Edgeworthstown, 1 January 1824

On the first day of the new year and on my 56th birthday I cannot do better than write to my dear friend Sophy Ruxton who has for so many days and years of my life so especially contributed to my happiness & comforted me in all my sorrows & rejoiced in all my joys & borne with all my faults ...

Mrs E ... yesterday and took Mrs Strickland and me to see Mr & Mrs Dease and Lady Theresa Dease – who seemed really glad to see us [187]...

Mr Strickland was an old friend of Mr Dease ... [*he*] has arrived from England & has been here about an hour ... [*He spent*] a day in London with Capt. Beaufort with whom he is charmed ... [*Captain Lyons*] told Mr S that the first year of their expedition they reached the land where they found the *Esquimaux*; the *Esquimaux* told them that this canal was an isthmus of about 40 miles across & that when crossed, it would bring them to the open sea – They found these *Esquimaux* understood their charts and maps and they drew

---

185 Maria's niece, and Maria's sister Emmeline King.
186 The famous poem beginning 'Ruin seize thee, ruthless king'.
187 The Deases lived at Turbotstown House outside Castlepollard. Like the Stricklands, they were Catholic gentry.

for the English a chart of the peninsula – Capt Lyons tried the coast along the peninsula … and as far as they went found the drawings and accounts of the *Esquimaux* perfectly accurate … It is remarkable that the lady *Esquimaux* were the best geographers and most accomplished draughtswomen – On the next expedition it is thought that party will try to cross the Isthmus by land and another of which Franklin is to be the conductor is to go by Mackenzie's river – I wonder he has the heart to go again[188] …

Early in January, Sophy, the second youngest of Maria's half-sisters, became engaged to her cousin, Captain Barry Fox. Barry, who had been on active service since the Peninsular War, had just been left comfortably off by his grandfather Lord Farnham and had resigned his commission. It was hoped he would buy an estate in Ireland.

TO FANNY EDGEWORTH
Edgeworthstown, January 1824

My dearest child – Is it not delightful – all we could wish for her – His letter of today is still better than that which you saw – full of manly sense & tenderness without one word of fudge and such generous consideration for Lucy[189] which endears him tenfold to me & assures, I think, the happiness of his wife – when he ceases to be a lover, he will be an excellent husband.

Nothing can be more composed, dignified & charming than her confident & her simple frank decision & avowal that he possesses her whole heart …

Oh my dearest Fanny, how happy I shall be when I see you – as happy. I ask only that of heaven – as happy – that is all I ask – no matter how [*or*] with whom – I ask not for fortune or any [*other*] thing for you – but as happy, that's all –

TO AUNT RUXTON
Pakenham Hall, 21 January 1824

… We, Mrs E – Fanny – Lovell – and I – are very glad to find ourselves once more at Pakenham Hall – and to see Lord Longford surrounded as formerly by his friends in the old hospitable Pakenham Hall stile – himself always as

---

188 John Franklin's first expedition to discover the North-West Passage in 1819 had ended in near disaster, with more than half his men dying of starvation and the survivors living on lichen and chewing their leather boots.

189 Lucy was still an invalid.

cordial, unaffected and agreeable as ever – Since we dined and slept here last, which was in 1817, the house has been completely new modelled – chimneys taken down from top to bottom – rooms turned about from lengthways to breadthways – thrown into one another & thrown out of one another & feet or inches added to the height of those below by raising the floors of those above – and the result of the whole is that there is a comfortable excellent drawingroom, dining room & library – all rather too low for their size but this cannot be helped and in my opinion is of little consequence – The bedchambers are admirable and most comfortably furnished with all that the most luxurious sleeper or waker or sleeper awakening can desire – No frippery, no tables covered with china toys – to be knocked down.

Mrs Smyth of Gaybrook & her daughter & Mr Knox are here. I have been so lucky as to have been seated next to Mr Knox at dinner yesterday & breakfast this morning and I hope to be near him at dinner today if manoeuvring can do it – he is very agreeable when he speaks and his silence is "Silence that speaks" – He has promised to come & spend a few days with us – Lovell gets on very well here and with good tact – nothing too much about his school.

By the by you ask me about the Lambert boys … Their father came from Dublin to spend some days with us for the express purpose of seeing with his own eyes the school to which he has put his boys. No less than three deputations had been sent from different quarters to warn him of the dangers he ran in sending his children to such a school – and such a master. Among other strange stories he was assured that Mr Edgeworth had an immense log of wood out of which he had scraped his own coffin – This he kept constantly at the schoolhouse & to this he chained boys by the leg whenever they were to be punished – keeping them sometimes three days & three nights without food …

The story reflects the huge difficulties faced by Lovell in his brave attempt to run a non-denominational – and classless – school in Ireland.

TO FANNY EDGEWORTH
Edgeworthstown, 10 July 1824

… Bess Ruxton & I and Richard passed a pleasantish day at Headfort – Lord Bective, Lord Kildare – Mr Coddington & half a dozen more Meath gentlemen … came to breakfast at B. Castle being a committee appointed to determine

Pakenham Hall in the 1820s, after Lord Longford's latest 'improvements', carried out by the architect James Shiel.

the site of a new jail ... He [*Lord Bective*] begged us to come to dine too ... – So it was settled all in a minute – & off we went. Lady Bective appeared very well in her new grand house which is in a great confusion of furniture half unpacked & old & new & but little of either – She is very obliging and bears her Ladyship honours neatly – provokes no envy – neither sets herself up nor lets herself down – She must be as much surprised as the little Mary in the story of sayings & doings ... now she finds herself in the grand house, mistress thereof & sitting on the hard stuffed sofas – She shewed me some of the beautiful things which they found in the old chest directed [*there*] by the good old aunts ... – There was Chinese paper for the diningroom with the most beautiful border of natural flowers I ever saw from China – Lord B had a mind to send it to the King – but she sensibly said "Keep it for ourselves – we can't afford to make presents to the King" – ...

Do you recollect hearing from your grandpapa of a Mr Smith of Ansville[190] who married a beautiful young Catholic heiress years ago and used her cruelly – snatching her prayerbook from her hands etc, after promising that he never would interfere with her religious sentiments – in short, broke her heart. All the time of their marriage Mr H. Harman [?] was joking with him about

190 Now Annesbrook House, Co. Meath.

marrying a Catholic after all his professed hatred of Catholics – "I will lay you any wager that you'll turn Catholic yourself yet, you'll be found some day in a Catholic chapel" – "Done" – Mr Harman paid down his guinea – the bet was put in writing – and there it rested for many a year – But after the death of the pretty creature whose heart he literally broke [*he*] married again and according to the wishes of all ... he found in the second one [...] who ruled him with a rod of iron. But she being a Protestant, no one expected he would lose his bet in her reign – Till a while ago it happened they were going through Kells, the Catholic archdeacon, a relation of the first wife, saw them at the inn & invited them to come to his house to see some pictures (daubs in my opinion) said to be original Rubens – The lady chose to go to see them so they went – and the archdeacon next invited them to look at an altarpiece, a Guido which Lord Headfort had given them – She went to see it & her husband followed her into the chapel – forgetting his wager – Mr Harman heard of it, found witnesses to prove the fact – claimed his bet – Mr Smith in vain pleaded the spirit of the bet was that he should never be found turning Catholic – Mr Harman held him to the letter – ... At last it was decreed that Mr Balfour should decide it – and a few days later he pronounced according to the written wager produced to him – Mr Smith is to pay the £500 – Everybody rejoices – he is rolling in gold and Mr Harman has a large family & few £s.

What possessed me to write this long story I cannot tell – the habit I believe of telling you, my dear child, whatever diverts me ...

Following her father's teaching, Maria had always been a convinced supporter of Catholic Emancipation, which had been blocked ever since the Union by two successive Hanoverian kings and a long-lasting Tory administration. The struggle to achieve it was now hotting up, especially in Ireland. The original Catholic Association run by the professional classes had been dissolved by order of Parliament. Daniel O'Connell, a brilliant lawyer and orator, had almost immediately set up a new Catholic Association with membership set at a penny – soon known as 'the Catholic rent'. Supported by the priests, it attracted a huge popular following but alarmed many of the surviving Catholic gentry.

Following repeated bad harvests, rural violence had also flared up under a new mythical leader, Captain Rock. In 1824 a book by that title appeared, defending the Catholic peasantry's fight against unjust tithes and rapacious Protestant landlords.

TO AUNT RUXTON
Edgeworthstown, 4 August 1824

[*Mrs FE*], Mrs Waller, Zoe and I drove yesterday to Turbotstown to pay a visit to Lady Theresa Dease – found her as agreeable and much better looking than ever …

The Deases are going to England and to Wales – and then to the Continent to spend two years … He has done a great deal at Turbotstown & has laid out much work to be done while he is away.

I find that several of the higher classes of Catholic gentry are on different pretences or reasons leaving Ireland. They seem to wish to get out of the way – Mr Dease is an exceedingly conversable man – He talked to me of Captain Rock which he had just been reading and we agreed in opinion as to the wit and talent which are displayed in that performance. He observed that it has in writing the same brilliancy & the same power of capricious allusion which Canning displays in speaking … As to the motives of the writer, he thinks as we do that the love of nationality prevailed over all nobler views[191] – We then talked of "Captain Rock detected" – Pray read it – At least the beginning of it which is a very interesting fabric of a story. It pretends to be written by a Munster Farmer. The object of the book is to shew that if tithes were abolished the poor tenants would gain nothing – that the landlords would gain all – that the distress arises not from the oppression of the church but of the land holders – There is much ability in the book – much sense and truth – But in my opinion it will serve neither church nor state – but is more dangerous than Capt. Rock himself – more intelligible by the common class of people & the moral they will draw from it is "Let us attack the rent & get rid of them since obviously the tythes is not enough."

This book, as Mr Dease informs us, is written by a Mr O'Sullivan – formerly of Maynooth – but being rejected – not for want of talent but on some other account – he turned …

TO SOPHY RUXTON
Edgeworthstown, 7 August 1824

… Francis and Pakenham arrived this morning by the mail and filled their mother's heart and all the house with joy …

---

191   The author was in fact Thomas Moore – the famous poet and songwriter.

We are reading Red Gauntlet – the first volume exceedingly tedious – all except Wandering Willie's story … I thought I should have fallen asleep as I was reading out loud and I have thought that if Walter Scott had fallen asleep & written in his sleep, there must have been more imagination & genius in his dreams … Nothing yet equal to Waverley & The Antiquary …

The Edgeworthstown schoolboys have been acting She Stoops to Conquer & Old Poz.

Some of them act admirably – How Goldsmith would have been delighted to see his play thus represented by Irish boys … We have been exceedingly entertained & think it good amusement for boys teaching them to speak and move before numbers … The last audience was I think 200 at least – 3 carriages – Mr Fox … was surprised & delighted – Mr & Mrs Whitney & lords are among those who go to the theatre tonight …

TO SOPHY RUXTON
Edgeworthstown, 27 August 1824

… We have had for these four days past a house full of company – one of those rendezvous times like what you may remember of yore when everybody from different parts came pouring in unexpectedly & from morning to night – Yesterday we were prepared by Dr McGovern, the Catholic bishop who was engaged to dine on a Godsent haunch of venison – Dr and Mrs Donohue came in the morning & sat by while Mrs O'Ferrall & Mrs Williams & Mrs Cox talked & talked & talked – And scarcely were they cleared out when Mr & Mrs Napier arrived & very glad we were to see them – Scarcely were they seated when in came Mr Hunter from St Paul's churchyard.[192] Then arrived Mr Butler and Mr Hamilton – and presently returned Mr Donohue & the Catholic Bishop to dinner & Mr Whitney … –

Hunter's coming in for a Catholic bishop here & a Catholic confirmation was curious – two men in greater contrast … could scarcely have sat opposite to each other, Hunter was much struck by his liberality – He went to the chapel today & says he had a sermon from a Mr O'Byrne that would have done credit to any clergyman …

Mr Butler holds his place firmly in my affections – the more I see of him, the more I like him … His friend, Mr Hamilton is the most unassuming

192 Maria's publisher.

gentle simple creature I ever saw – Though much has been done to make him think himself a lion, he does not seem to have the least idea that he is one – He has both the simplicity and the candour which make true genius.

This was Maria's first encounter with William Rowan Hamilton – a brilliant young mathematician from Trinity College who was to become a lifelong friend. The flood of guests were followed by two Commissioners of Education coming to inspect Lovell's school. This was a further attempt by the Tory ministry to grasp the nettle of educating the Irish poor. An earlier commission of 1811 had provided funding for non-denominational schools through the Kildare Place Society, enshrining the principle that all Bible reading should be given free of instruction. But the principle was not acceptable to the Catholic hierarchy and the schools were suspected of Protestant proselytizing and were increasingly boycotted by poor Catholics. The new Commissioners had been chosen with care by the Viceroy, Lord Wellesley, Wellington's brother.

TO SOPHY RUXTON
Edgeworthstown, 3 September 1824

… The Commissioners [*of Education*] who came to us the day before yesterday to dinner were Mr Blake, Lord W's secretary & Mr Grant – From their names we guessed that one must be Irish and the other Scotch – but when I saw them appear I mistook Mr Grant for Mr Blake – Mr William Grant is a full faced high coloured large *affaire de tête*, dark eyes full of benevolence, openness and good humour – I set him down for a jolly Blake[193] – But on the contrary Mr Blake is a pale thin acute wary courtier looking Scotchman – He has been a lawyer & left the bar to oblige Lord Wellesley … he has a good deal of humour – tells anecdotes and Irish stories admirably – and makes use of his humour to make his way in the world – Humour & diplomacy make an excellent mixture … He is a Catholic & liberal but liberal more for not caring much about the whole thing … than from benevolence …

The next morning was spent at the school – Lovell let them see it without showing it off to them in the least – They were very much pleased – Mr Butler and Mr Hamilton being there with them was advantageous as they were both

---

193 A well-known clan of Catholic landowners from Galway.

excellent judges – one of arithmetic and geometry – the other of classics – and of the attention paid to religious instruction …

Mr Grant went to see Harriet's school with which he was delighted – The tears really came into his prominent benevolent eyes – I never saw Harriet look so pretty as she did … as when showing them that school – I am sure I was not the only person there who admired her – that is one comfort …

Meanwhile the chronically sickly Fanny and Honora were both at Cheltenham taking a cure, staying with their newly married sister Sophy, and Barry Fox. Sophy and Barry then planned to spend the winter in Naples and had invited Fanny to accompany them. The plan sent Maria into a flurry of preparations and advice.

TO FANNY EDGEWORTH
Edgeworthstown, 2 September 1824

… Your mother and I as soon as we got [*the Commissioners*] out of the house began a review of your wardrobe. We hope we have not sent you any despairs but we found a great many – & more old shoes & gloves than I could have conceived! I wish you had seen us holding council but I have no time for diversion – I enclose a list of all we have sent – Mrs Moffat [*dressmaker*] has put satin on the tabard according to your desire – I, according to my own, send the gauze trimming if you should like to let Smith put it on for you – if not, give it away.

… You will laugh at our sending you one old silk stocking – but the other not to be found, we opined you had taken it with you by mistake & may be glad of its fellow – The same thing about an odd long white glove.

You have only one pair of short white gloves – & no long pair – provide accordingly.

You have no muslin worked or unworked skirts fit to be seen abroad – we send you two rugs with valencienne edging merely for the sake of that edging to which you may get new muslin – But you must shell out some money & buy yourself some decent habit skirts …

You have no white satin shoes but a good new pair of white silk.

… In a box you will find a duplicate of the list I enclose – but do not disregard it because it may save you trouble in a hurry in unpacking …

TO FANNY EDGEWORTH
Edgeworthstown, October 1824

During our visit to Mr & Mrs Napier's I heard and did as much as I could for you – Mr and Mrs Pollard were there – after a long conversation all I could learn from them is that they prefer Rome as a winter's residence – there you see all the Italian & English society worth seeing at the houses of the ambassadors – French – Austrian – to whom your own ambassador will procure you invitations ... that travelling is so easy & commodious through Italy that all advice is superfluous ... Mrs Napier & Mrs Pollard agreed that a steady ugly English maid would be a great convenience – I would advise Sophy to do whatever Barry wishes about the maid ... You are both so helpful that you could do without her but if either of you shd be ill she wd be a comfort & the comfort of her needlework when you are stationary could balance the inconvenience of her to take care of on the journey ...

> *Maria had originally planned to travel to Italy with them herself and spend the winter with her widowed sister Anna, now living in Florence. But Anna had died suddenly and instead her children were invited by Lovell to stay at Edgeworthstown.*

TO SOPHY RUXTON
Edgeworthstown, 6 January 1825

... I have to give you the most charming accounts of Honora and Lucy – Honora has gained flesh and strength and spirits without fever – She is now upon the sofa opposite me writing with a candle beside her on a bracket (I have had a mahogany bracket put up at each side of the chimney piece to push up or down ... this is my new year's gift to the sofas & they seem to like it well) – You see, we have two sofas opposite to each other – Mary Beddoes & I are upon one ... Honora & Anna [*Beddoes*] on the other – & SOMEBODY sitting in the middle talking by turns to each end – Who can that be? – Not Harriet – for tea is over and she has ascended to Lucy's room – not Mrs E or William, nor Mrs Beaufort nor Louisa for the coach has carried them away from us some hours ago to a large dinner – poor souls! & full dressed bodies! to Ardagh to dine in a room large as a barn & cold as the temple of the winds – with Lady Fetherstone & Sir George & 2 Foxes & other unknown.

But to return to our unknown in the middle – the joy of 2 sofas – whoever can this be – a gentleman it must be to constitute the happiness of two sofas full of ladies – who? Lovell? No, he is constituting the happiness of schoolboys as usual night & day – but who is the joy of the ladies?

My nephew, Henry Beddoes – and the joy of ladies he certainly will be, not merely of old cousins and sisters but of all who engage & be engaged by prepossessing manners & appearance – & by the promise of all that is amiable & intelligent – I am delighted with him – He would charm my mind & even though I have thus praised him, my uncle would like him – & you – Oh I will say no more – but that he is not as pretty a youth as his childhood promised – he has been bronzed over by four years midshipman's service, 3 in the Mediterranean ...

He had never seen his sister since his mother's death till they met this morning – He was much moved – He did not till he saw Sophy and Barry and Fanny at Genoa know even where they were ... A letter Anna wrote to Plymouth to tell him of Lovell's invitation here found him just in time to work upon his Captain ... a most good natured man, to procure for him leave of absence for three weeks while his ship is refitting. Straight he ran up to Captain Beaufort and a round robin from all the family praying him to come over here – freighted himself with packets 7 parcels for Ireland – landed & made his way to 31 Merrion St – all strangers to him one hour – friends, family friends the next – he dined these & got into the mail at night – And at about 7 o'clock this morning Lucy walked to my mother saying "Mother, there is Foster making such a barking in the hall I am sure something must be the matter!"

Out went my mother in dressing gown & nightcap & in the hall she saw Foster barking at a gentleman ... The gentleman looked at her & she at him

"I do believe you must be Henry Beddoes!"

It is 13 years since he was here before – and oh how much has happened since then – Yet here are the walls & pictures & chairs & table all the same and most of them in the same place – he recollects them all ... and the tree he used to climb – now grown old – So goes the world – & so will go when we go no more – Let us enjoy what we have left as much as we can & do as much good as we can & keep our health as well as we can & be thankful – The bible society & the Catholic priests would perhaps think one very wicked for not putting this in other language – but of all Dr Johnson's sayings to Boswell that which I like best as most applicable to the present time is "My dear Sir, avoid cant."

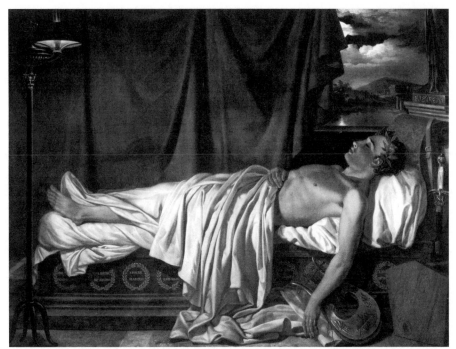

Romanticized view of Byron's deathbed at Missolonghi. Maria's nephew Henry Beddoes reported he died in 'an absolute hovel ... without any bed of any kind.'

TO AUNT RUXTON
Edgeworthstown, 10 January 1825

... Henry Beddoes tells us that Lord Byron was extremely beloved & highly thought of by all he heard speak of him at Missolonghi, both Greeks and his own countrymen. He had gained public esteem by his latter conduct. He raised a regiment there at his own expense and supported it, at least the soldiers, entirely from his own funds – Lord B had not the least idea of his own danger till the last day of his life & would not let his servant send for a physician & would not be bled. Henry B who was on the spot confirms the truth of this newspaper account but the place he died in was more wretched than I had formed an idea of even in my romantic imagination – He died not in the worst inn's worst room – or on a battered bed with tapestried curtains never made to draw, but in a hovel, an absolute hovel without any bed of any kind – lying upon a sack! The English officers all went away from the place after he died – All the Greeks went into mourning & every mark of public respect was paid to his memory

TO MRS EDGEWORTH
Black Castle, 10 April 1825

I have some hopes that the boy who undertakes to deliver this letter and Bessy the pony safely to you may be as good as his word, because he is only a boy – not an angel – I would not have trusted a pony to any Angel upon earth – Sophy Ruxton warrants the boy trustworthy if not put into temptation beyond the strength of boy or man to bear – that of having more money than he knows what to do with – I have given him but just what will bear his expenses and those of the pony – without whisky – to Edgeworthstown – viz 5 ten pences … Give the boy two ten pences to bear his own expenses back again – and not one farthing more – Trust the rewarding him to me if he brings me from you a certificate that the pony is safe in wind & limb …

The directions which Michael the sage gives for the future health of the pony are thus – it should be kept out at grass some time longer as it has been at grass & must not be pampered with oats too much suddenly – It should be taken up in the morning from the field & kept in the stable every day however till it is ridden – and not at first ridden hard – lest its wind should be broke – which is now sound – I am charged to repeat that none must attempt to leap it even so much as a potato furrow – Anything else it will do to please you – Anything in life! – I am desired further to keep a secret – Therefore I tell you that "it will draw capitally in gig or jaunting car or anything at all". But it is better this should "never be known" because there is nothing in the world ruins a pony equal to making him draw which causes him to stumble & he is never good for a riding horse after!

Yesterday I met a famous judge of horses and ponies who asked "Ma'am, did you get Hamilton's pony? – Then you have the best pony in Ireland – The best roadster – the gentlest creature – Nine year old – Aye, but there's ten years work n him – I'd have given twelve pound for him myself – but I didn't hear of it – You did it all too quick!"… The extreme look of disappointment of the gentleman shewed me the value he set on my bargain …

Whether I am cheated or not I neither know – nor much care, provided the pony answer its purpose – the adding to the happiness of my dear Francis & Pakenham and contributing to make them ride well which is an accomplishment every man & gentleman should have …

Pray send me by [*the boy*] a five pound note – Also Crampton's recipe for curing the cramp – pray do not forget this – for Mr Fitzherbert suffers much from cramp ... Send me also for Sophy Ruxton the recipe for aperient which I have in my bottle – she tried it once and liked it – and I have only an inch in my bottle left ... Yesterday my uncle was seized with sharp pain – swelling – inflammation in his foot – The gout *bien prononcée* – and there he was on the sofa all day – & there he is likely to be all day today – but in excellent heart – for the gout is ... a sign of "Long life to your Honor!" at 80 – In the midst of all this my aunt has had but one headache – has been as docile as a lamb about taking medicine (if lambs ever take medicine) – She is wonderfully well & I cannot believe she is 80 – I look – I listen – I think – I feel it is quite impossible she is 80.

All the time I am near 60 myself – and forget entirely – This you know is proof that I am quite well – Not a spot, Ma'am! I walk alone & in concert two or three times a day in these most beautiful walks which I love & admire more & more ...

Maria's uncle John Ruxton died three months later.

TO SOPHY RUXTON
Edgeworthstown, 24 July 1825

My dearest Sophy,
The bearer of this letter, a poor awkward creature, has just brought tears to my eyes by the most delicate & feeling manner in which he spoke to me of Black Castle – And of all the feelings of the country people who knew him [*Sophy's father*] – and of their sorrow for my aunt's trouble & yours – The astonishingly just and acutely fine discernment of character these people have! – And the nice tenderness with which they touch the mind that grieves is wonderful – None but those who have felt sorrow could do it.

I send for my dearest aunt one of those rose peonies she wished for – I hope she will go out with you to see it planted – I know she will from kindness to her own little Maria – I shall be sure she will be in her garden a quarter of an hour at least – I send some books – keep box and all that you may have no trouble or she either about recollecting whence & where they came ...

Sir W. Scott sent us word he would be this day in Dublin – He stays about 10 days or a fortnight there – & in the County of Wicklow – and will then come here & from hence to Killarney – Mr Butler has been engaged to meet him here – He liked Mr B much ...

The Archbishop of Meath's Irish heart burst out in tears all down his yellow cheeks when he spoke of Black Castle and never did I hear one [*more*] just – short – pathetic eulogium – I did not know that he knew all & each of you so well.

TO SOPHY RUXTON
Edgeworthstown, [?] August 1825

… Sir Walter Scott punctual to his word arrived on Friday in good time for dinner – he brought with him Mrs Scott [*daughter-in-law*] and Mr Crampton – I am glad kind Crampton had the reward of that day's journey with him – Though frequently hid from each other by clouds of dust they had as they told us never ceased talking – They like each as much as two men of so much genius & so much knowledge should & we rejoice in being the bond of union …

Scarcely had Crampton shaken the dust from his shoes when he said "Before I eat & what is more before I wash my hands I must see Lucy" –

As she was not prepared for this immediate visit she was at first agitated but he knew how to quiet her & soon made her laugh – he bunched her all over like a fat sheep as he said & was delighted he told us by the state in which he found her … He thinks (and with all the humility of hope & gratitude I repeat it) she will perfectly recover – perfectly straight as well as he thinks she will be. He says she must now sit up in a chair & be carried in a wheel carriage for the construction of which he gave orders …

Captain and Mrs Scott & Mr Lockhart were detained in Dublin by some repairing of their carriage … They came about eleven o'clock – Mrs E, who has always everything managed in the best manner, had supper & fruit & everything refreshing in a few minutes and put timid Mrs Scott & her shy Captain as much at their ease as it is possible for them to be – So much so that Crampton whispered to me

"It is witchcraft – I have seen them in other houses – It is positive witchcraft" – …

Sir Walter Scott delights the hearts of any creature who sees, hears & knows him … – He is most benignant as well as most entertaining – the noblest & gentlest of lions & his face, especially the lower part, is exceptionally like a lion.

Mr Crampton, Jephson & he were delightful together – and Lovell appeared to great advantage – not too much or too little of anything – The band after dinner by moonlight … at a little distance till Sir W.S. begged

*Engraving of
Sir Walter Scott
that he presented
to Maria.*

to hear it nearer – The Scotch tunes – the first he had heard except his son's regiment since he had left Scotland – delighted him ... All went on well from that – boys playing leapfrog delighted Sir W. Scott – Next day all went to the school for a very short time & saw a little of everything worth seeing ... The religious instruction, it being Sunday, was going on as we went – Catholics with their Priest in one room – Protestants with Mr Keating in the other

... More delightful conversation I have seldom in my life – I don't say never – heard than what I have been blessed with these three days – I feel it is a PERMANENT blessing that Lovell enjoys it so much ...

We set off at 7am on Tuesday for Killarney – Sir W.S. on account of his son's short leave of absence ... must be back in Dublin in 8 or 9 days from this day.

We dine & sleep at Judge More's at Lambrook [?] on Tuesday – reach Limerick on Wednesday – Friday we hope Killarney – William will meet us at Killarney, we trust – Anacreon [*Thomas*] Moore wrote to Scott saying how delighted Lord Kenmare etc – We are not sure whether his Lordship is at home. If he is of course he will do all he can for Sir W.S. – We hope to have a stag hunt

NB [*Sir W.S.*] is charmed with [*Mrs E.*] and all her useful and agreeable qualities – Lockhart too – who has put so much sugar in his acid that he is now quite palatable ...

The expedition to Killarney lasted just over a week, the party consisting of Scott, his son and daughter, and Lockhart, Maria and Harriet. William Edgeworth, who was laying out the road at Glengariff, was also able to join them there. For once Maria was too busy to write letters and perhaps too overwhelmed by the huge crowds that turned out to greet the party everywhere they went. (Their boatman at Killarney told Macaulay twenty years later that the pleasure of rowing Scott had made him miss a hanging that day!)

They returned to Dublin in time to celebrate Scott's birthday on 15 August at his son's house in Stephen's Green, and he and Maria took fond leave of each other, never guessing they would not meet again. Returning via Black Castle, Maria heard the delightful news that Harriet had accepted her long-term suitor, Richard Butler, the rector at Trim.

TO HARRIET EDGEWORTH
Black Castle, 27 August 1825

... My beloved sister, I may now without constraint let my heart swim in joy as it does – And it swims secure and fearless – I am now sure of the only point of which I ever doubted – of all the essential questions. Of his being all that can ensure the happiness of a good reasonable and cultivated woman I have long felt convinced – I think your happiness as safe as mortal happiness can be. For I know the decision of your character & that once your esteem & your affections have been touched, it is forever – I never saw a man look so happy! – He most kindly told me that he could not think his happiness complete till he had communicated it to me – Thankyou my dear Harriet for permitting him to do so – How very cold is thankyou to what I feel as I write it ...

Dearest Harriet – I am your happy and affectionate friend & sister – How shall I – we – live without you – I will never think of that – Your mother does not – Now if Fanny gets but well, I will ask no more of Heaven!

The upper lake at Killarney, painted by Sir John Carr in 1806, with a bugler demonstrating its famous echo.

TO MRS EDGEWORTH
Black Castle, 5 September 1825

… So you have another daughter almost settled to your and her heart's content with every reasonable prospect of happiness that the world can produce – And by her own merit and by her own choice without any manouevres on your part or my part – what satisfaction![194] … Thank God it has ended happily – Never did I see a happier creature – And this repaid for all the anxiety I have felt on his account – Well might he afford to go through some pain to obtain such a treasure as he will – for life – For life! …

As to the livings – It is very good to have £400 a year – and for all I can make out he will have it and will not, as I originally feared, be cheated … He hopes to be back at Edgeworthstown tomorrow – I think he told me if his horse (who is not in love) can do it for him – (By the by I wish he would learn to drive or look as if he could drive a little better – true woman! – Not that I care, only that it would please my aunt.)

… I wish … to have notice in time for a scheme I have to ask their acceptance of a carriage – With all the building etc he will have as much as he can do with his money the first year or two – and he is so much my friend & I may say has been so long my friend that I hope he would not dislike from his point of view my doing this – tho' on the other hand it is natural he shd wish

194 This was hardly true as Maria had been promoting Mr Butler for some time.

to give his wife her carriage himself – Consider you, dearest mother, what will be best & how to do it. I have in Mex[*ican*] bonds of my own saving £200 or 250 for this purpose or any other to which it can or might be better applied for them ...

Shocked at the bleak state of Mr Butler's rectory in Trim, Maria's letters throughout the summer were full of plans for providing Harriet with suitable furniture and other comforts – which entailed yet more frequent visits to Black Castle nearby. Her beloved Aunt Ruxton was still living there with her two daughters, though the house was now the property of her son. And at home she still had her adored favourite, Fanny, for company.

TO FANNY EDGEWORTH
Black Castle, 21 October 1825

I beg you will no more fret your tender soul and frail body concerning my body which is now sitting on a sofa in the drawingroom as well as ever you could wish & I wish I could give you some pounds of the flesh it has to spare & some sinews of its strength.

   ... I have been reading with breathless interest Legros's *Histoire de Napoleon et de la Grande Armée* – the most striking picture of ambition & war – of the strength & weakness of human nature, body & mind that was ever drawn – and the most useful because the best authenticated as to the feelings of the conquerer at the height of glory – & the depth of disgrace. It is the most valuable piece of historical biography I ever read – superior as a lesson to princes & people to Plutarch's life of Alexander or any other conqueror.

   I might have waited to have said all this to you till we meet – but I could not; I am too fond of you & too well used to pour out my mind of whatever fills it – warm from head or heart – By two strong sympathetic chains you hold me independently of all other causes of affection – by your sympathy in literature and in science – and what a delightful equality between us, in spite of the difference in our ages ...

   Adieu, my dearest – we have a fund of happiness which poor little Bonaparte never had except when he stood hammer in hand to unpack the box of books at St Helena – or watched the air pump making ice for him at his utmost need ...

VII
DECEMBER 1825 – APRIL 1830

SINCE HER FATHER'S *death Maria had spent much of her time away from Edgeworthstown, enjoying the financial independence given by her substantial literary earnings and the £500 a year left her by her father. She had seen her role mainly as giving support to her much-loved stepmother and providing her younger half-sisters with the* entrée *into the outside world where she was now welcomed not only as a celebrated author, but as a delightful and entertaining guest. After years of acting as her father's amanuensis, she had had little to do with the overall management of the Edgeworthstown estate. Half the estate was already Lovell's, and the family had unanimously appointed him trustee for the other half, which provided annuities for his stepmother and siblings. Taken up almost entirely with his school, Lovell had already handed the trust account back to his stepmother who oversaw the farm and kept the books meticulously. In December 1825, however, he confessed to her and Maria that he had run up huge debts on his half of the estate, and had been borrowing at high interest rates. The school was haemorrhaging money, fees were not being paid – and the estate rents had fallen sharply in the bad harvests and general agricultural depression of the 1820s. The sum owed was over £26,000 – nearly £3,000,000 in today's money. It was left to Maria to devise ways of saving the family estate and home at the eleventh hour. She turned to Sneyd, who was now living in England, as the family member most likely to help, enlisting his wife Harriette as an intermediary.*

TO HARRIETTE EDGEWORTH
Edgeworthstown, 23 December 1825

I enclose a letter for Sneyd from Lovell which will be very painful to him – The only means I can think of to lessen the pain is to enclose it to you who have so much the ... power to soothe him.

Read both Lovell's letter to Sneyd and Mr Little's to me[195] which will explain the business as far as we know ... it ourselves.

The first page of Mr Little's is in answer to a doubt which I suggested the moment I was made acquainted with the affair which was but a few days ago – My doubt was of the legality of the mortgage – You will see that Mr Little by producing counsel's opinion etc satisfied all doubts on this point – Lovell's having decided to write in openness to Sneyd and his having yesterday told William are the only consolations ... we have in this misfortune. However great the evil it is always a satisfaction to know the worst and to feel that when this is known the whole family can join together in whatever retrenchments or other necessities we can devise for supporting the credit & happiness of the whole as far as is possible.

The trust accounts and rents being in Mrs Edgeworth's hands and the trust accounts not being in the least affected by these debts incurred by Lovell must be another satisfaction.

.I suggested to Mr Little the plan which he speaks of and approves in his enclosed letter – That if Sneyd could by his credit and the assistance of his monied friends raise the £20,000 and have the mortgage made to himself the lands would not pass into the hands of a stranger – I will if Lovell allows me receive the rents of this his settled estate, the income of which as Sneyd knows is £1500 per annum – It is well paid – and I will undertake to pay Sneyd the interest of the twenty thousand pounds he raises in the mortgage – This appears to the best – I might say the only means of saving the credit of the family and preserving whatever can be preserved of that estate in future to Sneyd.

If Sneyd cannot command the whole sum, perhaps he could the 5 or 6 thousand – and that would be a relief to Lovell – But the other would be best for Sneyd – and believe me, dear Harriette, that is an object as near the heart of all this family as it is to yours – Lovell suffers severely – I am sure you will have the kindness to write as soon as you can for you can imagine the anxiety

---

195 Little was one of the bond holders for Lovell's debts.

we shall endure till we hear from you – especially till we know how you and Sneyd contain this blow – Dear Sneyd and Harriette, believe me your sincerely affectionate sister, Maria Edgeworth

It was soon clear that help would not be easily forthcoming from 'monied friends' in England, where a severe banking crisis had led to stocks falling sharply. Leaving, as she told Sneyd, 'not even the smallest pebble unturned', Maria had even approached her father's old manufacturing friends in England. But the family rallied and the Edgeworth tenants proved generous in volunteering to pay their rents ahead of time. By March Maria was writing to Sneyd that 'if we brothers and sisters join together … ten or eleven thousand can be raised' which would prevent the immediate necessity of borrowing from an outside source. As for Lovell, he was now suitably chastened.

'He now devotes himself entirely to his school in the most steady manner … no more sound of music is heard, no feasting or revelry … He says he really thinks he lost his understanding – that he never calculated – How could it all happen or what became of all the money we cannot conceive. But waste and jollity and foolish generosity – and no accounts – will in 8 years get through £15,000, a little trifle of fifteen hundred a year, please yr Honor …'

Almost at the same time, news reached Edgeworthstown of Sir Walter Scott's near financial ruin. Ballantyne, his printer in Scotland, had collapsed into bankruptcy owing £130,000. Scott, a part-shareholder in the printing works, honourably stepped in to guarantee the full debt by placing his house and income in trust to creditors, and refused all offers of help.

TO SOPHY RUXTON
Edgeworthstown, 5 March 1826

… A few days ago I saw a passage from a letter from Mr Morritts to Mr Strickland which puts us at ease about Walter Scott – Mr M wrote to Sir Walter to ask what truth [*were*] written reports [*of Scott's financial straits*] – Sir W assured him that though he loses a great deal of ready cash he has enough left to live well & comfortably – He does not lose Abbotsford – nor is he obliged to part with his library – In short he adds – I lose only the trappings of prosperity –

I like the manly & truly philosophic expression – Mr Morritts says that Scott writes and speaks on the subject with unaffected gaiety … Scott wrote to Harriet that they may only reform from keeping open house – Lady S. will rejoice at that …

TO AUNT RUXTON
27 May 1826

… You will have seen from the papers the death of Lady Scott. In Sir Walter's last letter, he had described her sufferings from water on the chest – but we had no idea the danger was so immediate. She was a most kind-hearted, hospitable person – and had much more sense and more knowledge of character and discrimination than many of those who ridiculed her. I know I can never forget her kindness to me when I was ill at Abbotsford …

Sir Walter said he had been interrupted in his letter by many domestic distresses – the first two pages had been begun two months ago … in answer to a letter of mine enquiring about the truth of his losses etc. Of these he spoke with cheerful fortitude but with no bravado – He said his losses had been great but that he had enough left to live on … that he had great comfort in knowing that Lady Scott was not a person who cared about money and that "Beatrice" as he calls Anne Scott [*his daughter*], bore her altered prospects with cheerfulness … "and poor Janie proffered her whole fortune as if it had been a gooseberry." …

The domestic distresses which had interrupted the course of his thoughts were the illness of his dear little grandson, Lockhart … and then Lady Scott's illness and death. He says that the Letters of Malachi Malagrowther cost him but a day apiece[196] …

Meanwhile, plans for Harriet's wedding to Mr Butler were fixed at last – and her modest dowry was safe.

---

196   A caustic attack on the government's proposal to ban the issuing of banknotes after a series of bank failures in England. The government abandoned the attempt and Scott's portrait still appears on Scottish banknotes in recognition of his defence.

TO HARRIETTE EDGEWORTH
Edgeworthstown, 1 August 1826

The time for the marriage has never been fixed until this very morning and in fact I cannot absolutely say fixed as it hovers between the 12th & the 14th … Capt. B[*eaufort*] who came over to visit the works of [*his*] company … cannot delay his return beyond the 15th or 16th – He takes Aunt Mary back with him to Byrkley Lodge – Oh how much we shall have to part with at once – William B[*eaufort*] performs the ceremony.

Sophy & Barry come to us today and stay till the marriage – It happens that the Prelate has appointed to hold his visitation at Trim on the 18th and Mr Butler MUST be there to receive them at his own house – It would be impracticable for Harriet to appear there so soon in the midst of all these bigwigs and black men … A kind thought of Barry's and Sophy's has obviated all difficulty by offering their house at Cloonaugh[197] – They will stay here during the four intervening days [*and*] Mr Butler, leaving Harriet for one day at Cloonaugh, proceeds to Trim to receive the big wigs … and returns next morning on the wings of love or legs of a gig and bears away his prize in triumph towards Kilkenny … to his father's

… Sneyd is very wise and very kind in the warning he gives about settlements which should be duly finished before marriage … But in fact the affair is here reduced to a nutshell. Mr B's lawyer draws up a deed settling upon H the amount of her own two thousand pounds fortune – & that is all that can be done at present – When his uncle's bequest of £500 per annum landed property comes into his hand he will, I am sure, do more …

Here I am got into the middle of money business to you though I said I would keep all that for my letter to Sneyd – but habit has wrapt me in this of late – I verily think I am turned into a jewess & a mere money changer – Whatever I think of ends in – money – debts – bonds – securities – interest etc.

There is some relief in my heart which I must give you the pleasure of telling Sneyd – that I think I shall be able to get through without selling any part of the paternal estate to strangers … I have struggled and will struggle on – I have lent all I possibly can – and William's purchase has been a great help. Without dear Sneyd's generous assistance we would not have gone on even so far …

197　Barry Fox's country house in Co. Offaly.

I would not upon any account tell Lovell that I think we can do without selling to strangers … his mind is inconceivably little governed by past experience of pain & he has so little resolution as to economy that I could not answer for the consequences – He says truly that he is not fit for prosperity – he can do admirably in adversity – with incomparable … resignation to the punishment which he candidly says he deserves – I alternatively admire his temper & – I will say no more – but that his conduct has been truly manly & generous to us all about his new trust deed – without which Mrs E's children would have been at this moment penniless – & William & Honora bereft of all the fortune their father left them …

With Harriet happily married as well as Sophy, Maria was increasingly concerned for Fanny who was now twenty-eight with no suitors in sight. Pinned down by financial worries and accounts, she could no longer afford to take her on jaunts to England or Europe.

TO FANNY EDGEWORTH
Black Castle, November 1826

My dearest child – Wherever my body is, my heart is with you – I am grown so humble in my wishes to heaven about you! I think I carry on a kind of cheating in my own mind like what children practice when they say to themselves – "Now, I will not hope or expect such a thing that it may come true" – I tell myself that I will not expect to find you much better that I may be surprised – what folly –

I trust that Heaven has some angel of a man in store for you & that this blessing has been kept to the last for your mother that she may have the sweetest last – Get well my dearest! That is all I ask – I know all the rest will follow of course …

… I rejoice that you have the delight of Cecilia[198] – thankyou for telling me whereabouts you are.

So you like Delville the lover – Look at Mme de Staël's memoirs (Regent's time) – and you will see resemblances to young Delville & his way of going on in the old castle.

---

198 Fanny Burney's second novel. Originally published in 1789, it had remained hugely popular and ran to fifty-one editions.

"Oh Ma'am" said Mrs Gibney a few days ago to Margaret "Let nobody ever think of marrying a man that has been profligate in the hope of his reform after marriage – for if she does Ma'am! – it is the foolishest thing that ever woman did!"

This was [*said*] most feelingly for Mrs Gibney had done this most foolish thing & had to see it to the last hour of her husband's abominable life and it is well it is no more –

I could not help thinking, when I heard her moral speech, how well it would have been for Lady Byron if she had heard it before marriage – Her ladyship & Mrs Gibney have come to the same conclusion at the last …

Meanwhile she was keenly following the final stages of the battle for Catholic Emancipation. Francis Burdett's Catholic Relief Bill had passed through the House of Commons the year before, but had been blocked in the Lords, opposed both by the ailing Prime Minister, Lord Liverpool, and the Duke of Wellington. Her hopes lay with George Canning, Liverpool's successor, but he was also ill and had almost died in January after an all-night vigil in an unheated chapel for the funeral of the Duke of York. Her old friend Dr Holland, who had once attended the unfortunate Queen Caroline, was now physician to both Liverpool and Canning, and sent her regular bulletins on ministerial health.

TO SOPHY RUXTON
Edgeworthstown, 23 March 1827

… How much depends on Canning's health – and [*his*] continuing in power …

You see that Mr Peel keeps a severely marked line between his own opinions & those of the violently illiberal – The best thing for this country is that the majority of Irish members vote greatly in favour of Catholic Emancipation. This … will help keep the country more safe than all the police or dragoons which Peel or Wellington could send – the conclusion which the very acute Paddy will draw from this is that – The measure must & will be assured and that it would not differ of the price of a cow to poor men whether it be done this year or the next – While maybe if he'd join the Cath[*olic*] board or the likes to meddle to much … he might get left in the lurch in a Revolution as afore times and hanged – as poor men are apt to be – in lieu of the rich that "set 'em on".

Something like this reasoning will, I trust, keep us from civil war this year – and on patiently till the Chancellor dies – It is not treason to imagine the death of a Chancellor – But nevertheless keep my opinions to yourselves …

Edgeworthstown was still receiving a stream of visitors, including the 'philosophers' or scientists whose company Maria most enjoyed.

TO HARRIET BUTLER
Edgeworthstown, 16 July 1827

Be it known to you that Dr Brewster[199] is here – & William and Sneyd – and Mr Collyer and Mr Davidoff & Mr Cooke and Mr Francis & Pakenham Edgeworth – The 2 Miss Beddoes, the 5 Miss Edgeworths including Miss Cecilia, and Mr Tom or Tommy Rothwell was here till 9 o'clock this morning – when he departed per Scarrifbridge coach.

All the above persons & Lovell & Mrs E are well lodged & well fed etc by Mrs E's admirable management without any appearance or bustle or difficulty – And certainly Scotch, Russian, English & Irish do pay well by their various conversation.

I never heard such in this house since long before the year 1817 – It reminds me of former times & I rejoice to see that such persons still come to Edgeworthstown – My dear Harriet, I wish you were here & you should have half my end of the longer bed for the shortest woman – We should only be 3 in a bed – But this is not in the least what I intended to say to you (Private).

I had asked young W. Hamilton to come here before I knew that all these people would come together & now I really am in an agony lest he should come & my mother shd not have a bed to put him in – I really cannot give him a third of mine tho' he is a 2nd Sir Isaac Newton – I don't know when Davidoff leaves – I wish he may stay for he is one of the best bred, most amiable & variously informed young men I have seen – (Sir Walter Scott, as Brewster tells me, is distractedly fond of him & so is Brewster himself)[200] – But still while he & William are here there is no bed for Hamilton …

---

199 Sir David Brewster (1781–1868) was a Scots physicist famous for his experimental work on optics and polarized light. He reported his visit in a letter to his wife: 'A more extraordinary family for talent, mutual affection & everything that can interest I could not have conceived.' He became one of Maria's regular correspondents and a mentor for her youngest half-brother, Pakenham.

200 Count Orloff Davidoff had come to Edinburgh in search of Enlightenment ideas, which he later applied to his vast estates in Russia.

'The Balance of Public
Favor' (1827) – Moore's
romantic novel Epicurean
outweighing Sir Walter
Scott's Life of Napoleon.

*Sir Walter Scott, meanwhile, had completed at breakneck speed a nine-volume
life of Napoleon, which paid off nearly a third of his debts.*

TO FANNY EDGEWORTH
Rostrevor, Co. Louth, 21 August 1827

I am charmed by Scott's life of Napoleon in spite of all its faults – which were
many – It has life in it – it carries one on – on – on – through revolutions –
battles – everything – and its morality is excellent without the author ever
moralising – The everyday common talk style, though it at first shocked me as
unbecoming in an historian, is wonderful for keeping the reader awake – or at
least ME reader awake – I have slept sometimes over grand histories ... I like
the moral enthusiasm of Scott far better than the mocking wit of Voltaire –
To interest his fellow creatures a writer must be interested in them – always
laughing will not do – Man has a serious regard for himself – and woman
ditto –

I think Scott's life of Napoleon is as fine a moral history as Macbeth is as a tragedy on the fatal effects of selfish ambition.

After all Bonaparte was right to dread the power of the press – It is an overmatch for his cannon.

His fame depends more on this life of him than on all his generals & courtiers put together ever said to or of him …

Maria's reading also embraced a diary from the revolutionary days of 1798.

TO MRS EDGEWORTH
Black Castle, 6 September 1827

… I am afraid I shall learn to swear from the bad company I am keeping in Wolfe Tone's diary[201] – Very entertaining it is indeed after he gets to France. I think he was made for domestic life & not for a head of revolution – or even Chef de Brigade except as to the uniform & epaulettes – It is always most interesting and amusing to see the human heart laid out without disguise in all its little weaknesses and vanities – For most I like him all the better … Many of the preachers of humility I know are shocked past all enduring with his barefaced vanity – the naked truth of vanity always shocks these humility prudes & they draw their drapery carefully around them and then they reprobate others – & adjust their pretty veils in the most becoming manner conscious & trembling for all they have to conceal – Without a veil & with only just a decent rag to cover me, I am, dearest mother, ever your affectionate &, above all, sincere Maria E

TO SOPHY RUXTON
Edgeworthstown, 27 September 1827

… The day before yesterday we were amusing ourselves by telling who of all our acquaintance among literary and scientific people, we should wish to come here that day to Edgeworthstown if a fairy were to give us our choice.

---

201 A founding member of the United Irishmen, Wolfe Tone had gone to France to act as their liaison with the new French revolutionary government. He was captured during the abortive landing by Napper Tandy at Lough Swilly in 1798 and escaped hanging by cutting his own throat. His diaries were published by his son, a former officer in Napoleon's army.

Wolfe Tone as Chef de Brigade in 1798. His diaries, edited by his son, published in 1826, made him a national hero.

Francis said – Coleridge and I said Herschel[202]– "What of all people in all circles in the whole world" said Francis who understood I did not seek for one of his poets "Yes – the whole world" ... persisted I ...

Yesterday morning, as I was returning at half after eight from my morning walk, I saw a bonnetless maid, letter in hand on the shrubbery walk in search of me.

To my surprise when I opened the letter, it was from Mr Herschel! – and that he was waiting for an answer at Mr Brigg's inn in Edgeworthstown! There are coincidences enough to spoil me for a novelist! For they would not be believed in a book ...

And now he has spent twenty four hours here, and that he is gone, I am confirmed in my opinion; and that if the fairy were to ask me the question again, I should more eagerly say – "Mr Herschel, ma'am if you please"... All the family are much of my opinion that he is one of the most agreeable and unaffected of all the savants we have seen. He is not only a man of the first

---

202 John Herschel (born 1792), a brilliant mathemetician, astronomer and chemist. Maria had visited him in England in May 1822 and spent all day with him 'looking into telescopes'.

scientific genius but his conversation is full of information on all subjects –
And he has a taste for humour & playful nonsense though with a melancholy
exterior … something dried bone [?] in his face & peculiarly dark hair.

Mr Babbage, the friend of whom he spoke, is a gentleman of fortune
who has great mechanical invention – he has distinguished himself by a most
ingenious mathematical machine for calculating logarithms – We knew him in
London & he showed us this truly wonderful machine – We saw Mrs Babbage
[at the] same time … But she is dead … Babbage is in dreadful affliction &
Herschel brought him over here to begin a course of travelling – he is going to
the Continent for some time …

Mr Herschel spent an hour at Lovell's school and seemed delighted … –
He was particularly pleased by the registry the boys keep by turns of the weather
– for the purpose of determining whether the moon has any influence … He
says that the keeping of a register of this sort … is good training to experiment
in general … and teaching to keep them from superstitious ignorance – he has
promised to send us a copy of Pringle's directions on chemistry …

[Herschel] saw the Giant's Causeway on a stormy day when the waves beat
up against the stony rocks & added to the sublimity of the scene … Then he
went from the Sublime of Nature to the sublime of art – He arrived at the
place where [Colonel] Colby is tracing the l [?] … and saw the instrument …
the measure of which was [to] the twelve thousand part of an inch …

I cannot tell you how often I wished for you, my dear Sophy, during the day
Herschel spent here now how much I regret that you would not hear his variety
of conversation – but you shall have as much as I can cram into a letter …

There follow four closely packed pages of travellers' tales relating to science.

There is enough of science for one letter. Then now for some nonsense &
diversion in which Herschel, I assure you, abounds …

Have you heard of the live camel leopard – twelve foot high, Ma'am, if he
is an inch & not come to his full growth … He is now living happily, they say,
in Windsor Park with some kangaroos for humble companions – Herschel
is well acquainted with him & was so fortunate as to see the first interview
between him and a kangaroo – The little kangaroo – stood – gazed for one
instant – and the next leaped at once fairly over the camel leopard's head –
After this he got over his fears as people do – even of lions – and he and his
great friend became hand in glove …

TO FANNY EDGEWORTH
Black Castle, 10 October 1827

... £25,000! earned in the last year by Sir Walter S[*cott*]! What would the philosopher's stone have been to Sir Walter Scott ...

Scott had just reissued a collected edition of his novels. To Maria's pleasure, the introduction included a tribute to her. 'Without being so presumptuous as to hope to emulate the rich humour, the pathetic tenderness and admirable truth which pervade the works of my accomplished friend I felt that something might be attempted for my own country of the same kind as that which Miss Edgeworth so fortunately achieved for Ireland.'

TO FANNY EDGEWORTH
Edgeworthstown, 14 May 1828

What did you think when you read in my letter of yesterday when you came to the words "The servants' hall chimney has been on fire"?

We have had a most happy – and narrow escape [*from*] having the whole house burned – Most fortunately the fire broke out by day – if it had been in the night, nothing could have saved us – and nothing would have saved us either by day or night but the extraordinary courage, zeal, activity, steadiness & obedience of the people who came to our assistance – 30 men & boys who went on unremittingly for above 3 hours from 7 o'clock in the morning till half after 10 carrying water up, up, up ladders & staircase & pouring continually, continually, continually down the chimney till at last the fire was got under and extinguished – the total extinction & complete safety was not effected till half after seven o'clock in the evening ...

... Lovell & I first met in the study, he carrying the tin box with the title deeds – I undertook the carrying out of all the papers with 2 men he left me – Mrs Smith's son & Dargan – most steady they were – in less than an hour's time they had carried out all the presses of leases etc, boxes of surveys & every rent book – The top of Mr Hind's [*the land agent*] table in which were his accounts & I know not what & it was impossible to open the locks –

First I tried to get the things out of the study window – impossible opening from top – too high up – weight of presses – breadth of table – imposs – The men actually carried the whole alcove mentioned through the hall – down the stairs – while every instant bucket men were ascending – how it was done Heaven knows – Honora & I carried out all my papers & Lovells – and my mother's – letters – (pigeon holes) money, accounts, books all laid on the grass before library window – my father's picture on verandah – all the library side of the hall pictures, Mr Day etc.

The quiet at front of the house seemed most extraordinary! – as if it knew nothing & nature knew nothing of what was going on – But what is still more extraordinary, my dear Fanny, believe me if you can – I whom you have seen such an egregious coward in small or no danger in a carriage felt all this time without fear – absolutely as if the magnitude of the danger swallowed up fear – I was absolutely bereft of feeling & could think & did think as coolly as I do now – and more clearly – I cannot understand it but it is fact …

Maria's eight-page letter included a moving description of the sweep and his 'climbing boy' who had been sent to clear the still smouldering chimney. Numerous parliamentary attempts to ban the practice had failed or been ignored and climbing boys were too often asphyxiated by fumes or smothered by soot.

… He clawed down honeycombs of soot – The boy was many hours getting up – The man [*his master*] outside (standing at the foot of maids' stairs) applying his mouth & ear from time to time to encouraging the child – There's my brave boy – Do you hear me – are you faint? He was most humane & the boy every now & again tried to sing – But at last grew quite silent & the man had tears rolling down his black face – Lovell shockingly frightened – But the boy at last spoke again – he had struggled on & … working with a hoe at top of his chimney had opened a passage – & at half past seven o'clock the poor little creature got into the air & sang out – his professional song of triumph

… Neither Honora, Lovell or I have suffered in the least – We have been solacing ourselves with speeches on Cat[*holic*] question but I dare not enter into that – I only wish the anti-Catholics could have seen how poor Catholics were labouring here at the very time hazarding their lives to save the property of Protestants – They are a most generous people – & are even honest when honesty can take the shape or colour of generosity – wretched boys in rags refused shillings from me afterwards saying "You gave me one before, Ma'am" when I could not properly remember which I had given to & they might have been doubly rewarded – But they were upon honor & scorned to take advantage –

A 'climbing boy' with
his pet owl, drawing by
Honora Edgeworth.

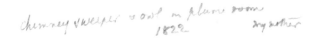

They all had breakfast at [?] intervals in the kitchen – long tables –
stirabout – immense dishes milk & beer – fast day – poor creatures – would
not touch meat …

TO FANNY EDGEWORTH [*staying with her sister Sophy Fox in Offaly*]
Edgeworthstown, 16 May 1828

All going on well post fire … I wish you would write a few lines to Lovell
congratulating him upon his having saved the house – which I do think he
really did by his exertions – Praise from his own family & from his equals or
superiors is most advantageous to him[203] …

He is at this moment reading to us Mr Grant's speech – He has been with
us reading or hearing every evening. The debates [*on the Catholic Emancipation
Bill*] are most interesting – We think of each speech as you do – except that
you over rated Burdett – I think he had better have left the Treaty of Limerick

---

203 Since the financial crisis Lovell had taken refuge in a different part of the house.

– I think both sides proved that that Treaty meant only religious liberty for Catholics without political rights ... I think Peel's argument was conclusive in showing that after the treaty a bill was brought in to petition for the Catholics to be burgesses & to practice trade in companies – Now these were much inferior privileges to that of sitting in parliament ...

I am half listening to Lovell reading & half writing – I am afraid I am not intelligible ...

Goodbye my dearest – It is shameful to do two things at a time – If I was Lovell, I would not read to two ladies who are scribbling to a third ...

Maria's youngest half-brother, Pakenham Edgeworth, was now just sixteen and had left Charterhouse to go to Edinburgh to study Oriental languages in preparation for entry to the East India College at Haileybury. He was already a keen botanist, an interest which Maria had helped to foster, and was to become a noted plant collector in India.

TO MICHAEL PAKENHAM EDGEWORTH
Edgeworthstown, 10 June 1828

My dear M.P – I wish you were an M.P and I prophecy you will be one before you are 40 – but cannot be before I have been dead and buried ... So I shall have to never get a frank out of you ... – Meantime I am heartily thankful to that indefatigable kind franker, Lord Rosse[204] ...

On the 24th May we drank health and happiness to you – and as much wealth as is consistent with the first and contributes to the last – more I never wish you to have – so pray do not when you go to India tire and fret yourself into a liver complaint for the sake of a few hundred or even thousand guineas more – Don't come here as yellow as the gold you bring in your pocket – Bring less & keep your colour as the colour of a good Christian – But you will not be gone to India these two years so that I am a little premature in talking about your return ...

My peonies and yours are in charming blow – There never was anything so beautiful as my double scarlet Turkey anemones this year! – Sophy and I admired your *weed* garden yesterday and wished you were with us ...

---

204 The Earl of Rosse had recently been appointed Postmaster General in Ireland. Maria's letters to him show her shamelessly begging for his assistance in franking letters!

Do you recollect that old woman who is Quinn's dairymaid and factotum – who doated on all his children – Lately she took it into her head that she would emigrate to America – Nothing that could be said would prevail upon her to give up the scheme – At last the day for her departure came – Little Beaufort who is a most determined little fellow went up to her and said "If you go, I go – I will go with you." His father & mother expostulated. He answered to his father "You have another son now, Sir" He packed up his clothes for himself – and made gifts & legacies of all the goods he could not carry with him – he gave his goat to his sister & his peas and potatoes to another – and bequeathed his old jacket to another ... The old woman could not stand it – She was so touched by the boy's affection for her that she burst into tears and said she would never go – to take him from his father and mother ...

Grandfather's Tales[205] are admirable – the life of life is in them – far superior to any of the last novels. Have not yet been introduced to The Fair Maid of Perth.

Where do you think I got The Grandfather's Tales – from a bookseller at Longford.

The world's improving, Sir ...

In the autumn after a visit to London, Fanny finally became engaged to her long-term suitor, Lestock Wilson, whom Maria had persuaded her to reject eight years before. Their reunion in London had been arranged by Fanny's uncle, Francis Beaufort, who had seen Fanny's increasing depression living at home. Now Maria had to convince not only herself but her friends and relations that it was for the best. In time she was to recognize Lestock's sterling qualities – and to rely on him for financial and other advice. In the short term, she could not conceal her pain.

TO SOPHY RUXTON
Edgeworthstown, 30 November 1828

... I wrote a few lines last night with Fanny's letter to my aunt mainly to assure her in the first place that I was perfectly satisfied – This in truth comprises the whole of what I think & feel – She has a very different view of life now from what she had 8 or 9 years ago and though we may regret for him that so many

---

205 A new book of short stories by Sir Walter Scott.

years of happiness have been lost to him, yet I am of the opinion that neither he or she would have been so happy had they married as I am sure they will be now – She had not sufficiently known her own taste & her own heart … The early first love which there certainly was with the addition of 9 years of tried, agonised yet enduring affection on his part now altogether give all the strength & firmness to attachment which ensure happiness – She loves him gratefully, tenderly, truly – She feels the delight of giving pleasure to a noble heart devotedly attached to her …

They are to be married on New Year's day which they were both so kind as to choose from other days … because it is my birthday …

And now that my first wish, my most ardent prayer to Heaven is granted & that my dear Fanny is going to be married to a man I think worthy of her by the nobleness of his heart … how can I not have reason to be most happy, most grateful to God? – But there is a deadly sickness across my joy when I think of the separating from her. It wrings – it wracks my heart – But this is selfishness – and I must keep it down as well as I can …

TO SOPHY RUXTON
Edgeworthstown, 1 January 1829

Fanny's wedding day

… Fanny will always be the same Fanny – But Fanny Edgeworth is now Fanny Wilson! I can hardly believe that she is gone! I feel it – and long must feel it with anguish – selfish anguish – But she will be happy – Of that I have the most delightful conviction. Therefore all that I now feel is only surface sorrow & it will pass away …

They left the church door a little after eleven – a very fine sunshiney day it has been – They will reach Cloonaugh about 3 – There everything has been arranged for them in the most gentlemanlike and gentlewomanlike manner by dear Barry & Sophy – They will have fields quite retired to walk – & horses to ride …

The final ordeal remained of presenting Lestock Wilson to Aunt Ruxton, now living in a villa outside Dublin. Like Maria, she was snobbish and would have perceived a London broker as below the salt.

TO MRS EDGEWORTH
31 Merrion Street, Dublin, 15 January 1829

… We found my dear aunt in her own chair by the fireside dressed most nicely in a cap which Sophy had been doctoring … for half an hour to make it becoming and very becoming it was

"I have had more pains taken with my appearance, my dear, than if I had been the young bride – And here is Fanny – the same dear little Fanny as ever" (in her purple cashmere) "But you must have disappointed the Miss Simpsons sadly, my dear, in not being decked out in some finery for they have been waiting, I'll answer for it, to get a peep at the bride as she came in" etc – Then she turned to Lestock "My nephew, my nephew who has been so kind to me already" – Most graciously she received him – she looks so very well that it is difficult to believe she has been so very ill … all that remains is weakness in her limbs. She cannot stand more than a minute or two without fatigue …

It was a most happy day – Lestock appeared to such advantage & Fanny enjoyed the pleasure of seeing him please and seeing my aunt shine upon him – I never saw him so completely at his ease – talking so agreeably & so sensibly on various subjects – animal, vegetable & mineral – the China voyages – & the Hong merchants to whom I was never introduced before – I cannot tell you how entertaining he was – "I can't conceive what people can mean by complaining of his want of conversation" said my aunt to me …

Meanwhile, Maria found the streets of Dublin seething after the recall of the popular Viceroy, Lord Anglesey. He had written a letter publicly calling for the Tory ministry to bring on the Catholic Relief Bill, and been peremptorily sacked by the Duke of Wellington.

TO MRS EDGEWORTH
31 Merrion St, Dublin, 19 January 1829

… An immense concourse of people – cavalcades & carriages innumerable passed by here today – We saw it – and you will see it all in the newspapers. Banners with constitutional agitation picked out in black – Mobility & Nobility in black crepe hat bands etc – Lord Anglesey's two little sons riding between two officers in the midst of the hurricane of mob struck me most – One of the boys a little midget no larger than Johnny seemed to stick on the horse by accident or by mere dint of fearlessness – The officer put his arm round him once & set him up & the boy's head looking another way – & the horse keeping on his way through such noise & struggling & waves multitudinous of mob …

TO MRS EDGEWORTH
31 Merrion St, Dublin, 20 January 1829

… [*The Miss Cramptons*] told me that Lord Anglesey showed their father the letter that the Duke of Wellington wrote to Lord A recalling [*him*] – It had been settled that Lord A was to go before he wrote said letter & this had been announced to him in very civil terms but after the appearance of Lord A's letter in print the Duke wrote without measure "The King's Council have been astounded by your Lordship's letter – after which it is impossible that you can continue to hold the Ld Lieutenancy of Ireland. Even till the arrival of a new Viceroy you are desired forthwith to give up the sword of state to the Lords' Justice."

The Ladies Paget were in outrage & exclaimed that they would tear him to pieces! – that the Duke would not have used less ceremony in discharging a footman. So much for Castle gossip …

By February Fanny had reached her new home in London and become the main recipient of Maria's news – and views. The battle over the Catholic Relief Bill was reaching its climax. After Daniel O' Connell's triumph in the Clare Election, both Peel and the Duke of Wellington had recognized that the bill must be passed to avoid outright civil war. The Duke was now campaigning tirelessly to ensure its passage through the Lords.

TO FANNY WILSON
Dublin, 14 February 1829

… I cannot touch upon politics for it has now struck eleven and I might be up till past 12 if I said half I wished to say on that topic – I rejoice – and admire the Duke of W – sum total – Leslie Forbes' speech is as like himself as possible & as like his pitiful appearance after the election at Edgeworthstown [*when*] he asked if I thought the Catholics would ever vote for him.[206]

206 Lord Forbes, son of the neighboring grandee, Lord Granard, had been elected the Tory MP for Longford in 1826.

I liked Lord Anglesey's speech about putting himself aside when the interests of millions of people were in question.

How wise of the Cath[*olic*] Association to put themselves down.[207]

All the Catholics of whom I have heard the sentiments receive their promise of emancipation in the best possible manner –

"Yes, now everyman may educate his son with the hope that he may go forward according to his merits – Curran's son was only a weaver" – Harriet Butler told me this was said by some of the Catholic people in their neighbourhood.

TO FANNY WILSON
Dublin, 16 February 1829

… I am almost ashamed to go over my opinions of old speeches to you because the fresh swelling tide of new interest in politics must have swept away all traces of the past in your mind.

Of Grant's speech which you tell me was beautiful I can find only a few lines in the newspapers I see …

Mr Peel's – indifferent – as well perhaps … I hear that he is turning back again under the notion that the old chancellor may prevail upon the king to go back & say the Duke has gone further than he intended – If so, Peel is lost forever to public opinion – Difficulty will only stimulate the D. of Wellington & he will never give up that to which he has put his hand, accustomed as he is to victory – He now has won the crown of civil glory – civic crown – to me …

Maria's enthusiasm for the Catholic cause had encouraged her to a new adventure while in Dublin.

TO FANNY WILSON
[?] Edgeworthstown, 9 March 1829

My dearest, you used always to like to know what was the uppermost thing in my mind – the reigning folly or madness of the moment and so you shall now as if you were alone with me in my little room & sitting opposite to me on my little stool – I am quite full of a nunnery, or rather of a nun – quite enchanted by a nun.

---

207 The Catholic Association had been revived by Daniel O'Connell in 1825, but his political rival Richard Lalor Sheil had now agreed to its suppression as part of the deal for Wellington's Catholic Relief Bill to get through Parliament.

... Mr Strickland [*told me*] ... that he has just been breakfasting with some of the very happiest people he has ever seen – Nuns – That he had been always averse ... to nunneries & nuns – But that this institution & the sight of its effects had made him feel and acknowledge this exception – Indeed the principle is different from all he had ever known – Not exactly *Soeurs de la Charité* – they attend chiefly the sick. But these Sisters of Mercy (I think he called them) attend those who are bereft of all human aid – condemned criminals etc & administer to the mind diseased as well as to the body – They have a house of refuge for young girls who might be driven by want ... into early vice – These are kept separate from penitents for whom there is another asylum. In short said Mr S. – other nuns are selfish creatures at best withdrawing themselves from social feelings & social duties to secure for themselves future happiness ... These, though as it were dead to the passions & pleasures of the world, live for all its best purposes & devote themselves to be useful, actively useful to humanity. All the superintendents & acting sisters of this establishment are ladies of birth – many of them having been or being possessed of grace, beauty, wit in [*eminent?*] degree ...

I expressed a strong desire to see these happy useful angelic people – He stopped short in his walk – You shall see them – let me etc – Could I go to breakfast with them tomorrow.

But they breakfast so early & live so far off – Oh, no, no, no, you could not – Oh yes yes I can – I will if I may – and if I may bring Harriet Beaufort with me ...

... Now for this nunnery business – Sunday morning, seven o'clock

Up & dressed & coffee a cup each – down – but threatened with insuperable difficulty – Every carriage of every kind in Dublin engaged this day because it was to be the entrance of the Duke of Northumb[*erland, the new Viceroy*] ...

When they managed to procure a carriage, Mr Strickland could not go with them but sent his friend Mr Bodenham to escort them instead.

... Enter through a court – large patched building in Stanhope Street – Stoneybatter – Porch pretty – passage with view of garden at further end – admitted into nice little parlour – corner chimney – breakfast laid out – Mr B introduced us to his sister – who appeared almost instantly – about your age – pretty figure – face at first I thought plain – marked slightly with smallpox – but what but youth & beauty could look tolerable in that hideous dress – hers was a white headdress, however she had taken the black veil – But though not handsome, she had the air of birth & perfect natural good breeding …

Enter Reverend Mother … a handsome composed Irish woman with a governing look yet benevolent &, when she smiled, great sweetness – But evidently not a woman of the world or of the intelligence & higher culture of Miss Bodenham.

Chocolate – admirable – tea – coffee – marmalade made by Scotch rect[ory] – as reverend mother told me – we have everything as good as we can – we do not put our point of virtue upon ascetism of this kind.

During breakfast – such conversation as I have scarcely ever heard in my life from Miss Bodenham – Scott, Napoleon – Madame de Genlis' memoirs & works & character – Madame de Sevigné's letters – anecdotes of all the most interesting persons whom she had met & intimately known in England – France – Italy –

Mr Bodenham's conversation is too much that of a London diner out, a dealer in anecdotes. But his charming sister is quite free from the littleness … in that profession – she had all the touch & go of a practised converser, but beside that all the polish of a wellbred person & beyond that again all the ease of a person above vanity … Quite separated from the world, looking back without envy and without acrimony – what you might imagine the conversation of the dead to the living might be if a wellbred angel came to meet you …

I was obliged after many movements of the reverend mother to recollect at last the business of the day – and to see the establishment – Excellent – laundry – girls of refuge in silence at work – ironing – earning – & learning to be servants – accounts settled once a month – saw account books – annual income I believe about £800.

Hospital – Bedrooms – all well arranged & all the regulations judicious – But I will pass over all this to go on to what will be of most interest to you –

Mr B[odenham] was not allowed to accompany us through all the places but he was summoned to rejoin us in the "Room of Recreation" – a handsome square high room the size of drawingroom in 31 [Merrion St] – Pianoforte! Reverend Mother, Yes we admit every kind of innocent recreation and you would be surprised if you heard the noise and merry voices in this room at our hour of recreation –

I then ventured to ask Miss Bodenham if she would play for us (I assumed she could). She never stirred till the Reverend Mother asked her.

Great was my astonishment indeed when she played – You know I have not the affectation of admiring music when I don't feel it – But it was impossible not to feel hers – She played one of Handel's finest pieces – Alexander's Feast … Her brother accompanied here … The manner in which her assurance wakened in playing with her beloved brother in pieces they had so often played together many years past … was most touching, most striking – I scarcely ever felt or saw anything that touched me more – She played all these from memory …

In walking through the passages with her this day I could not resist saying to her

"How is it possible that you could be allowed to be a nun – I wonder some man did not carry you off!"

She suddenly made some kind of genuflection & drew a little back as if she asked pardon of heaven for me – & the Reverend Mother either coming up by accident or called by a sign took me in hand & talked to me insipid talk about a garden …

The next day Mr Strickland & I journeyed down together to Edgeworthstown – and had a vast deal of conversation about Miss Bodenham. In perfect innocence I let out all my enthusiasm purely for my own satisfaction – He seemed delighted & repeated

"You do appreciate Eliza! You are willing to know her – She is a most superior creature – Such is the power of religion etc" – and once there was a look which did strike me as beyond friendship …

It occurred to me at that time … that Mr S. might think of preventing her taking the black veil.[208]

I had asked the reverend mother whether there was any discredit attached to the novice declining to take the veil during the 2½ years of the novitiate – She said not in the least. It is a frequent occurence. …

I repeated this in talking to Mr S – But upon the whole my impression is that he thought she was fixed in her fate and he had no intention to try to make her change it – He told me that every argument that human could devise, every power of persuasion tried to prevail upon her not to leave her house & go into this nunnery …

Her brother had been almost frantic when he first found she had left home – She took the opportunity when he was gone to a Worcester Music meeting

---

208 He had been recently widowed.

and when on his return he heard it, he ordered horses and pursued her – but too late ...

Mr S bought two small pigs of some rare breed at Mullingar – the children of a sow of horrible bulk – The pigs were put in a hamper & led to the front of the carriage & Mr S said they could pass for a hamper of claret.

They squealed most of the way to Edgeworthstown.

So things are mixed – tedious & sublime in this world – I cannot help it – So it is – must finish ... Charles Fox will soon be here for dinner – 5 o'clock ...

Two weeks later came the news that the Prime Minister, the Duke of Wellington, had fought a duel with Lord Winchelsea, who had impugned his honour during the Catholic Emancipation debate.

TO FANNY WILSON
Edgeworthstown, 25 March 1829

When I came down to breakfast this morning I was received with a universal cry from the breakfast table of great news – Extraordinary news.

Extraordinary indeed that I guessed in vain that the Duke of Wellington had been assassinated – My kind Aunt Mary said "You knew!" and I guessed that he had been challenged but never did it come into my head that he had sent the challenge.

Oh my dear child how I wish I had seen or heard you when you were reading the letter of the D[*uke*] and Lord Winchelsea and all the account of the transaction ...

I think the Duke's first letter was admirable – his second natural but not prudent ... The general of an army should not hazard his personal safety in time of action when his life is of so much consequence to ... great national interests – What might have become of Ireland if the Duke of W had been shot in a duel at this critical time.

... If he were bound by public opinion to notice and demand satisfaction for every fool's insult, this puts his life & his power to serve the country at the mercy of every fool like Lord W[*inchelsea*] ...

Old Mrs Colville diverted Aunt Bess the other day with her housekeeper's complaints of a white hen that had got such an ascendancy, ma'am, over the cock that it is quite scandalous – There she is 'ticing him, Ma'am, up into the trees – and she governs him entirely ...

With the bill for Catholic Relief safely through both Houses of Parliament, Maria's letters to Fanny returned to more down-to-earth concerns.

TO FANNY WILSON
Edgeworthstown, 13 April 1829

I was quite surprised this morning by your mention of the vein of sand – it seemed as if you had been at my elbow! ... This lucky vein is the smallest conceivable – about 13 loads – which is about 13 shillings – be this more or less – The two houses I am going to build are between Garret Keegan's and Burke's – where there is ample room enough for [*them*] ... The houses are of the plan enclosed – of which my mother has made me out a nice working drawing – glued on board by Michael the universal, and now lying in the wet ground before Andy Steel & 3 other masons who are working away at the foundations ... Another man, Desmond who has not, I believe, the honor of your acquaintance but who distinguished himself by many pigsties and a dry wall capped and pointed [?], is now working away also at the dry walls of the new yards of the new houses which have risen to their full height (without their cap) of 5 feet above ground – Same time, Behan, the deaf, the intelligent and the neat-handed, is shoring away at a great rate and clearing gripes of ditches to secure dry lodging and little gardens for the future lodgers & occupants of these new tenements – carts loaded with stones – and carts loaded with lime & boys & men loading, drawing or carrying away – the various vehicles are all in activity – and Conolly is quarrying at Tuites – and Mr Bell, the most obliging of master builders & architects is buying timber & slates for me in Dublin – and I am almost frightened at the activity & bustle ... myself has made – But I have calculated & know that I can pay – & that I shall be paid 5 per cent which is all I want or will take for my money & Lovell will, I hope, at the next year's end touch £10 for a plot which hitherto brought him nothing.

The employment is good for me – taking me out continually every possible morning – and always in your plaid – your dear plaid which is delightfully comfortable ... My mother has given me her old black bonnet of beaver and has lent me *sine die* the fur pelisse which little William Beaufort gave her and thus equipped and comfortable ... in borrowed feathers I sally forth mounted on real pattens 2 inches high or more – I hope you see me, my dear, this instant as you used to do from your window.

*Irish family eating
their dinner.*

Is it not this power of bringing before the eye friends at a distance by making little black marks on paper more really wonderful than the fairy glass – not only the pictures, but the thoughts! – the feelings!

Be pleased to see me going at 8 o'clock to the widows' houses – (their yard, formerly puddleduck and worse, now is well paved, clean and nice as you could wish to see) – The widow Campbell, your old friend – ie, the old woman to whom you were a friend – had been confined to her bed with stitches and I went to see her – found her sitting up by her fire with her white hands nicely pinned across & her poor thin yellow face & dark eyes looking as cheerful as it was possible for sickness & misery to look – a little girl beside her sweeping up the hearth & her son appointed to her sitting with hands on knees skinning an excellent manly looking potato, a flat basket of hot dittos before him on a stool, a tin can of milk, his mother happily full – and when I asked is this your youngest son? – His mother's eyes doating on him as she murmured, Yes and the best of boys he is to me, – These poor people have a happiness in their sympathy & affection for each other unknown to the brutal selfish stupid Birmingham artificer whose enjoyment (wife & children nothing to him) is in a draft of porter …

The Duke of Wellington must now indeed feel that he is a happy as well as a great man. He has certainly prevented a cruel war and has by his civil courage saved both England & Ireland. The Catholics in their moment of triumph behave wonderfully well – with a noble spirit that strikes, as Henry Hamilton wrote, … even those who were formerly least favourable to their cause. …

Maria ended hopefully with a report from the Abbé Langan – son of her father's old steward – of how local Catholics viewed the bill's disenfranchisement of the forty-shilling freeholders.

Many of the freeholders themselves were quite content – glad of it for they knew they got nothing by the freeholds but trouble and just drinking, drinking & getting into trouble for or against the landlords at election time – They thought what was true – that they were driven like beasts – or cajoled or forced to perjure their soul, & no thanks to their bodies – He [*the Abbé*] does not think that Catholics have the least idea of getting rid or to ask to be rid of tithes – for, said he, I found they all understood as well as we do that the landlord pays the tithe not the tenant!! ...

Maria's views in this case were an extreme case of wishful thinking.

TO SOPHY RUXTON
Edgeworthstown, 26 April 1829

... Mr Butler who called at Wilson's hospital[209] on his way here saw a letter from Lord Longford to Mr Brown – a very sensible letter – in which he observed that now the [*Catholic*] Relief bill has passed & is law he hopes & wishes that no further opposition should be made – That he opposed the measure as long as he could but now Opposition can do no good & demonstrations of difference of opinion can only do harm, he submits & wishes all who can be influenced by him to submit with a good grace to the law of the land.
　　Very wise & good –

Another case of Maria's wishful thinking. Lord Longford had caused his brother-in-law the Duke of Wellington a great deal of trouble in the House of Lords by heading a group of die-hard anti-Catholics, but Maria had always had a soft spot for him.
　　Meanwhile Maria's brother William, the engineer who had been laying out roads in the west of Ireland, had come home with a shocking cough and fever. The Ruxtons' doctor from Navan was called in and confirmed the local doctor's view that William was suffering from the family disease: consumption.

---

209 A Protestant boarding school in Multyfarnham, Co. Westmeath.

He died two weeks later on 8 May. Maria's stepmother was desolated; she had brought up William from when he was a four-year-old child. Maria, who had already lost so many siblings, took the loss apparently philosophically – at least in writing to Fanny.

... He has done all the good in his power to his fellow creatures even to the last of his life ...

As for myself ... I go out every morning at half after seven – and find that brick & mortar supply me with health. The mind has a curious power of making itself take to new things – seemingly the most unassociated to former habits ...

But she was in fact severely cast down by William's death, brought on, she believed, by the harsh conditions he had endured in his profession, building roads in remote parts of Ireland. She had just started on a new novel, her first attempt to write one since her father's death, but she put it aside in disgust as 'miserable stuff' to report instead to Fanny on more cheerful events.

TO FANNY WILSON
Edgeworthstown, 5 August 1829

... We had a wedding a few days ago & I wish you had seen it – Peter Langan's eldest daughter to Pat Green of the Hall – very well suited in age – looks – everything. It had been going on many a month – Green's father wanted £200 – they split the differ & Peter gave £150 but begged it might not be mentioned & would not have it known on any account that he *would* give so much – The marriage was all rightly done – no running away & acting [*out*] of anger, penitence & forgiveness – So we were all particularly glad to grace these proper nuptials with our presence – Grandmamma [*Mrs Beaufort*] – Mamma – Honora – Maria – Lucy walked to Peter Langan's – day fine – He came out to receive us a face shining with the oil of gladness – smooth & smooth shaved – (the sun illuminating his countenance as when we came home after the rebellion [*in 1798*] – a few years older than at that time – but little the worse for the wear) – He ushered us with an air which many a gentleman might have envied – led us through kitchen with blazing hearth & preparations of roasts & baking & pots of flesh like the wedding of Trimalchio the rich – & through another door the boiling of pot[*atoes*] seen in the yard ...

Go on to the main rooms – a bedchamber of good size – remarkably clean & nice with nice patchwork quilt & pillows white as snow – two windows, plenty of light. In this room was the bride, a very pleasing neatly dressed bride with Mrs Michael Langan, mistress of the ceremonies & bridesmaid – a sister-in-law – & Mary Ivers & Betty Langan & another bridesmaid all very neatly & plainly dressed seated on a range of chairs at one side – & opposite a range for us – a great french chest at the end of the room under the window – this served for table.

Enter a flock of black priests – Mr O'Donoghue, Mr Slievin- "Give me leave to introduce Mr Higgins (our bishop that is to be)" – in a whisper, & two more names forgotten.

There was rather an awkward waiting for the bridegroom – and many slipping out to look up the hill to Green's to see if anybody was coming. Meantime we talked to the new Bishop who could tell of Paris & Rome & the illumination of St Peter's – But I did not like him half as well as our cordial jovial Dr McGovern – He is too slimy and *apprêté* – "Oh Mr O'Donoghue! – Don't *anticipate*" – with his hands crossed below the round of his stomach …"No likelihood I am sure – as such a thing as my being a bishop! Oh!" – and many prudish ridiculous faces – If affectation be ridiculous in a woman, nauseous in a man!

At last a whisper brought the joyful tidings that they were on the hill …

When we returned, all was ready – Mr Slievin was to perform the ceremony – and he began by throwing over his shoulder the great broad ribbon cincture – "Did ye never let anybody marry you two before?" "Never, please your Reverence" – Then he gave a short exhortation on the duties of the married state – plain & well said ending with "But if ye don't be kind to one another and live together according to Holy Mother Church, it is the most miserable state, this of marriage."

Holy Mother Church made into one rumbling word was repeated sundry times in several sentences of similar meaning & then, suddenly changing his tone, he said in the most brutally ordering tone in which the Catholic priests give directions to their flock as labourers speak to a cow or horse when they are drawing them through a gateway – "Down on your knees"

Down popped bride & bridegroom & as the space was too small it was not easy. But when they were jammed down Mr Slievin stood close over them, with his little prayer book over their heads, between every mumbling of Latin giving directions of what they were to do –

"Now" (in the same tone Garrett Keegan would speak to the cow)

"Now – your Lord's prayer – say yr Lords prayer" –

Both in Latin mumble "Dominus domini" – I could hear nothing –

"Take her hand – no, th'oder – Will you have me" – (the same as our marriage ceremony)

But then came the ending with worldly goods – & this differs – with the gold & silver I thee endow

"Where is it" – (in a low voice) "& have you the ring" –

Bridegroom "I have somewhere" and he felt through his waistcoat pocket – out came two crowns & a sovereign & in the hurry, down they slipped on the ground – and all the time the priest was mumbling prayers overhead – the groom below with his long hands scrabbling up the money, which he did happily get together right in time to pass into the bride's hand … Poor creature – her hands shook so she could not hold these wordly goods & down rolled the money a second time …

It was probably the first time Maria had attended a Catholic service. She reported the sequel to Fanny a week later.

… I saw the bridegroom yesterday again and when alone in the study with me as I was congratulating him on his having such a nice wife, he said smiling "She cost me dear, Ma'am" – "How so" – "I could have had another girl with £200, a relation of my own too – But she was very homely & I could not fancy her – It is all fancy you know, Ma'am – But my friends were not satisfied & would not let the marriage be unless I got £150 – So it hung for several months – and at last this was the way I settled with Peter, my father-in-law. He was to give me some £150 down afore my people – and I promised after the marriage should be over & they not knowing, I would give back the £50 – and so I did – So there it is now" – I gave him joy & assured him I thought he would be much happier than if he had the other £100 & the other woman whom he did not fancy – "Well I think so, Ma'am, that's what I feel."

I told him that it was the feeling we all had in our family that it was better to marry for love than money – That none of my sisters had married rich men but they were all happy without riches.

"Why then, Ma'am, I thought Miss Fanny that's settled in London had great riches with the gentleman she has married" – "No, she has not, I assure you – but she has what is much better, love & happiness & so I hope will you."

He made a graceful bow of his head, & his whole face lighting up seemed to say I'm much obliged to you, Ma'am – for this is a prize more than the odd hundred …

In September, Wordsworth called on a tour of Ireland with two industrialist friends from Cumbria – Maria was not well and confined to her sofa, but still able to send a full report on to her aunt. Unlike her admiration for Byron and Scott, she had never been an enthusiast of Wordworth's poetry.

TO AUNT RUXTON
Edgeworthstown, September 1829

I am now able, with the consent of all my dear guardians, to write with my own hand to assure you I am quite well.

I enjoyed the snatches I was able to have of Wordsworth's conversation – and I think I had quite as much as was good for me and for him in my opinion – He is sensible – but has an abundance, a superfluity of words and he talks too much like a book & like one of his own books neither prose nor poetry … as if he were always speaking *ex cathedra* for the instruction of the rising generation and never forgetting he is MR WORDSWORTH – the author and one of the poets of the lake – But under all this slow slimy circumspect <u>lengthiness</u> there is a vein of real humour and whenever this breaks through and he lets himself laugh & describe naturally without picking his words or thinking of his character he is very amusing and agreeable – At all times he is I am persuaded a really good man. He has a good philosophical bust too though very plain – a long thin gaunt face, much wrinkled and weatherbeaten … of the Curwen style of figure & head[210] … but with a more cheerful and benevolent expression – He has contrived very comfortably to travel all over Europe with different rich travellers – I hope they were none of them so impatient as I am of long-winded speakers … Mr Marshall & his son with whom he came here seemed to dote …

My guardians turn their eyes reproachfully upon me – Mr William Hamilton has been with us since the day before Wordsworth came – and we continue to like him …

---

210 John Curwen, a well-known agricultural improver and friend of Wordsworth, had visited Edgeworthstown in 1813.

William Rowan Hamilton reported that Maria had deployed 'a great deal of her usual brilliancy' in her conversation with Wordsworth and even succeeded in drawing the younger industrialist 'whose talent for silence was profound' into discussing 'the formation of the solar system' after tea.

Meanwhile, a cousin, Mrs Anne Edgeworth, had died, leaving unexpected legacies to most of Maria's siblings. Maria's share was a pair of diamond earrings. She sent the earrings on to Fanny in London, asking her to arrange their sale through her old friend Mr Hope.

TO FANNY WILSON
Edgeworthstown, 10 October 1829

I hope the diamonds came safe to hand.

Now I will tell you the purpose for which I intend them.

"To help build" a market house in this Edgeworth's Town – a desideratum for which all the wise heads have been long laying themselves together in vain for want of the *je ne sais trop quoi.*

If the thing can by the use of this simply [?] be accomplished I mean to inscribe Mrs Anna E's name on the markethouse in some such way as follows –

This market house built by a pair of diamond earrings left to Maria Edgeworth from Anne E, daughter of John E. etc -

I think that her finding herself [?] … near her father's constant haunts wd be gratified by this.

My mother & Honora & Aunt Mary & all the 7 sages of Edgeworth's Town … not only make no objections but approve. So does Bessy Mills of the crane and George Hinds of the study.

Follow a good example

When you can if you can.

The first step towards the market house is – sell the diamonds – Now Mr Hope to whom I have imparted my wishes most kindly undertakes to act the part of diamond merchant for me – and you will probably receive with this note a line or two from him and you will plan, my dear, in consequence to give – send or deliver the valuables as he may require – I only hope they prove valuable. But he wisely warns me that the London market has been glutted with diamonds and the ingenious French rogues have contrived to lower their value incalculably & irrecoverably by an art they have invented of making small worthless diamonds coalesce into larger ones.

So in all probability my market house will never have a stone of it laid. The days of Arabian tales when diamonds worked wonders are over alas! One thing however I have gained – the pleasure of a most kind & entertaining letter from Mr Hope which I will send you first frank …

Mr Hope sold the diamonds well and Maria was able to build the handsome two-storied Market House that still stands in the main street of Edgeworthstown.

By late November Maria had recovered strength for a prolonged visit to her 85-year-old Aunt Ruxton, who was now living in a comfortable seaside villa outside Dublin. She had undertaken to organize the sale of Sneyd's old house in Baggot Street. Sneyd and his wife, now both confirmed valetudinarians, had bought a house in Kent, much to Maria's disappointment. She had hoped he would return to take over the running of the family estate.

TO FANNY WILSON
Bloomfield, 15 December 1829

… Lord Rosse has paid me a visit here of 2 hours – a delightful visit – He is the most agreeable aimable old school nobleman – So fond of his son & proud of him & it is delightful to see how such reality & simplicity of affection. Dr Heussler is printing in his journal as fast as he can the account of Lord O[xmantown]'s improvement in the telescope … I saw a letter from Brewster saying that he considered this to be the greatest improvement in the telescope that has yet been made. The speculum is three feet in diameter – first made of coarsest brass – in various pieces polished down most carefully … and then he applies about the thickness of a shilling covering of [tin?]

TO FANNY WILSON
Bloomfield, 22 December 1829

… Mr Napier, who has some of old Napier's bones in him & is very agreeable moreover, persuaded me to go with him and Mrs N to see an ingenious mechanic who has brought over to Dublin a machine for filing & planing iron. Also a chamber circular saw which rabbits & dovetales etc. The machinery & the machinist McKenna, a simple hearted clear-headed man who I am afraid will be ruined, were well worth seeing and I thought I was doing finely too as an Irishwoman by giving his patriotism 40 minutes [?] of praise. But all the time I forgot that I was standing in a draft of wind & then I stood in a cold garret … with my attention at full stretch so that I did not feel till I got back into the carriage … By the time I reached Mr Napier's house I had such pain in hip & back that I could not stand & she most kindly put me body, back & all between the blankets of her own bed and drew the curtains round me and left me to repose …

Crampton, dear kind Crampton, came to see me on Sunday late and found me just come out of my room for the first time – He sat down for half an hour by firelight & talked so agreeably & instructively, opening in all he said such noble views … that my aunt, like my father, was quite enthusiastic in his praise when he departed –

"My dear Maria – What a man that friend of yours is – What scenes of fresh knowledge he opened to us in a few minutes – And what a charming manner – and what a voice" …

I cannot think any pleasure of vanity, none that I have ever felt I am sure, is in any degree comparable to the exquisite delight of being absorbed in admiration of another – Since the happiness of my days with my father I have seldom enjoyed this, but whenever I have, I find age has not dulled my sense of it …

TO FANNY WILSON
Edgeworthstown, 5 January 1830

… Harriet is reading to our great delight The Antiquary every eve[*ning*] and we are doing our best to get The Rivals on your recommendation. Crampton gave me a clever opinion of the author Mr Griffin[211] – a simple youth of 22 – who answers yes, Miss and no, Miss – holding the ends of his fingers together while he sits on the edge of a chair.

Miss Crampton asked him where he found the beautiful old songs & snatches of poetry in The Collegians –

"In our shops in the back lanes of Limerick there is often bits of ballad strung together … I would often be turning them over always – and I met with the things."

Honora will not let me say more …

---

211   Gerald Griffin, son of a Limerick brewer. His most famous novel, *The Collegians*, 1829, was adapted
       as a play, *The Colleen Bawn*. He later renounced writing to become a Christian Brother and died of
       typhus in 1840.

Reading aloud in the library after dinner –
from left, Aunt Mary Sneyd, Harriet, Maria and Mrs Edgeworth.

In the New Year, Lestock Wilson reported Fanny's health precarious and her
mother left for London, taking her youngest daughter Lucy with her as fellow
nurse.

   Maria was left in charge at Edgeworthstown. She was now running both
parts of the estate with the help of a kindly local agent, Mr Hinds, and sent
reasssuring instalments of news and gossip to London.

TO MRS EDGEWORTH
Edgeworthstown, 23 January 1830

It is of the greatest comfort to us all … that you are with Fanny when she
needs you so much … I cannot express to you how glad we are that you did
not delay your journey and that it has been so happily accomplished – Every
time the storm winds blew after we knew you safe we blessed Heaven – and
Lucy having borne sea and land & excitements of all sorts so well it is quite
wonderful …

   You will have the comfort of hearing from all hands now scribbling fast to
you that all is going on as well as possible here … Aunt Mary's cold … quite
gone and Honora well – and myself perfection.

   Ho[*nora*] gave an excellent dinner yesterday to the 9 times bulk of
common Colonels & to his thin subaltern Mr Scott (who seemed quite

daunted by him) and to Mr and Mrs Willoughby Bond & Major B – Farrell the long-armed man of figure & Mitchell the little man of parts and poor lame Reger [?] ... and all went off WONDERFUL considering the mistress was away.

The Colonel is a Falstaff size of man with a great deal of humour & told several good stories of John Kemble learning or <u>not</u> learning to ride in his riding house when he was an old man – But what pleased us best in the Colonel was the liberality and humanity with which he spoke of the Irish – He has been a year in Ireland quartered in all parts as he said and "Upon my word I think if the Irish had fair play, there would not be a finer people upon earth" – "When a man comes to me to be enlisted – or for whatever he comes, I make no difference between Catholic & Protestant – Go to Heaven your own way say I – only do your duty – Be a good man that's whether you are Catholic or Protestant – churchman or atheist."

This from a military man & the kind of conciliatory tone will do much good – I took to him directly and he saw it and went on and parted excellent friends ... Francis fell quite in love with the Falstaff colonel.

... I have been much entertained with Shipp's Memoirs ... There is a chapter of advice to young men going to India which of course interested me for P[*akenham*][212] – I think it would be worth your looking at again when you are surrounded by all who can give you information – I observe he says that young men take out too much expensive outfits of clothes which do not usually <u>suit</u> & they are cheated at the selling ... I am aware that he is with the <u>military</u> and P in the civil line – But a portion of what he says may be applicable ...

TO MRS EDGEWORTH
Edgeworthstown, 18 February 1830

Ann Tighe told me yesterday <u>behind</u> <u>my</u> <u>back</u> ... that she knows an infallible cure ... which she learned when with Mrs Strickland and which assuredly cured her after trying all other things.

Tanners bark boiled in plain water – strained off – applied with a syringe two or three times a day – kept in a jug – a quantity of it & just warmed tepid – every time. ...

---

212 Pakenham, Maria's youngest sibling, had just passed top in his exams for the East India Company and was due to embark shortly for India.

If you know all this – or don't CHUSE to – no matter – I have eased my own mind of it – and I hope not burdened yours – and it costs me only 5 minutes … out of my 4 allowed hours[213]

They have this minute to open the window in the library it is so fine & sunshiny a day – snowdrops plenty – and your abominable black turkeys & cocks gobbling and pulling them up – and much worse pulling up anemones. I wish you had seen the passion Gahan [*the gardener*] was in yesterday & the running he made in half a dozen directions at once … and the dirt, gravel – stones he threw – cursing them all the time & the kitchen maids … & the gate & the yard & everything he could lay his tongue on – How I did laugh all the while – tho' ready to cry at the devastation & prophecy "Then, Ma'am, you won't never have anemones this year more than last."

He took to replacing the bodies of the dismembered anemones … with a tenderness only his love of plants could feel …

I enclose 3 of Lady R[*omilly*]'s letters about Lord B[*yron*] which I think might amuse that dear F[*anny*] on her sofa now that your heads – or ours at least – are shock-full … of Lord B's marriage and separation – Put it which way we all most make sense of it – But what a goose Lady B must be to WRITE now – was he a liar outright or mad – if mad he might have been unconscious of the frightful things he did – v. Lady R – But what purpose did he have in acting so as to frighten Lady B out of her house when she was willing enough to go – and sure he would not kill his own child ?

Be it as it may – one thing is clear – that Mrs Leigh, her sister-in-law, was double dealer and scribbler of letters and of what she had no business to tell …

TO FANNY WILSON
Edgeworthstown, 19 February 1830

> *Re the proposed biography of Sir Humphrey Davy who had died of a stroke in Switzerland the previous May.*

… I have written to Mr D. Gilbert who wrote to me about Sir H.D's letters. My father left me none of his and I have none – except with mere compliment – I know of no anecdote of him fit for publication – I could not well furnish Mr D. with the only one I know – that my father advised Sir H early not to

---

213 Maria's family had imposed strict limits on her time for writing letters.

tell lies – and that he really did not hate him for it afterwards – I am not sure that he took his advice.

Your description of Sir Humphrey's last book is most touching – and beautifully composed. I detest more & more since I have looked last night into Leigh Hunt's book on Byron this trade of making prey of the dead ...

TO FANNY WILSON
Edgeworthstown, 27 February 1830

... Lord John Russell's speech on enfranchising Leeds, Manchester & Birmingham is quite worthy of you – and independently of all association with you [*I*] should ... have listened to & admired it – Honora read it to Aunt Mary this morning – We feel sadly still without our reader Harriet – our talker & our sunshine over everything – and her husband too – we miss him very much. He conversed a great deal & very kindly to Aunt Mary at dinner & tea – Francis & he kept up a continual battledore & shuttlecock of arguments from Hamlet to Plato – & Leigh Hunt to Shelley.

Leigh Hunt's life or anecdotes of Byron are really odious – such a mean wretch – afraid to strike yet willing to disfigure & insult the dead – Moore says well of him – "kept his cold venom till his friend was dead" – Hunt's anecdotes of his own school life (having the insufferable conceit ... that everything relating to himself must be interesting to the public) are entertaining ...

TO MRS EDGEWORTH
Edgeworthstown, 8 March 1830

... Opposite me sits Camilla our new cousin – & Richard [*Fox*] her delighted husband – she does not look as if she thought she had married a fool & he looks happier than most of the wise men I see – NB. What is the use of wisdom but to make ourselves happy – I like Camilla very much – She is perfectly free from affectation – frank but not forward – gentlewomanlike & ladylike, but not polished nor with the manners of the world – But with good family manners, domestic liveable habits – an amiable temper – capable of employing herself but I guess not literary tastes – talks a good deal and as if she had known us all her days – An agreeable voice, something of a lisp ... Her tone is of course Scotch – but not broad accent ...

TO FANNY WILSON
Edgeworthstown, 11 March 1830

My dearest child – My happiness at the close of the day is to write to you –
This packet will contain an unusual number of my follies – (at 63!) –

The packet inscribed To be opened with care no doubt you will expect to
be something worthy of care & you will be surprised to find nothing but violets
smothered in sea sand – As Honora tried with moss I am to take the reverse
of wrong from right in trying dry sand – Pray let me know in what state the
violets get to you.

The paper patterns are of a black velvet beret and velvet kind of stomacher
& cape which I saw last night on Mrs Richard Fox, otherwise Camilla, and
which I thought would become you – or Lucy – But you in particular – and
at 12 o'clock at night I ran to Evans who ministers to my fancies delightfully
quickly & begged her to tell Mrs Fox's maid that before she packed up the
said accoutrements in the morning she would cut the patterns for me –
accordingly here they are – Camilla looked an old picture in them – very
like the large Vandyke at Wilton – which you and I had the pleasure of
seeing together – It is the cheapest headdress that can be worn as the Scotch
economists have found & it does for half & whole dress … The stomacher
was made of black velvet with an edging of black blond [?] round the edge.
This was fastened to the dress on which she wore it but might just as well be
moveable ornament – I think it would most particularly suit your shape &
whole neck & shoulders – it could be worn with any cachemere gown – (in
satin with white muslin for Lucy -) … The dress with which this stomacher
[*was worn*] by Camilla was a plaid silk. The whole was a wedding present
from "Aunt Caithness" along with a superb black veil – Aunt Caithness you
are to understand is Lady Caithness & is to Camilla what Aunt Farnham is
to Richard –

But to stick to my own affairs – I think this stomacher cannot be very
old fashioned as it was part of this recent bride's paraphernalia – I hope it
is not by this time running the streets of London – I have an image of you
looking elegant in it – and my hope that reviving health, my dear child, is
bringing back the very few thoughts you ever had about dress – At any rate
you will forgive with a smile my old habits of considering you as my guide,
philosopher & doll –

What happiness it is to me to have such an object of fondness, sick or well, absent or present as you are & have been and ever must be to me – I do really believe you are now getting well – & that your mother will have the reward of seeing yourself again before she leaves you – Do not let her think of that for a great while yet – For indeed everything goes on smoothly here & she is still more useful to you than she would be to us ...

TO MRS EDGEWORTH
Edgeworthstown, 26 March 1830

... Francis breakfasted in my room yesterday morning settling down on my green cushioned armchair to coffee, egg, and bread and butter (so help me Heaven! I speak truth) at a quarter past seven by my watch hanging before us – and why this unwonted entry? – Because he had appointed overnight to drive who do you think in the gig with him to the Hills – Garret Keogh.

Gahan rode Dick the pony alongside of them – and F had plenty of sandwiches and bacon to fry and a knife and fork packed (Don't mention it to Hertford College[214]) in Pakenham's tin Botany case which never saw Bacon before! It is as well as ever after it this morning. They had all a good day in their own opinion – and F says he was never at a loss for conversation with G. Keogh all the way there and back and as he is not a lover of low company methinks this speaks highly for Garret.

They went over the whole farm – and Francis is delighted with their improving state and with all the people, Jameson Pat & ALL ALL! Luckily all were in their holiday clothes it being the grand Lady's Day.

There were 4 improvers of bog with little stone cabins on the edge of the great Serbonian or Carolinean bog which he particularly liked to see – He admired an old man of 60 so much for setting about to build a house for himself and reclaim bog.

By the way, <u>60</u> now appears to me not at all old – rather the first bloom of old age – no more.

These people carry the lime down on their backs 2 miles sometimes stone by stone ... When I catch Mr Hinds again we have great projects for 40 bog cabbineers – More of this in the days of May when please God we shall be thinking of you, Ma'am – of your being apt to come soon – thereabouts ...

---

214 Pakenham was now attending Hertford College, Oxford, in preparation for his departure to India.

Edgeworthstown, 12 April 1830

…. Sophy and Barry and Maxwell – Mary Anne and Charlotte – [*Sophy and Barry's children*] have all been here since between one and two yesterday – They are one and all delightful – They are the nicest, dearest happiest best behaved children I ever did see and the most engaging – The library is now so happy and <u>littered</u> not lettered – The bricks are all about the floor! – The two castr'd stools in rapid motion whirling about their two characters – Barry has little delicate Charlotte on his knee on the sofa which is now in the bow-window – found by Francis to be a charming place! … Sophy is at the pianoforte now in its summer place …

Aunt Mary is netting and has beside her on the library table – what do you think? …

A bullfinch which Barry brought her so like our own dear Bullie that I can hardly believe it is not the same – Only he cannot say Bully Bully pretty Bully – But he has a sweet natural song of his own – Honora thinks him much handsomer than the last Bully – but she never had a proper sense of my poor late departed Bully.

We have Lord Byron's life but I have not begun it yet …

TO AUNT RUXTON
Edgeworthstown, 3 May 1830

… It is very happy for your little niece that you have so much the habit of expressing to her your kind feelings – I really think that if my thoughts and feelings were shut up completely with me, I should burst in a week – like a steam engine without a snifting-clack, now called by its grander name of a safety valve …

You want to know what I am doing and thinking of – of ditches, drains and sewers – of dragging quicks from one hedge and sticking them down into another at the imminent pleasure of their green lives – of two houses to let, one tenant promised from the Isle of Man and another from the Irish Survey … Then I am thinking for three hours a day of "Helen" – to what purpose I cannot say.

Helen *was her proposed novel, the first she had seriously attempted to write since her father's death.*

VIII

JULY 1831 – AUGUST 1834

BY THE AUTUMN of 1830 *Maria's stepmother was back at Edgeworthstown and Fanny was reported better. The chance of going to London to stay with Fanny herself was irresistible to Maria. It would give her the chance to see old friends and extend Fanny's social circle. She was also looking for material for her new novel,* Helen, *which was to be set in England. In August she set off for a last visit to her beloved Aunt Ruxton, now fading fast, in Dublin, and then to stay with Sneyd and his wife at their house in Kent. She reached London in December. After nearly six years in rural Ireland, she found the social and intellectual excitements of London almost intoxicating. Thomas Moore, who met her at a Whig breakfast, reported her rather scathingly as suffering from 'overactivity of the tongue'. Maria wrote ecstatically to Honora (10 February 1831).*

I am just come home from breakfasting with Sir James Mackintosh[215] ... Fanny was with me, double! double!! joy and pleasure ... Oh what it is to come again within the radiance of genius. Not only every object appears so radiant, so *couleur de rose* – But I feel myself so much increased in powers, in range of mind with a view *d'oiseau* of all things raised above the dim dim fog & bustle & jostle of commonplace life ...

---

215 Eminent Whig historian and politician. Appointed Professor of Law to the East India College at Haileybury, he would have taught Maria's youngest brother, Pakenham.

How can anyone like to live with their inferiors – prefer this to the delight of being raised up by superior talk, bright regions of genius. The sense of having even this perception of excellence is a pleasure so far beyond what flattery can give – Flattery is like a bad perfume – Nauseous & overpowering after the first waft ...

In February she wrote her stepmother a moving account of her visit to the former Kitty Pakenham, now Duchess of Wellington, lying bedridden, a tiny, pale, shrunken figure in the splendid drawing room at Apsley House. On 9 April she called again, only to find the poor little Duchess had died the previous day, the Duke at her bedside. She was given a lock of Kitty's hair and left Apsley House just as the crowds were collecting to smash the windows in protest against Wellington's opposition to the Reform Bill.

The political drama over Reform proved so thrilling that she did not tear herself away till early June. She declared herself, after initial doubts, for 'the Bill, the whole Bill and nothing but the Bill' and described in detail to her stepmother the extraordinary shenanigans in the House of Commons. She returned eventually in July, now travelling comfortably by train and steam packet, and bringing with her the ten-year-old son of old friends, the Moilliets, who was to attend Lovell's school at Edgeworthstown.

TO FANNY WILSON
Shelbourne Hotel, Stephen's Green, Dublin, 9 July 1831

I am perfectly well and was the same all the way from Liverpool ... a passage of about 13 hours. I landed at 6 o'clock at Howth and reached Dublin by half after 7 and found Peggy [*the housekeeper of 31 Merrion St*] quite in despair at having no bed for the young gentleman – One she had for me to which the painters have not yet come. I recovered her from despair as well [*as*] I could and enquired for the nearest cheapest hotel – Shelbourne's on Stephen's Green – I made recovered Peggy lead me to it and found it full – crammed all but one very dirty sitting room and bedchamber smelling insufferably of stable – 9 shillings per day – Waiter & chambermaid scarcely awake and barely dressed – but while we were parlaying a red eyed thin faced man put his head between their shoulders – "My name's Burke, Ma'am, and I've just learned your name's Edgeworth and you're as welcome as life to the best room in my house for anything at all! Only not a room have I vacant till after 12 – then the tenant will be gone & you shall have a proper drawing room – & your young gentleman – if you will take what you see till after breakfast".

So I did – and a very bad breakfast we had – and a worse dinner – everything truly Irish in the old worst sense – too much show – too much dirt – and not a word without flattery – or lying – One of Burke's unanswerable speeches finished with "Ma'am, I admired you before you were born" –

This made even Theodore Moilliet smile, albeit he has almost as little comprehension of humour as his father ...

I have not told you, but without my telling you, you must know what I must feel returning where no Aunt Ruxton is – and passing by Bloomfield – & all the places associated with that most dear, most kind & loving best of all friends ...

Mrs Ruxton had died in November just after Maria's departure for England.

TO FANNY WILSON
Edgeworthstown, 1 July 1831

(St Swithin's day & very showery it has been)

Here I am again at my scribbling work in my little corner in the library at my little table – quite well – quite happy – and with the surplus of unexpected happiness in having Harriet here – I had the most delightful journey from Trim with her – & such talking! Oh such talking! both in the carriage & ever since I came here – I am indeed a very happy little creature & old as I am I have the keenest relish of the highest happiness of being so loved at home & of loving all at home so thoroughly – How miserable people must be who come back to an unhappy disunited home. The place in the middle of haymaking looked remarkably cheerful and pretty ...

But oh! I must tell you that my room has been made so nice by your kind mother – New carpet – new bed – white & green same as before the bed – the carpet beautiful & a cover over the box form [?] in the window which now makes a real sofa – Upon this the ladies sat to see the unpacking – and great was the diversion! And laughing & wondering how so much & such astonishing things could come out! – The ironmongery box, the little box in which I used to keep Helen was the first unpacked ... Harriet liked all the little things I had bought her ... The watch chain she said was exactly such a one as she had seen Lady Lansdowne wear years ago & she had always wished to have one like it … You see how rightly you judged – I am anxious that you who so kindly helped me in all my choosings should share my pleasure …

Honora liked her comb & its vandyked top – my mother without knowing that the red shawl was for her fell into admiration of it and exclaimed "Well, Maria, I am glad you have bought yourself such a handsome shawl that will do you credit".

When I told her that I had another of exactly the same value which I like much better & that this was hers & chosen with the hope of suiting her taste, she grew very red & gave me a kiss, dear good kind soul that she is, God bless her. She is your own mother & the moral of you, as Mary Bristow says, in kind heartedness – …

All the lower region offerings succeeded to heart's content. Especially Mrs Evans' worked ginghams made a great sensation … Of the people who do not live within the house I have as yet seen only Margaret & Mr Hinds and Marianne – all well & good … and like their souvenirs quite as much as you could wish for me – Poor Gahan I have not yet seen, he has pleurisy – and I was afraid for him – he is a very valuable person – Garret Shea gone [*till*] tomorrow – he is in some domestic trouble with his beautiful vixen –

Mr Shaw looks moribund with a black silk cap over his shaven skull – Have not been to Molly Bristow yet …

I cannot describe to you how excessively happy I have been these last 3 days – I did well enough when I was in Hampstead Hall – etc etc but this is my own home & there are the people after my own heart – Even if they were not my own by nature, they must be by choice – My spirits dance within me – and ideas spring faster than I can utter, and brighter than I can paint …

TO FANNY WILSON
Edgeworthstown, 1 August 1831

… I am deepening the bed of the Edgeworthstown river … Francis and I have just been walking down there. And what shall I see when I get there, Garret, said I. Mud and some gravel and stone, Ma'am, said he. And Francis lifted me over the ditch & I saw gravel, mud & stone – And saw the water run – and came home content.

What use in talking when the water runs – The job is done and it has been many a year doing – and never would have been done but for my plaguing Barny Woods' heart out.

His heart has been put in again & spirits raised this day by the watch

Francis Edgeworth
– a sketch on his
return from Italy.

which Mrs E has presented to him & he goes red with delight and redder when I give him chain & seals – Never was chancellor so much delighted …

Yes, my dear, I am going on with Helen [*her novel*] much to my satisfaction – that is, going over all we did and reforming it all.

> *A few days later there was a new family crisis to deal with. Francis, precociously brilliant, had to his mother's consternation left Trinity College, Cambridge after a year, declaring himself an atheist, and proposing to earn his living by writing. He had then gone to Italy for several months – before returning to Edgeworthstown for the summer. Now aged twenty-one, still with no job prospects, he declared his wish to propose to Miss Hamilton, a sister of Maria's favourite mathematician, William Rowan Hamilton. He would then take her back with him to share his life in Italy where two could live, he claimed, as cheaply as one.*

TO FANNY WILSON
Edgeworthstown, 12 August 1831

… [*Francis*] declares he feels no passion – only a sense of suitability – and a desiring of having a companion who will join in all his pursuits & sympathise with him in love of poetry, the arts etc. And she can & will – She is not pretty & he is sorry for that – She has not a pleasing voice – is not elegant – polished

– he sees all this & moreover that he would not wish to marry her if he were to live in England instead of Italy …

Then there is also to be considered that, with his present opinions on religious subjects & his ardent desire to make converts & to tell all he does & does not believe, he never will do for this country – I heard him on his notions yesterday till I really was convinced that he is beyond the power of reason on this subject – and that he has a strong ambition to propagate his strange opinion – that he would like as he said to go to the faggots – He seemed rather to regret that faggots are out of fashion – I told him H[*amilton*] dared to say he might get himself comfortably burned in Spain even nowadays if he tried – The upshot of all this … about Miss H is that he will not make any proposal – She is not pretty …

My dear – I am excessively fond of Francis – he is so very amiable with all his extravagances – poor fellow, he is always quoting to me my father's marrying so young – & thinking what my father did – felt & thought – so like him in some things & unlike him in others …

These last two days have been rain, rain, Irish July rain – and I have had the satisfaction this morning (which I got up at 6 o'clock to enjoy) of seeing the swollen river of Edgeworthstown keeping between its banks so beautifully & running away at such a rate – Barney Woods & I stood looking over the bridge in the morning sun and crying Success to ourselves! Never was a better job done there these 16 years, concluded Barney!

And conceive my added delight in wandering through the muddy streets and stepping like a child in the puddles on purpose to prove how well my *caoutchoux* boots keep out wet – Not a drop entered in – dry as a bone for breakfast my boots …

In London, the uproar over the Reform Bill was reaching a crescendo – Maria feared that 'the House of Commons would soon batter itself to death'. And at the seaside in Co. Down with Fanny, she discussed immediate practicalities that might help the family finances, which were still heavily burdened with Lovell's debts.

TO MRS EDGEWORTH
Rostrevor, 25 September 1831

There has been much sense put into my head by Fanny – that when this bill [*the Reform Bill*] passes there will probably be a sudden rise of stocks – And when the mass of bodies find they have not gained by it there will be a fall – Now if Mr Hinds[216] does not sell at the high moment he will not be able to sell afterwards & I cannot have his money. Therefore I beg you will request that he will immediately write to his broker to order them whenever the stocks rise to 831, the point at which he tells me he can sell. He should sell without waiting in hope that it should rise higher. Let him order that the two thousand be placed to my credit at Hoare's …

She returned from Co. Down via Armagh, where another mathematical friend, Dr Romney Robinson, was now head of the Observatory, and retailed the latest instalment of scientific gossip to Fanny.

TO FANNY WILSON
Edgeworthstown, 1 November 1831

… My journey to Armagh with Mrs & Dr Robinson was delightful – She never speaking or talking at all & I sitting back in the middle in the way in which I used to do between you & Harriet – certainly his flow of ideas and variety and accuracy of information scientific & literary are quite astonishing – His prodigious memory, retentive & recollective both in superlative degree, has not encumbered his inventive faculty, nor in any way impeded the march of intellect by the vast baggage they bring to the field – In fact none of it is rubbish-baggage – all is treasure well weighed & counted & packed for use not show – admirably packed – so that he can get at anything he wants at the moment of need – During the 4 days I was at the Observatory my mind was taking in … taking in – more than it could hold – and I often wished, dear, for you to make it all clear to me for he explains scientific things so admirably that, ignorant and impractical as I am, I could and I did perfectly understand at the moment – yet it was all gone! – or confused – the old & the new – and all the improvements that he has made or projects …

He shewed me all the experiments in the polarisation of light which Herschel showed us with an excellently contrived apparatus of his own which I perfectly longed that you should see – But I dare not be your witness [?] over particulars …

I was particularly pleased by his estimates of Wollaston, Herschel – Kater and Babbage of all of whom he told me anecdotes that agreed with our own

---

216 Acting agent for the Edgeworth estate.

experience and judgements – He spoke of Babbage with more force … than I could venture to do – of the meanness of his personal animosities – of this being utterly unbecoming [*to*] his superior genius both as man & philosopher.²¹⁷

Robinson had observed that some persons … worked upon Babbage's irritability for their own base purposes – repeating to him what was said behind his back by this or that member of the R[*oyal*] S[*ociety*] just to set him to fight their battles – not caring what became of his reputation – Babbage was made to see this at last and said frankly to Robinson "I think you really care for me – and I thank you and feel it" –

I was very glad to find that Babbage has this candour & feeling – R[*obinson*] after pointing out to him in his book a sly covert stab at Herschel, reminded him of H's kindness at that time of distress. Babbage burst into an agony of tears – I believe he is now as good friends as ever with Herschel – I thought all this did Robinson great credit …

I was to have left the Observatory on Saturday but when all packed and chaise at the door it rained and blew such a storm that I really could not go. Stayed till Monday … found that … I could go in a coach which had just begun to run (to oblige me) by Slane to Dublin so got up at five o'clock on Monday morning, – dark rain and blowing desperately.

… Dr Robinson was so good as to go with me though he had been talking till one o'clock the night before …

In the coach as soon as the grey light of morning made them visible, I saw opposite me a thin mild sort of man with a cleric hat on his knees and a fat 2-volumes bound in one kind of a jolly mortal who might have been a Catholic priest or a prosperous whiskey selling shopkeeper. The thin man was a priest, a country curate and the thick man I know not what but a <u>wag</u> gratis and many a joke he cut upon the mild priest who never soured, always smiled benignantly or Jesuitically. One instance will tell all – I was at work (Honiton border)²¹⁸ – I threaded a small needle –

(Priest) "Well as long as I have lived" (he could not have lived very long) "I never saw that done and would not have believed it possible."

(Wag) "No? Why then, your Church believes more extraordinary things possible."

---

217 Charles Babbage had published an attack on his fellow scientists the previous year, inspired by pique at not having been elected head of the Royal Society as Sir Humphrey Davy's successor.
218 A kind of lace.

Presently came in a huge bang-up-coated self-sufficient bear of an English agent, with a fur cap on his very handsome head, set at an angle of insolence.

(Wag) "Sir, you have the advantage of us in having a lady on the same side with you."

Down flopped the gentleman without the least pretence of care for the female and it was well he did not extinguish me – I shrunk and was saved. Much politics and three newspapers were unfolded and handed by the bear to all but the female. Almost all sentences began or ended with "I have no hesitation in saying" – or "Decidedly – decidedly". He was not without sense or even liberality but he made both almost odious. He talked of hunting men as if they were animals. I thought he must be either a Revenue officer or an agent and I afterwards found that he is agent to both Lord Bath and Mr Shirley. He shall be in my books, I promise him, whenever I get to Ireland again. I am much obliged to him for he has given me many ideas that will work out well …

A month later a new crisis with Francis erupted. He had gone to London to look for tutoring work and almost immediately proposed to an unknown Spanish girl – Rosa Eroles – whom he had met in his lodgings. (The story reads like a preview of La Bohème.) Fanny was distraught at having failed to prevent the engagement and Maria wrote immediately to console and advise. The bride, though penniless, must be treated as 'a sister' even though – horrid possibility – she might turn out to be a Catholic. Francis' mother had 'wisely and kindly' already invited the young couple to Edgeworthstown. Maria sent a long letter to Sophy Ruxton putting the story in the best possible light.

TO SOPHY RUXTON
Edgeworthstown, 27 December 1831

… Nothing could be more just than Margaret's reflexion that we should not add the evils of family discord to any other – Upon this plan we have all acted and – how to make the best of it is the general thought of the whole family – And the more we see and hear, the more materials for making good of it we find.

In the first place it might have been so much worse – And it was to prevent it being much worse that Francis married – He left Italy to avoid a sort of connexion which young men of the world could not have blamed but which besides its real immorality might have led to the most fatal worldly consequences – besides the degradation of his tastes – As Margaret truly observes he might easily have been worked upon to marry a mistress & this would have degraded us all …

In the present case his motives were excellent and there is a sort of consistency in his inconsistency which I must do him the justice to explain to you – And for this purpose I must turn him inside out … He came over from Italy determined to look for a wife – to save him from doing worse – He found he could not be happy without a female companion living at a distance from his family in that exile to which his income & his determination not to go into any profession rendered necessary. He found after a year's experience that he could live in Italy upon half his income – How he managed it I can't tell – but he certainly did live upon it. He then imagined – these were his words to his mother "That it was quite selfish not to share his superfluous wealth" with somebody – some female companion. He looked out & saw in Ireland 2 sisters, the names I do not like to put on paper … First he thought one would do then the other. The one was a person of considerable literary abilities – the other of great sensibility & who wrote very pretty verses – He was on the point of proposing for sensibility – went up to Dublin for his purpose – But upon his mother's, Honora's and my advice to stay a bit & see a little more without committing himself … It was quite evident to Honora, myself & Mrs E that there was not the least passion or love in case of either – He said so himself …

We much prefer what he has chosen – even for our own sake … I for my part could not have lived with either of these sisters – tho' I believe them perfectly good – and clever too.

Well, but to go on with Rosa – His first account was a letter to my mother of the romantic adventure of his first seeing these Spanish ladies & their black eyes … when he was shown into their room at his lodging house by mistake – Though Francis honestly showed he was disposed to fall in love with Rosa, we did not feel frightened when he ended his letter with "But you must not be frightened, my dear mother".

Fanny unluckily was obliged to go out of town with Lestock to pay a visit to the country. Francis' last words at parting with her were "I would propose to Rosa if I was sure … she would refuse me". Fanny fancied he was secure leaving him in this line of mind – But no sooner was the weight of her prudential influence off his mind, then off he went to his donnas – Rosa came to open the door … and she said "Oh it is you" in a rich soft voice which encouraged him when he found himself alone with her to say "May I take the liberty to ask if you are engaged" – "No Sir" – Then he proposed in what words he did not tell but her reply was "Do your friends, your family, know what you are doing – And do you know that I have no fortune and no accomplishments except paying a little on the pianoforte … and knowing how to embroider well" … The candour of this made him love her all the better. "Then Sir, I should tell my mother …" She did so. His proposal was immediately accepted subject to the approval of the father who was living in Limoges … Francis wrote directly to his mother astounding her with the news … Fanny on her return equally astonished – Sneyd who was [*told*] in turn acted in the most kind & judicious manner – He wrote to Lord Holland to enquire whether these people really were what they said they were [*people of good family who had had to flee Spain*] – They had referred to Lord Holland's family who as they said had been very kind to them. … Meanwhile notwithstanding all Sneyd could say, Francis hurried on & had his banns published in St Pancras church to have all ready for their arrival.

The first comfort we received was from Lord Holland's reply … that the Eroles family are what they said they were … Miss Fox [*Lord Holland's sister*] went to see Fanny … & assured us that at least they were perfectly respectable though poor & earning their bread as immigrants … quite independent of all considerations about station – or birth – The next thing comfortable is that they are all united – very fond of other … and pulling together in adversity …

Fanny's account of [*Rosa*] pleased us "Rosa is a sort of person of whom I think I could grow very fond" – These words were balm to all our souls – Both Fanny & Sneyd describe her as not handsome but with fine soft eyes and with beautiful hair …

Francis calls her SIMPLICITAS – and values her all the more for knowing nothing – He will have much to teach her – and that will employ & attach him all the more – So all is for the best … She is between 16 & 17 but Fanny & Sneyd … think she has very good sense and remarkable … steadiness of character & understanding – When Sneyd urged her to nag Francis to follow some profession, she answered "Sir, everything cannot be done in a day – We must take time, Sir" …

Francis, duly married in St Pancras, swept his Spanish bride off to Italy without visiting the family home. His best friend had fallen in love and married Rosa's sister, Mariquetta and the two couples were to share a house.

Maria's letters turned on the political scene at home – O'Connell had stepped up the so-called Tithe War and had launched a new campaign to repeal the Union, the Catholic Relief Bill having failed to deliver his followers to the promised land. Tithes were now largely unpaid and in the west of Ireland, tenants were reported to be refusing rents. Edgeworthstown was still a relative oasis of calm.

TO FANNY WILSON
Edgeworthstown, 10 January 1832

... You ask ... about the state of our county – we are at present at peace still – except constant beatings of poor people suspected of being anti-reformers – No decided opposition yet to paying tithes – and all our rents paid – But there are symptoms that make us fear this will not last long – As Mr Mills said to me the other day "While ever Mr O'Connell lives, there can be no peace or security" – Mr Strickland said much the same – He gives O'Connell up as a bad or rather a mad man who has made popular applause his only motive & to whom excitation is now so essential that he cannot live without it & is blind to all other interests. He – S[*trickland*] – says that if a hundred thousand were put down before O'C[*onnell*] upon condition he wd never harangue a mob again he would [*not*] accept it or if he took it, break his word ...

December 1832 saw the first elections in Ireland since the Reform Bill. The Whig party's vote had virtually collapsed in Ireland, leaving its traditional supporters such as the Edgeworths with no option but to support Tory candidates against O'Connell. In Longford and elsewhere O'Connell's candidates swept the board, much to Maria's dismay.

TO HARRIET BUTLER
Edgeworthstown, 22 December 1832

A note has arrived this morning from Lovell – the first words of which are "All is lost" – he tells us nothing more except that he goes to Castle Forbes with Lord Forbes tonight – Mr M. O'Rourke [*?*] and Luke White are the members for the county of Longford –

The hills are blazing with bonfires and there are screeches of boys triumphing in the town – I hope that the night will pass without any murder

*A triumphant
mob runs wild
after the election.*

being committed – we have only 2 police now. We had some hopes of the
poll brought home to us at 12 o'clock last night by Morgan when Lord Forbes
[*the Tory candidate*] was 18 or 22 ahead. At eleven o'clock this morning Barry
Fox passed by in a coach on his way here – he could not stop but left word
at the gate that all was going on well! What made the change afterwards we
cannot guess –

Almost all our Catholic tenants have voted against us – they declared
to me they could not do otherwise, tho' they all said they wished it. James
Woods! – is an arrant coward so I was not surprised at him – Caffrey was
almost beat to a jelly last election for voting for his landlord – I really don't
wonder at his not daring to expose himself again – But Garret Keegan has
behaved infamously – telling superfluous lies … Now at least we know whom
we cannot trust … The evil cannot stop at this election – It is not as in former
times only losing an election – "Visions of tumult, spare my aching sight" – I
wrote to Lord Lansdowne a few days ago … a warning to waken in time his
fears for his Irish territories – which, if there be (and what is to prevent) a
dissolution of the Union, will soon cease to afford him rents & presently pass
into other hands. His great grandfather's Survey of Ireland may help in this
business in a way he little expected.

No more croaking till we meet – I have no knowledge if Sophy Fox and
her little ones will come … The King's County election, I fear, will detain her.

The alarming political outlook for landlords was compounded by the further collapse of Lovell. Breaking his promise to his family, he had run up another £3000-worth of debts (over £300,000 in today's terms), gone to Dublin to try to collect unpaid fees for his school and was found by Fanny and Sneyd in alcoholic despair in a Dublin hotel. His horrified family decreed that they could no longer share a roof with him – and he agreed to go to England for a cure. Financial disaster was staved off once again by Sneyd who agreed to buy the remainder of Lovell's land.

Maria remained surprisingly calm; she had long been aware of Lovell's secret drinking. Her beloved Fanny was back with her at Edgeworthstown – and her new novel, Helen, *was nearly complete. In May Harriet read the completed draft out loud in the library to the assembled family, including Aunt Mary Sneyd, now bent nearly double with age, who showed 'great interest'. There was approval all round. Sneyd wrote to his wife that it was in 'Maria's best style …' He and Harriet walked round the lawn when the reading was over, 'the owls shrieking and flitting by in pursuit of bats … The library, as we looked in at it through the windows with all its walls and pictures lighted up by the lamps looked beautiful. I thought how my father would have been touched to look in as we did on his assembled family …'*

J.G. Lockhart, Sir Walter Scott's clever son-in-law, had offered to act as Maria's agent with publishers and procured an advance of £1100, almost as much as she had earned for Ormond, *twenty years before. As she wrote triumphantly to her youngest brother Pakenham in India, Lockhart had told her it was the 'largest copyright that was ever given for a novel'.*

Pakenham, now in his first district in Saharanpur, north-east of Delhi, sent long bulletins home about his work, which Maria found intriguingly relevant to Irish problems. She forwarded his letters on to a new acquaintance, Professor Jones, whose lectures on political economy she had attended recently in England and sent Pakenham Professor Jones' seminal book on Rent. Her long letter to Pakenham gave the full melancholy story of Lovell's financial collapse and departure.

TO PAKENHAM EDGEWORTH
Edgeworthstown, 10 September 1833

… [*Lovell*] is now living at Liverpool. It is most melancholy to think of his banishment & I cannot tell you how it has really wrung my heart – He has such a mixture in his character of what is highly benevolent & generous and of such incongruously good temper with what must be despised and can never be depended on that I am in a continual seasick <u>seesaw</u> of pity and indignation – contempt & admiration, but the upshot of all my feelings is that I would do anything in the world for him but live with him again ... Upon the whole I am convinced and so is Honora & Fanny & above all Harriet that he was so little at ease in our society & always glad to escape out of the room that he is happier living far away from us ...

The school at Edgeworthstown is now to be <u>let</u> ... We have paid off nearly all the debts and are now repainting & repairing & hoping to find a good, substantial & moral ... & economical master who will take it on his own account. Poor Lovell, it rings my heart when I think of all the pains he has taken with that school ... And it cost him immensely. When C[*harles*] Fox asked him how did such sums of money go ... He answered – The <u>School</u> and <u>wine</u> ... Two or three wine merchants were his creditors for hundreds of pounds each ... Lifting up hands and eyes, one of them exclaimed how <u>could</u> so much wine be drunk in one house.

It is come very nearly to what was said of my great grandfather by the judge when his wine merchant's bill was brought into court – "This gentleman's coach horses must have drunk claret."...

That summer Edgeworthstown received its usual quota of visitors from England. Sir Culling Smith and his wife, the former Isabella Carr, brought their baby and nurse at Honora's suggestion to leave at Edgeworthstown while they fulfilled a long-laid plan to visit Westport and Connemara. They asked Maria if she would join them – and on impulse she accepted, and set off in their heavy coach on 4 October for the unknown.

TO HONORA EDGEWORTH
Mr Pounders (Ballinasloe), 7 October 1833

I have not repented yet, my dear Honora, and I hope that nothing has yet occurred at home that ought to make me repent of indulging myself in this extraordinary excursion.

The grey horse of whom Mr Briggs boasted so much ... was as willing as ever but not quite able to draw us the whole 20 miles to Athlone ... His poor shoulder was worn raw to the size of half a crown under a vile collar ... as we at last discovered … was the cause of his refusing to put his shoulder to it when we were to go up hill … I am sure my aunt Mary would have loved Sir Culling S[*mith*] for his humanity & gentleness to the horse … We walked up every hill of the 2nd stage and were not at all tired …

The road is beautiful along the banks of the Shannon to Athlone and the sun shone silver bright upon the water & its many little wooded islands … I persuaded Lady C.S. to get out and sit in the barouche seat with her husband, he looked so lonely on his perch without her – They were very happy and so was I – and thanks to you, my dear Honora, for the sandwiches & gingerbread which last Sir Culling in particular likes and consequently desires his double thanks for his double portion – We were, I cannot tell you how many hours, going from Athlone to Ballinasloe because the road for many miles was absolutely full of sheep and their drivers & boys shouting & pushing and trying to make a way for the carriage … When we came to a narrow bridge we stuck fast … A very gentlemanlike officer on horseback … with his soldiers made way for us – and while we were waiting patiently who do you think came up to the side of the carriage & said "Ha! – How do you do, my dear Miss Edgeworth" – Mr Strickland! He was receiving rents & just heard my name at the inn and made his way after us – He is to be here this morning & will settle where we are to meet again … We did not arrive here till between 6 and 7 – But were dismayed to find the family at dinner and the house as full as ever it could hold of various branches of the family … The inns were full … a guinea a bed for 5 must certainly be paid even if they could be procured …

However these most kind hospitable people made out a nice little room in their full house for me … & next door there was found 2 empty rooms for Ld & Lady Wandescourt [*?*] who most luckily had been detained. So Sir C & Lady Smith were lodged there & though the bed is not so large as mine at home they have contrived to sleep & be thankful …

Mr Strickland has been with us here these last 2 hours – we stay here till luncheon – set off at 3 that we may reach Loughrea tonight before dark – Mr Strickland advises us … to drive through the beautiful park of Garbally and to go 5 miles out of our way … to see the ruins of Kilconnell famous for containing chambers full of bones of the thousands … who fell at the battle of Aughrim … We shall pass through the village of Aughrim to see the field of battle etc – all which will be fine to tell of as Sheridan said to his son when he proposed going down to the bottom of the coalpit.

The scene of this day's fair at Ballinasloe is to me admirably worth seeing – The fairgreen is before these windows … The sun is shining upon the green filled with horses & horsemen riding to show their horses – leaping & galloping – all full of spirit …

TO HONORA EDGEWORTH
Oughterard, 8 October 1833

These few lines are to let you know that we are at present at Outerade [*Oughterard*] and in good health – We were very near spending the night in the streets of Outerade – but, thanks be to heaven, it ended otherwise in very good beds after having eaten a very good John Doree and a beef steak and a few praties – We saw the town of Galway yesterday and then the very house & window from which the famous mayor of Galway … hanged his son who was a very great scamp – There is a marrow bone & Charles' head over the doorway in stone to this hour – And there are many curious Spanish gateways & old Spaniards' houses in Galway & Milesian relics – which we had not time to see all – but we saw the new docks that is to be and the broad Atlantic which I never expected to see … And I could have gone off straight to America that minute & no more about it if I had been so minded … Having called up the landlady & consulted I got a list of all the quality & literati that inhabits the town of Galway … [*and*] with Sir Culling and her Ladyship's approbation … wrote to the Doctor of the Infirmary which we preferred before all the others tho' there were titled names & O's … and just before he came into the room by great good luck I opened (in the history of Galway which Mr Strickland had bought me … the day before) on a passage in which there was the greatest praise ever you saw of the man coming upstairs – and the thanks of the whole county & country … for his skill and humanity in the time of fever & famine. And when he came into the room I knew I had seen his face before which was very red & goodnatured & Scotch … and he recollected me immediately and reminded me that he had dined at my father's table at Edgeworthstown the year of the rebellion, '98 – and praised my father almost till the tears in his eyes … It was he took us everywhere as I mentioned and would have taken us to the infirmary & the world's end but we had not time …

It was dark just as we got here – & the ugliest country ever you saw, parts of it all desolate and stone walls throughout & great rocks like giants' thumbs sticking up through the bogs and boiled rocks that look as if they had just bubbled & coiled up in great blobs on the shores of the lake – And then there came trees – and gentlemen's improvements very handsome – and a blacksmith with whom we stopped to talk and will mention more particularly on Wednesday week when we shall be at home if alive … We have been very well – never better – and fine days every day – none finer … We are going on the lake, Lough Corrib – as soon as we have breakfasted …

In my opinion we shall stop at Westport this night. But I never know (nor anybody else) so early in the morning …

TO HONORA EDGEWORTH
Ballinahinch Castle, 12 October 1833

… I wrote yesterday to tell you that we had arrived safely here at night by lantern light after having been passed or rather having been carried carriage and all without horses over such sloughs on the road as I never saw before – We have been most hospitably received and most fortunate for us that we reached this shelter for the morning after our arrival, Lady C. Smith who had several touches of rheumatism was totally disabled – seized with such violent pain in her knees that she could not stand or move – I dreaded a rheumatic fever … James' powders etc and lying in bed all yesterday have, I hope, prevented that danger but she is still incapable of moving …

On Thursday I hope we may get on to Westport or if able to Castlebar – But I see it is impossible that we can reach home by Wednesday next – All Sir Culling & this poor tortured sufferer can say is that they hope they may be able to reach Edgeworthstown by Saturday to dinner – Sir C with a spirit I much admire, especially as I shall profit by it, sent off a messenger to Castlebar (30 miles) yesterday for our letter … They will be here tomorrow night …

TO HONORA EDGEWORTH
Ballinahinch, 15 October 1833

… The gossoon who [*Sir C.S.*] sent to Castlebar from hence went on Saturday, I suppose, took some short cut across the mountain else he could not have been back so soon. The letter from you was read by Lady C.S. … [*and*] gave her much pleasure both from the assurance that her child was well & that she was not a plague to you … She was charmed by the baby stretching out her arms when Mamma was mentioned …

At the moment she is getting up and for the first time is to be brought downstairs for an hour or two wrapped in fur cloak – The dreadful rheumatic pain is gone – Ether, turpentine & laudanum in equal parts applied – and acetate of morphine gave her sleep ... Though her courage is pain proof – yet I am more afraid of her doing too much before she is equal to it – A relapse on the journey and in some wild place where no shelter could be procured might be fatal – I CANNOT in common prudence ... allow her to travel till ... she is able at least to stand – & to walk – and to walk a quarter of a mile too – for that last she may be forced to do the next stage we have to go – of 17 miles of execrable sloughing road without human habitation or shelter – and Mr Martin who is used to the country assures me it would be absolutely impossible for us to get to Westport from this place though it is only 43 miles – After what we have already gone through & the hazard of breaking this all-enduring [?] carriage I will never attempt it. The only alternative is to be bould & imp'dent – and to beg a night's lodging halfway between Ballinahinch and Westport, [at] Mr St George's at Delphi – It is a lodge which Lord Sligo built in the mountains ... and contains 17 *lits de maître* – Well! Well! One way or other we must get into some of them – Mrs Martin has written a note to beg for us – and she says that if the family are at home they will be happy to see us – and if they are not! – What do you think I propose to do? To take possession of the house & treat the servants as if they were our own – like the man in the Arabian tales who took possession of the Sultan's pavilion, all the supper prepared for him & his friends & was found asleep on his sofa ...

Ballinahinch, 17 October 1833

From day to day I have been hoping and wishing my soul away – The post did not go from this outlandish place yesterday and today I can only say that I hope we may be able to move on Monday – but I have no certainty – Lady C. Smith is now out of pain but her feet are so much swelled and inflamed that it is impossible that she could walk ... It would be rashness and folly that might cost her her life to let her attempt to proceed on her journey – Sir Culling too has been seized with a fit of asthma and has been so ill ... that he has been forced to take to his bed ... In my opinion his health is very hazardous ... The physician is a young man & his chief merit is saying little and doing less. Mrs Martin (who is a Mrs Bushe sort of person) has much experience &

judgement in illness and she has been of great comfort to us all – and she is most particularly agreeable to me – putting me in mind of my aunt Ruxton by a sort of original humour and quiet good breeding …

If we can move on Monday we must be in the carriage by 8 o'clock in the morning … and the postillion with these 4 horses which we brought from Galway undertakes to carry us to Westport before it be dark – There are two sloughs between this place and the Killeries, but from the Killeries to Westport there is a new road … Nimmo's delightful new line of road … Poor Nimmo! His works were taken out of his hands just before his death – Mr & Mrs Martin had the highest opinion of him[219] – You will understand my having become really fond of them both when I tell you that they were truly fond of William – Mrs Martin has repeated to me many of his conversations with her in his own words which I would not fail to recognise as his – She knows you perfectly from his description & calls you Honora – "That Honora he doated upon" – I cannot tell you how much she has fastened upon my affections and what a comfort I take in her … At such a distance from my own family to have found one who really seems to know you and Fanny & Harriet & my mother so well – Mrs Martin is a cousin of Mr Kirwan, the President of the RIA, my father's and my old friend & she tells me that he had early inspired her with a strong desire to become acquainted with Edgeworthstown – How strange & at what a providential time it has been brought about – The kindness and hospitality we have received surpass anything that I ever before met with …

Miss Martin (Mary) the only daughter of this house is quite an original character … a slight figure – classical hair – not red but auburn – altogether like one of Leonardo da Vinci's pictures – She is about 18 – there is an estate of £10,000 per annum in these wilds – an estate which Sir Culling says if improved would be worth a hundred thousand a year – She has never stirred from home – She is to go to London with her father & mother next spring – and what a new world for her & with what new eyes she will see it – She has read a good deal both of modern & ancient literature – Homer in Greek! – is well acquainted with all the beauties of Euripedes, Aeschylus etc as well as all French literature & all modern English – Scott – Byron – and down to the last volumes of Harry & Lucy – Nimmo gave her a taste for science – She is perfectly simple in her manner but has an independence of opinion & mind

---

219 Alexander Nimmo, famous Scottish engineer and architect who had died the previous year. William Edgeworth had worked under him laying out roads in Galway and Connemara.

Sketch of the lake from Ballinahinch Castle in Connemara, given to Maria by a fellow guest.

expressed with fearless gentleness that might be called brusquerie & yet is not – not in the least like Miss Clarendon [*a character in Maria's novel,* Helen] ... I did not intend to have said a word about her till we met, my dear Honora – But when I began, I could not help going on – as if I were sitting by your bed in the morning – and how I wish I were ...

[*Postscript*] Psalms & lessons for the day read by Mr Martin every morning before breakfast – and before dinner – Evening lessons & prayers – I have regularly been ready but I know you will not believe it ...

Maria's hopes of returning home were dashed when Lady Culling Smith shortly afterwards suffered a relapse, and in the end the enforced stay at Ballinahinch lasted for nearly a month. Eventually the Culling Smiths' coach managed to reach Westport and the party then travelled by stages back to Edgeworthstown. The adventure was to produce one of her best and longest letters (forty closely written pages) to her brother Pakenham in India (later published by his grandson Harold Butler as Maria Edgeworth: Tour in Connemara, *Constable, 1950). In the meantime she sent an account of the Martins' astonishing culinary arrangements to her stepmother who was still in England on a cure with two of her daughters.*

TO MRS EDGEWORTH
Edgeworthstown, 20 November 1833

... All the luxuries of life abounding for the table – but not always the necessaries – Venison the best Sir Culling Smith declares he ever tasted – almost every day – an island for a deerpark & a red haired odd kind of ½ gentleman retainer for a gamekeeper – to hunt and shoot the deer ... Salmon every day when in season ... Hare soup as good as at Mullingar ... all kinds of game and a little woman who learnt under Dick Martin's French cook and is one of the seven wonders of the world sending up dinner at the shortest notice that would do honour to a London tavern & from a kitchen dark as Dame Leonardoes and all in holes the floor & no conveniences of any kind – not even an oven And yet hot rolls ... and bread of all sorts ... all baked in a temporary oven of a great iron pot ...

The kitchen all day long haunted by ragged loungers & the labourers dining in it & then laying down to rest ...

You don't believe me – I cannot help it, but there it is true ...

By January 1834 her stepmother was still in London with the ailing Fanny and Lucy, and was now growing concerned for her third daughter, Sophy Fox, who was also showing consumptive symptoms.

TO MRS EDGEWORTH
Edgeworthstown, January 1834

... I am very glad to tell you that Mr Peacock [*the Edgeworthstown doctor*] thought Sophy much improved yesterday [*and*] ... says he does not apprehend any danger ... So as it is a mystery I can only repeat his words like a parrot ... I hope this will be some comfort to you, dear <u>old</u> mother as Fr[*ancis*] now calls you – Oh how I long to see him ...

Mrs Blackhall has ordered 270 cards – Mrs Blackhall – at Home – Quadrilles.

The County of Longford wonders at being so fine! And I wonder where she found the 270 people to send the cards to in this & the neighbouring counties – highways & all inclusive.

Mrs Blackhall told Sophy that she doats upon gaiety. I think she will not

*Harriet reading to the
aged Aunt Mary Sneyd.*

do for the County of Longford. We have excused ourselves in the plea of being
engaged with the company at home ...

Harriet Butler is so agreeable & so useful! Helping indefatigably Honora
and me at accounts and reading ... Ney's Life to Aunt Mary all evening & at
all odd times.

George Bristow to whom I carried a loaf of sugar this day is up – Honora
carried Lucy's purple ribbon to Molly & both she & Molly much pleased with
it – and George's eyes twinkled with delight ...

TO FANNY WILSON
Edgeworthstown, 7 February 1834

> *Maria had called on her father's old friend Admiral Sir Thomas Pakenham at
> Coolure just outside Castlepollard to thank him for helping with her brother
> Pakenham's appointment in India. He was about to move to a healthier station
> at Ambala.*

... The good Admiral who I like better to call Admiral than Sir Thomas met us
on the steps in a sort of embroidered skull cap which ... looked as if had been
[*made*] by one of his daughters out of bits of old carpet. He looked very like his
old self – and scarcely more worn or older than 26 years ago ... his mind quite
alive all the time we were there ...

*Admiral Pakenham's
unmarried daughter
turned 'farmeress'.*

Miss Bess [*Admiral Pakenham's daughter*] came in and was more agreeable and less frumpish than I ever saw her – The house is now well served – very proper butler & footman – quite well appointed – but what concerned us much more, the two daughters were extremely attentive to their father and in a very agreeable manner as if from real love & not mere duty work & for the love of God – Do not think I mean anything wrong or irreverent by that last speech – But you recollect to what I allude – my poor dear aunt Ruxton's crying bitterly when her son Richard in one of his fits of sanctity said to her "All I do for you, mother, is not for love of you, but for love of God"... [*Maria was still resolutely agnostic.*]

She reported the visit in full to Pakenham three days later.

TO PAKENHAM EDGEWORTH
Edgeworthstown, 10 February 1834

... Pray send us the plan of your new Bungaloo whenever you build. I hope your two faithful servants that you really like will accompany you to Amballah – But I am afraid you will miss your friend Atherton and your kittens – I wish I was one of those kittens ... I should wish to be your white furred cat with the pretty spots ... and I dare say you would allow me to sit upon your shoulder and purr-purr-purr – while you were writing.

My dear Pakenham foolish as I am I am so old that I am afraid I shall never be able to see you again and this thought comes across me and gives a twinge to my heart.

I hope your steam ships will be carrying your letter with the <u>speed of light</u> across the Red Sea and then overland in no <u>time</u>, please your honour ...

Sophy's letter has told you of ... the death of poor Francis' boy on whom he so doted ... He and Rosa are now at Fanny's – she says he looks as if he had suffered much but his spirits are even. I have no doubt that these realities afflicting and all the ... exertions he has made will be of permanent use to him & will bring him from Plato to the necessary duties of life. But I need not prose about it. You will know what I mean ...

[*She reported further on her new novel,* Helen, *due to be published in early spring.*]

You may be sure that I have desired Fanny to send a copy ... Oh how I wish Harriet could fly over and read to it you ... I should tell you beforehand to prevent any disappointment that there is no humour in this book, nor any Irish character.

It is impossible to draw Ireland as she is in at present in any book of fiction. Realities are too strong – party passion too violent to bear to see or care to look their faces in the looking glass – The people would only break the glass & curse the fool who held the mirror up to Nature – distorted – nature in a fever – we are in too perilous a case to <u>laugh</u> – humour would be out of season – worse even than bad taste – Whenever the danger is over as the man in the sonnet says "We may look back on the hardest part and laugh" ... Meanwhile I am preparing materials for an Irish story – providing such as may leap clear of politics and polemics & be interesting still if possible without them by waking the natural affections which are of all times – and in which the Irish are rich indeed.

I never forget what Sir Walter Scott once said to me. He urged me "To explain to the public why Pat who gets forward so well in other countries is so miserable in his own ..."

A difficult question – I fear above my powers – But I shall think of it continually & LISTEN & LOOK & LEARN ...

Helen *was finally published in May. Although it was received with largely favourable reviews, it did not have the immediate success of her novels twenty years before, whose first editions had sold out within days. There were now a host of racier 'silver-fork' novelists (depicting romance and scandal in high society)*

competing with her, and Maria's initially slow-moving plot was against her.
(The plot of Helen *– in which the heroine is sucked into lies to protect her*
friend – was later to inspire Mrs Gaskell's great unfinished novel, Wives and
Daughters.*)*

TO FANNY WILSON
Edgeworthstown, 23 June 1834

… Do not be angry with Mr Lockhart – I am sure he did all for the best – I am
quite convinced that he wrote that beautiful review of Helen which appeared
in I forget what paper in which the characters were said to live & move around
the reader. I think that Lockhart gave Bentley [*Maria's publisher*] the choice
of either publishing in the newspapers or in the Quarterly & that he chose the
newspaper puff and perhaps no publisher chose rightly – The book I believe
from what I hear in remote lands & Dublin not famed [*for*] buying books has
sold well – and there is the publisher's point & test …

TO FANNY WILSON
Edgeworthstown, 25 August 1834

[Helen *was to go to a second edition*] … I enclose Harriet's list of corrections
for second edition – and beg you to add any of yours & Francis's that you may
have been so good to make – I quite agree with all you think of Col. Stewart's
criticisms – especially as to the effect produced on the moral character by
sympathy & generous admiration for virtue & abhorrence for vice & contempt
for meanness. [*Colonel Stewart, son of her old Edinburgh friend, Dugald Stewart,*
had written Maria a long criticism of Helen, *claiming the moral was too heavily*
drawn.] And I am quite convinced that this general impression or general
effect is better to aim at than any peculiar moral confined to any one virtue –
It must also leave free scope to genius or invention and give greater chance of
the whole fable & character being more like life & reality – This is the beauty
& excellence of Scott's novels – You shall see that if I write again that old as I
am, I profit by good suggestions …

    Only 2 things give me pain in Col. Stewart's criticisms – One of them was
in his first letter … The sentence something about flying a kite, appending
myself as a tail to Walter Scott's kite – this simile referred as I conceive to my
eulogy of Scott in Helen & I felt it at first as implying that I did meanly …

Engraving of the library at Edgeworthstown, early 1830s. Maria was angry to find herself included.

in courting popularity by praising him. But Harriet has dashed this out of my head – ... scolding me well too for having so much misunderstood the man – So there's an end to that & the thorn clean out of my mind ...

The other thing that pained – not offended me – is his undervaluing altogether the utility of moral fiction. Not the impress made at the moment on the mind but his believing that it has seldom or ever any effect upon the conduct or character of human creatures – Then my feeling was "My good God, what do [*I do*] it for?"

But luckily I've collected some credible assurances from persons who had no interest ...

IX

JANUARY 1835 – DECEMBER 1838

HER NOVEL PUBLISHED *and enjoying a mild success, Maria returned in her letters to politics and elections. Melbourne's government had fallen and Robert Peel had been elected to office as the Tory prime minister: in Maria's view, a decided change for the better. As she wrote to Sneyd a few weeks later,*

the late Ultra-Reform Liberals went far and had they continued in power would have overturned everything both in England and Ireland, would have let upon us the ragamuffin democracy, cried havoc etc ... The Duke of Wellington ... has had the leisure to repent the error which turned him out before, viz that he could have no reform. Mr Peel has guarded well against this in his address on his return.

Even O'Connell was now apparently showing signs of restraint. Maria's stepmother was still in England with two ailing daughters; Maria sent back the latest reports from Trim. Harriet's rectory there had now become a favourite staging post en route to and from Dublin.

TO MRS EDGEWORTH
The Rectory, Trim, 28 January 1835

... It was well for me that dear Harriet came for me and took me down in her own carriage & Veger [*the Butlers' groom*] with us for the horses had been so horridly worn out and rawed by the elections that the poor nags ... stopped ... at every *montant* and it was all the [*driver*] could do to get the horses on to the Black Bull – and the roads so deep in mud ...

You know the result of that election, O'Connell's son & Grattan – O'Connell's son, Mr B[*utler*] says, is quite a gentlemanlike young man & spoke well and Mr Butler would not cut O'Connell's own head off if he never spoke worse or did worse than he did at Trim. You know or shd know that O'Connell went down to Trim – had himself proposed merely to have the advantage of speaking his speech – Mr Butler who heard it says it was exactly the ditto of what he spoke in Dublin. He thought him very eloquent & with a fine voice & great variety of tones – evidently studied tones – affected pronunciation – diet de-et of Poland etc.

Richard Fitzherbert[220] boldly attacked him and asked why he had pressed the dissolution of the Union & then changed his opinion about it – He replied he had not changed – but he was as great an anti-Unionist as ever – only is waiting his time ...

Now Heaven grant the present Government with their strengthened hands, discretion and firmness enough to prevent a revolution ...

In Edgeworthstown O'Connell's party had swept the board again. Barry Fox, Maria's brother-in-law who was one of the trustees for the family portion of the estate, took the view that the Edgeworth tenants must be punished for their disloyalty to their landlord by suspending the old favour given them fifty years before by Maria's father of paying their rent at the end of the year, the so-called Hanging Gale. Maria, caught between Barry and her father's old practice, appealed to Sneyd, who now owned the rest of the Edgeworthstown estate. Her letter shows her tact and passionate desire to keep family harmony, and her belief in her father's principles, which she also believed – rightly – would ensure the family estate's survival.

TO SNEYD EDGEWORTH
Edgeworthstown, 12 February 1835

I was absent in Dublin having my teeth taken out and put in at the very time when the Longford election terminated. The evening I returned home, Barry,

---

220 Richard Ruxton had taken his uncle's surname after inheriting.

looking out from one end of the library table, where he was sitting, to me standing at the other end and said: "Maria, I have prepared some work for Hinds tomorrow when he is to come. I have sent to the tenants who voted against their landlord – Woods, Langan and Dermod – and ordered them to bring in their rent – the hanging gale. I am determined to make an example of them".

I am sure by his countenance and manner of speaking, as well as by his knowledge of what I had said and done on a former election, that he was in doubt at least as to my approval of this step. But as he did not explicitly require my opinion, only announced the fact to me, I was dead silent. I own I was surprised and sorry – sorry particularly about Dermod because, setting aside my own opinion of the politically right or wrong which might have nothing to do with the decision, I felt that as your agent I should never have taken such a step without your orders and knowing your opinions by your letter on the election (which I had not, by the by, shown to Barry). I was the more embarrassed and anxious. Assuredly, I neither then, or at any time, gave any sign, direct or indirect, of approval. And so doubtful, I am sure, did Barry feel as to your and my approval that the next morning he asked me: "Maria, who do you think ought to be consulted and to act for the trust estate about these tenants and for the other estate?" "You, Barry", said I, "should act as your brother Charles' representative as trustee of the trust estate in conjunction with Sneyd as the other trustee – as to the other estate, you know it is Sneyd's. He has bought it and I act as his agent and should always refer to him". He replied something about your being at a distance and that the two estates must follow one rule. I spoke of Dermod, said he was your tenant and that I, not Mr Hinds, received his rent! And I said that I could not do anything about him and his rent without referring to you.

That day (Mr Hinds being here), I in the study with him, Dermod is announced before he could hobble up the backstairs. Barry entered and said: "Here's Dermod has brought in his rent. But what is to be done now? Maria won't receive it, I suppose?" Considering that it would not be kind or right to Barry to show that there was any doubt in my mind as to what he had done, as I was sure with the best intentions, I immediately answered: "Yes, Barry, I will receive Dermod's rent and hold it till I hear from Sneyd". Accordingly – exit Barry – entered Dermod, hobbling and bent … and followed by his young son, who presently fell to crying. I endeavoured to keep automatically to my receiver of rents and I fell to counting the money …

The thoughts of the number of years I had received rent from that old good tenant in my father's time all worked upon me. I am ashamed to tell you my finale – that tears began to flow and though I twinkled and rubbed them out and off they did come – and Honora came in and Mr Hinds was by and it was all shameful. But I never said an overt word to Dermod, approving or disapproving what had been done. But told him I should let his landlord know all about it and I gave him a receipt in full to November 1834. But I entered his rent only in pencil in the book till I should receive your ultimatum. This I never said to Dermod, but to Barry. I gave him a glass of beer, which he drank to "Captain Fox's good health" anyway – and his landlords ...

To Maria's relief, Sneyd gave her his full backing to reinstate the Hanging Gale for his tenants six months later. In the meantime, Peel was still clinging on with the help of Edward Stanley, the former Chief Secretary for Ireland who had defected from the Whigs over a bill to disestablish the Church of Ireland and attempted to set up a central party.[221]

TO MRS EDGEWORTH
Edgeworthstown, 5 March 1835

... I hope the present ministry will stand with the assistance of Stanley and his *modérés* – You wrong me, I am exceedingly interested <u>now</u> in politics because all our fate & fortune & domestic life altogether hang upon this point – Will they be able to prevent those who have no property & no education from overwhelming by their numbers those have some property & some education ...

TO FANNY WILSON
Edgeworthstown, 3 March 1835

... James Kelly (the pale faced weak minded but very good Kelly whom I believe you will recollect as tenant of Kilcourney [*sic*] living at the tidy home & smart lawn beside us) has [*a son*] grown too big for the paternal home and he wishes to make his own way in the world – in the new world he thinks will

---

221 Stanley was also author of the famous 'Stanley letter' of 1833 that had defined government policy as providing 'joint secular and separate religious instruction' in schools attended by pupils of all denominations, which had been exactly the principle on which Lovell Edgeworth had earlier attempted to run his school.

do best – He has asked me twice about it and he has shewn me the subject –
a goodlooking slight made youth who does not appear to me robust enough
even for Back & Settlement work in America or in the Canadas. He has been
educated in Lovell's school, understands arithmetick (you can grasp about how
well) – makes a good hand but has not learnt bookkeeping – appears not
bright but ... very willing & well disposed to turn his hand to anything either
indoors or out – by which he can earn independence ...

TO FANNY WILSON
Edgeworthstown, 14 March 1835

... Both the young man & his son fully sensible of what Mr Ralstone [*the
emigration officer in London*] said of the lowly spirit necessary to get on in
America – He is quite prepared & willing to do all the needfull in a store –
including sweeping floors ...

"When I sweep my own stables & stableyard" said Kelly Senior "why
wouldn't he sweep the Store – what ever it is" ...

*In early April Peel was forced out of power by a combination of Whigs, radicals
and O'Connell's party. After the meeting in March known as 'The Lichfield
House Compact' O'Connell had agreed to suspend his Repeal campaign in
return for immediate reforms from the Whigs.*

TO FANNY WILSON
Edgeworthstown, 10 April 1835

... My mother's arrival & Sir Robert Peel's speech have completely filled my
head & almost turned it – Sir Robert Peel's is one of the finest most dignified
farewell speeches I have read. I am glad so much virtue & magnamity is left
in England – Lord Forbes ended a note to me about the Longford Infirmary
with these words "The British Constitution died last night".

Sir Culling Smith thinks it but just beginning to live – He wrote me word
by the same post that he has sent over his bailiff to look at a property which
he is going to purchase in Galway and that now he thinks English capital will
flow to Ireland in security.

"God help your poor head" I thought ...

Lovell's school had been closed since his financial collapse and had been somewhat
of a white elephant for the family. It was now to be let to the Church of Ireland
as a school for the sons of distressed clergyman – a possibly dangerous step in view
of the ongoing battle over tithes and Church disestablishment – and a long way
from Lovell's original dream of educating across religious and class barriers.

TO FANNY WILSON
Edgeworthstown, 15 May 1835

… The archbishop seems at present to be quite content to pay £50 a year for
the school premises, though has not been able to set the school a-going again
… Dean Murray & Mrs Murray have persuaded Mr Stuart to return as rector
– they think he will be happier here than anywhere else – Being near them
too is of great advantage – It is of the utmost importance to us to have a mild
sensible clergyman here as the times require great discretion & command of
temper – and our Catholic priests are violent and rude …

Edgeworthstown, 30 May 1835

… Andy Burke is to go to America – to an uncle in New York who invited
him & took his sister with him – He is a very good boy & went away with the
best of characters from priest & Mr Keating … He wrote to his father from
Liverpool & gave him excellent advice not to be taking too much also many &
affectionate thanks to his always being a good father to him and having fitted
him out so well – and his hopes or his trust that he shall in a few years be able
to repay, and that he shall return "and walk the streets of Edgeworthstown in
splendor" – … in a new blue coat and brass buttons …

Oh my dear Fanny, we have just heard of Lord Longford's death and very
very sorry we are for the loss of that excellent man – Little did I think when
but a few weeks ago he was sitting in the library beside Aunt Mary – she so
ill – he to all appearance in such jovial health – that she would outlive him –
that he would be gone so soon – that I then received his last cordial shake of
the hand – his last affectionate Pakenham look – He was to have been over
here, was asked to breakfast here on the 10th. Though we heard he had been
ill, I disbelieved it quite till I had the enclosed from Lady Longford – and it
does appear from this how unaware of his danger she was at least the other day.

How shocked she must be – ten children – and her eldest only 17 – abroad.

The traditional way to murder a landlord: shooting at him from behind a wall. From Realities of Irish Life *(1856) by William Stuart Trench.*

She is a woman of strong mind and a strong sense of duty – God help her …

Neighbours were buzzing with stories of renewed attacks on landlords.

TO FANNY WILSON
Edgeworthstown, 25 July 1835

… Mrs Bond at Sonna gave us an account of an attack upon her husband at their home … in the county of Armagh – a discontent or dishonest steward who feared his accounts should be looked into was the performer …

One night he fired in at the hall two shots with pieces so oversized that they lodged in an opposite door. Mr Bond would have been crossing the hall that instant but for something or other – And Mrs Bond as she told me in her insipid way … would also have gone into the hall to look what was the matter but that she thought some furniture had fallen down.

In short no harm was done by these shots except to the doors & clever Mrs Lyons observed "Pah – you know if he'd wanted to murder the man he would have shot from behind a hedge on the road & not shot that way into the hall door at random – without knowing was he in it – 'Twas only to frighten them away" …

In August there was a welcome distraction. A huge gathering of scientists, or as Maria still called them 'philosophers', had been arranged to meet first in Dublin, then at Markree, the Coopers' house in Co. Sligo; Mr Cooper was a well-known astronomer with his own Observatory. Maria did her best to capture some of the scientists in passing – or on their return journey.

TO FANNY WILSON
Edgeworthstown, 18 August 1835

… Such conversation before breakfast – Mr S[*trickland*] came fresh from Dublin where he had spent the splendid scientific week seeing and hearing the philosophers foreign & British …

First he told of the handsome conduct of Sir John Jobson who [*put*] his new steam vessel the William Penn at the disposal of the philosophers to bring them over free to Ireland – He accompanied them – and as soon as one cargo of 40 or 50 had been landed … he put his vessel about and returned for more … It was a beautiful fine day – a Sunday – The whole company of philosophers of all sects & parties & countries under one awning on deck assembled at prayers – Mr Sedgwick was the person who read prayers and when he had finished he was called by the whole congregation round him for a sermon – He had none – he was quite unprepared – But they said it was the finest sermon that could be heard – and the effect noble!

It struck me very much – touched me much to hear Mr Strickland, a Catholic and warm enough in his politics to lay aside all party feeling and with true benevolence & true religious elevation of mind describe and exalt in facts.

Oh, if Mr O'Connell's heart could so feel what his heart might do for Ireland – and for ages yet unborn …

We invited Robinson – Alison – Roget – Greenough & Hamilton here.

Roget staid but one day & never received my note – Greenough answered very kindly but could not come – is going abroad with Lord I forget who.

Hamilton & the rest are gone to Mr Cooper in Sligo to see his great telescope – Whether they will come here or not I do not know …

TO FANNY WILSON
Edgeworthstown, 11 September 1835

… Sir John & Lady Franklin called in on the way to Mr Coopers and spent a day here … Sir John is a downright honest singlehearted Boniface of a

person whom one should never suspect of having starved to an atomy[222] ...
Lady Franklin was walked by Mrs E to see the spire & cottages & seemed
very judiciously curious ... She was much more agreeable than when I saw
her in London.

You know Professor Hamilton has been knighted by our Lord Lieut[enant]
– and Lord Mulgrave did it so well – Spoke so well and what is more was so
good that Lord Cole was so much pleased that ... he immediately went to
Lord Ex's levee where he had never been before – this suspension of party
feuds is the real advantage of this meeting to Ireland. But I was going to tell
you that Sir William Hamilton is here – quite unchanged by the honours that
have been paid him – very kind and so full of ideas that I cannot take them
in fast enough & really cannot hold them – "It is the Euphrates pouring into
a cup".

He shewed me a letter from Herschel which he has just received which
delighted me so much I asked him leave to copy it for you – and I send it
you herewith & hope it may afford you pleasure in the reading it to Captain
Beaufort & perhaps Harriette E and my own dear Henry [Beddoes], I hope
he will activate a taste for science & the excellent abilities God & his father &
mother gave him ...

> By autumn 1835 the Whigs' new conciliatory policy in Ireland was well in place,
> directed largely by the new Under-Secretary of State, Thomas Drummond, a
> Scots engineer who had worked on the Irish survey and knew rural grievances
> at first hand. Maria had met him in London in 1831 and had 'fallen quite in
> love with him' as she wrote to Harriet. His first act was to ban the use of military
> force to collect tithes, much to the army's relief: the Protestant clergy were to be
> supported instead from a government hardship fund. A party of young Scotch
> officers called at Edgeworthstown and told a sad story over dinner of one attempt
> at tithe collection.

TO FANNY WILSON
Edgeworthstown, 5 October 1835

... Mr Garsten told us that in parts of Ireland he has hard duty in going out
to collect tithes and last year especially with an old clergyman who lived 50

---

222 See footnote 191. He had led a famous attempt on the North-West Passage and been trapped in the
ice for months. On a later attempt he and all his crew were to die of starvation.

years in one parish where he hoped he was beloved – He was so tender hearted that he could not bear to take the money at last – till Capt Garsten stepped forward seeing it was necessary "You must not make a fool of us, Sir – We have been brought out here to have your tithe paid & you must receive it" – Thus he took off the odium as much as he could and the people seeing the military in earnest found their due – But the poor clergyman's heart was really broken by all he had gone through – "I'm sorry to tell you Ma'am he died a few weeks afterwards – I am clear he died of a broken heart" …

Maria however was not convinced that the temporary alliance between O'Connell and the Whigs would last.

TO FANNY WILSON
Edgeworthstown, 12 October 1835

… As to O'Connell – I am clear that no ministry could buy him because he has sold himself to the devil of popularity and [*could not*] get himself back again even if he would – He must be a slave to the huzzas without which he cannot live – (You know in old books of Heraldry they say that the Lion has a spur or goad at the end of his tail with which he lashes himself up to fury) …

I believe I told you in my last that we have written to invite Mr & Mrs George Moore here – They answered by letter with prompt acceptance – And whether they will come Tuesday or Wednesday next – or some later day – is by no means a matter of indifference to the kitchen – for there is Mrs Smith standing with face full [*an*] ell long while the new oven is being set and the whole floor covered with bricks & mortar & masons & aprons flitting about – She said to yr mother "Oh Ma'am if it had pleased God that Mr and Mrs George Moore had chosen any time but just this to come upon me." …

Maria had been put in touch with the Catholic Moores of Moore Hall in Co. Mayo by her friend, Mr Strickland. George Moore had been a close friend of Sir James Mackintosh, the famous Scottish historian whom she much admired and had met in London. (See her letter to Honora, February 1830.) Fortunately for the cook, the Moores postponed the visit until after Christmas when Maria arranged to have the Butlers and Sir William Hamilton there to meet them. First impressions were mixed.

TO FANNY WILSON
Edgeworthstown, 5 January 1836

... Mrs Moore is very clever – & very coarse – & strong – more than vulgar
if I may be allowed to make a distinction – Vulgar is common & there is
nothing common about her – nor in ... any of her habits or qualities – She has
uncommon strength of mind & violence of temper & activity – & decision – &
courage & cowardice – The cowardice of superstition & visionary fears – of
spirits etc – dreams & prognostics to the most extraordinary degree ...

She is very entertaining, exhaustingly entertaining to me – for I listen till I
am ready to drop – and Harriet sends me out of the room to lie down.

Mr G.M himself is a most pitiable spectacle – at first, till we perceived that
he was paralytic, we could hardly refrain from laughing at the oddity of his
ways of looking, moving, speaking – But now it is tragical – to see such a wreck
of a man – He has a great deal of information on book matters & worldly
anecdotes of rather stale date but all concerning Mackintosh of course very
interesting – He is writing a hist[ory] of the French Rev. – He is of the opinion
he tells me that it was not Rostopchin burnt Moscow – but that the French set
fire to it. From this sample I cannot say I augur well of his historic judgement.

The young man must be much improved since you saw him in his selfish
cub state – He is very clever & Mr Butler says he must have applied intensely
to have acquired all the knowledge re gas – His mother ... will tell me their
family hist[ory], giving me anecdotes of his loves at Munich & his being
pigeoned at play etc – I think she has in some difficult circumstances saved
both her sons from ruin by her decision & by the strong influence of their
affection for her – through ALL.[223]

*She wrote a further description to her youngest brother, Michael Pakenham,
in India.*

TO PAKENHAM EDGEWORTH
Edgeworthstown, 29 January 1836

... Mrs Moore ... was all in black velvet pelisse and furs and smiles and delight
to see Mrs E – whom she had longed to see ever since she was born & before
I believe.

---

223 The Moores' two sons were both addicted to racing and gambling: Augustus was killed two years
later steeplechasing in England.

And she was delighted to present to me her son Augustus who is a youth whom Sir W. Hamilton pronounces to be of the first mathematical genius of the age – and who was now returned from Munich and where moreover his kind communicative mother whispered he had lost a lot of money at play [*and*] had been taken in by an Irish friend & pigeoned by a half French half German adventuress "Oh mother, if I could once see her in the gutter … how I should rejoice to give her one good look of contempt …" – That single speech paints the youth with all his strong passions, violent temper … He would make a good enough hero to match Miss Martin about whom he was very curious. But his mother would not hear of it because she is a Prot[*estant*] & he is a Cat[*holic*] …

Mrs Moore … is an amazingly <u>bigotted</u> – liberal – clever – governing – vulgar woman with more than the quantum sufficiency both of Irish vulgarity & Irish humour.

You may perhaps remember having heard Fanny talk of her – Mrs Strickland took Fanny to Moore Hall about 8 years ago … It is curious that she repeated to us … the very same poem of Anacreon Moore which she had repeated to Fanny "The Irish Advent" – I enclose them to you – But the lines are nothing without her voice, rich round brogue & gestures accompanying – her eyes turned up repeating "Oh willow tree" at every break – and the perfect ease & freedom from exaggeration with which she repeated and acted it …

Mrs Moore is excellent to hear and see when one is safe & sure she will go away in a day or two or a week at farthest – but she would be intolerable to live with or have in one's neighbourhood or within 50 miles – A violent temper – and not scrupulous of means … in the midst of all her liberalism in politics and all her dashing thorough going cleverness …

Most of the remaining letter was a response to Pakenham's latest Journal from Ambala. India was now a new and fascinating subject for Maria's enquiring mind.

We have you up to 25th August last Journal, letter and all – God bless you and success to Steam Navigation. Never was brother in India in the 8th year of his absence so fresh and full in the actual presence as in the hearts of his family I believe as you are and have kept yourself by that wonderful Talismanic journal which keeps you in our eye.

Dr Farrell who dined here last week observed that your tastes for botany, reading and drawing and the interest those tastes give you wherever you go ... will preserve you in good health and from that *ennui* and the *mal de pays* which seizes so many young men in India – They think that there is something the matter with their body – politic and all the while it is their mind – impolitic that is sick & weak. Indeed it must require a degree of strength of character & energy of which we who have never lived out of family society and in the solitude of foreign faces & customs & country ... can scarcely form an idea ...

I do not know if you <u>can</u> now care about the Edgeworthstown school for the sons of distressed clergy. But I will spend 6 lines upon it – just to tell you that I think it will all now do – Subscriptions from the generous English, some of £500 and some of £50 per annum have poured in and there is now an <u>income</u> of between £500 & 600 – on Monday next the Dean of Ardagh & committee meet at E'town to choose a schoolmaster – on which the whole will depend – his salary to be £300 per annum – There are to be two other masters – £12 is the very low sum which each boy admitted is to pay for board & tuition – to be fitted for college – and <u>any</u> profession – The Provost of Dublin has given an exhibition – The school is to open after Easter – and there is an <u>end</u> – I mean a beginning to the Edgeworthstown school history ...

The Edgeworthstown school reopened in April, with a ceremony attended by all the local clergy, and Maria took a firm liking to the new headmaster, Mr Murphy.

TO FANNY WILSON
Edgeworthstown, 23 April 1836

... There are now about 17 scholars at the E'town school – The Archbishop was here yesterday in high delight with its opening & fair promise – Dean Murray addressed the boys on the subject of Truth – I wish we had heard him – but by some mistake we did not understand when or how it was to be – However good Mr Keating came ... after it was all over & gave us his version of it ... supplying with gesture, emphasis and tears in his eyes all that was better literary composition in the Dean's address –

"Oh 'twas uncommon good, Ma'am! Now if you'd heard it! – Oh it came from the heart – And it went to it – It did to mine I'll swear – I am convinced there was not a young chap that would not be the better for it all his life long" –

Then Mr Murphy, headmaster, read to me the regulations for the boys – To be up at half after 6 – Breakfast at ½ 8 – bread & milk & stirabout if asked for –

Dinner at 3 – Meat every day – beef, mutton & sometimes pork – Bed at 9 – Mr Murphy happened to see the boys all ranged in the schoolroom as Mr Keating & he were going their rounds & asked "Why don't you go & play boys, not sit here waiting for dinner?"

"Oh sir" said a boy putting his hand to the smooth head – "my hair would be lassed – and Mr Hall would not be pleased."

"Oh if Mr Hall desired it, all is right" said Murphy

I am glad that the boys begin with order – Heaven's first law was in trifles – and still more glad that the masters begin with pulling together …

In June Fanny reported hopeful news of Francis – now with a wife and new baby to support, he had applied for the post of Keeper of the Queen's Prints at Windsor. Maria hastened to find the necessary references.

TO FANNY WILSON
Edgeworthstown, 14 June 1836

Oh, my dear Fanny, this very day I received your first letter about Francis, … I have great hopes for my Grace of Canterbury as he has always been good to me. Mr Abercrombie [*the Speaker*][224] I know little but of the little I do know I have made the best – or worst impudent use I could – reminding him the evening we passed at Joanna Baillies' when Francis, then a boy, sat behind his back on the sofa swallowing his conversation with evident good taste as Joanna, I remember well, observed – Trust me, I said neither too much nor too little for Francis to these high & mighty ones – but referred to Cambridge – Thorpe & Peacock – for literary qualification – to Captain Beaufort for character … I have this morning in consequence of your second letter … written to Lord Lansdowne …

Alas for Maria, rumours of Francis' atheistic views had already leaked out into Establishment circles and her string-pulling was in vain. She was much offended by the refusal of her old friend Thomas Spring Rice to recommend Francis.

---

224 James Abercrombie, later 1st Lord Dumferline, Speaker of the House of Commons.

TO FANNY WILSON
Edgeworthstown, 16 September 1836

... Honora returned to us yesterday to dinner after having spent a day with poor dear Sophy Ruxton[225] ...

[*She*] arrived just in time to see a Scotch gentleman R. Graham who had arrived a few hours before her yesterday morning – Mr Butler had been quite impatient for her arrival particularly on this account as he, albeit unused to matchmaking, suggested the Lord Lynedoch's near relation might do.[226] Mr Butler was very droll about it & in high rejoicing when ... after the hour we expected and given her up, Aunt Mary's carriage with Honora in it drove up from Tuite's gate – she all blooming with joy at coming home to us, not knowing that we had a knight *in petto* for her ...

Mr Butler only was with me in the library and our first notion of him [*Graham*] and his cotton umbrella were not particularly favourable ... [*He*] is too leg-tied & shuffling & uncertain to give an idea of a highbred gentleman. However after he was seated & had got through the first introduction, reading of credentials etc, he appeared very gentlemanlike ... in conversation – And was altogether agreeable – told us a great many curious facts – ... was bred to the bar – mentioned that in a very tiresome complicated law reading of mountains of papers and parchments ... he suddenly came to some letters of Sir Walter Scott! – He said he cannot describe the relief they were to him – it was an oasis in the desert with sunshine & fresh water too – He says that they were exceedingly good letters of business ... yet so playful & offhand that they might have been inserted in any of his own novels ...

Mr Graham told another anecdote which has not yet slipped through my mind – One who was a schoolfellow of Bonaparte told him that Bonaparte's love of conquest showed itself very early. The boys had all little gardens – Bonaparte never rested till he has persuaded them or forced them one and all to let him have them – and when had possession he portioned them all out again to his tribunes ...

---

225 Sophy and her sister Margaret were now living in a pretty cottage at Swinnerton on the Boyne near their old home at Black Castle, but Sophy was suffering from chronic pain.

226 Robert Graham, then aged fifty-one, was the nephew and heir of Lord Lynedoch, a Scottish landowner. His journals (Four Courts Press, 1999) record 'a most agreeable day' at Edgeworthstown, and a visit to the new school. He also noted that 7/8 of the local population were Catholics and 'the party I was with expect, like all the rest of the country I have come through, to be swallowed up by the catholics'.

In mid September Maria paid a long-promised visit to the Moores at Moore
Hall in Mayo, accompanied by her stepmother and Harriet and Richard Butler.
She reported the expedition in full – the original letter is twenty-four pages long
– this time to her sister-in-law, Harriette, in Kent.

TO HARRIETTE EDGEWORTH
Edgeworthstown, 30 September 1836

... You say you should very much indeed like to read an account ... of our
tour to Connaught ... Since you desire to hear about it, I will gladly conquer
my laziness for a stronger motive I cannot have than to do anything that may
amuse you ...

Honora told you we were to stop at Lough Glynn in our way to Moore
Hall – the distance being between 70 or 80 miles from Edgeworthstown –
And some of the Roscommon & Mayo roads are ... execrably patched with ill
broken stones ... which horses abhor & scarcely any carriage & much less one
near 20 years old can be expected to stand.

I believe you know that the present Lord Dillon is really possessor of Lough
Glynn and that Mr Strickland is his agent – Mr Strickland is at Leamington
for his health at present – and 2 of his daughters, Harriet & Kate keep house
in his absence – and half a dozen young brothers, some mere children, with
them – Just at the time we had offered to spend a day on our way with them,
over came Lord & Lady Dillon & thus we met them at Lough Glynn – There
was a great awkwardness necessarily from the difficulty of knowing who was
to act master & mistress – The excellence of the Miss Stricklands' education
& the principles of good manners founded in good sense were fairly and most
agreeably shown in this ... unprecedented situation – They did it all admirably
– Harriet S said to my mother as she met her in the steps "My dear Mrs
Edgeworth I have never seen you since –" (her mother's death she meant to
say) but could only throw her arms about her neck & quite over powered
burst into tears – My mother hurried her off down a dark shrubbery walk for
all the crowd of Dillons' servants etc – And I, like a fool, following her out
of the carriage without a rag on ... caught cold & a headache & in the hurry
afterwards of dressing for dinner the head became so intolerable that it was
[*with*] the greatest difficulty that I could sit at dinner without fainting ...

I can tell you nothing of this dinner but that it was like a dream where
all the strange voices were bawling about I know not what – Lord Dillon

is very ugly & rather a fool and yet he has glimmers of sense every now & then & whatever he has goes so straight to the purpose that it serves by its truth – as we saw next day at dinner in a set between him and his uncle Lord Oranmore (*ci-devant* Dominick Browne of Castle McGarrit) – His Lordship, I guess, is more rogue than fool – lives in high company in London & piques himself upon his English & being able to live grandly upon less than nothing, being head & ears in debt – Someone witty called him Lord Owingmore – and the name fitted so much that – one is afraid of saying to him instead of Oranmore – (Is it not odd that he should have taken that title which I used in The Absentee …) [*Maria's novel.*]

Lord Dillon is a great friend of Cat[*holic*]s – a great radical & among many things said to Mr Butler "I am an O'Connelite and a great radical and I thank God for it" – The more polished Lord Oranmore abuses church & churchmen (though he is a Protestant) and then turned round to me & asked whether Mr Butler was a clergyman – to which I replied "Yes he has the honor to be a clergyman, my Lord" – Then he begged pardon …

Lady Dillon behaved kindly enough to the Stricklands – She is rather a pretty & prudent seeming young wife who will have a hard task with her goodnatured radical fool of a Lord – But still he is a Lord & Lord of Ditchley [*a great English house*] – which is a great comfort – She enjoys much the being Lady Dillon & seeing Ireland and all the barbaric rejoicings for her arrival at Lough Glynn. At night between 9 & 10 was suddenly heard a burst of noise indescribable at the hall door – yells, screams, huzzas – and such a blaze of light when we ran out of the diningroom into the hall that we might have thought the house was on fire – in flames.

But it was only rejoicings – from a crowd of hundreds of ragged subjects assembled bearing in their hands & flourishing high in air great pikes to which huge blazing wisps of straw were fastened which streamed to the sparkling night … wild figures … craving, intelligent, grinning, pathetic, cunning faces crowding up below to the very high steps on which the Lord and Lady stood, and the sea of heads as far as the eye could reach ending in darkness visible. It was one of the most striking sights I ever saw – and would have been the finest study for a painter – I wished for Wilkie – but more for Mulready who has Irish genius … In the county of Roscommon … there is a red dye and a deep blue which the Italian painters love and which added much to the picturesque effect of these barbaric rejoicings – Some groups of women & children – young & old – some disfigured [?], some graceful – sat on the lowest steps or leaned against the piers and there was one prominent face of intense curiosity, that of a bare necked red-haired man, half rogue, three quarters savage, stretching neck in front to listen to the lady which can never leave my eyes.

The object of the whole … was to obtain leave to hold a market, I believe at Lough Glynn. Petition referred by my lord to Mr Strickland the agent – and cause adjourned till his return – So with a whoop and a screech and a brandish of yet unextinguished torches, they beat them against the ground and disappeared.

Next day we went on to Moore Hall – Only 30 miles … But such roads! – and such hills and such mistakes of roads – The people we saw in Mayo … spoke little English and understood less … so that when we asked the way to Moore Hall – they understood Brown Hall or Mr Browne & an unlucky woman so mishearing directed us down a bog road to which our county of Longford black lane leading to the bog could not compare in cowpathishness – We went astray several miles and were obliged to walk many for our horses, though stout, could not draw us …. The short of it is we did not arrive till 9 & ten at night – Soup just upon the table and we given up – But most cordially welcomed & fortunately it is a house where it is impossible to be too late – They breakfast between 11 & 12 – The rest in proportion.

To my astonishment I found Moore Hall which I had fancied would be a delapidated wild kind of hand-to-mouth house … a most excellent house, beautifully furnished in the best taste with all the comforts & luxuries of life --- --- dining room – bedrooms – library – drawing room – The library especially [*is*] a most liveable and elegant literary one – papered with a sort of gothic paper representing colonnades of pillars & fretwork arches above & all manner of tables & armchairs & low & highbacks … bookcases with networked doors opening easily – none higher than you could reach – books – well chosen … all around two rooms, for this library opened into a study of Mr Moore's with a snuggery & charming writing desk for himself.

The summer drawing room papered with a green trellis paper – the prettiest I ever saw – Large windows to the ground open upon a balcony from which you see … a clear sparkling lake below, wooded and islanded – and with a sort of spoon shaped cape – The house & plantations are on a peninsula.

Mr Moore is a thinnish, palish, tallish, gentlemanlike, flat backed, head up person – He is as I am sure you know a literary man – friend of Mackintosh [*the Scottish historian*] … with lives of Ripperda – Alberoni – Pombal – all worth your reading & he is now engaged on a history of [*the*] French Revolution.

A view of Moore Hall given to Maria by Mrs Moore.

He has had a stroke of the palsy which has dreadfully disabled his writing & his organs of speech ... But when his understanding & powers of speech are not fatigued he converses remarkably well, ... and his store of information from books [*is*] of the best sort, ancient classics and modern French – history, belles lettres and anecdotes galore ... and of all the Parisian wits and politicians from Bonaparte & Talleyrand down to the underlings – and back to Mirabeau and Duclos etc – So you may guess he is never silent for want of something to say worth saying – nor were we ever tired of hearing him – only sometimes it was very difficult to make out what he said ... one word running into another ...

Well tried his good nature and good temper are daily by his wife and son – Yet they both love him & only love power better – Mrs Moore is as great a contrast in person to her husband as can be conceived – fat – large – full blown – brown & ruddy with prodigeously fine large expressive grey eyes & long lashes of which she makes sovereign good use ... strong expressions – strong as Mrs Siddons – of horror or indignation for causes small or large – then suddenly melting into almost feminine tenderness & sweetness of look & voice – like a storm that ... blows over in an instant – blue sky, sunshine – & no trace [*that*] there has ever been a cloud.

She is a woman that, take her all, such as I never saw the like and am not sure whether I should ever wish to see anyone the like. And yet I should be very sorry to think I was never to see her again – & still more sorry that I was to live within ten miles of her ... She would never be satisfied even if you submitted to be completely ruled and trampled upon – she would never be satisfied unless you got up directly and declared that she had not trampled &

that you were free and her equal – and then she must have all your sympathy & all your advice in all her schemes and hates & loves & prejudices & superstitions. Oh Superstition! She is the strangest mixture I ever saw of audaciousness of mind and weakness of superstition … Down on her knees confessing ∴ to any vulgarian beast of a priest, calling him a beast all the time – and when one of them differed with her at some election work, a priest that lived in the house, she packed him off one morning with as little or less ceremony than you would a footman – rolling up his half year's wages for him in a paper on which she informed him that she had no further occasion for his services etc. The note was published in some Dublin paper – and she was – and is called her Catholic Majesty – and all this she told me herself – with exultation … Never was a person more thoroughly competent in this world's business and to ruling over all worldly creatures & affairs from garret to kitchen & kitchen to stable & cowhouse & kennel inclusive & husband inclusive.

"Mr Moore, hold your tongue for God's sake!" "So I will, my dear, for your sake"! replied he in the most gentle, kind, not abject manner – "Your head aches and I will not say another word …"

She was at that moment sitting with a bottle of hot water under her feet & [a] young lady friend rubbing her temples with *Eau de Cologne* which she poured from a vast cut glass bottle in her hands … She had just returned from visiting alone as she does every month the burial place of her son – where she has a monument to him in the midst of a beautiful little garden full of flowers. The entrance is shrouded by a weeping willow … The next day when Harriet Butler and I walked to see it, there were the flowers half withered which she had left upon the son's tomb.

She has a bust of this son, veiled, in her bedroom and one night by candlelight she took … all of us, one by one, to look at it unveiled. It is most beautiful …

Next day in the back yard … in the stables

"What's all this! – Whose horse is this? How came he here and oats eating – How's this! – Out with him! Off with him! How dare you? … To the outhouse [?] – Off! Off!

And all this in a tremendous voice that all the yard might hear …

She is, as I told you, an incomparable actress – Tragic – I dare say she can be – Comic I am sure she is – The Irish character with all its humor, all its faces, all its brogues she gives without the least exaggeration … Then she has exquisitely good taste for poetry … all the best passages in Scott, Byron,

*Mrs Louisa Moore – Maria
dubbed her 'Her Catholic Majesty'.*

Moore and many others ... pouring out with a fluency and ... accuracy of memory that never called for the least admiration ...

One day at dinner when she was ruling her husband for his good about some vanilla cream of which he was not to have one spoonful – he across the table to me quoted Rousseau's saying of Madame d'Houdetot *"Elle est la surintendante de mes privations"* –

By this you may conceive the apropos & quickness of his recollections – & the contrast between the literary ... sort of his wit – and the ... strength & power of his wife – her Catholic Majesty – he is always a King Consort – and as to Catholic – not at all I opine – When she went to mass & carried her son off under her arm or under her thumb, he remained at home saying to us "I am an invalid you know " – Then he told Mr Butler that the summer drawing room or any other room he pleased was ready for him to read prayers in for us as there was no church within 5 miles – Afterwards her Cath[*olic*] Maj[*esty*] said laughing or playfully "We must have this room purified after these heretics & their prayers".

I have not told you that our bodily fare all the time was excellent – Breakfast, luncheon, dinners – excellently served and neither too much or too little – silver dishes & china … and servants all good – and attentive & well dressed … bedrooms all attendants, female and male well appointed and well attending – her own maid had lived with her 23 years – her housemaid 14 – others proportionately … This tells well for both master and mistress …

In this county of Mayo, I might say in Connaught throughout, there are a few of these potentates – and magnificent great houses planted about – and all the rest between poor & base – Stone walls, no hedges – no trees – bogs black & interminable – rocky wastes – fields seemingly covered with showers of stones – verdure patches round or between the stones which cattle know how, impossible as it seems, to fatten on …

We made several excursions – One day we spent boating on their lake &, doubling the cape of their peninsula, saw a strange wild stony coast and a deep black part of the lake and then came to a beautiful point of view – and Castle Caragh – Mrs E took many sketches, both of the country & ruins of castles and abbeys – I wish you could see them

We went another day to Westport – Lord Sligo's – his place beautiful & magnificent – his house well enough – the most striking thing in it was half a cannon fished up or cast ashore from wreck of Spanish Armada – But the present and living wonders are the town & bay & prosperous country & people made at Westport by the exercise of one individual – the late Lord Sligo – …

We dined late but well at Lough Glynn where we had the affectionate Stricklands comfortably to ourselves – Lord Dillon having gone off to a public dinner at Castle McGarritt with his uncle Ld Oranmore – How Lord Oranmore, owing more than his worth ten times over, lives and entertains in silver & gold better than anyone else without the philosopher's stone remains a mystery insoluble to any of us – though we have ourselves a pretty tight notion of what estates can do buttoned up to the chin with debts – However we are not of the worshipful … Company of Rogues of which I shrewdly suspect his Lordship hath the freedom & we don't know all the cunning & craftmanship of that legendary coining company – So be it – Our credit may outlive theirs though we may be stinted … meanwhile.

But to return to Lough Glynn – On the morning before we left we saw at our bedchamber window an assemblage … of many of the troops of torchbearers and huzzars whom we had seen by firelight the first night, now by day-light in their natural characters & genuine misery as beggars – some with brickdust coloured jagged skimped petticoats & kerchiefs on heads – the bettermost sort with ragged blankets – & literally I believe sheets, torn sheets, wrapped around them – & the worse [?] with lower limbs as well as feet all naked & so starved & worn that they looked like spectres or corpses in grave clothes of wretches risen from their tombs after having been first starved to death.

I have no doubt that several of these were dressed or undressed for the occasion to make an effect upon the English bride, Lady Dillon – But the starvation, the thinness, the wretchedness could not but be real & Time had been at work giving every touch of wretchedness which only he can give – I never saw a more dreadfully odious sight – I cannot imagine how anybody … unaccustomed to such sights can endure them & live – and think of living in the country where it must take half a century with capital incalculable at command & industry, exertion & discretion in both landlords & tenants which few – few – few! can boast or hope to possess to remedy or banish this curse – this misery.

I would not take a million a year, a palace, a territory well planted to boot, and a lease of 3 lives insured to me … to pass 10 years at Lough Glynn with such objects appearing before me every morning of life – Mr Strickland has a strong mind & unconquerable exertion – and he has done much in 20 years and yet how much remains to be done – and his health injured. …

And this was the last of Lough Glynn and we found ourselves at home – and were glad to find ourselves on good roads & in sight of hedges & trees & good cottages – and in short in a civilised country – Our own home too looked most comfortable! … Harriet Butler & Mr Butler left us this morning – and here I have not a word more to tell …

Maria never travelled west of the Shannon again, but she remained fascinated by Mrs Moore and kept up a regular correspondence with her.

In December there was a new election in Longford. The Tory MP Lord Forbes, son of the neighbouring grandee, Lord Granard, had died suddenly from a brain tumour. This time it was the Edgeworths' cousin, Charles, Barry Fox's brother, who stood against O'Connell's candidate, Mr White. As the priest claimed to have secured every Catholic vote for White, the election result seemed a foregone conclusion but Maria still pulled out all the stops to help Charles Fox. It is difficult not to feel sympathy for the Edgeworths' tenants involved.

TO HARRIET BUTLER
Edgeworthstown, 23 December 1836

I hope I have done some little good (and no harm) by coming home, as I have secured I hope Dermod's and Kelly's votes, to whom I drove out through the snow on the ground that day, and after deep struggling internally each of them gave me their promise. Dermod was as white as a sheet and each particular bristle of his beard half an inch long seemed to feel the struggle of his mind.

"Oh Ma'am, the priest in – and I so set upon – and a lone cripple. But I will tell you what – I am much obliged to you, and my family, as you say, and myself was always so obliged to your father – the best of landlords – that I cannot, when it is put to me by yourself, I cannot refuse you. I should not die easy in my conscience if I did. So there it is – let the priests do their worst. I will vote for you. But, dear Miss Edgeworth, would you let me stay till the last day that I might get in as it were unknownst?"

"No, that is impossible, you cannot do it unknownst, and as you feel it right to do it boldly."

"Then so I will. Send a carriage of any kind for me when you will. I will go."

Now I hope he will be steady … Mr Kelly's conscientious struggles you shall hear of when we meet …

TO SOPHY RUXTON [*Fragment*]
Edgeworthstown, n.d. January 1837

… The election is over – of course we know that Mr White must be the member.[227] So he is with a majority of the fourth day – but not till the 4th day – But Charles Fox has made a noble start … and having shown he has power & will to support the conservative cause for four days, no one can reproach him with rashness for having stood this contest – The Conservative interest in Ireland must, at least ought, to feel obliged to him – The gentlemen of the Conservative side did not act zealously together – If their head, if Sir G[*eorge*] F[*eatherstone*] had not sacrificed to a 10 year old pique the interests of this county, & of this country, his own principle too in politics, Charles F would have been at this moment our member.

---

227   Luke White was in fact far from a dangerous radical, but a member of an up-and-coming county family and heir to a wealthy Dublin bookseller.

... The violence has been beyond description or belief on the part of the priests, raising mobs, forcing voters etc. The pleasantest thing I have to say I keep till the last – that Lovell made such an excellent manly speech that he has done himself infinite credit & much obliged both Barry & Charles[228] ...

I don't think C.F. is much disappointed – I believe (but do not talk of it, pray, yet) that there is to be a petition – Some gentlemen talk of substituting – CF declares that he will not be at any more expense – I am sure this election has cost him fifteen hundred – and that is enough for the public good – If the petition goes on – that is effectively raised by small sums – they will be able to strike off more than the present majority of voters and CF would be then seated just as Lord Forbes was after his petition ...

Captain Harte, Lord Forbes' agent, called over to warn of further local disturbances.

TO MRS EDGEWORTH
Edgeworthstown, 26 February 1837

... Captain Harte is become quite grey headed and looks careworn – I am sure he has suffered much and was sincerely attached to Lord F – He showed the judgement of affection in what he did not say as in all he did say – Lady Forbes intends to come over as soon as she can to superintend the removing his body and building some mausoleum over it as he wished in the old parish churchyard. Harte agrees with us in high opinion of Lady F's attachment to her husband and her truth of mind & truth of character ... The 2 children are very fine children – especially the youngest – She wished to have lived at Castle Forbes for the next 2 years – But it is thought that the affairs being in Chancery, the Chancellor will not let to her but as most advantageous let it to the best bidder during their minority. Harte tells me that Lefroy[229] is determined upon bidding for it and he will probably have it – and so be it – He will be a good kind tenant and a MAN is necessary to keep the people in order – The change made in that whole Forbes neighbourhood since Lord Forbes' absence & more since his death is dreadful – I believe ... Another attempt has been made to assassinate Amos – the good steward (fired at over a hatch

---

228 Lovell had returned briefly from exile in Liverpool at his stepmother's invitation.

229 Thomas Lefroy was a successful self-made lawyer who had bought a neighbouring estate, just outside Longford town. He rose to be Lord Chief Justice of Ireland and has become posthumously famous as the man with whom Jane Austen had once been in love.

door – escaped) – Amos now never steps out without a man with a gun with him – never is out after dusk & is determined to stand his ground ... They detest him as Scotch – and fear him as strictly honest & just ... In such a state of lawlessness poor Lady Forbes could not live – but she will come over ...

Family tragedy struck soon after. Maria's stepmother had returned to Clifton with her third daughter, Sophy, now showing all the signs of consumption. Fanny, who was still ailing, joined them and the two sisters were installed on sofas in adjoining rooms. Sophy died suddenly in early March, leaving four children. The two youngest, Waller and Charlotte, had been left at Edgeworthstown.

TO MRS EDGEWORTH
Edgeworthstown, 7 March 1837

Most dear and tender and ... best of mothers and friends, I pray that your own strength of body, your own most precious health may not be overpowered by this affliction. The end came so rapidly that you were not prepared for it ... If the shock was great for us, what must it have been to you! The mother! I am sure in spite of yourself you had not given up all hope till that fatal wonderful moment that separates the living from the <u>dead</u> – Oh how much that one word says when once one has seen it – I had always trusted to her youth and to her being of your blood & of your constitution. But however great the shock of the suddenness of parting there is consolation to you that her sufferings were much less than if she had lingered and her perfect preservation of her angelic mind, her serene temper ... to the very last must be soothing recollections ... Think how happy she was in having you & her husband & Fanny ... with her – And Maxwell and Mary Anne – and knowing that her two other darlings were so well taken care of and so tenderly loved by her Harriet – yes – and Mr Butler who really loves them ...

The children are well – In Waller's innocent gaiety there is something very touching – and almost shocking – Charlotte older was more than proportionately more affected ... – she was all day unhappy ... and came fondling up to me and to whoever she saw without speaking – but only leaning her head against one – and trying to amuse herself with pictures – 5 o'clock Mr Butler that kindest of friends has just arrived – the children are twining round him just as he was their own[230] ...

---

230 The Butlers, who were childless, were to bring up Sophy's children as their own.

TO FANNY WILSON
Edgeworthstown, 9 May 1837

How do you do – I long to know how you & Lucy go on now you are bereft of my mother – You were very brave & generous to send her to us – Here she is at her old place at the library table writing either to you or Lucy

– And Barry at the opposite end writing to Charles – There are marks of mental suffering in the face.

Barry has even the first day of his arrival been called upon by various persons wanting redress of wrongs – He will feel that he is of use to them & to us – and to his manly mind that will be the best comfort – The return to this place must be dreadfully painful[231] – Annaghmore worse –

I am glad he had just at this moment the pleasure of hearing of Charles Fox's complete success – so well deserved – so honorable for him![232] … The striking off of those bad votes is in itself an indemnity for the past and a security for the future. This committee have had an opportunity of seeing something of the Irish priests themselves and of tracing [?] their influence upon voters – They must have been shocked at the violence and the perjury –

The labour they have gone through has had excellent results that Parliament must in consequence of their report … make some reform in the mode of registering votes in this country – One district definition of what constitutes a good vote would do away at once with the recounting for the registering barristers – and would prevent the cheating at elections & the squabbling …

The effect even at this moment is felt in this village and all the neighbourhood in the immediately altered tone of the people – Their being relieved of their dread of the priests and the beatings – As they say we have been worn down between our priests & our landlords – and they are rejoiced when the pressure on one side is taken off …

TO FANNY WILSON
Edgeworthstown, 5 June 1837

… I am sorry [*Sismondi*] has been too severe in his remarks upon Lady Stafford.[233] – I do not agree with him there as to the facts – The main

---

231 The house in Offaly that he and Sophy had bought two years before.

232 Charles Fox's election defeat in December 1836 had been overturned on appeal.

233 Maria and Fanny had stayed with Lady Stafford nineteen years earlier at their splendid house, Trentham Park. Sismondi, an Italian economist, had published an essay in 1834 claiming evictions from the Staffords' estates in Sutherland as the worst example of the Highland Clearances.

point which can hardly be denied is that things and people could not have remained in the state to which they were when these dislodgements took place.

5 people could not live on the land that was but just sufficient to support one or two – Then the people must have starved or eaten one another or emigrated – and the whole remaining question is whether the means taken to remove them were too much hurried or not – productive in short of most happiness or misery.

I think Sismondi in this point is too irrational & not philosophical or accurate as to his facts …

Sismondi has undertaken a difficult task when he is to estimate the happiness of others – he would want my mental thermometer.

In June Francis and Rosa arrived from Italy, bringing their son, little Willy, to meet his cousins, the little Foxes. Edgeworthstown once again was filled with children.

TO FANNY WILSON
Edgeworthstown, 23 June 1837

You will like to know from each and all of us our impressions of the boy & the mother – Rosa and Willy – Good in the first place – very good and agreeable all – Rosa appears to me much improved in appearance – her skin less yellow and her eyes fine and more bright … and the same clear decidedly honest and intelligent countenance – full of life & feeling.

The boy – not the least like his father – nor like any Edgeworth – but like a Murillo child in a picture and in reality a very fine boy – observing and quick – and with a fine happy temperament – The dear young cousins of his all clustered round him and formed as pretty a group as ever you could wish or could draw … Many a nice drawing of yours I have already so I should not be greedy or as Major Taylor pronounced it greddy –

Willy has not yet got come to his powers of noise – a little shyness is to be worn off before he can make the most of all the means of happiness & noise which he now contemplates, hushed in smiling repose in his mother's arms, looking down upon the playful crowd around her –

Poor poor dear Barry – when he sees the mother with her son – and his own – and thinks of what a mother they had – and if she was …

Francis appears to the greatest advantage – He is in a difficult delicate position – in which he shows – good sense – good taste & that perfect good breeding joined also to good natural temper & some self control.

... Yesterday soon after Rosa came – Francis said to me – "It must be so painful to Barry – I am almost ashamed to have a wife – to have Rosa here with her boy."

And he kept himself in a sort of background subdued state – Francis is a most amiable as well as agreeable creature ...

TO SOPHY RUXTON
Edgeworthstown, 29 July 1837

... I find Francis much improved ... His good sense is growing up apace and will regulate his genius – His disposition & his temper are really naturally so amiable that they have in a wonderful way held him to good while principles have been forming ... Rosa is the very wife that Prudence would have chosen for him – How lucky that Love for once went right along with passion without knowing it ... My affection for Rosa increases – and my esteem & real admiration for the clearness of her understanding and the nobleness of her mind – She is infinitely more agreeable to me than more literary people who have only to pour out secondhand opinions from books ... There is something original in her and a mind still new and true, unfolding itself and making me unfold mine – I never heard more accurate or more beautiful discrimination of character than she showed in giving me her opinion of Fanny and Harriet Butler ...

Rosa is teaching me Spanish – and Francis is laughing at me for learning a new language at 70.

I have been reading Miss Martineau's 3rd vol[*ume*] on America – Very clever she is – and I think she has a most courageous mind and enthusiasm for good – But I cannot agree with her democratic mania and her notions of the rights of women – There are more striking and useful facts in Miss Martineau's book than I ever read on America except de Tocqueville – But all her facts in my opinion go against her theory that a majority should be the foundation of all good government[234] ...

---

234 Harriet Martineau, social theorist and lecturer, much feted by the Whigs. Her account of America caused huge controversy there because of her support of the abolitionists. Maria admired her but also rejected many of her economic theories as impractical, especially her 'anticharity principles' on the grounds that they were inhuman in practice and would create a race of 'political, philosophical Thugs' (a reference to the Indian sect described by her brother Pakenham).

TO SOPHY RUXTON
Edgeworthstown, 6 October 1837

Francis and Rosa and their little boy were leaving.

… This house will be quite dull without him – And I do not know how we will bear the loss of Francis & Rosa now that we have been 3 months together – How much Francis is improved in worldly wisdom and how much of the over abundance of genius has been reined in – Entertaining, affectionate, agreeable, charming tempered to live with he is! Heaven knows when we shall meet again or how or where – As life advances how heavily these parting thoughts prey upon the heart – I have become more and more attached to Rosa – the originality of her mind and warmth of her feeling are peculiarly suited to me – She is very dear to me …

This was Maria's last letter to Sophy Ruxton. Maria's seventieth birthday brought the shocking news of Sophy's death.

TO FANNY WILSON
Edgeworthstown, 1 January 1838

… Last night I heard of the death of Sophy Ruxton who had been for the greater number of years more truly my friend than anyone now living – and more strongly and intimately associated with those I earliest loved … Though she had been so long declining … it was unexpected. Till within these last few days I had hoped she might as Dr Brown said live for years – I had believed too easily … and did not want to leave home when Louisa Beaufort came …

– And now – oh my dear Fanny, when it is irreparable how … bitterly I reproach myself …

She is gone – that poor helpless looking Catherine [*the maid*] was indefatigable in her exertions, was how great and most useful support to the last … When she first saw that there were symptoms which she knew to be of imminent danger … she ran out of the room & said to Margaret "Oh Ma'am her legs are swelling" – & she could not utter another word but fell on a bed in a swoon.

Poor Margaret[235] – How few know her or what she feels, or cares for her – You do – & so do I – and it wrings my heart to think of her – Especially as now she will feel that she showed half the affections she felt – & that she never felt half enough …

Harriet's rectory in Trim was conveniently placed to offer comfort to Margaret, and was by now almost Maria's second home.

TO MRS EDGEWORTH
The Rectory, Trim, 21 February 1838

I am very well and as warm and comfortable as possible only the day is too short for all that is to be enjoyed and the evening and night is gone before I have threaded 3 needles.

Harriet has read in the evenings Emma all through & Pride & Prejudice – And I liked them better than ever – And the last thing she has been reading is Frazier's Persian Princes in London – Oh so delightfully entertaining a true story …

Tell Honora that Waller [*Sophy Fox's son*] does indeed deserve the map of the rivers she sent him … He traced almost all the rivers through the different maps and has drawn almost all the rivers through their courses – Never was a present better suited or better timed …

Trim, 23 February 1838

The frozen goose did well notwithstanding his being a goose and frozen … It has arrived safely – yesterday – and gives plenary & universal satisfaction – and special delight to Mary Anne & Charlotte … by the moment of its arrival – They were actually equipped in bonnets and cloaks to go with us to Summerhill to pay a visit to Lady Georgina Hill (now its lady) when in my going into my own room to put on bonnet – there was a fat parcel on my table!

… First and chief good – the zebra bootikins and their fellows! "Good dear dear Grandmama" – and their destined feet were in in a trice and "Oh how nicely they fit! And how beautiful! Oh look, Aunt Maria" And how comfortable in the carriage.

---

235 Sophy's younger sister who had shared the cottage beside the Boyne with her.

Mary Anne   au Bain

'Mary Anne au bain';
Sophy Fox's children
were brought up by her
sister, Harriet Butler.

And Waller was full as much delighted as if all of them had been on his own feet at once. The first thing he said when he opened his eyes in the morning (and my eyes scarcely open) was "Goodest grandmamma! Is she not, Aunt Maria – The zebra bootikins ... you remember – I shall write to her myself – and I won't forget zebra – She must have a great deal of money – I wish she was as rich as a Queen! And she'd make me a Prince – I daresay, wouldn't she – The caps for Charlotte – did you see! Purple ribbons so nice!" – and much more said no doubt ad infinitum – but that Mary Jones and the tub entered ...

Dr Butler pounced upon the Quarterly Review with hawk bright eyes – and has been devouring it ever since – garbage and all. By garbage I mean the extracts from "The Reign of George 4th" which, whether by Lady Charlotte Bury or not, Mr Butler declares are most scandalous & detestable and not fit to be read – therefore he began to read them to us. But we preferred Northanger Abbey which Harriet is now reading to me every evening – As you know, Sir Walter Scott sent us to it – to see if he was right in liking it – and I say ditto to Sir Walter[236] ...

---

236 She had revised her scornful earlier opinion on *Northanger Abbey* when she first read it in 1817.

TO FANNY WILSON
Trim, 22 April 1838

I have not yet finished the 7ᵗʰ vol of Scott's life – Only got as far as Ballantyne's letter to him on the first appearance of failure in his powers – and his answer quoting the archbishop to Gil Blas.

It is very melancholy and affected me so much that Harriet took the book from my hands and would not let me read more … I am sorry Lockhart has condescended to EULOGISE Scott or to draw any character of him but what is so truly – so admirably brought out by his whole life and through the whole work. Lockhart's preface to the 7ᵗʰ vol. is excellent …

> *She had just received a long letter from Mary Martin of Ballinahinch. Mary's father had been sent to prison for violent threats during a dispute over land.*

Mary Martin wrote me a most characteristic letter – I could not blame her enthusiasm about her father or her indignation against Judge & Jury & Government by whom in her way of seeing the case he had been so shamefully treated –

She ended with saying that when Government affords no protection to those whose property is forcibly taken from them it cannot be wondered at that "Connemara Chieftains still put on their tails and in the old way fight it out and run their chance of being sent to jail by the jury afterwards."
Upon which Mr Butler when I first read it exclaimed "I should not wonder if Miss Martin were to go out with her tail herself" –

Upon which hint I wrote a sedative to her – administered with all the kindness & all the address in my power.

I hoped in short "that she knew her *Métier de Reine* better than to enact a mere barbarian chieftainess" –

For after all we must confess that Force is the ultimate law of Kings – and Queens[237] …

I recollect that I have not told you what I think of Balzac's stories – I am afraid that by what I said at the beginning of *Père Goriot* I led you to believe that I liked it better than I really do.

---

237 Maria remained a close confidante of Mary Martin; the poor 'Princess of Connemara' was to be bankrupted nine years later by the Great Famine and to die on an emigrants' ship to America in 1848 after marrying a distant cousin the previous year.

I cannot after all express too much admiration for Balzac's GENIUS which is of the highest order – But he seems to me to be completely destitute of moral sense – Not only does he not care for right or wrong but he does not recollect that he shd appear to care for it and that as a writer must depend for much of his powers over human creatures not destitute of moral sense and consequently of sympathy & moral repulsion.

Père Goriot is a kind of fantastic King Lear … But parental love so … PERVERTED & running into moral deformity of the most shocking kind – a father sharing in corrupting his own daughters and wishing he could strangle their husbands – the husbands he had given them! …

[*Balzac*] is a kind of Mephistopholes … detestable to me – a great genius – but an evil genius – And not a fine Satanic Miltonic evil genius – But a Parisian Dandy devil with his French perfumes "*Parfaite Amour*" and "*Mousseline des Indes*" mixed with the stench of brimstone and Sulphur …

Maria's denunciation of Balzac covered eighteen closely written pages! However, she later relented somewhat and much admired Le Curé de Campagne.

TO FANNY WILSON
Edgeworthstown, 17 June 1838

… I am not sure whether my mother mentioned to you that she and I paid a visit to Lady Longford who is now at Pakenham Hall with her son Lord L and all her daughters. She has lost much of her beauty by suffering, but she is all the more interesting – Her manners much improved in warmth and no matter what the manners when one reads the heart through time & feeling – I think she will reside at P. Hall – & do her duty – and make her son love & respect her – He is an amiable looking youth – I should not guess on much talent – In the guards – But does not love drinking or gambling – and if she gives him his head may run his own course well – and I think she will. Her daughters are unaffected charming girls.[238]

There is a wooden bridge now in place of the Float – same tolls paid as at Float.

Mr Butler is charmed with Sidney Smith's letters – their wit and sense – and he declares that they do not shock him as a clergyman or from a cleric

---

238 Maria's optimism was misjudged. The 3rd Earl was to die in unsavoury circumstances in London aged forty-three.

& that they contain almost all his own opinions – I think they will not lower Sidney Smith's reputation as a writer what ever they may do as a party friend – A man who bespatters on both sides cannot be liked by either party – Nor can a man who speaks the truth, I fear[239] ...

TO FANNY WILSON
Edgeworthstown, late July 1838

.... We are reading Miss Martineau's last book on America – she is as strong in body as a horse or an elephant – and except for her feeling HUNGER & weakness in hunger I should say as to bodily feelings "Since our natures naught in common know – From what foundation could a friendship grow." ...

I think ... that she writes from high & good motives – But that she is audacious & self opinionated not only for a woman but for any human being not ensured infallible ... (she publishes slap dash her opinion & the names of individuals most rashly & cruelly without feeling for the pain she gives & the mischief she does)

... I think Tom Beddoes is the strangest creature I ever heard of – this comes of an early fancy to be ORIGINAL ... I am very sorry that I gave myself the trouble of writing to ask him here ... This is the second time he has raised a letter out of me on false pretences – He shall never have a third – I am really provoked at a son of my beloved sister, Anna's ... not allowing me to love as I should have wished to have loved her son[240] ...

> *In late 1838 there was a change of cast in the family circle. Francis Beaufort, now official Hydrographer to the Royal Navy – and a widower – had come to Edgeworthstown during the summer and proposed to the shy 42-year-old Honora. Honora was at first hesitant to abandon the care of her aged Aunt Mary and deal with London after the quiet years at Edgeworthstown. Maria encouraged her to make the leap, and in November she married Francis and left for England. Maria wrote via Fanny to reassure her that all was well.*

---

239 Three Letters to Archdeacon Singleton on the Ecclesiastical Commission. The famous Anglican preacher and wit, Sydney Smith, had studied moral philosophy under the Edgeworths' old friend Dugald Stewart in Edinburgh and later helped found the *Edinburgh Review*. Maria had met him numerous times in London and much enjoyed debating with him over Irish subjects. His eldest daughter Saba had married Dr (later Sir) Henry Holland, another close friend.

240 After a dazzling literary debut at Cambridge, Anna's eldest son had gone to Germany to study medicine, but was expelled from several German cities in turn for preaching extreme democratic ideas. He eventually ended in Switzerland but committed suicide in 1849.

*Thomas Lovell Beddoes,
Maria's nephew.
He committed suicide in 1849.*

TO FANNY WILSON
December 26 1838

... Aunt Mary said to me yesterday "My dear Maria, when you write to Honora or Fanny, will you tell them how very kind and attentive Lucy is to me and what an agreeable manner – she really suits me[241] ...

---

241 Lucy, Maria's youngest sister, had returned to Edgeworthstown to take Honora's place as her aunt's companion.

X

JANUARY 1839 – DECEMBER 1844

1839 BROUGHT ANOTHER *change of cast. After much discussion it had been agreed that Francis should return to take over the day-to-day running of the Edgeworthstown estate from his stepmother and his 71-year-old elder sister. He was now the putative male heir to the estate, given that Sneyd had no children; he had a wife and three children and could not earn enough to support them by tutoring. But the year began ominously with the shooting of a landlord in Offaly. Barry Fox sent a first-hand report.*

TO FANNY WILSON
Edgeworthstown, 4 January 1839

... You will have seen in the newspapers before this reaches you the account of Lord Norbury's being shot – too true – Harriet Butler has a letter from Barry this morning which confirms the intelligence – You know B[*arry*] is with Lord Charleville at Tullamore holding sessions there – This poor Lord Norbury had been with them the day before – was returning to his own home at 4 o'clock in the evening – was shot by a man who was behind a hedge but a few yards from him – It is surprising he was not instantly killed – he was shot in the shoulder – when Barry wrote it was not certain whether Lord N would live or die – This poor Lord Norbury was a most innocent goose or gander who could not have offended anybody one would have thought. And spent a great deal of money among the people – Barry does not mention what was supposed to be the motive – I suppose that it will turn out that some tenants have been turned off his estate – But the usual course in such cases is to shoot the agent as he is considered the proximate or efficient cause and moreover he is generally more obnoxious for having more coarseness of manner towards the lower classes & more resources to annoy them. Really, though I wrote a story called The Absentee, I begin to think that it is but reasonable that a country should be rendered safe to live in before we complain of ABSENTEES[242] ...

Two days later Ireland was hit by the great hurricane later known as the Big Wind. Beginning in Mayo around noon, it swept across Connaught, Ulster and northern Leinster, destroying buildings and haystacks in its path. Maria was in Harriet's rectory in Trim and reported the town 'a most deplorable spectacle' with half the houses unroofed though the rectory itself suffered little but a fallen apple tree.

TO MRS EDGEWORTH
Trim, 23 January 1839

Harriet and the children and I went to Black Castle yesterday – Except for one large elm there is no loss ... that is of any consequence near the house ... Most of the trees which the storm blew down are better down & they have only to carry them away & give whatever can be useful to the poor people either for repairs or firing – and be thankful they came off so well. Boarded panes numerous in front of the house ... 39 large panes broken – and the skylight of the great staircase almost all the glass demolished. ... [*But*] what is this to the poor Martins' dreadful account of the loss of lives and shrieks of the living reaching their ears from the surrounding lakes and hills ...

Mr Egan's house that was bad enough before the storm was completely demolished ... And Archdeacon Pakenham invited the whole family to come to his house for a month or whatever it may be necessary to fit up another residence for them ... They have to feed 14 of the family ... children and servants included.

---

242 Who killed Lord Norbury has remained a mystery until this day. Contemporary accounts confirm
Maria's view that he had been an innocuous and generous landlord; but his father, the first Lord
Norbury, had been notorious as a Hanging Judge and as the man who had pronounced the death
sentence on Robert Emmet.

Who says there is no good left – Henry Pakenham really has a good large heart – What <u>mixture</u> of good & great & little in human creatures. They say he is a <u>plaguey</u> person to live with, so fussing about little things and fretful.

His own man's expression which Harriet has just told us is "My master is <u>briary</u> this morning" – But I'd rather live with his <u>thorns</u> of temper & all because he has a warm heart – and can be easily pleased – and the thorns can be pulled out …

Francis and his family made the crossing to Dublin safely and arrived at Trim a week later much to Maria's relief.

TO FANNY WILSON
The Rectory, Trim, 1 February 1839

At this instant I am as happy as happy can be – Rosa is lying on the sofa beside me and Francis in the tub armchair opposite the fire reading a Review … of Sir Walter Scott's works and Harriet is at the round table working hard for me, turning Irish acres into English for a new Rent Book intended for Francis' initiation into Agent's duties – To complete your idea of my present felicity, comprehend that behind the sofa on which I sit is a band of merry young ones – Willy's [*Francis' son*] joyous laugh heard clear above all, while some are shooting peas from an old spring gun & some from a new pistol, a present not yet a day old to Waller …

Here they are happy – arriving late on Thursday, coming through drifts and with tired horses but Willy not the least bit tired & bright eyed and willing and ready to talk about everything! He is a delightful boy – & Waller and Mary Anne and Charlotte are so fond of him that it does the heart good to see and hear them altogether …

Harriet also relieved Maria of another burden. Years earlier she had begun a story that she believed her father had instructed her to finish. Even twenty years on, his commands were sacrosanct.

TO FANNY WILSON
Edgeworthstown, 16 February 1839

… My dear, you will be very glad to hear that I have completely freed myself from that millstone which has been weighing me down – Take for Granted

… Harriet believes that he [*Richard Lovell Edgeworth*] did never augur well of it – And she told me that she remembered reading it to him – and she heard him say "That is commonplace. That will never do" or words to that effect.

In short Harriet quite satisfied my conscience – and moreover had the courage or kindness to seize upon the chapter which I had with me and burn it without reading it just as I had hoped; and when I got home I took down ALL to the kitchen fire & stood by while every page (I am sure 5 or 600 pages) and every scrap relating to that tale Take for Granted burned to black film – And much relieved I was when I had secured myself against the shame of it ever being read by my friends – much more published.

And now my mind is free & I will take care to begin nothing of which I have not considered the end – And nothing which I do not feel I really like to do …

A month later she had a serious fall, which she sketched and described in detail to Harriet. The sketch shows that Maria, as she had always maintained, was no draughtsman.

TO HARRIET BUTLER
Edgeworthstown, 13 March 1839

I hope the frontispiece which I have sketched for you will make you laugh – and very glad I am not to make you cry! I assure you I had a narrow escape of being a cripple on your hands – and your dear mother's for life.

How I escaped breaking my legs I know not – so entangled were they among the rungs of the broken ladder, as ladder and I came down together – how I cannot conceive. I had made the least struggle I <u>must</u> have broken both legs, but I let the ladder do just as it pleased – and one half was so good as to fall clean off one foot without doing a hap'orth of harm to foot or leg. And the other half of the ladder was content with scraping the skin two half-crowns' worth off my shin-bone, but not cutting through to the bone, leaving most considerately a cherry-red film or skinnikin underneath …

My first distinct thought – after <u>myself</u> – was how glad I was the ladder did not break with Willy [*Francis' son*] whom I had let go up it the day before. Finding I could stand, I got to the door and called out to Lockie [*the maid*] most manfully, desiring she would go for my mother (<u>your</u> mother was <u>my</u> mother then, observe, as she always is in time of need). She had not left the breakfast table, so was with me with the speed of morning light – and doctored and

Maria's drawing of herself falling off a ladder aged seventy-two.

surgeoned me and gold-beater-skinned and sticking-plastered and garlanded me – and gave me essence-of-Pity-and-Love mixed properly which did me all the good in the world. And when I was bandaged and dressed, Francis carried me upstairs most nicely ...

July saw the closing of Lovell's old school, which had been taken on by the Church of Ireland three years before, for lack of funds. Maria expressed herself relieved; the school had gone downhill and its pupils were running wild and drinking in the town.

TO FANNY WILSON
Edgeworthstown, 9 July 1839

... You will in a few days see in the newspapers an advertisement of the Premises lately occupied by the school at E'town etc etc.

Mr Trench has this day sent the half year's rent in full on 25th June – and desires me to consider premises are given up & now in our possession. The boys are all gone home – Mr Murphy to his living in Clare – He will return to pack up and pack off – He has behaved very well towards us – sincerely & honestly – Sorry to leave US but glad to get away from a place which circumstances had rendered painful to him – He and the Dean ... hope that the place they have taken at Lucan (Spa House) will be really more advantageous not so much in point of money but the possibility of keeping the boys under proper moral discipline – They will not have a village full of whiskey shops to run into – They will have to run a mile at least first and to climb over walls almost impossible – if any ever be to schoolboy impossible –

You know I must be sorry for the loss of the rent for Lovell & CSE & less considerable advantage to the Town. But as I am going to tell you, I am not so sorry as you might think I must be for the departure of the school ... the truth is that I do not finally believe that the Institution will last much longer wherever it is and I would rather that the noise of the fall should not be at Edgeworthstown – Dean Murray is doing all he can to encourage the Irish clergy, Bishops especially, that if they do not help their own clergy nobody else will – He will never be able or willing to keep it up by begging every year in England ...

Francis rode to Sonna the other day – and liked Hugh Tuite ... & Old Mrs very much – "aimable" & very kindly civil to him but not entertaining or agreeable – and he had a bad dinner or something that did [not] agree with him ... Too much sage, he says, in an omelette – or too much gooseberry fool – and claret – all jumbled together by his ride home after a hot day – in short he was very sick when he got home – and when we shall persuade him ever to pay another visit to anybody I do not know – and am very sorry as he ought to be seen by the gentlemen of the county.

I am learning algebra from him & am detestably stupid but he does not tell me so – not even now that I am too old to learn – as firmly as 20 years ago he pronounced about chess.

I find in Francis a perfection which I should never have expected in him – and which pleases me more for the unexpectedness. He is very punctual and as regular in the hourly duties as if he had been bred up at the foot of Harriet herself. He is at this moment (after 3) at the Loan Fund, stifling in the market house where he does business for the good of the people for 5–6 hours every Thursday – They have given out at least £1150 –

TO MRS EDGEWORTH
Edgeworthstown, 28 August 1839

... The Butlers are at the breakfast table this morning enjoying all the good news which Honora read from your letter to her and to me. The oval table was quite full with young dear bright faces like former times – only the eyes much larger and brighter and darker in some of these faces – Mary Anne's superb and Maxwell's and your Spanish grandson's "flashing Spanish eyes" like those which did for his father at first sight ...

Barry [*Fox*] who took the dressing of his young ladies into his own hands at Annaghmore & declared that nobody should have anything to do with it, has certainly done them up wonderfully well – and shown much taste and judgement too, consulting Crampton about committing them to the *peine forte et dure* of stiff stays – I am glad he forbids the bands – the whalebone bands at least – only a stiff boddice for dacent support – (Francis, your precious paradoxical son made a fine misguided argument in favour of ramming human creatures into stiff stays on the strength of the Scriptural expression "Gird up your loins"). NB His own Rosa all this time wears no stiff stays ...

I wish as you do that poor dear affectionate Barry may find a companion & wife suited to him – young yet not too young – fashionable enough to please him yet not too fashionable etc – etc – etc – in short a nice phoenix with a bank note of £20,000 or so in her paw (if a phoenix has a paw) and insured against all accidents

Rosa is going on quite well and now opposite to me dressed in her muslin gown with the white muslin roses – quite beautiful even after washing – her little Maria is charming. I never saw so pretty an infant ...

But in the autumn Francis and Rosa were summoned unexpectedly back to Italy to look after Rosa's sister Mariquita who was severely ill; and Maria found herself once again in charge of the estate.

TO HONORA BEAUFORT
Edgeworthstown, 20 October 1839

I am quite well and have done all the rent receiving without suffering from it – Indeed I was most kindly helped by Mr Hinds[243] who came over on purpose

---

243 The Edgeworths' former land agent who now had his own farm in Co. Westmeath.

… I told him that my mother had been saying to me the very hour he came … that she was almost afraid of the responsibility Fr[*ancis*] was taking in himself in this agency – afraid that he might not be able to make the tenants pay regularly on time at every quarter … to [*make*] the regular payments on which the keeping of this establishment depends – I told him also that we feared Fr[*ancis*] being not yet sufficiently acquainted with Irish politics to get well through politics, elections etc & finished by asking his opinion … whether he thought it would be prudent for Fr[*ancis*] to take this agency.

"Then candidly, Ma'am, putting myself out of the question, I do not think it would … I do not so much feel the difficulty about the rents & the quarterly payments – I could get him in the way of doing all that – But I shd fear that he is not yet sufficiently acquainted with politics in this country & parties to steer clear of factions and once committed he would be lost … And then the charge of embroiling himself with his own friends and relations perhaps in case of elections".

You know, my dear Honora, we have felt all this and Mr Hinds … showed me both his sense & honesty … But then the alternative – his [*Francis*] not being with his mother and all of us – for he is resolved not to stay here unless he can earn his bread …

We have till next Gale [*rent collection*] in April & keep Mr Hinds till then on tenterhooks …

TO FANNY WILSON
Edgeworthstown, 1 April 1840

… We were much shocked by death of Mr Drummond[244]– Quite unexpected – unprepared we all were for [*it*] – No doubt his ill health brought on and his death hastened by over application to the duties of his office and over anxiety – For all I read of his evidence last year before parliament I formed a very high estimate of his intelligence & zeal in doing his duty and his sincere wish to do good in and to this country. Also I formed a higher opinion of his abilities as a man of business from that evidence than people in general here have held or professed to hold …

---

244 Thomas Drummond had worked earlier as an engineer on the Survey of Ireland and from first-hand knowledge had been able to implement a huge number of beneficial reforms as Under Secretary of State. Maria had met him in England in 1831 and had always much liked and admired him (see *Letters from England,1813 – 1844,* p. 538).

Maria in her bonnet totting up estate accounts.

I do not think I am at this moment biased much by the private feeling for the kindness he has shown us – He was to have come down here, very lately wrote to promise he would come to E'town & bring his wife whenever he shd be free from the turmoil of public business – as he plainly said whenever he should be leaving Ireland for not till then he said he could be spared.

He has been taken away, snatched away. He died with business on his back if ever a man did.

I wrote yesterday to Crampton about him and asked him to beg to have some public testimonial to Drummond's merits – of what sort he can judge best …

In September another of Maria's heroes passed through Edgeworthstown, Father Mathew, the famous temperance reformer from Tipperary. Two years before he had set up a campaign whereby followers would take a simple pledge of total abstinence and in return receive a medal. At the height of the campaign he was to attract over three million pledge-takers. Maria herself received a temperance medal, but never seems to have met him in person.

TO FANNY WILSON
Edgeworthstown, 22 September 1840

Father Mathew passed by this gate yesterday going to Ballymahon – stopped and left his respects "And that he was in great haste on business but would do himself the honour of calling on Mrs & Miss Edgeworth very soon" …

Edgeworthstown, 1 October 1840

… The 1ˢᵗ of October is come and gone … and no Francis – … Tomorrow I hope we shall hear something of him or I shall grow quite sick at heart …

We have 3 Foxes, 2 Beauforts, I think & Baby[245] – 8 young people in the house – and very cheerful it is – Harriet the youngest of them all. Harriet asked one of the girls in her school today if she knew what a <u>prisoner</u> meant ?

"Yes – <u>A man taken by a Peeler and put in prison."</u> …

Francis returned to his farm duties in late October much to Maria's relief and she left for London in early December 1840 to stay with Fanny, who was pregnant (she later miscarried). She came back in June to find Edgeworthstown at its best, and her stepmother, who had been ill with rheumatic fever, just recovered enough to venture outside.

TO FANNY WILSON
Edgeworthstown, 15 June 1841

… Your mother has been out in the landau this fine day – Francis carried her downstairs and across the hall and she walked up the steps and into the carriage herself and sat up like a lady – Francis & Lucy & I and baby put next to her … We drove along the Mullingar road about as far as you and I used to go when you were last here … And your mother … enjoyed herself seeing the face of nature and the lawn so pretty and her own well grown hedges and Francis' oats and the sheep and cows and calves and all the waking interests which have been torpid or dead … so long – and which now to light and life rising. The people on the road who knew her looked so glad to see her …

I must tell you as the most agreeable *chasse douleur* that all Francis' accounts and all the business he has done for me has been perfectly well done – And all

---

245 Francis and Rosa's youngest child, Maria, had been left at Edgeworthstown.

I have seen of his changes indoor and out done with much prudence and with both common and uncommon sense.

Your mother assures me that she completely approves of all he has done out of doors – And he has not entered into any speculation or laid out any money of hers – but she willingly supplied him with all the money which she would herself have used in farming – The crops she says & she hopes will repay ...

There is the fatal knock – and I have not time to add more ...

Later, same day

... I do not think I ever did [*Francis*] justice or anything like justice in the hurried account I gave you of his doings here and his mother's approval of them and him – manner and matter.

She told me that the land which he has taken into his own hands came in the first place from petty exchanges with tenants of the trust estate of little bits and corner fields which join the demesne grounds and prevent the necessity for passes and interference & rounding off the Demesne, giving at the same time equivalents to the tenants exchanging – and each paying their respective rents to Trust as before ... You know your mother holds the Demesne from Lovell and pays rent for it as he does for the Trust. Francis is to pay this rent and to make it out of farming and cattle etc – He made drains and fences and altered the course of a little stream ... in order to drain certain fields well and to include a road to a tenant's farm and house where none was before except in the bed of said river at certain times of year.

This has been his most expensive improvement – We have walked all over the ground and seen the water running which proves better than words or levelling that the grounds are drained and the drains have been judiciously laid out ...

He has this year done all that the better farmers are doing – in the particulars I cannot enter as I am ignorant – But I am assured by your mother that she thinks he has done all for the best with prudence ...

Nothing in short has been done ... with head in Plato or merely to follow whim or wilfulness.

... About the calves – for which we laughed at FBE so comfortably – Well, the calf madness has turned out very profitable – Though he lost two sets of twins! – But the prices for which he sold the others brought him up ... And at one point all our cows almost were sick and cow doctors predicted death and total loss – Francis was excessively interested and anxious for their cowships and calveships and the men in the cowhouse and stable caught the master's anxiety and they were up night and day and in short only one cow dead OUTRIGHT and another PINES but may live to see another day.

I was much amused by seeing the place he had racked and bushed in for his calves and admired the facility with which his mind has turned from the high ABSURD to the low useful –

And delighted to see how he loves his home and all that it contains and how he is loved by his mother ...

News had just come of the death of Sir Walter Scott who had died at Abbotsford, his home in Scotland, aged sixty-two, worn out by the efforts to pay off his creditors.

TO FANNY WILSON
Edgeworthstown, 1 September 1841

I am glad I am only a little taper and have never burned at both ends – or flamed – flared – and waned ...

With Francis farming and 'equal to all agent business', Maria had planned to spend the winter again with Fanny in London but was taken ill in November and was slow recovering. And in May, Pakenham, Maria's youngest sibling, returned home on leave after eleven years away in India – and there was a joyful reunion at Edgeworthstown to greet him. Only Sneyd was absent, still suffering from imaginary ills in Kent.

TO HARRIETTE EDGEWORTH
Edgeworthstown, 16 May 1842

... I should not at first have known Pakenham again I think if I had met him without being told he was an Edgeworth. He is so bronzed and his countenance & whole appearance so different from that of the youth from whom I parted eleven years ago – But now & then the old young Pakenham comes out – He has a most official man of business appearance – calm & penetrating and accustomed to power. He is most tranquil & concise & clear in giving orders or in narrating or summing up information – of which he has abundance.

But it is his perfect freedom from pretension or affectation ... that is delightful in him, his affection and simple easy tastes are all as fresh and pure as though he had never seen the world and been a man in authority saying to this one go and more – live or die.

Pakenham's love of his mother is quite touching and you may conceive how touching to her – In truth she has since his arrival, and with Honora & Fanny and with Harriet and Mr Butler and the two young Foxes (now turned into handsome young ladies) and with Rosa and her William and Mary all surrounding her, been as happy a mother or grandmother as she deserves & more I cannot say ...

In June Maria received an unexpected honour that pleased her immensely. Her old friend, Sir William Rowan Hamilton, now head of the Royal Irish Academy, wrote to tell her she had been elected a member. It was an honour accorded hitherto only to two women, Mary Somerville the Scottish mathematician and Caroline Herschel, who had worked with her brother on his famous telescope. Maria's passion for scientific knowledge had only increased with age – and she took it also as a posthumous tribute to her father, who had been a founding member of the Academy.

That autumn she was once again planning to go to London when she was struck down by a serious attack of her old enemy, erysipelas.

TO FANNY WILSON
Edgeworthstown, 28 January 1843

You shall see how short a note I can write to you with mine own hand.

To certify, to prove to you – how slowly I am going – how prudent and admirable I am. "Oh we are indeed a glorious family" – So much better than glorious I have found mine own, so loving, so affectionate, so <u>affective</u> to use one of father's favourite words that they are pulling altogether with the able and steady aid of <u>Dr</u> Butler's favourite physician. Dr Clifford actually dragged me from Death's door which was more than half open (pulse 120) ready to receive me.

When I have strength enough to let out all the mirth and facetious pleasanteries upon the past which Dr Quiet & Diet insist upon, Dr Merryman not allowing me to be let out at present – you shall have them – *Le malheur passe!* is good for much better than to be forgotten ... Good to make us laugh heartily – For past kindness we can give only tears, sweet tears of gratitude ...

How can I be thankful enough to Providence and proud enough of myself for having known and dared to tell that I felt I was unequal to the journey to London at the time appointed.

I <u>must</u> have died on the road – at a railroad station or at poor dear slow Mrs Moilliet and Mr Moilliet's watery eye would have disappeared altogether.

TRUTH for ever – Huzza –

TO FANNY WILSON
Edgeworthstown, 8 February 1843

... I really don't know myself and almost doubt of my own identity – all my feelings and motions ... seem so different ... But I know now what it is to be not only sick but weak – all the pains and penalties of weakness quite unknown to me before I have now become too well acquainted with – and instead of running about I now creep as slowly as may be and think it a trial to mount the Alps – that is the stairs ...

Francis and Rosa have been to Lord Rosses'. Francis was delighted with his manners, his cook, his butler, his whole establishment and beautifully furnished castle and good natured self. Pakenham so delighted with his science and his telescope that he would stay two or three days longer – They met there Southern [?] and McCulloch and the Robinsons, Dr and daughter. They will come here, I mean the Robinsons, next week and Harriet Butler ... and I will only stay an hour at a time in the room – So help me God ...

In March she went to Trim to convalesce in Harriet's rectory and enjoyed the celebrations for St Patrick's Day from her bedroom window.

TO FANNY WILSON
The Rectory, Trim, 17 March 1843

... In the morning the Temperance band sent up to ask whether Miss E would like to hear a tune by choice (or else Mr Butler fabricated that message and gave me the honours paid to himself). However this may have been I contentedly took the compliment and answered I should be delighted – and I was delighted.

Through the open double bastions [*of the town*] in poured a band profusely gay with blue ribbons and blue scarfs flying – and the high priest with a broidered scarf and coat of blue and white, pendant floating, mounted on as black a horse as you have ever <u>seen</u> with body clothes and ears and all decorated, followed by another attendant priest very seriously dressed in black and mounted too but on a younger horse that would not stand while the band played – and played exceedingly well … The mound of heads and bodies … extended as far as could be seen up the street & under the ivy tower. I saw from my bedchamber window for I was not allowed to go down the steps …

And it was very pleasant to see Mr Butler bare headed shaking hands with the priest and so kindly speaking to all without Catholic or Protestant distinction and encouraging this harmless mirth – this most innocent enjoyment – Why should not the lower classes have this amusement and pleasure as well as the higher – And especially in this case where they refrain from all that is hurtful and have cured themselves of a vice – they should be paid in honour and innocent merriment and sociability – with sympathy from their superiors.

I cannot bear that people should suspect something bad & politically mischievous <u>underneath</u> …

The same quantity of will and energy ill directed might in some time here raise an insurrection …

O'Connell is here at this moment roaring away to the mob in Trim

Such quantities of laurels were begged and cut and dragged from this garden yesterday to adorn his stage.

But he had a very poor reception – no respectable people – Flood the shopkeeper the best of them!

I asked Dr Clifford who has just been here & who had been talking to many of the knowing and the unknowing what he could make out from the people that they expect O'Connell should do for them.

"Why" "the butcher answered me" said Dr Clifford "We expect that when he gets a <u>repale</u>, the Irish gentlemen will all be obliged to reside at home and kill their own mutton and spend their money in Ireland and at home in lieu of abroad and in England."

Dr Clifford saw O'Connell and says he looks well but much aged though as impudent and clever as ever …

Bess Fitzherbert's gardener brought her one day (lang syne) a fine geranium called O'Connell or so he told her.

She dashed it out of his hand and broke pot and all exclaiming "O'Connell! Out of my sight."

Maria was still too weak to accept an invitation from her favourite scientist, Dr Robinson, to Armagh, and to bring with her her youngest sister Lucy. It turned out to be a fortunate refusal: Lucy went without her and Dr Robinson, a handsome widower of fifty-one, proposed. Lucy was now thirty-eight, fully recovered from her old spinal complaint and badly in need of an occupation and a husband.

TO FANNY WILSON
Edgeworthstown, 18 May 1843

I feel quite sure of the pleasure, the joy you have had for Lucy since your mother's last letter – I had hoped, I had almost expected the event but I the more rejoiced and strange contradiction to say so, I was the more surprised at the accomplishment of my dream, my most ever waking hope – I am very very glad that I decided not to go to Armagh. It was much better not only for me on my own selfish health account but there was no interference you see – It was all from their own spontaneity and people like to find that – it was all their own doing.

... I wish you could see how happy and blooming your mother looks – Rosa says that the morning she read Lucy's first intelligence of this happy event she came into the room saying "I have not for years received a letter that gave me so much pleasure as one I have received this morning! Here it is" ...

My dearest Fanny, perhaps, perhaps you could come and see her with your dear eyes – Lestock ... <u>might</u> bring you and Captain Beaufort might bring Honora and Pakenham will be here and then once more in her life, a life well deserving such happiness, she would have all her children, all her sons in law, all who are dearest to her round her in the home she has kept for us all.

It is a dream too delightful to be realised – I am just now spoiled and intoxicated by the joy of the accomplishment of one dream and I am like a child dreaming again in hopes of having it accomplished.

By the autumn Maria was strong enough to set off for London. She reached Fanny's house in early November 'quite well and not the least tired'. The journey from Dublin by steam packet and train now took less than twenty-four hours;

Daniel O'Connell addresses the electors in Trim, 1843, from The London Illustrated News.

a huge contrast to her travels half a century before. She was back at home five months later. Francis was not well, suffering from mysterious stomach pains. In May she went with him up to Dublin to consult doctors, travelling this time by boat up the Royal Canal from Longford.

TO HARRIET BUTLER
Dublin [?], 16 May 1844

… I sat under boat awning from 9 – 4 – and no more – and I was not tired to death – nor near it … And between the two cabins on the boat – one for the quality, such as the quality was, & another for riff-raff whom I never saw but sometimes smelt – spirits – there was a little intermediate den with a window & table for refreshments – eggs – tea – bread – butter – steaks & potatoes as bespoke by different parties – half a dozen at a time with ramming and cramming … I could not sit upright, but … crouched …

To her relief the Dublin doctors reported nothing seriously wrong …

Marsh says there is nothing the matter with Francis' liver or spleen but the fault is within colon – He advises warm baths and application of warm cloths to the part.

She returned by coach to stop at Harriet's rectory.

TO FANNY WILSON
Trim, 14 June 1844

… The day before yesterday for the first time this three weeks I put foot out of doors and walked leaning on Mr Butler and Harriet to see the greenhouse.

Quite delighted, enchanted by the sight! The house nearly as large again as I had pictured to myself and so beautifully filled with geraniums, fuschia, rhododendron and lady's slipper of all sorts, sizes and hues – that it looked like an established conservatory of the first rate order and as if one fairy patroness of lucky childhood … had brought all together with a wish in full blow defying times and seasons.

Harriet set me down on her garden stool to rest until I had supped full of pleasure.

But I was so weak that it was too much for me and it was as much as I could do to get home leaning heavily and at last lying prostrate on my sofa. … But I do not like to make what is called a poor mouth (what sort of mouth is it, I wonder). I am regaining my strength wonderfully and much sooner than after my last year's illness …

I told you how delighted I had been with having Harriet read Mme de Sevigné while I was bedridden … it annihilates time and space – We have another book which she got for me knowing it would interest me – the life of Griffin, the author of The Collegian – a very singular character – not affected – but really original. Pray get and read the book.

In September, she was strong enough to go with her stepmother to stay with the newly married Lucy in Armagh.

TO HARRIET BUTLER
The Observatory, Armagh, 18 September 1844

... It is more delightful to me than I can express ... to see Lucy so happy & to see her mother see it all.

I sleep in the same room & same bed with my mother as we did at Trim and fine talking we have ... and though the walls have ears and these walls are so thin we need none of that discretion which Caroline Hamilton said the fairy at my birth denied me – we care not who overhears – we say no harm of nobody – we have none to say.

All the things are amazingly improved in the house since last I saw it – Lucy certainly made use of her time while Robinson was in London & has painted and papered and garnished and arranged furniture so that I should never have known the house ... The diningroom is made into the sittingroom – light and delightful with white summer curtains fringed & floating and a beautiful Brussels carpet in knots of flowers which you can almost smell ... The diningroom ... has a fine portrait of Robinson ... a boy full of genius – & romance sitting upon a rock with a very clean frill to his boyish collar. The bedchamber we sleep in has been papered with flowery paper – very pretty ... It is admirable and delicious how well and completely she has turned her mind to all that can make her house and her house-band and all belonging to her comfortable and happy.

Lucy has got or has – a very good cook, one who knows how to serve up "with dignity" as Lady Belvedere said. If she has but a potato she wd serve it with dignity. NB – The potatoes are very good ... and the potato crops here, tell Mr Butler, are all remarkably fine ...

It is marvellous to me and almost laughable if it was not admirable to see how PUNCTUAL Lucy has become – to the hour punctual – to the minute – Prayers – breakfast – dining out – coming back all to the second watch consulted so like you that I could not believe it is the LATE Lucy.

Well, well, how principle & sense of duty plus Love can work wonders even in conquering Habit – the greatest of all conquests. These metamorphoses are as wonderful as any in Ovid & rather better, methinks.

Robinson at home is more agreeable and not less wonderful than Robinson abroad – the "abundance" is equal to Mackintosh in literature & in science, you know, out of sight superior. In home life his amiable qualities and amiable temper appear to the greatest advantage and improve his conversation –

making it more conversation like – and with more give and take – I mean more take or give – Lucy and he are better suited than I expected – Her genius sees & feels his in the most gracious manner ... & she feels that difference which will keep her imagination in happy useful wonder all her life through ...

She and her stepmother were taken by Lucy on excursions to the neighbouring big houses, the magnificent Palladian Caledon in Co. Tyrone and Dunally, 'one of the most beautiful places I think I ever saw' – but Dunally's owner, Mr Cope, was a drug addict with 'glazed opium eyes'.

Back at Edgeworthstown, she and her stepmother were still doing all they could to encourage Francis to dine out with the local gentry. But it was an uphill task in the intellectual desert of Co. Longford. A dinner with Sir George Fetherstone proved a total failure.

TO FANNY WILSON
25 October 1844

... Your observation upon the advantages of Francis' going out into society and mixing with the people of the county I must approve and even admire for these were almost the very words I had been saying to your mother last night when we were *tête-à-tête* in our snug in the library while F and Rosa were gone to dine at Sir George and Lady Fetherstone's with a model party – 2 brides and their grooms expected – Mr and Mrs O'Connor and Mr and Mrs Jephson.

The bride and bridegroom who Francis and Rosa did meet – Mr and Mrs Jephson – were not much worth seeing – but still they furnish the County of Longford and have furnished Foxhall – to which they are engaged for 2 years certain ... But what could tempt her with a very good fortune to marry the man she has married is inconceivable – He is by all accounts a yahoo dandy – coarse, awkward creature that looks as if he never stood in a room before and yet decked in gold chains and pins – ... His father would never give him any education and being a drunkard himself kept his wretched son like a beast in the stables – and after his death left him a large fortune. – Sir George Fetherstone was left his guardian – put him to school and college – but hard to bring into training a boy of fifteen! – who did not know how to read, write or speak, much less to think ...

The dinner at Lady F's was very stupid and Francis vows he will never go to such another – and that he may safely vow. My mother and I were so happily engaged reading Lord Rosse's account of his telescope and talking that we did not know it was half after 12 – Francis looked at the clock and roared SHAME!

I think that Lord R has spoken handsomely and justly and discreetly of Herschels, father and son and I earnestly hope Sir John may feel it soon – All that Lord R says of his writings and his disappointments and his progress by 15 years' perseverance is admirable – and exceedingly interesting – I shall like very much to go to see the telescope and much more to see Lord R. But till the great show time is over.

We had never heard of the dreadful catastrophe you mention of Father Mathew – We are all in amaze and dismay.

Since I began this note Mrs E and I have been to Longford and paid various visits and of everybody who could be supposed to have heard we asked "Have you heard [word] of Father Mathew lately – what – "

Mrs Curtis, wife to the head of constituency in Longford, was the only person who had heard anything – and her informant was the Packet newspaper – That a man had arrested him for a debt for the price of medals.

Had first kneeled to take the pledge from him – Then started up and arrested him – Then kneeled again and begged his pardon.

Oh my dear Fanny, I cannot let you know how grieved I am by even suspicion lighting upon such a man – So much good he has done.

Pakenham, her youngest brother, was still on prolonged leave from India. He was to stay with a friend in Scotland, where Maria hoped he would find a wife.

TO FANNY WILSON
Edgeworthstown, 31 October 1844

… Pakenham would be able to see much more of a young lady in a week at home and in the country than in a season in town – And I think it is now or never with him in that affair – if it is – or ever is to be.

You may well laugh and say I am dreaming and so good night to you.

[*Postscript*] … I should be very very sorry that it never should be – I think so many years happiness of his later life are at stake – An old Indian Batchelor abroad or at home would be such a wretched creature – isolated or only an old uncle with a good fortune – but no heart and soul to share with.

Well, well, I can do nothing in that matter but wish and wish my soul away …

I see in today's paper a statement about Father Mathew which acquits him of all but imprudence, spending money before he had it on works of public utility – building churches etc – But the want of prudence and foresight and punctuality are absolutely to be deplored as a public misfortune in such a man – destroying such a vast power of doing good.

Many of the poor people in our neighbourhood have lately broke their pledges – Garret Keogh – Gahan's brother and others. Alas! Alas

In November she was still debating whether she was strong enough for another visit to Fanny in London – she had fainted unexpectedly at dinner – and money was short. She needed enough to pay for school fees for her nephew Willy, Francis' oldest boy, now nine. Shortly after, she had another relapse; she wrote to Fanny to reassure her.

TO FANNY WILSON
Edgeworthstown, December [?] 1844

… At 12 o'clock this day I was so hungry that when an egg and bread [*and*] butter came into the room my mouth literally … watered as when a child it used to do for grapes not sour – At one o'clock I was mounted up (via armchair) upon the dressing table in my own room looking from window …

I was very happy and warm and not catching cold as even your mother allowed and I was overseeing not overlooking four labourers and Gahan executing a delightful improvement in my garden which I planned just before I was taken ill and which I have every reasonable hope of having finished tomorrow and perhaps of living to see blowing in April and perhaps May and June when rhododendrons are profuse in blow in this happy boggy native soil – I drew and scrubbed out yesterday in my bed the plan of the intended improvement for Gahan to study all Sunday evening and I here enclose my full copy of the same, like the griffonage which Humboldt published of S. America Hieroglyphics and like the Irish hierographic scribble of the elven bottle which you may remember.

Observe that line representing an embankment, Ma'am & <u>Sir</u> if Lestock be, as I hope, beside you.

The middle of that half circular embankment is about a yard high raised above what the earth was at the back of my shrubbery – About a yard wide at back – and from the front it now all slopes off gently and sweetly dug to the edge of the little gravel path at the back of my garden beds –

All the rhododendrons which were scattered over my back settlements in unequal heights have this day been most carefully taken up, not a fibre of their roots hurt and in order of their height they have been ranged over the bank – And I saw Gahan with one hand on his hip and another in his mouth standing in front of his work before he quitted in irrepressible admiration.

So I came down from my dressing table and begged a bottle of raspberry vinegar from Rosa who made a good quantity with her own hands last autumn for Francis to give to the tenants instead of whiskey which you know the pledge takers cannot touch …

It would make you laugh – as it made Rosa laugh in her armchair till she rolled at an interchange which she saw between Cassidy and me about this raspberry vinegar and the coals. Enter Cassidy heavy laden with coal scuttle – grunting like hippopotamus …

Miss E "Set down that coal scuttle, Cassidy and draw the cork out of that bottle if you please."

"What is it Ma'am" quoth Cassidy leisurely putting coals upon the fire.

I say "Do not put on any more coals yet – Leave the coals there – go to that bottle – draw the cork."

"Is it draw the cork? Which bottle?" (There was but one)

Seeing me prepare to rise to do it myself – and pitying my weak condition and impatience he gutteraled a "Och!" and saw and pulled the cork.

Miss E to Cassidy – "Now – no – not the coals – But [go] into my garden and bring Gahan to this room directly – and bring a decanter of water, tumbler and … spoon".

All of which he did really in no time – for "Och" he understood how it is with me, he'd have put a girdle round the earth in 40 minutes to please me – soon as any Ariel ever breathed.

Gahan had a delightful tumbler – How refreshing it seemed and more than convinced him that he had been working hard all day and had had the responsibility of all the transplanted rhododendrons on his own shoulders – By the by his hair is grey and grizzled over with the responsibility and cares of office he has had these 2 years.

We begged that he would take the bottle of raspberry cordial … home with him for Mrs Gahan to have ready for his own use or pleasure. No courtier could have more gracefully, graciously accepted – his eyes on Rosa as he bowed.

"When Mrs Francis made it – my wife will be most thankful – and better, more refreshing never was – Thankyou Miss E that was always good to me."

It is quite worth while as I feel it to get well to enjoy as I do animal and vegetable and mineral and intellectual pleasures …

XI

JANUARY 1845 – MAY 1849

THE YEAR 1845 *began well for Maria. Sir Robert Peel was still firmly in place as Prime Minister and seemed to have brought a framework of law and order to Ireland. Agrarian violence had diminished. Daniel O'Connell, her old enemy, had been forced to call off a monster meeting for Repeal at Clontarf and had been briefly in jail. The farm was thriving under Francis' management; tenants were paying rents, and the house was full of happy children. Maria's birthday began with a delightful exchange with an elderly tenant.*

TO FANNY WILSON
Edgeworthstown, 2 January 1845

… Peter Langan came here yesterday to wish me a happy new year … Then suddenly in his ecstatic way he exclaimed "Well! There! Now! Is it not wonderful what sons in law your mother has, God almighty bless her with them – She has a right. But now look at 'em – All so good & shuitable but is it not wonderful" –

And then we went through them all – "There's Mr Butler – the Reverend and he's a good man sure if ever there was one – And Captain Fox, the Major – Oh the raal gentleman – and Miss Lucy's doctor that I don't know myself but I hear a wonderful deal! AND Miss Fanny that is Mrs Wilson – Oh! Och! – He is the man!"

It is impossible to give you the emphasis or look or ... throwing out of the hand and arm to give an idea of the extent of his feeling & judgement.

I own I was gratified – flattered if you will – and I ended by giving him what I found he came to ask me for "A picture of my father" ... and I wrote an inscription at the bottom of it saying that I have known Peter Langan as an excellent improving tenant – & for above half a century.

The first gale of rent I received from him was 55 years ago as he reminded me.

But before I put this inscription into his hand it occurred to me to ask whether he knew what is meant by CENTURY – "Oh – what is it – What would it be then?"

I told him the name for a hundred years and asked "How many years are there in the half century?" "Would it be fifty, sure?"

Harriet Butler (the suspicious) when I told her laughed & said it was all acting simplicity ...

Be that as it may – you will acknowledge that Irish tact is required – for flattery perhaps Lestock will say, for good manners I say – which all depend upon good feeling and quick sympathy with others – Peter went off assuring me that he'd rather than £50 – aye £100 "have what I'd writ for him there".

Gentlemen may laugh! "I see Lestock laughing" ...

TO FANNY WILSON
Edgeworthstown, 3 March 1845

... Poor Sidney Smith! Little did I think when I heard him in your library making Hunter laugh *à gorge déployée* with an account of his last illness in which he said he could not recollect whether there were 39 muses or 39 articles – that it was the last time I was to hear him!

And Rogers still the dead alive![246] And that wonderful old Tom Grenville (who never was an admirer of mine) – I wish he had been still alive to vivid intellectual enjoyment that is worth living to be old for indeed – and what a wonderfully lasting bright link he is between past generations and the present day going back to Horace Walpole! ...

---

246 Samuel Rogers, poet and London wit; he was the original for the pretentious Horace Churchill in Maria's last novel, *Helen*.

TO FANNY WILSON
Edgeworthstown, 16 April 1845

... I wrote to Mrs Sidney Smith yesterday – Her note to me was most touching
– most charming – so simple and true ... I think pretty much as you do, my
dear, about the pamphlet[247] – why, I think better – I mean I think highly of
the wit & humour ... and I think this playful jocular mode of dealing with the
subject ... will have great effect ... and he is prepared for all the abuse which
it will meet with ... I have no doubt that it will do good – when people laugh
they do not hate one another quite so bitterly – His way of parlaying with
O'Connell is admirable. About the Catholics & chapels etc ... I regret all the
exaggeration & ignorance as much as you do – They are however so absurd that
they will do no mischief – People will vent their abuse upon his ignorance –
and his sense will remain & operate. In the main he is right about the payment
of the Catholic clergy if – if it can be done, it will be done now the matter is so
boldly brought to [?] – But where is the money to come from? The Catholic
priests are better paid as to actual income now than the Govt could pay them
– tho' that income is raised as Sidney says in an unfit manner ... There is no
exaggeration in the pamphlet on these points. But great exaggeration about
the hovels of chapels – compared with churches.

It is a great pity that SS did not travel in Ireland & see these things with
his own eyes before he wrote ... It is very difficult to me to write to Mrs Smith
without saying what was false or hurting her feelings uselessly[248] ...

TO LUCY ROBINSON
Edgeworthstown, April 1845

Your mother has gone and I am both sorry & glad ... sorry for my sake ...
but glad for her and for dearest Fanny's and good Lestock and very dear
Honora's ...

Dear, dearest Frances has been showing me since I came home all his
improvements here in farming and building and draining and all the

---

247 'A Fragment on the Irish Roman Catholic Church', in which Sydney Smith called for the Catholic
    clergy to be paid by Government. It caused much heated debate and ran to six editions.
248 Maria had written two years before begging him to come to Ireland to see 'all our manifold
    grievances' for himself. See *Memoirs and Letters of the Reverend Sydney Smith*, Volume I, 1855.

wonderful improvements that have been made by Cowen in that part of the school premises which he has taken – made a Bakery – and a Chandlers and a shop – and a dwelling house all complete with separate entrance staircase and offices …

The people here are all busy making the most of the fine weather and blessing God for it and not troubling themselves about O'Connell or any of his nonsense and wickedness. There is a great national difference between agitation and activity and the country people here at least seem to feel and understand this. It comes home … to their pocket and I shrewdly suspect they will not much longer pay O'Connell's rent – His prestige is gone – I hear that he is much depressed … The Law has him now – and the Attorney Gen. says he will not let him slip …

But how I have got to O'Connell I know not …

TO FANNY WILSON
Edgeworthstown, 8 October 1845

… Pakenham is at Armagh & will stay there 3 weeks … Harriet & Louisa Beaufort are gone, I believe, this day to Armagh. How they will all fit in with Pakenham there

> "I can't imagine, I declare
> But 'tis none of my affair" –

My affair – the pianoforte is come – is in its place … where the old one … stood of yore and it fits the place much better, admirably, leaves room for music stand at one end and armchair at the other end – and enough room & verge enough for Mr Butler in said armchair to work himself backwards and forwards over whether the Church is in danger or no newspapers! – The two extreme cases which work [*him*] to and fro the most.

It is an upright pianoforte – or rosewood beautifully streaked and highly varnished & perfectly plain … the legs are solid yet … becomingly curved … the top watered rich green silk … quite plain, stretched – no flutings to hold dust … It has all the new improvements – it is three stringed – I am told – and all this I repeat like a parrot …

My dear mother likes it as a piece of furniture & as a convenience for granddaughters & nieces etc … Rosa likes it for Willy & herself – Mary-Anne

& Charlotte will find it here and Harriet will be glad and that is all in all. I have not told Harriet that I have got it – or that I was about it – I shall be foolishly delighted to see her look of pleasure. NB. Foolish delight is as good as wise delight – if it lasts as well through life & hurts nobody ...

TO FANNY WILSON
Edgeworthstown, 23 October 1845

Francis had been ailing for several weeks.

... His cough continues, he has red spots in his cheeks which heighten in colour every evening. He eats very little – he has grown very thin. He is much depressed and thinks no physician can do him any good and that he wastes money and time upon them ... It is very melancholy – I have not offered to receive the rents for him lest I should further discourage him about himself ...

I do not think the cough at this time comes from diseased lungs – But one cannot tell how soon the danger may come & in what shape – It is certain ... that he is much out of health & apparently & obviously to all who see him at intervals wasting away ...

In September the first signs of a virulent new potato blight had appeared in Ireland, having already affected Europe and England. Maria's letters to Fanny turned from bulletins on Francis' health to the need to provide relief. Having lived through numerous famines and partial failures of the potato, she saw no great reason for alarm. Machines had been brought in that could apparently extract the starch from the potatoes before they rotted.

TO FANNY WILSON
Edgeworthstown, 9 November 1845

... We are laying out all the money we can raise ... to provide meal against the famine. I this moment asked Francis what I might say to you on the present state of the potatoes – "May I say that the potatoes are getting [*better*]? Or say that they are not worse" – "No, I do not think you may say any such thing". "What then, may I say?" "That nothing could be worse than the potatoes are in our neighbourhood – universal dismay this fair day ..."

We had today at breakfast rolls made of half potato starch, half oatmeal – for want of better (whenever it comes to that) – good enough …

Thanks to supplies of cheap American corn secured by Sir Robert Peel, food prices were kept low during the winter of 1845, and in Longford and its surrounding counties there was still no real distress. Meanwhile there was the happy news of Pakenham's engagement to a suitable girl, daughter of Professor Macpherson from Aberdeen.

TO FANNY WILSON
Edgeworthstown, 14 January 1846

… It is all happily out – and done for dear Pakenham and now I must write to you about it and pour out my joy … It has been for some time the warmest wish of my heart that this dear affectionate brother should find a wife worthy of him … I was almost in despair for him after his disappointments … I am glad that she is Scottish – glad that she is his friend's sister – & that he had had opportunity of seeing her in her own family – the best place on earth for an amiable woman to be seen in and judged of – I don't care for her having no fortune – He does not look for it and will have enough to support her in the manner of life she has been used to … It is well that she is of an age (25) to know what she likes and what she is about – The going to India requires some steadiness as well as love – Everything that I have heard promises well … The 10th Feb. is the day we have fixed, the Queen's wedding day …

Pakenham's new wife, Christina, was duly brought to Edgeworthstown to be inspected. Christina recalled later how odd it was to find the tiny 79-year-old Maria deferring to her 78-year-old stepmother as 'mother', but that she had never met two more able-bodied and able-minded old ladies. Maria took to her at once. Pakenham, who had been experimenting with photography with his old mentor Sir David Brewster in Scotland took a calotype of Maria in her white mob cap and shawl.

TO FANNY WILSON
Edgeworthstown, 19 March 1846

… Even from the first meeting I felt she [*Christina*] was not a stranger or NEW to us, nor did I think of her even as a bride but as one of us directly as if

Michael Pakenham Edgeworth on his return from India. A calotype taken in Scotland while he was staying with Dr Brewster.

Michael Pakenham's calotype of Maria, aged seventy-eight, at Edgeworthstown, taken in 1846.

she had always belonged to us – a bit of the family map that fitted in its place ... Her voice is very agreeable – some little northern or Scotch accent ... but always good sense & good nature & good breeding ... She has fine clear eyes with a steady truthfulness of expression that secured confidence in her directly ... She does not seem afraid of us – but as if Pakenham had taught her to know and like us all ... She is not pretty but well looking in the best meaning of the word – Her hair is dark and abundant – She looks well matched to Pakenham – there is but half an inch between them[249] ...

I think she will do well in India – she is well able to rough it and smooth it – she has no maid ... seems to be used to do for herself ... Pakenham is ten years younger and smoother with happiness – Quite himself before her and with her with all his little quips and cranks but with that softening of manner ... which LOVE naturally gives ...

Mr Butler always brings you down upon me when I am not as anxious as he thinks I ought to listen to long speeches in the newspapers ... Sir Robert Peel & Lord John Russell. "What would Fanny think of you?" Then I listen my

---

249 Pakenham was extremely short.

best but there is so much talking talking! I am told that we shall be ruined by Sir Robert Peel's corn measures[250] – and that no rents will or can be paid – and that various bankruptcies have already taken place in consequence …

TO FANNY WILSON
Trim, 2 April 1846

Potatoes – very good were to be had at the last market in Trim for 10s a barrel to 6d a stone – Excellent food at the poor house here – Indian corn at 1d per pound – No man can eat more than two pounds – a woman not so much …

TO FANNY WILSON
Trim, 5 April 1846

… I think I shall certainly if alive be with you – my dearest – in Oct. and meantime you will come here, won't you, with Lestock and Honora at the great gathering at home while Pakenham and Christina are still to be … with us.

I think Sir Robert's speech of thanks[251] was admirable and shows he has some soul tho' nobody would believe that – save myself. What party spirit is – *Mais je me sens d'aucun parti – Je ne suis que bon Royaliste …*

> *Later that summer Maria reported Francis' eyesight failing: he was no longer able to read or keep accounts. He was also racked with anxiety after the second failure of the potato crop as to how to provide and pay for local relief. Maria wrote to him from Harriet's house in September to reassure him that all the family would contribute. But by early October he was dead. Maria received the news while at Trim with Harriet. Luckily Fanny was still at Edgeworthstown.*

TO FANNY WILSON
Trim, 13 October 1846

My dearest Fanny,
Heaven help you. Thank God you are with Rosa at this moment – What a mercy that is under such affliction to this admirable wife – widow of our lost one.

---

250 The repeal of the Corn Laws that prevented imports of cheap foreign corn.

251 Peel had just resigned as Prime Minister after his party had split over the repeal of the Corn Laws – brought down, in Wellington's phrase, by the 'blackguard combination' of his own right wing and the radicals.

Every possible consoling idea you have suggested, with love and goodness never failing – I trust your health will not suffer … Mine has not & shall not – if I can by my exercise of mind or body prevent it – and if I can be sustained as I am by the utmost care and kindness of my incomparable sisters and mother … So much taken away – so much remaining for us on Earth – I am thankful – God's will be done – is the sincere and resigned feeling of my soul.

As you so justly say, my most judicious Fanny, it is best for his sake that it should so have ended – It is best for all – We could never have been sure of his recovery being permanent … He has had a good, useful & happy life according to his own wishes … happy according to the epitaph which he wrote when he was 6 years old "Innocent of ill and dying early – lamented" – Oh how lamented – I thought I was prepared. But who can be for such a loss –

Meanwhile the new government led by Lord John Russell had set up belatedly a huge programme of public works to give employment. In Maria's view much of it was misjudged, since it interfered with the normal cultivation of the land.

Edgeworthstown, 1 January 1847

… The tenants all who can are now very eager tilling their land and if they obtain seed all will be well – next year – if not all will be ill & worse than ever – Kitty who tells little truths told me yesterday when I sent her son the 4s.11d. … for the poor … that his own poor under tenanted lands are lying untilled because the undertenants are all employed in public works – and would not be let to come away to till their own lands – besides if the men did come away they would starve for they have only just enough to live upon their wages …

By the end of January 1847 the situation in Edgeworthstown was becoming desperate, and Maria was persuaded by the Edgeworthstown rector, Mr Powell, to write to the Quakers in Dublin, who were the chief source of charitable relief. Her letter to them of 31 January reported over 3000 people out of 5000 in the Edgeworthstown district alone in need of food. With no cheap supplies of American corn as Peel had provided the previous year, even those engaged on public works were paid too little to feed their families. The local workhouse at Longford was overflowing with those incapable of work and there was sickness and fever everywhere. To raise money by her own efforts, she proposed writing an educational tale for children as she had done fifty years before.

TO FANNY WILSON
Edgeworthstown, 31 January 1847

... I believe I am the more disposed to try to earn something for our poor because there is so little to give and that I have been prevailed upon by Mr Powell (much against the grain – against my grain at least) to write 2 begging letters for him or for the poor. One to Dr Harvey, the Quaker – Quaker Association – and another to the Ladies' Association. I have been all day except to church concocting a *morceau d'élégance* for the Quakers that should contain no falsehood and be palatable – & not demean myself in the cooking ...

Please to write me posthaste, my dear, whether you approve or disapprove of my writing a story for Chambers ...

My first thought is that a story might be written to show young people what children CAN do or should do in charity – What is real charity – or generosity in them – or false.

Begging half pence to give – false.

The girl at breakfast giving her own hot muffin – true ...

Erolino & Mary & David [*Rosa and Francis' younger children*] here have been knitting their fingers almost through, turning half pence to buy soup. Erolino was up at peep of day as Rosa found, knitting – delighted they were.

It occurs to me that a boy of 12 might show children some chemical experiments –

I wish you would consider what may be feasible – What safe – and whether advisable for children & could be made short and sufficiently entertaining ...

I think it is impossible that Robinson could think for me at present. ... You might see and learn from Faraday some hints for me ...

Maria had met Michael Faraday, a former associate of Humphrey Davy, several times in London and an article on Faraday's electrical experiments had just caught her eye.

TO FANNY WILSON
Edgeworthstown, 5 February 1847

[*More about her new book.*] ... There would be no false principle or maukish sentiment but sound moral and ... political Philosophy & economy

Push to the extreme the Martineau principle, say that you must [*not*] relieve misery to gratify your own feeling of compassion & that the comparable merits etc – But while so do[*ing*] the sufferer perhaps starves –

In following Miss Martineau's principles the human heart must be so steeled against human feeling that people must bear to see their fellow creatures starve …

Luckily the Quakers' Relief Committee in Dublin had no such intellectual quibbles and their response to Maria's appeal was swift and practical.

TO HARRIET BUTLER
Edgeworthstown, 9 February 1847

… Mr Powell instigated me to write to beg some relief from the Quaker Assoc. in Dublin. So very much against the grain, I penned a letter to a certain Mr D Harvey only to ask him to put our case before the committee – I prayed for some small assistance to enable Mr Powell & all of us contributors to soup shop & meal distributors to get us over the next two months, fearing our funds wd not be quite enough … Your mother moreover represented to me that many poor men & boys who can get employment (draining particularly) literally cannot STAND the work in the wet or do the work for want of strong shoes.

So in for a penny in for a pound – ask for lamb ask for a sheep … And I made Bould to axe my FRIENDS for as many pairs of brogues as could afford or as much leather and skins as they could give … as this would enable us to set sundry starving shoemakers at work.

Well, Miss Harriet, what do you think of this? And what says Mr Butler – laughs at me.

Very well, those who [*can*] may laugh

By return of post came a letter to Miss Edgeworth beginning with "Most respected Friend" or better … They granted us £30 for the soup shop and a cwt of food [*?*]

They offered us a boiler of 80 gallons if we had not one sufficiently large – They granted me ten pounds for the women's work.

They told me that they should soon have a committee for supplying clothing & that they would not fail to lay my shoe petition & our claim for clothing before them as soon as possible …

TO FANNY WILSON
Edgeworthstown, 16 February 1847

... I enclose a most efficient kind note from my good clothing Quaker –
Alley I believe is her name – I think the lines which Cowper wrote to Lord
Carrington might be applied to the Quakers

> "Who when the poor apply
> Will give them all things but her name".

A thaw has come on – 20 degrees of thermometer difference between today
and yesterday. The frozen pipes have thawed. But before they thawed great
floods in the China Closet & Observatory – Cassidy in great force and activity
– "Whatever man can do I can do" – And really he does a great deal – Puffing
as he goes.

But when I begin telling about the thaw I am thinking of Campbell the
cowman who has been prevented from setting out for Dublin by the frost –
Tomorrow he starts and he is to call on the Clothing Fund and bring down
40 or more garments ready made – Much needed! Most thankful we are for
them – The poor have suffered dreadfully by the cold – the price of turf has
trebled ...

Mrs Powell gave soup (most excellent it was) yesterday to 160 persons with
your mother – and gave tickets from you and from herself to about 20 of the
above.

The price of food has not come down – The Fiend of Frost rained on
everything.

There is an end to all I have to say about charity in this parish at present. I
liked what Sir R. Peel said about the Ladies of Ireland in his speech ...

Gahan is admirable in his active & judicious good nature as one of the
overseers of the work undertaken and he manages as well as it is possible to
employ the men at whatever can best be done in all weathers – and to keep up
their industry & spirit of independence as workmen without being a hard task
master – Mrs Gahan makes soup for the labourers. There is a great deal of real
charity in the world – It is not all talkie talkie talkie except with some – [?]

At a charity meeting at Longford more people made speeches saying they
were very sorry, very very sorry they were for the poor. A Quaker rose & said
"Friends, I do not know how sorry you are but I am five pounds sorry" ...

Peasants queuing for food: sketch by Louisa Beaufort, 1847. Maria appealed for leather for shoes so that they could undertake relief work.

TO FANNY WILSON
Edgeworthstown, 8 March 1847

My dear Fanny – Pray look at the motto of the seal of the enclosed from Lord John Russell – You know it of course, Che Sara Sara – never was it more appropriately applied than to this letter.

I wrote to him before we saw in the papers that the Bill had passed for the £150,000 for seed – I wrote when my mother was so vexed and I felt so indignant that his promises about the seeds (in his speech of Jan.) was not to be fulfilled – But I assure you I wrote with circumspection – And I like his answer – no judge or humbug in it – But you see he gets the blame off his own shoulders & throws it upon the Lord Lieutenant very dextrously. The end however is too serious to be diverted with tricks …

The people are dreadfully in want of seed – and discouraged. Mr Tuite who was here 2 days ago told us that the price of parsnips for instance was amazingly risen and the scarcity so great that quite beyond the possibility of tenants or of landlords either – He, a considerable landed proprietor, could only get one pound for love or money from a great seedsman, his particular friend as a particular favour.

I am sure that Mr T does not wilfully exaggerate … He reported that he met with two or three other members of the H. of C before he left London in the great seed shops and found sad scarcity – especially of the said parsnip seed – parsnips having been recommended by all the knowing ones, medical & agricultural, as the best food for Irishmen next to potatoes – the most nutritious & most productive.

But what is worse (if Mr Tuite is right) the parsnips are infected with the potato disease[252] – he gave witness to his own knowledge … and I never heard his own tongue speak with such little hesitation – They say I am a croaker but I believe many are now coming to the same opinion I have held for some months that there will be found to be a want of food in the whole world …

TO FANNY WILSON
Edgeworthstown, 9 March 1847

The skins are come – huge skins of leather for brogues, 40 more [*like*] 50 pair. The shoemakers may shake their elbows & the naked footed draining workmen rejoice – To the smell of leather to which you say Faugh! I say delicious! There is a parcel of clothes large as the tea table packed in brown linen now lying in your mother's dressing room delightfully encumbering the passage – It is full of 50 garments and 400 additional pieces of flannel thrown in by those excellent Quakers to make Friend Maria E amends for having delayed the clothing a few days – The parcels cannot be unpacked till tomorrow – too late today so I may take the rational recreation of writing to you.

The contents of parcel & the leather were to have been divided by your mother & Miss Powell – But Miss P who is at this moment come into the room to see the joyful sight has most judiciously in my opinion advised that my mother should have ALL (including all the trouble) as she knows best all the people and their wants.

What a mercy it is in the midst of these distressed times that instead of quarrelsome POWER loving ladies & gentlemen such as fell to quarreling on the Longford committee, we have Powells – especially for your mother who has such constant business with them about the poor …

You understand that our committee is consisted of US – viz Mr & Mrs & Miss Powell, Mrs E. Mrs Francis E and Maria E!! In short your mother is the committee – God help her.

---

252 They were.

In this day's Evening Mail there is a sensible speech of O'Connell. I see that the people in Parl[*iament*] as well as out are attacking Lord John about the seed business – Perhaps it will come to NON SARA ...

There is a monstrous waste of public money now going on salaries of 2-3/400 per annum to overseers or Instructors of Drainage etc. About half a million, as Mr Blackhall has calculated, is at this instant job job jobbing among these people who do no earthly good to anybody or anything in Ireland – I don't swear to Mr Blackhall's calculation as I have no means of verifying – But I know that we have seen half a dozen in this county & Mr Tuite says £1200 per annum is now to be spent in this manner in Westmeath.

Calculate, calculate what this money could do in buying seed or tilling the land. Is not Sir J. Burgoyne a jobber?

I am glad that Govt (Mr Labouchere at least) are now determined to turn the people from cutting down and breaking up roads to cultivating their gardens & tilling their fields "as far as can be done with safety to the public".

So there is a Government confession of the mistakes of their own doings! – It is now dangerous to undo – But it is idle to talk of past mistakes – the present so present and the future to immediately provide for – under the penalty of more famine – worse disease – desolation & death – next year.

It is said that numbers who have been employed in public works and numbers who have been employed at home are so much weakened that they cannot, really CANNOT work without being supplied all food.

Spite of all the soup shops & charity it is come to this – Spite of all I say. I would not venture to say in consequence of the gratis feeding – Because here must be the exception to the general rule – If thou dost not work, thou shall not eat. For here it has been – even if thou dost work, thou shall not eat.

Here is a calamity – national calamity – by the hand of God inflicted no doubt for wise purpose – but which all the wisdom of man cannot avert or remedy completely.

The vast number that have died it is dreadful to hear of – not in our county but in other parts of Ireland – too well authenticated are the facts, I fear.

What a most horrid address and resolution have been published in the papers by the Catholic Bishop of Cloyne & various other Cat[*holic*]s with venomed claws – Have you seen their Dispatch to Mr Labouchere & his very temperate answer – and PUBLISHING their opinion that the Protestant proprietors of the county of Cork are rejoicing at the prospect of the numbers dying of famine to thin the land.

Such unfounded calumny! When all heads and hearts of proprietors & clergy are straining every nerve to assist the poor …

There – now my mind is easier! Now I have worked off my indignation – My dear Fanny, I hope you will have some sympathy … if only for your mother & Rosa here.

Thursday morning

… Soon as breakfast was done, your mother went to work in the study on the skins of leather & the bale of Quaker clothing – good Mr Powell having come punctually to assist … and Cassidy standing by – Happiest of mortals! … and he is to rule over the shoemakers and the pawnbrokers' stamps and stamping

6 o'clock evening

Mr Powell has been to every house in the town – in some he found dirt & misery beyond what he had ever seen before – He could not stand many minutes in some houses but was obliged to run into the fresh air – Your mother has given up her whole day (but what day does she not give up to doing good) to this distribution – and by the list made out by Mr Powell she has distributed all the clothes that are made up …

Gahan is sowing oats – and is happy to have them to sow –

There are some circumstances that look a little better in the neighbourhood – There are more potatoes than we had any idea existed – Harriet Butler tells my mother that some of the little farmers built up their potatoes to prevent them from eating them during the winter months of distress – and now they are coming out for sale and for planting in the market at Trim – In the market for 7d – And at Tullamore 8d as Mary Anne Fox said – the usual prices at this time of year being from 3d to 4d … We find that the people are as eager and as forward in tilling their ground as ever at this time of year, and though many are much in want of seed, many more have seed oats than we knew of or imagined

… I am sorry to tell you that in spite of all good your mother does and the gratitude of the people, there are some or one at least vile – base – enough to steal from her. A sack of oats was stolen out of the stable a few nights ago. Gahan had been sowing oats and put the remaining sack into the stable at night – In the morning – gone. The window which had been shut was open, but that was only a sham – The sack could not have been got through that window, nor could it have been hauled over the yard walls – It must have been carried out through doors and gates. The theft must have been committed by some *habitué* and the keys taken from Gahan's house where they were kept – The thief was cute enough to empty the oats from the sack in which they were marked FBE and to leave that in the manger – I suspect Murtagh junior … who committed that audacious theft during the time we were at church … But he cannot be detected now – "No one can swear to their own oats" –

American friends and readers of Maria's books, including children, had also responded generously to her appeal. Her new story for children, Orlandino, *was about to be published.*

TO FANNY WILSON
Edgeworthstown, 25 May 1847

… I am extremely obliged to you, my dear kind Fanny, for not delaying to tell me your opinion of Orlandino for I was in the greatest dubitation about it – But I am delighted that you approve of it and that it has really entertained and interested you as Harriet told me … I have many letters of gratitude to write first to America to all the kind people who have sent us meal etc … I have heard of its safe arrival at Cove [*Cobh*] & at Howth & have received & written innumerable letters to Mssrs Scott & Co & Mr Unthank [*?*] of the Limerick Relief Committee.

And hope tomorrow that the meal has turned into money & lodged at Ball's bank –

I have been reading Peru to fit myself for writing to Mr Prescott[253] – I like it much … But the subject is more powerful than The Conquest of Mexico – The Peruvians were so happy or at least so contented before these horrid cruel Spaniards went among them.

I wish that Pizzaro and his comrades had been seized by the throat & their mouths pulled open & molten gold poured down into them, hot, hot, someone saying to them in Spanish "Glut thyself with gold of which thou art so fond!"

---

253 William H. Prescott (1796–1859) – famous blind American historian. He was a friend of George
      Ticknor, Professor of Literature at Harvard, who had visited Edgeworthstown.

When I read the volume of Peru, what do you think I was doing besides? Doing two things at the same time never comes to good it is said, but I find I can do two things at a time well.

While I read, I knit – chains for the Americans – Coral chains for the 20 young ladies who … have subscribed their pocket money for the little Rice contribution for our poor – All the House here have been helping me to make these chains which were the only things I could think of that without too much trouble or expense be fit souvenirs or tokens of gratitude.

One pound's worth of coral coloured braid suffices for 30 chains which are of different sizes …

In late May the news had reached Edgeworthstown that Maria's old enemy Daniel O'Connell was dead. He had died at Genoa en route to Rome, aged seventy-one. Maria's inveterate optimism resurged. She wrote to her friend the Reverend Richard Jones, the distinguished economist who had taught her youngest brother Pakenham at Haileybury.

TO REV. RICHARD JONES
Edgeworthtown, 14 June 1847

… This minute, after having in the last year gone through as much misfortune in this family as could well be and now, and for months, public distress, famine and fever surround us – yet. I find myself taking pleasure in the roses you gave me and grieving for a fern that has been killed by frost … Our harvests promise well, even the potatoes. But we must not brag or hope too soon …

The great good arising from the change of national food for this country will remain when the famine is over … The potato for many reasons is not fit to be the staple food … not storable – not employing industry or labour in its cultivation for the moral purpose – … affording nothing to fall back on in case of failure. I have letters of Ricardo's in which all the requisites for a sage national food are ably stated and the potato is the lowest in his scale … Yet and nevertheless [*I do not*] … unlike some Political Economists … consider it to be an evil in itself but a good that has been abused …

The death of O'Connell 'the great agitator' would now allow for a new turn in politics.

... The cry against Irish landlords, which has been unjust, will be completely put down by the humanity and most active exertions of the landed properties during the distress in Ireland. It is not fair to argue as to good or bad from a few incidents, but it is fair to take them into account. I could name at least ten or twelve great landed proprietors who have this season and last year lost their lives from overexertion and from fever caught in attending their tenants and the poor. And Protestant clergymen in great numbers have so zealously exerted themselves that they have won the affections of the poor Catholics and even their priests, convinced that they have not used any undue means of conversion, are much conciliated. This is a good which will survive the evil ...

A month later she was writing in the same optimistic vein to her old acquaintance Mrs Moore in Mayo that 'the conduct of Irish proprietors during these distresses must convince the English as it has convinced the Irish of their good will by their good deeds ...' and the 'union between the two countries will now be more strongly cemented than it has ever been.' As Mrs Moore's son George was now standing as candidate for the radical new Young Ireland party, it is unlikely that Mrs Moore would have agreed. And in the long run, nearly all of Maria's predictions proved sadly untrue – neither Irish landlords or Protestant clergymen were to be remembered as the people's saviours. But the potato harvest of 1847 was largely free from blight and temporarily relieved local distress. Maria's letters returned to other subjects; books, gardening, family affairs. Pakenham, her youngest brother, was about to return to India and had been promoted to Commissioner of his vast district. The Indian Civil Service was well paid.

TO FANNY WILSON
Edgeworthstown, [?] August/September 1847

[*fragment*] ... Two thousand, seven hundred a year – Delightful for Pakenham. Harriet Butler observes upon his economical resolution to spend only £700 & put by £2,000 [*that*] it will be well if he can put by £700 & be content to spend only £2,000 – But there is no saying what an economical wife & Scotch wife may do who has been bred up in a family of sixteen at Aberdeen without her parents ever borrowing or getting into debt & educating 8 sons for Professions ... Our poor dear Francis was struck with amazement when he heard Christina say this! Poor dear creature, the pain in my heart & the feeling of a knife in my eyes comes whenever I think of him & all he did – and did not live to complete ...

This was Maria's last surviving letter to her beloved Fanny who died after a short illness the following February. Maria appeared to take this latest death stoically. She had already lost so many siblings. Only four of her father's twenty-two children were still alive.

She continued to follow politics with passionate interest. In May her neighbour Mrs Lefroy, wife of Thomas Lefroy (Jane Austen's old dancing partner) – now Lord Chief Justice – brought her a thrilling first-hand account of the trial of John Mitchel, one of the radical Young Irelanders, for sedition. (He was deported to Australia.) 1848 was a year of revolutions everywhere in Europe. But she contrived to find yet other causes for hope. As she wrote to her old friend Professor Jones in July, the 'anarchist' rising in Paris in February and the murder of the archbishop of Paris might have had 'a salutary effect' on the Irish clergy. And another neighbour, Judge Jackson, just returned from the Roscommon assizes, had reported that a largely Catholic jury had convicted 'without hesitation' one of the assassins of a neighbouring landlord, Major Mahon of Strokestown – proof perhaps that the Irish people 'begin to go with Law'.

Her interest in science also remained as sharp as ever. A letter to her youngest sister, Lucy, was packed with queries on the latest discoveries. She was fortunate to have a distinguished scientist as brother-in-law.

TO LUCY ROBINSON
The Rectory, Trim, 1 March 1849

... To my infinite satisfaction, much more to my feeling than mere pleasure, your letter to Harriet Butler arrived ... I had been most anxiously longing to hear of your dear Robinson – and had heard nothing new since I left home.

How dreadfully he must have suffered with that horrid tooth and inflammation ... besides all the other dangers and torments ... Thank God! I trust he is now recovering – since he is very busy doing electrical and magnetical experiments, he cannot be very bad ... I wish he could come here and recuperate for even a few days – Oh how happy I should be! <u>We</u> should be – I would not quite kill him either with questions or with kindness. Questions innumerable I could ask him but I would be reasonable. But I have no hope that I <u>can</u> have my wish to see him gratified ...

I will therefore suggest to you, my dear, some of the innumerable questions I should like to put to him – and you may put or not as you see fit …

First, look at No. 1 of the enclosed lettters – , from Emily Jephson, not one of the Jephsons we dislike but the only one we like (by another mother) … about the guidance of balloons … The day before I received her question I had been reading in the Edinburgh Review a paragraph about the impossibility of guiding them – I remember Wollaston held to the same impossibility – against such hopes – What does Dr R think? …

Then another. What [*has*] Paley's observation touching the decomposition of water … added to our scientific knowledge.

Next – Does he think that licences or Patents would bring any advantage or the contrary to science? Is it not better to leave every one to their own peeping and prying and trying? Is it true that each patent might cost £340 …

I shall stay here another month at least. I am very well and very happy – and you may be sure that I am well taken care of and well treasured to my heart's content.

Back at home two months later she alarmed Harriet by continuing to climb the ladder to wind her father's clock.

TO HARRIET BUTLER
7 May 1849

I am heartily obliged and delighted by your being such a goose and Richard such a gander as to be frightened out of your wits at my going up the ladder to take the top off the clock! Know then that I am quite worthy of that most unmerited definition of man – "a creature that looks before and after" – Before I <u>let on</u> to anybody my doubts of my own capability of reaching the nail on which to hang the top I called Shaw [*the housemaid*] and made her stand at the foot of the ladder while I went up – and found I could no more reach the nail than I could reach the moon.

Prudence of M.E., Act 2 – Summoned Cassidy and informed him that I was to wind up the clock, and that he was promoted to take off the top for me – and then up I went and wound the clock – and wound it as I had done before you were born – as there is nothing easier … You see, I am not quite a nincompoop.

Honora by a note this moment read intends to come over in July ... So Maxwell [*Barry Fox's son*] is going to sea – and I shall never see him again ... I answered about the Governess' Institution. I send my lines –

> Ireland, with all thy faults, thy follies too,
> I love thee still: still with a candid eye must view
> Thy wit too quick, still blundering into sense
> Thy reckless humour, sad improvidence,
> And even what sober judges follies call –
> I, looking at the Heart, forget them all!
> Maria E. May, 1849

Two weeks later on the morning of 22 May, after a drive, she was taken suddenly ill with pain near her heart, and a few hours later she died in her little room at Edgeworthstown with her stepmother beside her. As her stepmother wrote,

'She had always wished that her friends should be spared the anguish of seeing her suffer in protracted illness; she had always wished to die at home and that I should be with her – all her wishes were fulfilled.'

Maria's bedroom, sketch by Lucy Edgeworth after Maria's death.

POSTSCRIPT

FAMILY LIFE AND affection had been all-important to Maria. In a sense her father's best gift to her had not been just to encourage her talents as his 'literary partner', but to provide her with a huge family of brothers and sisters, and a stepmother and friend of her own age. It was her family who provided the sounding board for nearly all her writing; Edgeworthstown was her rock to which she always returned with joy even after being feted in London and Paris and exposed to the glamour of grand Whig country houses. Ireland was her country, and she loved its people and only half wished it would evolve into a version of industrial England as her father had hoped. For most of her life she was also exceptionally lucky in that she was financially secure. It never occurred to her when she began writing that it would earn her serious money and she was much surprised when her father presented her with £500 in 1801 as literary earnings. Later on, she took immense pleasure in spending her earnings from her books to provide the *entrée* to social life for her younger sisters, to buy them pretty clothes and furnish their houses for them. But she kept strictly to her promise to her father that she should never touch the capital he had left her – and died leaving considerable wealth to her surviving family.

Maria was the highest-paid novelist of her generation except for Sir Walter Scott – at the peak of her career, she was paid a £2000 advance for her longest novel, *Patronage*, in 1812, and twenty-five years later, £1100 for *Helen* (negotiated for her by Sir Walter Scott's clever son-in-law, J.G. Lockhart). By the time she died her popularity had already dwindled. Silver-fork novels on high life had dominated the twenties and thirties, and 'baggy monsters' of social realism like Dickens' had just begun. (*Oliver Twist* was published in 1836.) Meanwhile Jane Austen, her contemporary, continued her discreet climb to fame among the discriminating, and in old age Maria herself highly recommended her novels to her youngest brother, Pakenham Edgeworth. Maria's heroines never had the charm of Elizabeth Bennett or Emma Woodhouse. Even her father had denounced them as 'flat and spiritless and stuffed with morality'. And many of her heroes were equally wooden, making romance unconvincing. Cupid in Miss Edgeworth's case, Byron had written wittily, was probably a Presbyterian (although Byron also claimed that his ideal wife would be like the sensible Emma Granby in Maria's satire on marriage, *The Modern Griselda*). Maria herself was well aware of her failings – and in 1825, when Sir Walter Scott was staying at Edgeworthstown, had asked him whether she should diminish the moral tendency in her stories. He replied with charming tact and a smile, 'Well, you know the rats won't go into the trap if they smell the hand of the ratcatcher.'[254]

Given Maria's own emotional nature, or what her father described as an 'inordinate desire to be loved', it is also odd that she should have failed to produce heroines with more 'sensibility'. But the affection and humour that permeate her letters often shine through her depiction of the 'uneducated classes' (who make almost no appearance in Jane Austen), especially in her Irish novels. J.G. Lockhart, in his life of Scott, recalled that while walking in the park at Edgeworthstown, Scott had claimed that more 'higher sentiments' were to be heard from the poor and uneducated than were to be found in the Bible or among the great: 'We shall never learn to feel and respect our real calling and destiny, unless we have taught ourselves to consider everything as moonshine compared with the education of the heart.' Lockhart reported Maria's eyes filled with tears, though she rallied with a witty quip to Scott. But her sympathy for the poor went with a firm conviction that men and women were not born equal, and that 'democracy' was a dangerous chimera – leading to tyranny and the excesses seen during the French Revolution. Only through a programme of general education could the poor be made fit for power, and in Ireland that was bedevilled by sectarian divides. Her brother Lovell's school had been a gallant attempt to transcend them – and it had failed, partly through his own incompetent management but also as the divides grew wider.

Among her own social circle, 'wellbred' remained her favourite word of approbation – and she was quick to note 'vulgarity' of mind or manners. High

---

254 Maria to Aunt Ruxton, 19 December 1825.

morals and discretion were for her the essential ingredients in being 'wellbred'. She was shocked by Madame de Staël's indelicacy in her early novels (though she much admired her intellectual powers) and found Lady Morgan's 1818 novel *Florence Macarthy* 'a shameful mixture of highest talent' with 'impropriety – & disregard for the consequences of what she writes … Oh that I could prevent people from naming me along with her – either for praise or blame.'[255]

In private letters or conversation she was happy to discuss scandal such as the breakdown of Byron's marriage or the Duke of Wellington's amours, but she refused on principle to let any of her private letters be published, even by her friend Lockhart, in his life of Sir Walter Scott; only her stories and novels were to be held up to the public eye. And she always baulked at writing reviews, which would have attracted vulgar public debate and set her up in judgment on her peers.

By an irony, it was Maria's private letters that brought her back to the public eye just when her novels were almost forgotten. Maria's stepmother had outlived her by sixteen years, dying at the age of ninety-five, and, encouraged by her daughters, had written a *Memoir* of her famous stepdaughter, using Maria's own letters to form the narrative. Maria's surviving sisters, Harriet and Lucy, probably selected and edited the actual letters themselves. Their *Memoir of Maria Edgeworth* in three volumes was not published until 1867, two years after Mrs Edgeworth herself had died – and then only in a private edition to be read by friends and the extended family. But the fame of the *Memoir* spread. In 1882, two writers used them as the basis for biographies of Maria Edgeworth: Helen Zimmern, and Thackeray's daughter, Anne Thackeray Ritchie, in her 1883 publication, *A Book of Sybils*. Twelve years on, Augustus Hare recast the *Memoir* in two volumes as part of an official 'Life and Letters' series. The world was reminded of Maria Edgeworth's extraordinarily attractive personality – the warmth, humour and sharp intelligence that had once dazzled the salons of Paris and London and made Edgeworthstown a place of pilgrimage for the great and good.

The same year as Augustus Hare's *Life and Letters* appeared, Mrs Ritchie set off on a pilgrimage herself to Edgeworthstown – in the steps, as she wrote, of Herschel, Wordsworth and Sir Walter Scott. She found Maria's half-Spanish nephew, Eroles Edgeworth, presiding hospitably in the old family home. His older brother Willy had died. Maria's favourite books were still lined up just as she had helped arrange them on the library shelves, and her little writing table was still in place under the library window.

---

255 See *Letters from England 1813–1844*, p. 167.

Edgeworthstown in the 1880s, with Maria's books still in place.

Outside, gardeners were working in the walled garden, lush with fruit and vegetables, and most of the parkland trees were still standing. Crossing the courtyard, Mrs Ritchie walked out into the village street of Edgeworthstown to find it neat and orderly with whitewashed cottages. Old women came out to curtsey in the doorways or threw up their arms in benediction, and local politics were discussed over the post-office counter with 'an aptness and directness' that much impressed her. Gladstone was gone and the great battle for Irish Home Rule was temporarily in abeyance. Goodwill and deference to the landlord appeared, here at least, still alive and well.

Eroles Edgeworth had been five when Maria died but he could just remember her tiny figure on her deathbed and all the household in tears. He also remembered being caught red-handed with a box of sugar plums and confessing he was about to eat them. He was brought to Maria for judgment: 'She at once decided he had behaved nobly in speaking the truth and must be rewarded – by keeping the sugar plums.' As Mrs Ritchie mused, it was a long way from Maria's own stern upbringing by her stepmother and father nearly a century before.

The last of the Edgeworths to live at Edgeworthstown was another nephew, Francis Ysidro, born three years before Maria's death. Educated privately

The Edgeworth family vault at St John's Church, Edgeworthstown.

at home, he soon showed all the precocious brilliance of his father Francis. He became an eccentric Professor of Political Economy at Oxford, invented several important economic theorems and was much admired by Maynard Keynes. He lived in Edgeworthstown intermittently until his death in 1926. Nine years later the house and its contents were sold. Photographs at the time of the sale show the house almost unchanged since Maria's day.

It was bought by a New York property developer who had been born near Edgeworthstown. In 1939 he presented the house to the local community. It was taken over by the Sisters of Mercy and drastically altered for use as a nursing home. Inside the house almost none of Richard Lovell Edgeworth's 'improvements' described in Maria's letters have survived: the elegant staircase that curled its way into the hall or the square pillars and deep casements of the library. The bay window with which he enlarged her tiny bedroom has long since tumbled off the wall, and all the parkland trees have gone. Only in the walled gardens can one sense the delightful world that Maria knew. Stone walls and flowerbeds have been restored by an enthusiastic horticultural training school. And in summer there are guided tours organized by the local history society from here to the handsome rectory and churchyard where Maria and eight generations of Edgeworths have been laid to rest.

THE DESCENDANTS OF
RICHARD LOVELL EDGEWORTH

1   By his marriage with Anna Maria Elers, *m.* 1763 (*d.* 1773):
Richard, 1764–98, *m.* Elizabeth Knight: 3 sons;
Maria, 1767–1849;
Emmeline, 1770–1847, *m.* Dr King: 2 daughters;
Anna, 1773–1824, *m.* Dr Beddoes: 2 sons, 2 daughters.

2   By Honora Sneyd, *m.* 1773 (*d.* 1780):
Honora, 1774–90;
Lovell, 1775–1842.

3   By Elizabeth Sneyd, *m.* 1780 (*d.* 1797):
Elizabeth, 1780–1800;
Henry, 1782–1813;
Charlotte, 1783–1807;
Charles Sneyd, 1786–1864, *m.* Henrica Broadhurst;
William, 1788–92;
Thomas Day, 1789–1792;
Honora, 1791–1857, *m.* Admiral Sir Francis Beaufort;
Sophia, *d.* 1785;
William, 1794–1829.

4   By Frances Anne Beaufort, *m.* 1798 (*d.* 1865)
Frances Maria, 1799–1848, *m.* Lestock Wilson;
Harriet, 1801–1889, *m.* Hon. Richard Butler, Dean of Clonmacnoise;
Sophia, 1803–36, *m.* Captain Barry Fox;
Lucy Jane, 1805–97, *m.* Dr Romney Robinson;
Francis Beaufort, 1809–46, *m.* Rosa Florentina Eroles; 4 sons, 1 daughter;
Michael Pakenham, 1812–81, *m.* Christina Macpherson: 1 daughter.

One child of the third family is said to have died in infancy.

MARIA EDGEWORTH'S
FAMILY CIRCLE

(roughly in order of appearance)

RICHARD LOVELL EDGEWORTH, F.R.S. (1744–1817), Maria's father. Married (1) in 1763, Anna Maria Elers; (2) in 1773, Honora Sneyd; (3) in 1780, her sister, Elizabeth Sneyd; (4) in 1798 Frances Anne Beaufort. Fathered twenty-two surviving children, most of whom he educated at home. Founding member of the Lunar Society in Birmingham, which was made up of leading scientists, chemists and engineers. Experimented in roadbuilding and carriage design, and invented a telegraph system eventually adopted by government during the Napoleonic Wars. Returned to live permanently on his Irish estates from 1782. Served as Lord Charlemont's aide-de-camp during the Volunteer movement. Elected to last Irish Parliament in 1798 and voted against the Union on principle in 1800. Prided himself thenceforth on his independence from politics but worked on the government board of education from 1806 to 1811 and, later, on the official enquiry into Irish bogs. Co-author with Maria of *Practical Education* and *Professional Education*, and her idol and mentor in all her pursuits, even after his death.

ANNA MARIA ELERS (1746–73), Maria's mother, brought up in Oxfordshire, eloped with Richard Lovell Edgeworth aged seventeen. Described by him in his *Memoirs* as 'prudent, domesticated but not cheerful', she shared none of his intellectual interests and was remembered by Maria as always weeping. Had five children of which four survived, and died in childbirth when Maria was five years old.

HONORA SNEYD (1751–80), daughter of well-off landowner, Edward Sneyd, of Byrkley Lodge, Staffordshire. Maria's first stepmother, she was remembered by her as dazzlingly beautiful, but cold, and a stern disciplinarian. Had two children by Richard Lovell Edgeworth. Began writing moral tales for children and working on a book of educational theory with her husband, but died of consumption before it was complete.

ELIZABETH SNEYD (1753–97), younger sister of Honora (see above). Her marriage to her brother-in-law less than a year after her sister's death initially caused scandal. But, cheerful and kind despite almost constant pregnancies, she proved an admirable stepmother and was much loved by Maria. She died like her sister Honora of consumption.

CHARLOTTE (1754–1822) and MARY SNEYD (1750–1841), unmarried sisters of Honora and Elizabeth. They were brought in to help with Richard Lovell Edgeworth's ever-expanding family and, after Elizabeth's death, lived semi-permanently at Edgeworthstown for many years, preferring it to their brother's luxurious house in Staffordshire. Much loved by all the family and in Edgeworthstown for their kindness to the poor. Helped Maria with copying and editing her books. Aunt Mary survived into her ninety-third year.

MARGARET RUXTON (1746–1830), Richard Lovell Edgeworth's younger sister, married in 1770 a retired army officer, John Ruxton of Black Castle, Navan in Co. Meath. Befriended and encouraged Maria from her childhood on and was adored by her almost as a mother. Sprightly, snobbish and highly sociable, she provided a wider social circle for Maria than that available at Edgeworthstown. Encouraged her to write her first real novel, *Castle Rackrent*.

LETTY RUXTON (1773–1801), serious-minded eldest daughter of the above. Maria was one of the few who could make her laugh, but never became her close friend.

SOPHY RUXTON (1776–1837), younger sister of the above. Became Maria's most intimate friend and confidante, and shared her interests in science and botany. Strong-minded and independent, she was Maria's most useful literary critic outside her immediate family.

MARGARET RUXTON (1780–1834), youngest sister of the above, used as a testing ground for some of Maria's earliest children's stories. After their mother's death, she and Sophy lived together in a pretty cottage beside the Boyne.

RICHARD RUXTON (1775–1840), brother of above, married in 1807 Elizabeth Staples (Bess). After his father's death he inherited Black Castle and the surrounding estate from a rich uncle and changed his name to Fitzherbert.

THE REVEREND DANIEL AUGUSTUS BEAUFORT (1739–1821), vicar of Collon in Co. Louth, and a distinguished cartographer and amateur architect. Produced a magnificent map of *Ireland, Civil and Ecclesiastical* in 1792 with an accompanying account of its topography. He became a close friend of Richard Lovell Edgeworth in the mid-1790s and later his father-in-law. Often consulted by Maria on educational and literary projects.

FRANCES ANNE BEAUFORT (1769–1865), Maria's last stepmother, eldest daughter of the above. A talented draughtswoman, she taught several of her stepchildren to draw and won all their affections by her tact and intelligence. Maria came to love her and confide in her as her dearest friend. Frances added six more children to Richard Lovell Edgeworth's family. After his death in 1817 she worked together with Maria to run the Edgeworthstown estate when Lovell Edgeworth, her oldest surviving stepson, proved hopeless at the task.

CAPTAIN (later Admiral) FRANCIS BEAUFORT (1774–1857), younger brother of Mrs Frances Edgeworth. Worked with Richard Lovell Edgeworth to lay the telegraph system in Galway in 1803–4 while recovering from a wound. Assigned to survey the South American coasts and then the Turkish coast of which he wrote an account in *Karamania*, published in 1817. Developed the so-called Beaufort Scale to measure force of wind (first used officially in 1833 on the famous voyage of the *Beagle*). Appointed Hydrographer to the Royal Navy and knighted in 1848. Married (1) Alicia Wilson, sister of Lestock Wilson (see Fanny Edgeworth); (2) Honora Edgeworth in 1838. Close friend and advisor to all the Edgeworths and a constant visitor to their house.

HARRIET (1778–1865) and LOUISA BEAUFORT (1791–1867), younger sisters of the above. Both clever and independent-minded, they became close friends of Maria. Harriet was the anonymous author of *Dialogues on Botany* (published 1819) and Louisa wrote an essay on round towers and was elected honorary member to the Irish Royal Academy. They lived much of the time in Dublin in the house of their aunt Mrs Waller, 31 Merrion Street, known as '*l'hôtel d'amitié*'.

ANNA EDGEWORTH (1773–1824), Maria's youngest full sister. Pretty, clever and vivacious, she married in 1794 Dr Thomas Beddoes who ran the Pneumatic Institute in Bristol. Beddoes' assistant, the young Humphrey Davy, was dazzled by her charm and they exchanged romantic poetry. She later briefly ran off with Davy's wealthy patron, Davies Giddy. Had four children; the older son, Thomas Lovell, became a famous poet. Henry, the younger, joined the navy. Maria became closer to her after she was widowed, and helped support her daughters.

EMMELINE EDGEWORTH (1770–1847), Maria's nearest sibling in age, though in childhood they seldom overlapped at home. Married Dr Beddoes' assistant, the Swiss surgeon Dr John King, in 1802 and lived in Bristol. Disliked by Richard Lovell Edgeworth, who thought her stupid and disapproved of her marriage. But she and her husband took on the care of her half-brother Henry when he became insane in 1812 and looked after three of Maria's younger half-sisters who were thought to have consumption in the 1820s and thirties.

HONORA EDGEWORTH (1774–90), ravishingly beautiful and talented daughter of Honora Sneyd; died of consumption aged sixteen.

LOVELL EDGEWORTH (1775–1842), only surviving child of Honora Sneyd. As a young man he disliked Maria, probably for her share of his father's attention. He was caught in France returning from Switzerland after the renewed outbreak of war in 1803 and held as prisoner of war at Verdun until 1814. Inherited the bulk of his father's estate in 1817 and set up a model school at Edgeworthstown aimed at attracting boys from across religious and class divisions. Although a gifted teacher, he proved incompetent at financial management and had plunged the family estate into debt by 1825. Maria took over the management, but seven years later he was back in debt again and had become a hopeless alcoholic. Sold his remaining interest to his brother Sneyd and lived in Liverpool for the rest of his life.

BESSIE EDGEWORTH (1781–1800), Elizabeth Sneyd's first child. There is almost no mention of her in Maria's letters. She died of consumption having been treated in vain at Dr Beddoes' Pneumatic Institute.

HENRY EDGEWORTH (1782–1813), consigned to Maria's charge aged three as part of her father's plan for educating his younger children at home without governesses or tutors. Sent to Edinburgh aged seventeen to train as a doctor, where he already showed signs of consumption and mental stress. He was sent to work under a doctor in Madeira in hope of finding a cure, but his letters home soon became completely incoherent; Maria offered to go to Madeira to care for him, but was refused permission by her father. Eventually he was brought back to Bristol and looked after by Dr King until his death.

CHARLOTTE EDGEWORTH (1783–1807), reported as beautiful and 'fresh as a rose', and became a talented artist. Went with Maria, her stepmother and father on their visit to France in 1802–3. Her stepmother's brother, Captain Francis Beaufort, fell in love with her on her return. Died of consumption aged twenty-three; her death caused frantic efforts to save her younger sister, another Honora (see below).

CHARLES SNEYD EDGEWORTH (1786–1864), probably his father's favourite son. Sent to Trinity College, Dublin to study law. Married a minor heiress from Staffordshire, Henrica (Harriette) Broadhurst in 1815, and bought a house in Dublin. But she suffered constant migraines and he gave up the law to travel England and Europe in search of a cure. Later settled in Kent, much to Maria's regret, but baled out the family estate twice during the crises produced by Lovell's debts. He and Henrica had no children.

HONORA EDGEWORTH (1791–1858), shy and dependable, acted as quasi-daughter and attendant to her Sneyd aunts, and was everybody's confidant. Gave much-needed emotional support to Maria just after their father's death, and helped her with editing and copying her later children's books. Francis Beaufort, recently widowed, proposed to her unexpectedly when she was forty-six, and after much encouragement from Maria, she accepted him and went to live in London.

WILLIAM EDGEWORTH (1794–1829), worked with his father as a surveyor and mapmaker, then under the famous Scots engineer, Alexander Nimmo. Helped to lay the spectacular road from Killarney to Glengariff and other roads in the west of Ireland. Died of pneumonia at Edgeworthstown aged thirty-five; Maria attributed his death to the harsh conditions in which he had worked.

FANNY EDGEWORTH (1799–1848), Maria's favourite sister and quasi-daughter. Noted for her prudence, she shared Maria's interests in science and politics. Married in 1829 her long-term suitor, Lestock Wilson, an insurance broker from London (brother of Francis Beaufort's first wife). Maria regularly stayed with her in London. Always sickly, she died suddenly during the Famine.

HARRIET EDGEWORTH (1801–89), described by Maria as 'our sunshine over everything', was the most lively and practical of Maria's young half-sisters, and before her marriage ran a school for girls in Edgeworthstown. Married the antiquarian Richard Butler, rector of Trim, in 1826. Maria made the rectory there her second home in old age.

SOPHY EDGEWORTH (1803–37), probably the least intellectual of Maria's half-sisters. Married her cousin, Barry Fox in 1824. Had four children, Maxwell, Waller, Mary Anne and Charlotte; died of consumption aged thirty-four. Her children were brought up partly by her sister Harriet (see above).

LUCY EDGEWORTH (1805–97), youngest and cleverest of Maria's half-sisters. Confined to bed with a spinal complaint from age of fourteen to twenty, but recovered fully and outlived all her siblings. Married, to Maria's delight, in 1845 the brilliant astronomer and mathematician, Thomas Romney Robinson, head of the Armagh Observatory.

FRANCIS BEAUFORT EDGEWORTH (1809–46), brilliantly precocious, he was sent to Charterhouse school in England in 1819 and from there to Trinity College, Cambridge. However, he left after two years without taking his degree, being unwilling to study mathematics and also proclaiming himself an atheist. Went to Italy determined to write and become a philosopher – having in Maria's phrase 'his head in Plato'. Returned in search of a wife and proposed on impulse to Rosa Eroles, daughter of a grand but impoverished Spanish family living in exile in London. Eventually returned to Edgeworthstown to act as agent for his brother, Sneyd. Died of possible brain tumour aged thirty-seven at the onset of the Great Famine, leaving four children. Two of them, Eroles and Ysidro, became the heirs to Edgeworthstown in turn.

MICHAEL PAKENHAM EDGEWORTH (1812–81), followed his brother to Charterhouse in 1825 and then enrolled at Hertford College (Haileybury) in preparation for the civil service in India. Served with distinction mostly in north-east India and became a noted botanist and Fellow of the Royal Society. Married Christina Macpherson in 1846. Their daughter, Harriet, inherited the bulk of the family letters, which eventually passed to her grandson Professor Sir David Butler.

MAIN EVENTS OF
MARIA EDGEWORTH'S LIFE

1763 – Richard Lovell Edgeworth (RLE) elopes to Gretna Green with Anna Maria Elers.

1 January 1768 – Maria born at Black Bourton, Oxfordshire.

March 1773 – Death of Maria's mother, Anna Maria, in childbirth.

July 1773 – RLE marries Honora Sneyd in Lichfield, Staffordshire.

Autumn 1773 to Spring 1776 – RLE and family at Edgeworthstown.

Autumn 1775 – Maria sent to Mrs Lataffiere's boarding school in Derby.

April 1780 – Death of Mrs Honora Edgeworth.

25 December 1780 – RLE marries Elizabeth Sneyd in London.

February 1781 – Maria sent to Mrs Devis' boarding school, Great Wimpole St, London.

June 1782 – RLE brings family, including Maria, to live at Edgeworthstown.

November 1783 – RLE attends National Convention of Volunteers in Dublin, acting as Lord Charlemont's aide-de-camp.

Autumn 1791 – Maria and children join RLE at Clifton, Dorset.

21 January 1793 – Louis XVI guillotined in Paris, with Abbé Edgeworth in attendance.

1 February 1793 – France declares war on Britain.

Autumn 1793 – Outbreaks of Whiteboys and Defenders in Co. Longford. Edgeworth family return to Edgeworthstown.

1795 – Publication of Maria's *Letters for Literary Ladies*.

1796 – Publication of Maria's *The Parent's Assistant*.

November 1797 – Death of Mrs Elizabeth Edgeworth.

March 1798 – Capture of United Irish leaders in Dublin.

May 1798 – RLE marries Frances Anne Beaufort (Mrs FE) in Dublin. United Irish Rising in Leinster and Munster begins.

21 June 1798 – Irish 'rebels' defeated at Vinegar Hill, Wexford.

22 August 1798 – French troops land at Killala in Co. Mayo and begin march towards Dublin; government forces defeated at Castlebar. Edgeworth family take refuge in Longford town.

8 September – French and Irish 'rebels' routed at Battle of Ballinamuck, General Humbert surrenders. Edgeworth family return home to find house untouched.

Autumn 1798 – Publication of *Practical Education* by Maria and RLE.

April 1799 – RLE, Mrs FE and Maria travel through Wales and Midlands visiting factories and friends, then on to London and Clifton.

June 1799 – Birth of Fanny Edgeworth at Clifton.

September 1799 – RLE, Mrs FE and Maria return to Edgeworthstown.

February 1800 – RLE attends last Irish Parliament and votes against Act of Union.

Spring 1800 – Publication of Maria's *Castle Rackrent*.

1801 – Publication of Maria's *Early Lessons, Belinda* and *Moral Tales*.

1802 – Publication of Maria's *Essay on Irish Bulls*.

March 1802 – Peace treaty of Amiens between France and Britain.

August 1802 – Napoleon elected Consul of France for life.

October 1802 – RLE, Mrs FE, Maria and Charlotte Edgeworth travel through Belgium to France and take house in Paris.

December 1802 – The Swedish diplomat Chevalier Nicolas Edelcrantz proposes to Maria and is refused.

March 1803 – RLE, Mrs FE, Maria and Charlotte escape to Dover just before war breaks out with France. Lovell Edgeworth caught in France and interned as prisoner of war.

April 1803 – The family returns to Edgeworthstown.

23 July 1803 – Robert Emmett's attempted rising in Dublin.

May 1804 – Napoleon crowns himself Emperor of the French.

1804 – Publication of Maria's *Popular Tales*.

January 1805 – Britain declares war on Spain.

1805 – Publication of Maria's *The Modern Griselda*.

October 1805 – Battle of Trafalgar, death of Nelson. Threat of French invasion diminished.

January 1806 – Death of Pitt.

February 1806 – Grenville forms Whig Ministry of all the Talents.

April 1806 – Sir Arthur Wellesley marries Kitty Pakenham in Dublin.

Autumn 1806 – Publication of Maria's *Leonora*.

July 1808 – Sir Arthur Wellesley joins Peninsula campaign.

1809 – Publication of first series of Maria's *Tales of Fashionable Life* and *Essays on Professional Education* (appearing under RLE's name).

February 1811 – Regency Act; Prince of Wales becomes Regent.

1812 – Publication of second series of Maria's *Tales of Fashionable Life*.

June 1812 – Lord Liverpool becomes Prime Minister.

July 1812 – English victory at Salamanca, led by Colonel Edward Pakenham.

March 1813 – RLE, Mrs FE and Maria leave for England, visit friends in Liverpool and Manchester, and then take a house in London. Maria hailed as literary 'lion' of the season. They return to Edgeworthstown in July.

January 1814 – Allied armies march into France.

March 1814 – Battle of Paris; Marmont surrenders to allies.

April 1814 – Napoleon exiled to Elba.

May 1814 – Lovell Edgeworth returns home.

October 1814 – *Waverley* published anonymously, with tribute to Maria in preface.

November 1814 – Publication of Maria's *Patronage*. RLE borrows Sneyd's house in Baggot Street for Dublin season.

January 1815 – Sir Edward Pakenham killed in Battle of New Orleans.

March 1815 – Napoleon re-enters Paris, Bourbons flee.

18 June 1815 – Wellington and Blucher defeat Napoleon at Waterloo.

July 1815 – Napoleon surrenders to the English and is exiled to St Helena.

13 June 1817 – RLE dies at Edgeworthstown.

21 June 1817 – Maria's *Ormond* and *Harrington* published.

August 1817 to July 1818 – Maria edits and completes RLE's *Memoirs*. Widespread famine in Ireland after repeated potato failure.

August 1818 – Maria travels to England with Honora to visit sisters Anna and Emmeline in Clifton, and submits RLE's *Memoirs* to Dumont and Francis Beaufort. Visits Sneyds in Staffordshire and returns to London. Returns to Edgeworthstown, June 1819.

May 1820 – Maria takes Fanny and Harriet to London and Paris, then on to Switzerland. *Memoir of Richard Lovell Edgeworth* published in autumn 1820. They return to Edgeworthstown, March 1821.

2 March 1821 – Napoleon dies on St Helena.

1821 – Publication of Maria's *Rosamund, A sequel to Early Lessons.*

August 1821 – King George VI makes state visit to Ireland.

1822 – Publication of Maria's *Frank, A sequel to Early Lessons.*

August 1822 – Partial potato failure in Ireland. Agrarian violence flares up under mythical Catholic leader, Captain Rock.

May 1823 – Maria brings Harriet and Sophy to Scotland and visits Sir Walter Scott at Abbotsford.

April 1824 – Death of Byron at Missolonghi.

1825 – Publication of Maria's *Harry and Lucy* concluded.

August 1825 – Sir Walter Scott visits Edgeworthstown, and takes Maria and Harriet with him to explore Killarney.

December 1825 – Lovell confesses to huge borrowings on Edgeworthstown estate.

1827 – Publication of Maria's *Little Plays for Children.*

February 1827 – Lord Liverpool resigns as PM after paralytic stroke, succeeded by George Canning who dies in August.

June 1827 – Daniel O'Connell wins by-election in Co. Clare.

January 1828 – Wellington becomes PM at King's request.

January 1829 – The Viceroy, Lord Anglesey, recalled from Dublin.

February 1829 – Wellington announces Catholic Relief Bill in House of Lords, declaring civil war only alternative to Emancipation. Forty-shilling freeholders to be disenfranchised.

April 1829 – Catholic Relief Bill receives royal assent.

Spring 1830 – Daniel O'Connell launches Repeal campaign.

June 1830 – Death of George IV.

Autumn 1830 – Wellington's ministry falls, succeeded by Whigs under Lord Grey. Struggle for Reform Bill begins. Maria stays with sister Fanny Wilson in London until July 1831.

7 June 1832 – Third Reform Bill receives royal assent.

December 1832 – First election post-Reform Bill; Repeal candidates sweep board in Edgeworthstown. Lovell Edgeworth confesses to new debts.

October 1833 – Maria leaves for tour of Connemara with Culling Smiths.

May 1834 – Publication of *Helen*, Maria's first novel since her father's death.

June 1834 – Lord Grey succeeded by Lord Melbourne as PM, who resigns in November. Brief conservative ministry under Peel, then Melbourne and Whigs return to office.

February 1835 – Lichfield House compact formed by Whigs and Irish Repeal party – O'Connell agrees to suspend Repeal Campaign.

Autumn 1835 – Thomas Drummond appointed Under-Secretary for Ireland. Compulsory tithe collection abolished.

September 1836 – Maria, plus Mrs FE and Butlers make expedition to Moore Hall in Co. Mayo.

February 1837 – Francis Edgeworth takes over management of Edgeworthstown estate.

1840 – Father Mathew begins campaign for Temperance.

April 1840 – Death of Thomas Drummond. O'Connell relaunches Repeal Campaign.

December 1840 – Maria stays in London with Fanny until April 1841.

September 1841 – Death of Sir Walter Scott.

September 1841 – Peel's second ministry begins.

May 1842 – Michael Pakenham Edgeworth returns from India after eleven years' absence.

Autumn 1843 to April 1844 – Maria's last visit to London.

July 1845 – First signs of potato blight in Ireland.

April 1846 – Peel repeals Corn Laws.

July 1846 – Second total failure of potato crop.

September 1846 – Death of Francis Edgeworth.

July 1846 – Peel resigns after his party splits. Whigs under Lord John Russell returned to power, backed by Peel.

January 1847 – Maria appeals to Quakers for famine relief supplies for Edgeworthstown. Famine fever widespread all over Ireland.

May 1847 – Daniel O'Connell dies on the way to Rome.

June 1847 – *Orlandino*, Maria's last story for children, published.

July 1848 – Partial recovery of potato crop.

February 1848 – Fanny Edgeworth/Wilson dies in London.

22 May 1849 – Maria dies at Edgeworthstown.

MANUSCRIPT SOURCES
AND BIBLIOGRAPHY

Manuscript Sources

NATIONAL LIBRARY OF IRELAND, DUBLIN

MS 10,166/7. *Edgeworth Papers*

(Edgeworth family correspondence from 1724 to December 1817).

MS 21,826. *Edgeworth Papers*

(Maria Edgeworth's letters to Fanny Robinson, later Mrs Charles Hoare).

MS 22,822. *Richard Jones Papers*

(Maria Edgeworth's correspondence with the Reverend Richard Jones).

MS 13346, MS 13371. *Mounteagle Papers*

(Maria Edgeworth's correspondence with Thomas Spring Rice, later Lord Mounteagle).

MS 11,132. *Rowan Hamilton Papers*

(Maria Edgeworth's correspondence with Sir William Rowan Hamilton).

TRINITY COLLEGE, DUBLIN

MSS 4018-9 and 4176-85. *Correspondence and Estate Papers of Sir Philip Crampton, surgeon.*

SPECIAL COLLECTIONS, NEW BODLEIAN, OXFORD

The Edgeworth family letters are catalogued as MS.Eng.Lett. Edgeworth. Because of their sheer numbers, Christina Colvin arranged Maria Edgeworth's post-1817 letters into separate folders for her various correspondents. The main folders quoted from in this book are as follows:

Maria Edgeworth to Mrs Frances Edgeworth, *fols: 696–702*

Maria Edgeworth to C. Sneyd Edgeworth & Henrica Edgeworth, *fol: 704*

Maria Edgeworth to Honora Edgeworth (later Lady Beaufort) *fols: 704–705*

Maria Edgeworth to Fanny Edgeworth (later Fanny Wilson) *fols: 706 –711*

Maria Edgeworth to Harriet Edgeworth (later Harriet Butler*) fols: 712–13*

Maria Edgeworth to Lucy Edgeworth (later Lucy Robinson*) fol: 714*
Maria Edgeworth to Francis Beaufort Edgeworth, *fol: 714*
Maria Edgeworth to Michael Pakenham Edgeworth, *fol: 715*
Maria Edgeworth to Mrs Ruxton, *fols: 717–718*
Maria Edgeworth to Sophy Ruxton, *fol: 719*
Maria Edgeworth to Harriet & Louisa Beaufort, *fol: 716*
Maria Edgeworth to Charlotte and Mary Sneyd. *fol: 719*
Drawings and albums used to illustrate this book can be found in MS. Eng. misc 902–903 and MS misc.30

Some Printed Sources for Maria Edgeworth's Letters

Memoir of Maria Edgeworth with a Selection from her Letters by the late Mrs Edgeworth (1867)

Augustus Hare (ed.) *The Life and Letters of Maria Edgeworth* (1894)

F.V. Barry (ed.), *Chosen Letters of Maria Edgeworth* (1931)

H.J. and H.E. Butler (eds.), *The Black Book of Edgeworthstown and Other Edgeworth Memories 1585–1817* (1927)

H.E. Butler (ed.), *Tour in Connemara and the Martins of Ballinahinch* (1950)

Christina Colvin (ed.), *Maria Edgeworth: Letters from England, 1813–1844* (1971)

Christina Colvin (ed.), *Maria Edgeworth in France and Switzerland: Selections from the Edgeworth Family Letters* (1979)

Edgar MacDonald (ed.), *The Education of the Heart: The Correspondence of Rachel Mordecai and Maria Edgeworth* (1977)

Select Bibliography

Brabourne, Lord Edward (ed.), *The Letters of Jane Austen* (2010)

Burney, Fanny, *Evelina* (1778)

Butler, Marilyn, *Maria Edgeworth: A Literary Biography* (1972); *Jane Austen and the War of Ideas* (1975); *Romantics, Rebels and Reactionaries* (1981)

Clarke, Desmond, *The Ingenious Mr Edgeworth* (1965)

Clarke, Isabel C., *Maria Edgeworth: Her Family and Friends* (1950)

Dedem-Lawrence, Catherina, 'Maria Edgeworth: A Sense of Place' (thesis)

Dunne, Tom, *Maria Edgeworth and the Colonial Mind* (1985)

Farrell, James P., *Historical Notes and Stories of the County of Longford* (1886)

Fraser, Antonia, *Perilous Question: The Drama of the Great Reform Bill, 1832* (2013)

Geoghegan, Patrick, *Liberator: The Life and Death of Daniel O'Connell* (2012)

Holland, Lady, *A Memoir of the Reverend Sidney Smith, Vol. I* (1855)

Holmes, Richard, *The Age of Wonder* (2008)

Hone, Joseph, *The Moores of Moore Hall* (1934)

Hurst, Michael, *Maria Edgeworth and the Public Scene* (1969)

Inglis Jones, Elizabeth, *The Great Maria: A Portrait of Maria Edgeworth* (1959)

Kelly, Linda, *Ireland's Minstrel: A Life of Tom Moore* (2009); (2013)

Kelly, Ronan, *Bard of Erin: A Life of Thomas Moore* (2008)

Knight, David, *Humphrey Davy, Science and Power* (1992)

Kowaleski-Wallace, Elizabeth, *Their fathers' daughters: Hannah More, Maria Edgeworth, and patriarchal complicity* (1991)

Lawless, Emily, *Maria Edgeworth* (1904)

Lynam, Shevawn, *Humanity Dick: A Biography of Richard Martin* (1975)

Lockhart, J.G. *Memoirs of the Life of Sir Walter Scott* (1837–8)

Longford, Elizabeth, *Wellington: The Years of the Sword* (1969); *Wellington: Pillar of State* (1972)

MacDonagh, Oliver, *The Emancipist, Daniel O'Connell* (1989)

Marchand, Leslie (ed.), *Lord Byron's Letters and Journals* (1924)

Murphy, Sharon, *Maria Edgeworth and Romance* (2004)

Ó Gallchoir, Clíona, *Maria Edgeworth: Women, Enlightenment and Nation* (2005)

Pakenham, Eliza, *Tom, Ned and Kitty: An Intimate Portrait of an Irish Family* (2010)

Pakenham, Thomas, *The Year of Liberty* (1969)

Ritchie, Anne Thackeray, *A Book of Sybils* (1883)

Somerville, Edith, *Irish Memories* (1918)

Treneer, Anne, *The Mercurial Chemist: A Life of Sir Humphrey Davy* (1963)

Uglow, Jenny, *The Lunar Men: The Friends Who Made the Future, 1730–1810* (2002)

Young, Arthur, *A Tour in Ireland, 1776–1779* (1780)

Zimmern, Helen, *Maria Edgeworth* (1883)

INDEX

Numbers in italic denote illustrations.

Abbeyleix cottages 149–50

Abbotsford, Scotland 249, 271, 272, 386

Abercrombie, James 352

Absentee, The 7, 27, 149n, 155, 161, 210, 355, 376

Ackland, Lady 141–2

Ackland, Sir Thomas 141

Act of Union 14, 15, 63, 66, 67

Aikin, John 39

Airey family 193–4

Ali Pacha's harem 194–5

Allen, James 201, 228

Allenstown, Co. Meath 117

Anglesey, 1st Earl of (Paget, Henry William 287–9

Annaghmore, Co. Offaly 381

Annesbrook House (formerly Ansville), Co. Meath 253

Apreece Jane – see Lady Davy

Apsley House, Hyde Park 312

Ardbraccan House, Co. Meath 98, 218, 221, 241

Ariosto, Ludovico 234

Armagh Observatory 13, 144, 317, 318, 393

Astley's circus 65, 158

Austen, Jane 11–12, 363n, 418, 422

    Emma 11, 198, 199, 369

    Mansfield Park 11, 187, 188, 189, 240

    Northanger Abbey 11, 13, 223–4, 370

    Persuasion 224

    Pride and Prejudice 188n, 369

Babbage, Charles 12, 280, 317–18

Ballantyne, James 271, 371

Ballantyne, Mrs 154

Ballinahinch, Co. Galway 13, 328–31, 371

Ballinamuck, Battle of 60, *61*

balls 30, 112, 119–20, 129, 170, 171, 192

Balzac, Honoré de 12, 371–2

Banks, Sir Joseph 115, 127

Barbauld, Anna L. 133, 185

    Evenings at Home 39, 50, 206

    Lessons for Children 205

Battle of Aughrim 326

Battle of New Orleans 194

Beauchamp, Lord 203

Beaufort, Daniel 14, 50, 51, 62, 67, 105, 132, 219

Beaufort, Francis 76n, 77, 89, *109*, 132, 142, 217, 225, 226, 260, 285, 347, 373, 390

Beaufort, Harriet 88, 93, 198, 216, 219, 231, 232, 290

    correspondence with Maria 70–1, 127–8, 179–80, 223

Beaufort, Honora (née Edgeworth) 36, 45, 62, 87, 88, 93, 110, 111, 122, 125, 131, 132, 134, 136, 138, 144, 147, 153, *163*, 166, 169, 171, 177, 182, 186, 189, 191, 192, 195, 204, 207, 210, 212, 215, 220, 221, 225–6 229–30, 234, 248, 258, 259, 274, 282, 297, 301, 303, 304, 307, 308, 314, 320, 325, 333, 342, 353, 354, 369, 373–4, 381, 390, 401, 420

    correspondence with Maria 107, 129–31, 132, 144–5, 221–2, 311–12, 325–31, 381–2

Beaufort, Louisa 88, 89, 99, 109, 198, 231, 259, 368, 402, 411

Beaufort, William 273, 294

Bective, Lord (Taylour, Thomas) 252–3

Beddoes, Anna (née Edgeworth) 12, 37, 38, *39*, 45, 106n, 107, 117, 148, 151, 168, 226, 244, 259, 373n

Beddoes, Anna (Anna's daughter) 259, 260

Beddoes, Henry 260, *261*, 347

Beddoes, Mary 259

Beddoes, Thomas 12, 37, 73, 106n, 107, 117

Beddoes, Thomas Lovell 117, 245–6, 373, *374*

Belinda 70, 128, 133

Bentley, Richard 336

'Big Wind' of 1839 376

Billamore, Kitty 13, 45, 59, 60, 87, 95, 104, 144, 145, 151, 154, 168, 177, 192, 207, *208*, 211–12

Black Castle, Co. Meath 33, 36, 38, 39, 40, 44, 45, 51, 86, 88, 97, 100, 109, 193–4, *195*, 200, 207, 216, 240, 241, 243, 263, 264, 266, 268, 376

Bodenham, Eliza 290–3

Bodenham, Mr 290–3

Bog Commissioners 127, 131

Bonaparte, Napoleon 12, 76, 80, 127, 128, 131, 135, 149, 178, 184, 206, 209–10, 236, 237, 242, 243, 268, 277, 278, 353, 357, *v*

Bond, Willoughby 305, 345

Bowood House, Wiltshire 172, 225, 240

Brewster, Sir David 276, 302, 404, *405*

Bristow, George 80, 204, 333

Bristow, John 168

Bristow, Mary 314
Bristow, Molly 13, 36, 37, 314, 333
Bristow, Samuel 13, 36n, 43, 59
Broadstreet, Simon 191
Buckley, Dr 192, 203
Burdett, Francis 275, 283
Burke, Andy 344
Burney, Fanny (Madame d'Arblay) 29n, 165, 173
　Cecilia 94, 142, 274
　Evelina 11, 27, 28, 29, 71
Bushe, Charles Kendal 11, 137, 144, 238
Bushe, Eliza 143
Butler, Harriet (née Edgeworth) 10, 92, 95, 96, 99, 110, 132, 153, 157, 158, 177, 180, 191, 193, 210, 211, 212, 221, 232, 233–4, 240, 248, 249, 258, 266–8, 274, 289, 303, *304*, 307, 313, 317, 324, 325, *333*, 337, 339, 348, 354, 364, 367, 369, 370, 371, 375, 376, 377–8, 388, 392, 400, 402, 403, 414, 415, 417, 418, 423
　correspondence with Maria 266, 272–3, 276, 322–3, 362, 378–9, 391–2, 393–4, 409, 419–20
Butler, Marilyn 8
Butler, Richard, 10, 12, 248, 256, 257, 263, 266–8, 272–3, 340, 348, 349, 353, 354, 355, 364, 370, 371, 372, 388, 389m 392, 399, 402, 409
Byrkley Lodge, Staffordshire 122, 129, 133, 136, 138, 215, 221, 226, 229, 273
Byron, Lady Annabella 229, 275, 306
Byron, Lord 81n, 138, 147n, 156n, 165, 171, 217, 238, *261*, 300, 306, 307, 310, 358, 422, 423
　'English Bards and Scotch Reviewers' 138
　'The Bride of Abydos' 172

Campbell the cowman 410
Campbell, Thomas 146
Canning, George 275

Carleton, Captain George 124
Caroline of Brunswick, estranged wife of George IV, 237–8, 275
Carr, James 228, 229
Carr, Sir John 156
Carrington, Robert (2nd Baron) 166, 169, 198, 240, 410
Cassidy 13, 397, 410, 414, 419
Castle Forbes, Co. Longford 13, 87, 88, 93, 97, 171, 233, 322
Castle Rackrent 7, 14, 21, 66, 67, 133
Castlereagh, Lord (Stewart, Robert) 61, 175, 180
Castletown House, Co. Kildare 83, 103n, 142n, 193
Catholic Association 254, 289
Catholic Emancipation 14, 15, 254, 275, 283–4, 287–9, 294, 295, 296
Catholic Relief Bill 275, 287, 288, 289n, 294, 296, 322
Charlemont, 1st Earl of (Caulfeild, James) 29, 30, 38, 63–5, 145.
Chantinee, Co. Monaghan 116
Chapman, Sir Benjamin 103–4
Chapman, Sir Thomas 160, 161
Chaptal, J.A.C. 68
Charlemont House, Dublin 63–4
Catherine the Great 85
Charles II 197n
Charleville, 2nd Earl of (Bury, Charles) 375
Charlotte Augusta, Princess of Wales 181, 182, 183
Chatham, 2nd Earl of (Pitt, John) 134
Chenevix, Richard 67, 72, 125, 127, 128, 130, 154–5, 233
Clarke, Mary Anne 123
Clifford, Dr 387, 389
Clifton, Bristol 11, 12, 34, 36, 37, 65, 165, 364
'climbing boys' 282, *283*
Coffey, Molly 135, 151
Coleridge, Samuel Taylor, 279
Collon, Co. Louth *176*, 177
Colville, Mrs (housekeeper) 293

Colvin, Christina 8
Connell, Pat 207–8
Conolly, Edward (formerly Pakenham) 142
Conolly, Lady Louisa 193
Conolly, Thomas 193n
Contrast, The 147
Coolure House, Co. Westmeath 108
Cooper, Edward Joshua 346
Cornwallis, Lord 56, 60, 61
Corry, James 116, 209
Corry, Letty 84, 116, 128–9, 209
Cosby, General 47
Crampton, Sir Philip 11, 18, 144, 230, 231, 234, 262, 264, 303, 381, 383
Cranalagh Castle, Co. Longford 66
Crewe, Frances Anne 96–7
Cuffe, Lady Dorothea 222
Curwen, John 300

Dallas, Charles 78
Daly, Lady Harriet 224, 225
dancing lessons 24, 27, 182, 226
Darwin, Erasmus 12, 22, 91–2, 160, 200
Davidoff, Orloff 276
Davy, Sir Humphrey 12, 106–7, 144, 151–2, 156, 306–7, 408, *iv*
Davy, Lady (formerly Mrs Apreece) 137, 148, 156, 165
Day, Thomas 222
　History of Sandford and Merton 205–6
Dease, Lady Theresa 144, 250, 255
de Charrière, Isabelle 72n
Defenders 14, 42, 48, 49–50
de Genlis, Madame 27, 28, 84, 172
de Lagaraye, Marguerite
　Chimie de goût et de l'odorat 41
de la Casas, Duc 210n
de la Kerouaille, Louise 197n
de Lespinasse, Julie 140
de Pompadour, Madame 82

de Salis, Count 139, 233
de Salis, Harriet (née Foster) 139, 177, 233
de Segur, Joseph Alexandre 128
de Sévigné, Madame 87, 234, 291, 392
de Staël, Madame 12, 127–8, 140, 149, 165, 171, 172–3, 197, 204, 210, 231–2, 234, 274, 423
Dickens, Charles 422
Dillon, Lord & Lady 354–5, 360–1
Drummond, Thomas 347, 382–3
Dublin 8, 13, 27, 31, 36, 60, 62–3, 122, 131, 134, 137, 138, 143, 144, 159, 160, 186, 189, 190, 191, 199, 200, 201, 109, 230, 231, 238–9, 286, 287, 289, 290, 302, 312, 324, 340, 391
Dublin Society 189, 198, 200n
Duffy, Brian 235
Dumont, Etienne 225, 226

Early Lessons 69, 70, 166, 187
  Frank 69, 70, 168, 169
  Harry and Lucy 169
  Rosamund 69, 70, 168, 169
Edelcrantz, Nicolas 10, 73, 222, 235
Edgeworth, Abbé de Firmont 15, 82, 83, 110, 190, 198
Edgeworth, Anna Maria (née Elers) 9, 22
Edgeworth, Anne 301
Edgeworth, Bessie 62, 63, 65
Edgeworth, Charlotte 35, 62, 65, 69, 73, 75, 76, 79, 81, 88, 92, 93, 94, 94, 95, 96, 97, 99, 100, 109, 115, 228, 229
Edgeworth, Christina (née Macpherson) 404, 406, 417
Edgeworth, David 408
Edgeworth, Edward 21
Edgeworth, Elizabeth (née Sneyd) 10, 27, 33, 34, 36, 38, 41, 47–8, 52
  correspondence with Maria 44–5
Edgeworth, Eroles 408, 423, 424

Edgeworth, Frances (née Beaufort) 10, 13, 14, 50, 51, 52, 55, 56, 58, 59, 62, 68, 69, 70, 76, 79, 80, 86, 87, 92, 93, 95, 109, 111, 119, 120, 121, 122, 127, 128, 130, 142–3, 150, 153, 154, 157, 165–6, 168, 172, 174, 181, 189, 193, 210, 212, 215–16, 221, 225, 227, 228, 237, 247, 251, 255, 266, 269, 270, 276, 297, 304, 311, 314, 354, 360, 364, 365, 378–9, 382, 384–5, 387, 390, 392–4, 395, 404, 412, 414, 420
  correspondence with Maria 15, 52–3, 78, 83–5, 97–8, 100–5, 116–17, 158–60, 216–19, 241–2, 244, 262–3, 267–8, 278, 287–8, 304–6, 307, 309–10, 316–17, 332–3, 339–40, 342, 363–4, 369–70, 376–7, 381
  Memoir of Maria Edgeworth 7, 8, 9, 55, 73, 121, 144, 186, 216, 423
Edgeworth, Francis 127, 132, 140, 177, 179, 180, 181, 187, 188, 191, 192, 193, 200, 245–6, 211, 212, 238, 244, 249–50, 255, 262, 276, 305, 309, 310, 314, 315, 315–16, 319–21, 332, 335, 352, 366–7, 368, 375, 377, 379, 380, 381, 382, 384–6, 388, 391, 394–5, 399, 401–2, 403, 406–7, 417–18, 425
Edgeworth, Francis (Maria's great-great-grandfather) 21
Edgeworth, Francis Ysidro 424–5
Edgeworth, Harriette (Henrica; née Broadhurst) 167–8, 175, 187, 189, 220, 225, 269
  correspondence with Maria 175–6, 189, 197–8, 198–9, 201–2, 204, 220, 228–9, 270–1, 273–4, 354–61, 386–7
Edgeworth, Henry 33, 41, 45, 62, 65, 67, 75, 81, 83, 88, 93, 95, 100, 110, 117, 157
  correspondence with Maria 91–2, 111–12
Edgeworth, Honora (née Sneyd) 10, 22–7, 23, 33, 182

Edgeworth, Honora (Honora's daughter) 33, 34, 35
  correspondence with Maria 24–5
Edgeworth, Jane (née Lovell) 21
Edgeworth, Jane (née Tuite) 21
Edgeworth, Lovell 10, 34, 35, 38, 39, 41, 43, 44, 46, 47, 62, 68, 73, 76, 80, 94, 115, 135, 139, 156, 174, 177, 178–9, 187, 199, 212, 215, 217, 221, 231, 240, 241, 251, 259, 260, 264, 265, 269–71, 281, 282, 283–4, 316, 322, 324–5, 363, 380
Edgeworth, Maria (Francis and Rosa's daughter) 384
Edgeworth, Mary (Pakenham's daughter) 408
Edgeworth, (Michael) Pakenham 8, 13, 154, 155, 177, 180, 181, 185, 191, 195, 196, 200, 211, 212, 225, 231, 245, 249–50, 255, 262, 276, 284, 305, 309, 311n, 324, 333, 367n, 386–7, 388, 390, 395–6, 402, 404, 405, 406, 416, 417, 422
  correspondence with Maria 284–5, 324–5, 334–5, 349–51
Edgeworth, Richard (grandfather of Maria) 21
  The Black Book of Edgeworthstown 21, 66
Edgeworth, Richard Lovell 7, 9, 10, 13, 14–15, 21–3, 30, 33, 34, 35, 36, 37, 38, 39, 42, 43–4, 46, 48–9, 50, 55, 56, 57, 58, 59, 60, 61, 62, 63, 64, 65, 66, 67, 69, 70, 72–3, 75, 76, 77, 79, 81, 85n, 86, 87, 95, 96n, 98n, 109, 111, 113, 114, 119, 121, 122, 123, 125–6, 127, 129, 131, 132, 133, 134, 135, 136, 137, 139, 140, 142–3, 144, 146, 148, 150–1, 152, 154, 156, 157, 158, 163n, 165–6, 177, 179, 180, 185, 186, 191, 195, 196, 196n, 198, 199, 200, 206, 208, 210–12, 213, 214, 215, 216, 218, 219, 220, 223, 224, 225, 226, 228, 230, 232, 377–8, 421, i

correspondence with Maria 24–6, 187
Memoirs 7, 9, 216, 218, 219, 220, 223, 224, 225, 226, 232
Edgeworth, Rosa (née Eroles) 319–21, 335, 366–7, 368, 377, 394, 397, 398, 402, 406–7, 412, 414
Edgeworth, Sneyd 62, 65, 69, 71, 72, 81, 84, 86n, 90, 95, 96, 107, 110, 111, 125, 130, 136, 137, 151, 158, *167–8*, 172, 175, 176, 178, 187, 189, 190–1, 197, 198, 201, 209–10, 211, 212, 217, 222, 223, 224–5, 227, 228, 269–71, 273, 276, 302, 311, 321, 324, 375, 381
correspondence with Maria 63–5, 69–70, 86–7, 88–9, 94–5, 117, 133, 136–7, 137–8, 139–40, 153–4, 161–3, 178–9, 193–4, 198–9, 202, 209–10, 220, 339, 340–2
Edgeworth, Thomas Day 36, 37, 171
Edgeworth, William 38n, 51, 62, 69, 70, 71, 87, 88, 93, 94, 95, 99, 110, 116, 122, 125, 127, 131, 136–7, 139, 140, 144, 147–8, 150, 153, 158, 159, 168, 193, 200, 212, 216, 217, 227n, 234, 259, 265, 266, 270, 273, 274, 276, 296–7, 330
Edgeworth, Willy (son of Francis) 366, 377, 378, 396, 402, 423
Edgeworthstown 8, 13, 16, 22–3, 27, 38, 39, 40, *41*, 42, 73, *109*, 227, 236–7, 269–71, 281–3, 294–5, 309, 313, 314, 316, *337*, 380, 403, 423, *424*, 425, *ii, viii*
Edgeworthstown school 14, 196–7, 206, 227, 229–30, 243, 244, 245, 248, 252, 256, 257, 269, 271, 280, 312, 325, 342n, 344, 351–2, 353n, 379–80, 402, 422
Edgeworthstown tenants and servants 114–15, *115*, 202, 235–6, 248, *295*, 297–300, 310, 402, 407
Edinburgh, Scotland 75

Edinburgh Review 92, 129, 145–6, 155, 223, 419
elections
    1832 322–3
    1835 340, 341
    1836 361–3
electricity 95–6, 408, 418
Elers, Paul 22
Elgin marbles 194
Emmet, Robert 376n
Enlightenment 15, 22, 276n
Ennui 7, 87, 121, 124
Essays in Professional Education 113–14, 129, 136
Essay on Irish Bulls 51, 74

Fallon's Inn, Longford 58, 59
famines
    of 1817 217–18
    of 1822 240
    see also Great Famine
Faraday, Michael 12, 408
Farnham, Countess of (Maxwell, Grace) 246, 247
Farnham, 2nd Earl of (Maxwell, John James) 56, 166, 247, 251
Farnham House, Co. Cavan *247*
Farrell, Barney 131, 305
Fetherstone, Lady 259
Fetherstone, Sir George 259, 362
Fetherstone, Sir T. 48
Fingal, 8th Earl of (Plunkett, Arthur James) 130, 144, 219, 239
Fitzherbert, Trevor 18
Float, Inny River 7, 86, 90, 372
Flood, Peggy 244
Forbes, Adelaide 93
Forbes, Elizabeth 9
Forbes, Leslie 288
Forbes, Walter (18th Lord) 94, 171, 245, 288n, 322, 323, 343, 361, 363
Foster, portrait of Maria's dog *226*
Foster, John Leslie 85, 126, 127, 130, 138, 163, *176*, 191, 205
correspondence with Maria 205–6

Fox, Barry 251, 258, 259, 260, 273, 286, 310, 323, 340–2, 363, 365, 366–7, 375–6, 381, 399
Fox, Camilla 307, 308
Fox, Charles 293, 325, 341, 361, 362–3, 365
Fox, Charlotte 310, 364, 369, 377, 403
Fox, Francis 147, 171
Fox, John 171
Fox, Judge 37, 56, 62, 85, 120–1
Fox, Lady Anne 37, 56, 57, 62, 70, 121n, 216
Fox, Mary Anne 310, 364, 369, *370*, 377, 381, 402, 414
Fox, Maxwell 310, 364, 381, 420
Fox, Richard 307
Fox, Sophy (née Edgeworth) 95, 96, 110, 132, 134, 153, 168–9, 177, 180, 182, 192, 195, 207, 211, 212, 221, 248, 249, 251, 258, 259, 260, 273, 274, 284, 286, 310, 332, 335, 364
Fox, Waller 364, 369, 370, 377
Foxhall, Co. Longford 69–70, 250, 394
France 10, 12, 13, 177–8, 183–4, 201, 209, 228, 232, 233–4, 421
French Revolution 14, 37, 47n, 67–8, 206, 278n, 356, 422
Franklin, John 251, 346–7
Franklin, Lady 346–7

Gahan (gardener) 13, 306, 309, 314, 396–8, 410, 414–15
Garnet, Ham 218–19
Gaskell, Mrs 336
Gautier, Madame 180, 233
Gaybrook, Co. Westmeath, 80–1, 114, 252
George III 14, 149
George IV (Prince Regent) 180–1, 237, 238–40, *v*
Gibney, Mrs 275
Giddy, Davies 107n
Gladstone, William 424
Godwin, William 51
Goethe, Johann Wolfgang von
    Sorrows of Young Werther 76

Goldsmith, William 256
Gordon, Sir A. 157
Gordon, James 183–5
Graham, Robert 353
Granard, Countess of (Forbes, Selena) 13, 82, 87, 233, 234
Granard, 6th Earl of (Forbes, George) 13, 43, 46, 48n, 233, 288n, 361
Grant, William 257–8
Great Famine 16, 371n, 403–4, 406, 407, 408 409–15, *411*, 416–17
Green, Pat 297
Greenough, George 106, 107, 346
Grenville, Thomas 232, 400
Griffin, Gerald 303, 392
The Collegians 303
Griffith, Richard 163, 196

Hanging Gale 340, 341, 342
Hamilton, Bella 158
Hamilton, Caroline (née Pakenham) 63, 119, 120, 130, 134, 142, 158, 163, 187, 201
Hamilton, Henry 130, 158, 295
Hamilton, Kitty 152
Hamilton, Sackville 158
Hamilton, William Rowan 12, 256–7, 276, 300–1, 315, 347, 348, 387, *vii*
Hardwicke, 3rd Earl of (Yorke, Philip) 85
Hare, Augustus 8, 423
Harrington 200, 217, 219, 226
Harte, Captain 363
Hawkins, Sir John 124
Headfort House, Co. Meath 93, 252–3
Helen 15–16, 310, 313, 315, 324, 331, 335–7, 400n
earnings for 180, 421
Herschel, Caroline 387
Herschel, John 12, 279–80, 317, 347, 382n, 387, 395, 423
Hill, Lady Georgina 369
Hinds, George (agent) 301, 304, 309, 314, 317, 341–2, 381–2

Hoare, Charles 141
Hoare, Fanny (née Robinson) 27 141
correspondence with Maria 28–32
Holland, Dr Henry (1st Baronet) 123, 145n, 182, 183, 187, 188, 191, 237, 238, 275, 373n
Holland, Lord (Fox, Henry) 321
Home Rule 424
Hope, Thomas 301, 302
Humbert, General J.J.A. 56, *61*
Hunter, Myles 133, 173, 180, 199, 211, 218, 256, 400
hurricane of 1822 241–2

Inchbald, Elizabeth 132–3
Ireland, William Henry 100
Irish Farmers' Journal 15
Irish language 32

Jackson, Frances 198
James, Sir Walter 46
James I 21
Jenkins, John 59
Jenner, Edward 77n
Jephson, Emily 419
Jephson, Mr and Mrs 125, 140, 167, 264
Jobson, John 346
Johnson, Joseph 50, 63, 67, 69, 70, 122
Johnson, Samuel 124–5, 245, 260
Jones, Richard 416–17, 418

Kater, Henry 317
Keating, George (vicar of Edgeworthstown) 150, 344
Keegan, Garret 323
Keir, James 12, 114
Kelly, Hugh 201, 228, 362
Kelly, James 342–3
Kemble, John 305
Keogh, Garret 309, 396
Keynes, John Maynard 425
Kildare Place Society 205, 257

Kilkenny 142–3
Killarney, Co. Kerry 106, 263, 265, 266, *267*
King, Emmeline (née Edgeworth) 35, 36, 41, 45, 62, 73, 117, 148, 157, 250
King, Emmeline (niece) 250
King, John 73, 157
Knight, Andrew 106

Labouchere, Henry 413
Ladies' Association 408
Lamb, Lady Caroline, *Glenarvon* 202
Langan, John 9, 13, 36, 37, 44, 66, 95, 119, 120–1, 146, 150, 168, 188, 207
Langan, Peter 297, 399–400
Lansdowne, 3rd Marquess of (Petty-Fitzmaurice, Henry) 15, 167, 169, 225, 240, 323, 352
Lansdowne, Marchioness of (Petty-Fitzmaurice, Louisa) 167, 197, 240
Lataffiere, Mrs 23, 24
Lavoisier, Antoine 68
Leadbeater, Mary 141
Cottage Dialogues 206
Lefroy, Thomas 12, 363, 418
Leigh, Augusta 306
Leigh Hunt, James Henry 307
Lennox, Lady Sarah (later Napier) 197
Leonora 76, 77, 86, 87, 97
Letters for Literary Ladies 162
Little, Mr 270
Lockhart, J.G. 324, 336, 371, 421, 422, 423
London 8, 10, 27, 73, 111, 122–3, 136, 141n, 156n, 165–6, 180, 226, 234, 285, 288, 299, 301, 304, 311, 332, 347, 348, 382, 384, 387, 390, 396, 408, 421, 423
Longford, 2nd Baron (Pakenham, Edward) 60, 154, 175
Longford, 2nd Countess of (Georgina (née Lygon)) 8, 203, 344–5, 372

Longford, 3rd Earl of (Pakenham, Edward Michael) 372
Longford, Lady 111, 119, 121, 134, 147, 152, 154, 175, 194
Loughglynn, Co. Roscommon 354, 355–6, 360–1
Louis XVI 15, 82, *83*
Lowe, Sir Hudson 236, 242
Lunar Society 12, 22

McGovern, Dr 256
Mackenzie, Henry 29
Mackintosh, Sir James 311, 348, 349, 356, 393
Madame de Fleury 121
Malone, Catherine 228
Malthus, Thomas 240
Manoeuvring 121
Mansfield, Lord and Lady 185
Marivaux, P.C. 46
Market House, Edgeworthstown 16, 301–2
Markree Observatory 346
Martin, Mary 330–1, 350, 371
Martin, Mrs 13, 329–30, 331–2
Martin, Richard 13, 329, 330, 331–2
Martineau, Harriet 16, 367, 373, 408–9
Mathew, Father 383–4, 395, 396
Melbourne, Lord 339
Mills, Bessy 301
Mitchel, John 418
Modern Griselda, The 38n, 77, 91, 422
Moffat, Mrs (dressmaker) 258
Moilliet, Theodore 234, 312–13, 388
Monaghan, Charlie 43–4
Montagu, Lady Mary Wortley 77
Moor, Sergeant Harry 43–4
Moore, Augustus 349n, 350
Moore, George 348, 354, 356, 358
Moore, Louisa 13, 348, 349–50, 354, 357–9, 361, 417

Moore, Thomas 13, *143*, 265, 311, 359
    Epicurean 277
    Memoirs of Captain Rock 255
Moore Hall, Co. Mayo 13, 348, 354, 356, *357*, 360
Moral Tales for Young People 69
Mordecai, Mrs 200n
More, Hannah 231
Morgan, Lady (née Sydney Owenson) 176, 189, *190*
    Florence Macarthy 423
Mount Kennedy, Co. Wicklow 225
Mulgrave, Earl of (Phipps, Constantine) 347
Mulhern, Peggy (née Tuite) 188, 233, 234, 235
Mulloy, Elizabeth 248
Murray, Lady Frederica 184–5
Murray, John 217

Nagle, Sir Thomas 238–9
Nangle, Anne 86, 95, 96, 105, 117
Napier, Mr and Mrs 259, 302–3
Nimmo, Alexander 330
Norbury, 2nd Earl of (Toler, Hector John) 375
Norbury, 1st Earl of (Toler, John; 'Hanging Judge') 130, 131, 376n

O'Beirne, Archbishop Thomas 98–9, 140, 217, 232, 264
O'Beirne, Mrs 217, 221, 232, 233
O'Connell, Daniel 15, 254, 288, 289n, 322, 323, 339, 340, 343, 346, 348, 361, 389–90, *391*, 399, 402, 413, 416, *vi*
O'Meara, Barry 242–3, *v*
Oranmore, Lord 355, 360
Orlandino 408, 412, 415
Ormond 7, 116, 195–6, 208–9, 211, 212, 217, 219, 226, 324
O'Rourke, M. (MP for Longford) 322
Oriel, Lord (Foster, John) 85n, 233
Oughterard, Co. Galway 327

Pakenham, Admiral Sir Thomas 13, 103, 108, *118*, 119, 120, 127, 132, 134, 142, 151, 157, 160–1, 193n, 333–4
Pakenham, Caroline 63, 119, 120, 130, 134, 142, 158, 163, 187, 201
Pakenham, General Sir Edward 108–9, 111, 147, 194
Pakenham, Edward, see Conolly, Edward
Pakenham, Henry (Archdeacon of Emly) 120, 152, 376–7
Pakenham, Hercules 111–12, 160–1, 167
Pakenham Kitty, see Lady Wellesley
Pakenham, Lady Elizabeth 97, 102, 105, 109
Pakenham, Louisa (Admiral Pakenham's daughter) 134
Pakenham, Thomas (later 1st Baron Longford) 7
Longford, 2nd Earl of (Pakenham, Thomas) 7–8, 60, 87, 102, 119–20, 130, 137, 151, 152–3, 160–1, 167, 197–8, 201, 202–3, 229, 251, *253*, 296, 344
Pakenham Hall 7–8, 13, 97, 112, 119, 121, 137, 152, 198, 251–2, *253*, 372
Parent's Assistant, The 50, 51
Patronage 10, 114n, 133, 147, 155, 162, 168, 169, 170, 173, 180, 203, 205, 232n, 421
Peel, Sir Robert 16, 275, 284, 288, 289, 339, 342, 343, 399, 404, 405, 406, 407, 410
Peyman, General 111
Pictet, Charles 72
Piozzi, Hester 124
Pitt, William 14, 89, 97n, 134n, 204
Playfair, John 137
Powell, rector of Edgeworthstown 407, 408, 409, 412, 414
Powerscourt, Co. Wicklow 224–5, 239
Practical Education 40n, 51, 65, 67, 69, 113, 136
Prescott, William H. 415

Quakers 408, 409, 410, 412, 414

Rancliffe, Lord (Parkyns, George) 94, 171
Rawdon, Lady Charlotte 140
Récamier, Madame 228
Reform Bill 312, 316, 322
Richardson, Samuel 11
Richmond, Duke of (Lennox, Charles) 135, 163n, 193n
Rising of 1798 14, 55, 56–61, 278, 297
Ritchie, Anne Thackeray 423–4
Robinson, Lucy (née Edgeworth) 92, 95, 132, 169, 182, 185, 195, 199, 207, 211, 212, 227, 234, 251, 259, 260, 264, 304, 308, 332, 365, 374n, 384, 390, 392–4, 423
correspondence with Maria 176–7, 191–2, 195, 200, 238–40, 401–2, 418–9, 421
Robinson, Thomas Romney 12–13, 144, 317–18, 390, 393–4, 399, 408, 418–19, vii
Rockingham House, Co. Roscommon 152
Roden, Lord (Jocelyn, Robert) 107
Rogers, Samuel 400
Roland, Madame Marie-Jeanne 49
Romilly, Lady Anne 172, 180, 198, 306
Rosse, 2nd Earl of (formerly Sir Laurence Parsons) 9, 284, 302
Rosse, 3rd Earl of 388, 395, vii
Rostrevor, Co. Down 100–2, 150
Rothwell, Thomas 128, 129, 245
Rousseau's system of 'natural' education 22
Royal Irish Academy 12
Russell, Lord John 16, 307, 405, 407, 411, 413
Ruxton, Bess 216, 252
Ruxton, John 26, 55, 85, 86, 116, 263–4
Ruxton, Letty 45–6, 66–7, 72

Ruxton, Margaret (née Edgeworth) 9, 26, 27, 35, 56, 66, 84, 89, 99, 101, 126, 145, 159, 195, 216, 218, 221, 268, 286–7, 302, 311, 313
correspondence with Maria 33–6, 38–40, 42–4, 46–8, 51–2, 58–9, 71, 76, 81–2, 85–6, 92–3, 95–6, 97, 110, 114–15, 119–20, 132–3, 135, 140–2, 147–8, 149–51, 156–7, 160–1, 166, 168–9, 170–3, 174–5, 180–5, 196–7, 198, 202–4, 208–9, 219, 223–7, 229–30, 234–7, 240, 246–7, 251–2, 255, 261, 272, 300, 310
Ruxton, Margaret (youngest daughter of above) 35, 37, 45, 78, 84, 101, 155, 159, 195, 218, 235, 236, 319, 320, 353n, 368–9
correspondence with Maria 96–7, 105, 121–3, 124, 126, 128–9, 155–6
Ruxton, Richard 47, 55, 72, 84, 85, 85, 100, 114, 158, 218, 238–9, 241–2, 245, 252, 334
Ruxton, Sophy 10, 35, 36, 39, 45, 50, 52, 73, 84, 85, 97, 101, 102, 105, 155, 159, 166, 175, 185, 194, 195, 209, 217, 218, 221, 225n, 235, 244, 262, 263, 353, 368, ii
correspondence with Maria 36–8, 40–1, 48–51, 55–8, 59–62, 67–9, 71–2, 75, 76–7, 79–81, 82, 87–8, 89–91, 93–4, 100, 106–7, 108–9, 113–14, 117–19, 120–1, 123, 124–5, 127, 137, 138–9, 142–4, 145–7, 148–9, 151–2, 154–5, 167–8, 169, 173, 177–8, 182, 187–9, 190–1, 195–6, 200, 206–7, 211–12, 248, 250–1, 255–8, 259–60, 263–6, 271–2, 275–6, 278–80, 285–6, 296–7, 319–21, 362–3, 367–8

Sadler, James 158–60
Sadler, Windham 160
St Patrick's Day celebrations 388–9
Saunderson Castle, Co. Cavan 68

Savage of Aveyron 72
Scotland 10, 156n, 184–5, 248n, 249, 386, 395, 404, 405
Scott, Anne 272
Scott, Captain Walter 264, 266
Scott, Charlotte 249, 272
Scott, Jane (née Jobson) 264, 266, 272
Scott, Sir Walter 14, 146, 186, 246, 249, 263, 264–6, 265, 271–2, 276, 281, 300, 324, 335, 336, 353, 358, 370, 371, 377, 386, 421, 422, 423
Antiquary, The 256, 303
Fair Maid of Perth, The 285
Grandfather's Tales 285
Letters of Malachi Malagrowther 272
Life of Napoleon 277–8
Peveril of the Peak 243
Redgauntlet 256
'Rokeby' 162
Waverley 11, 186, 188, 256
Selkirk, 5th Earl of (Douglas, Thomas) 113, 115, 222
Seymour, Lord Henry 60
Shea, Garret 314
Sheil, Richard Lalor 289n
Shelbourne Hotel, Dublin 312–13
Sheridan, Richard Brinsley 149n, 303, 326
Shiel James 253
Shipp, John 305
Sismondi, J.C.L. 365–6
Sisters of Mercy 290–3, 425
Smarmore Castle, Co. Louth 146
Smith, Caroline 401
Smith, Isabella (née Carr) 325, 326, 327, 328–9
Smith, Sir Culling 325, 326, 327, 328–9, 332, 343
Smith, Sydney 372–3, 400–1
Smyth, Mrs (of Gaybrook) 80–1, 251, 252
Sneyd, Charlotte 45, 58, 59, 76, 80, 109, 129, 136, 138, 145, 180, 191, 212, 215, 216, 219, 220, 226, 229–30, 234
correspondence with Maria 33, 65, 131, 133–5, 221–2

Sneyd, Mary 72, 76, 80, 82,
     89, 109, 110, 119, 122, 124,
     129, 136, 138, 145, 157,
     180, 203, 215, 216, 219,
     220, 226, 229–30, 293, 301,
     304, 307, 310, 324, 326,
     333, 344, 353, 373–4
  correspondence with Maria
     98–9, 133–5, 152–3, 221–2
Somerville, Edith 137
Somerville, Marcus 98
Somerville, Mary 387
Sonna, Co. Westmeath 67,
     72, 80, 100, 127, 130, 233,
     345, 380
Sparrow, Lady Olivia 120
Spring Farm, Co. Wicklow
     224–5
Spring Rice, Thomas, later
     Lord Mounteagle 15, 352
Stanhope, Lord Charles 97
Stanley, Edward 342
Stewart, Colonel 336–7
Stewart, Dugald 75, 90n, 92,
     336, 373n
Strickland, Mr 242, 250, 271,
     290, 292–3, 322, 326, 327,
     346, 348, 354, 356, 360, 361
Strickland, Mrs 242, 250, 271,
     305, 350, 360
Strutt, Henry 201–2
St John's Church,
     Edgeworthstown 146,
     147–8, 150–1, *425*
Sunderlin, Lady (Malone,
     Philippa Elizabeth) 228

Talbot, Mr 221–2
Tales of Fashionable Life 117
Talleyrand, Charles Maurice de
     210, 357
temperance movement 383,
     388, 396
Temple Michael 140
'This Is None of I' 121, *122*
Ticknor, George 415n
Tighe, Ann 305
Tipu Sahib 78
tithes 254, 255, 296, 344,
     347–8
  Tithe War 322

Tollymore Park, Co. Down
     107, *108*
'Tomorrow' 97
Tone, Wolfe 278, *279*
Trench, William Stuart *345*,
     380
Trentham Hall, Staffordshire
     226
Trim Rectory, Co. Meath 268,
     273, 339–40, 369, 376, 377,
     388, 392, 406, 418
Tuite, Hugh 380, 411–12, *413*
Tuite, Mrs 67, 100, 119, 120,
     125, 130, 135, 154–5, 233,
     234
Tuite, Sir Henry 119, 120
Turbotstown House, Co.
     Westmeath 250n, 255

United Irishmen 57, 278n, *iii*

Volunteer movement 30, *64*, *i*

Wakefield, Edward 139, 153–4
Wakefield, Gilbert 63n,
Waller, Belinda 105
Waller, Bess 80, 175, 245
Waller, Jane 105
Waller, Major 105
Ward, R. 203–4
Watt, James 12
Wedgewood, Josiah 12
Wellesley, Sir Arthur (Duke of
     Wellington) 15, 102, *103*,
     105, 112, 124, 134, 167, 175,
     201, 203, 275, 287, 288, 289,
     295, 296, 312, 339, 423
  duel with Earl of
     Winchelsea 293
Wellesley, Lady (née Kitty
     Pakenham, later Duchess of
     Wellington) 97, 102, *103*,
     105, 109, 112, 120, 121, 124,
     134, 152, 156–7, 175, 183,
     197, 198, 201, 312
Wellesley, Douro (son of Duke
     of Wellington) 183
Westport, Co. Mayo 331, 360
Whim for Whim 62
Whitbread, Lady Elizabeth 183,
     226, 240

Whitbread, Samuel 226n, 240
White, Luke (MP for
     Longford) 322, 361, 362
Whiteboys (Whitetooths) 14,
     47
Wilson, Fanny (née Edgeworth)
     10, 65, 70, *71*, 77, 83–4, 86,
     92–3, 95, 110, 137–8, 144,
     152, 153, 157, 158, *163*, 171,
     177, 182, 187, 191, 193, 195,
     207, 209, 212, 216, 217,
     218, 221, 232, 233–4, 240,
     249, 258, 260, 266, 274, 311,
     320–1, 324, 325, 332, 335,
     364, 367
  correspondence with Maria
     99–100, 210, 225–6, 230–3,
     237–8, 242–3, 248–50, 251,
     252–4, 258–9, 268, 274–5,
     277–8, 281–4, 285–7, 288–
     96, 297–300, 301–4, 306–7,
     308–9, 312–16, 317–19, 322,
     333–4, 336–7, 342–9, 351–3,
     365–7, 368–9, 371–4, 375–6,
     377–8, 379–80, 382–6, 387–
     90, 392, 394–8, 399–401,
     402–9, 410–16, 417–18
Wilson, Lestock 226, 285–7,
     304, 320, 390, 396, 399, 400,
     401, 406
Wollaston, William Hyde 317,
     419
Woods, Barney 314, 316
Woods, James 323
Woods, Margery 173, 241
Woods, Robin 173, *174*
Wordsworth, William 300–1,
     423
workhouse (Longford) 407
Wycombe Abbey,
     Buckinghamshire 240

Young, Arthur *32*
Young Irelanders 418

Zimmern, Helen 423